Praise for *Communal Reading in the Time of Jesus*

"The last few decades have witnessed a substantial move away from picturing the early church studying texts to assuming that most Christians could not read: orality trumped written text. Various efforts to balance the evidence have collided with one another. Enter this groundbreaking work by Brian J. Wright, who demonstrates how common 'communal reading events' were in both Jewish and Greco-Roman contexts. Reading and hearing are suddenly not so far removed from each other as some have thought. Wright's richly supplied evidence from primary sources is convincing; one wonders why these things have not been brought to light before. Wright's results are important, indeed seminal, not only to those who work in this field, but to our knowledge of early Christians who give every sign of being book-driven believers."

D. A. Carson, Research Professor of New Testament, Trinity Evangelical Divinity School

"A truly worthwhile, wide-ranging, and groundbreaking work! Unlike most publications, this book fills what was a genuine and essential gap in our knowledge of antiquity relevant to the New Testament. Although subsequent scholarship regularly debates some conclusions of any innovative work, it remains indebted to the foundations that such a work lays. This book exhibits careful methodology and thorough engagement with both primary and secondary sources."

Craig S. Keener, F. M. and Ada Thompson Professor of Biblical Studies, Asbury Theological Seminary

"B. J. Wright's masterly discussion of the communal reading of ancient texts, facilitated by an exhaustive analysis of twenty Greco-Roman authors from the first-century CE and the Jewish literature, is the bedrock for his investigation of the New Testament writings. The author's authoritative analysis of the New Testament documents demonstrates substantial continuities with ancient writers as far as communal reading practice, the strict control over literary tradition, and the broad spectrum of society involved in these public oral performances of texts from diverse geographic communities. This groundbreaking discussion provides another important pillar in arguments for the reliability of the New Testament oral and literary tradition."

James R. Harrison, Research Director,
Sydney College of Divinity

"This is a thorough study of an important topic, demonstrating that communal reading events were ubiquitous in the first-century world in general and in the early Christian movement in particular. Virtually everybody, it seems, would often hear texts read aloud. There are important implications for the much-discussed relationship of the oral and the textual in early Christianity. Texts were more available and more stable than we may have thought."

Richard Bauckham, Professor Emeritus of New Testament
Studies at the University of St. Andrews

"Communal reading has clearly been a neglected factor in understanding ancient literate culture. Recent attention to questions of literacy indicates that communal reading was an important part of the cultural experience of texts, as Brian J. Wright so ably shows in his extensive survey of the ancient evidence, biblical and otherwise. I commend Wright for bringing this to our attention, and, by doing so, for opening up areas for further exploration regarding how texts were used, how traditions were transmitted, and how ancients communicated."

Stanley E. Porter, President, Dean, and Professor of New
Testament, McMaster Divinity College

"People of all kinds regularly read their and others' compositions aloud in public in the ancient Mediterranean world at the time of Jesus. Christians regularly read the Hebrew Scriptures, along with their own literature in similar fashion. Public declamation regularly stemmed from or produced careful preservation of texts, sometimes from memory. Wright comprehensively surveys all this material, mounting an impressive case for all kinds of checks and balances in the preservation of early Christian tradition. A must read for anyone who still thinks that this tradition was largely uncontrolled and constantly distorted."

Craig L. Blomberg, Distinguished Professor of New Testament, Denver Seminary

"A focused presentation of the data relating to 'communal reading events' in antiquity has been long overdue, and Brian J. Wright's important research on this subject is to be much welcomed. *Communal Reading in the Time of Jesus* demonstrates just how common the oral recitation of written texts was, in a wide variety of social environments, in the first-century, Greco-Roman world. It helps us comprehend the larger cultural context for the public reading of Christian (and Jewish) Scriptures, and shows that audiences, at times, could even act as stabilizing forces on written texts that were read repeatedly in communal settings. Scholars of the New Testament and early Christianity should take notice!"

Charles E. Hill, Richardson Professor of New Testament and Early Christianity, Reformed Theological Seminary

"Brian J. Wright has shed light on important aspects of texts, reading, and literacy in the Roman Empire that are unknown to most interpreters of Christian Scripture. *Communal Reading in the Time of Jesus* will go a long way toward remedying this problem. I am delighted to recommend this important book."

Craig A. Evans, John Bisagno Distinguished Professor of Christian Origins, Houston Baptist University

"'Haven't you heard?' Jesus asked the crowd, assuming the Law had been read to them. How widespread was public reading and how may it have affected the preservation and dissemination of the Christian message? By surveying and analyzing numerous Greek and Latin texts, Brian Wright throws fresh light on the practice and underlines its relevance for the study of early Christian society and especially the composition of the Gospels. Through communal reading, he argues, people would know those texts and be alert to any changes readers might try to introduce. This is a notable addition to knowledge about books and reading in the earliest churches."

Alan Millard, Rankin Professor Emeritus of Hebrew and Ancient Semitic Languages, The University of Liverpool

"Why did early Christians write? When and where did they read? What did reading mean in the social contexts and practices of the first century? Meticulously sifting a wide range of evidence, Wright introduces us to 'a complex, multifaceted cultural field' that shaped that reading. His results demand a reconsideration of the whole process by which texts were controlled and, eventually, a canon emerged."

Wayne A. Meeks, Woolsey Professor Emeritus of Religious Studies, Yale University

"In this innovative study, Brian J. Wright brings to the forefront a matter that has been neglected in New Testament studies, namely, the role of communal reading in the first century. Wright's thorough analysis has implications for our understanding of literacy in the first century, gospel traditions, and the preservation of texts. We can be grateful for a work that opens new vistas in the study of both the ancient world and the New Testament."

Thomas R. Schreiner, James Buchanan Harrison Professor of New Testament Interpretation, The Southern Baptist Theological Seminary

"Ever since the publication in the 1960s of Gerhardsson's groundbreaking work, *Memory and Manuscript with Tradition and Transmission in Early Christianity*, there have not been significant advances in this highly important area of study until this highly important work of Brian J. Wright. He has demonstrated for the first time the importance of communal reading in the Greco-Roman world during the first-century CE and its relevance for the reading of the New Testament corpus for the first Christians."

Bruce W. Winter, Senior Research Fellow in Ancient History, Macquarie University, and former Warden, Tyndale House, Cambridge

Communal Reading in the Time of Jesus

Communal Reading in the Time of Jesus

A Window into Early Christian Reading Practices

BRIAN J. WRIGHT

FORTRESS PRESS
MINNEAPOLIS

For Daniella

An exemplary woman

A praiseworthy mother

A noble wife

Contents

Foreword

This book is an important contribution to our understanding of how texts were handled in early Christian circles and in their larger Roman-era cultural environment. For a few decades now, both in biblical studies and in classical studies, scholars have explored and debated a variety of questions about the distribution and usage of texts, the level and degrees of Roman-era literacy, the relationship between "orality" and texts, and the factors affecting the transmission and stability of texts. In the process, some earlier exaggerations and romantic notions (such as claims about an original "orality" in earliest Christian circles that involved the oral "performance" of texts from memory, rather than the reading of manuscripts) have been corrected.[1] But there continues to be a need for more data to be placed into discussion about texts and reading in the world of earliest Christianity, and one of the major strengths of Brian Wright's book is that it addresses this need, with a commendable abundance of primary sources drawn upon, which he submits to a careful and cogent analysis.

The rich body of evidence surveyed in chapter 5 on "communal reading events" in the Roman-era setting alone makes the book worth its price, and the appendix provides still more! That is, he documents amply the frequent, perhaps even characteristic, manner in which texts were used: one person reading from a manuscript while others listened. By giving attention to the provenance of his evidence, he is also able to show that this reading practice was followed

1. Larry W. Hurtado, "Oral Fixation and New Testament Studies? 'Orality', 'Performance' and Reading Texts in Early Christianity," *NTS* 60, no. 3 (2014): 321–40. Cf. also Kelly Iverson, "Oral Fixation or Oral Corrective? A Response to Larry Hurtado," *NTS* 62, no. 2 (2016): 183–200; and my reply, "Correcting Iverson's 'Correction,'" *NTS* 62, no. 2 (2016): 201–6.

trans-locally in various parts of the Roman Empire. In chapter 6, he shows further that this was the common practice among earliest Christian circles as well, and from the first century onward. In short, early Christianity reflected the reading practices of the Jewish matrix in which it emerged and, indeed, the reading practices of the larger Roman-era cultural environment.

One of the effects of Wright's study is to show that, whatever the levels of literacy in the Roman world, written texts were experienced and engaged widely and by people of various social and educational levels. For even among circles in which the great majority were illiterate, all that was needed was one person capable of reading out a text for the rest. So the low level of literacy that we assume (and it is basically an assumption) cannot be a basis for marginalizing the place and influence of written texts in the Roman world. Indeed, Wright adds further data to the growing conviction among historians of the Roman period that it was a time characterized by a remarkable salience of writing and reading of all kinds, from graffiti to inscriptions, and from letters and bills of sale to popular and elite literary texts.

Wright also notes rightly that the communal reading of texts functioned as one factor affecting the transmission of texts, particularly those that were read repeatedly. For as these texts were read, they became, so to speak, the textual property of the circle(s) of those who heard them read. Wright shows that people were often concerned to have a reliable version of the wording of texts and could object when any significant alteration was attempted to texts that they knew well. In making this point, Wright underscores a factor that is relevant for our estimates of how writings that came to be treated as scriptures, such as those that form our New Testament, were transmitted textually.[2] Michael Holmes noted how some early Christian texts, such as the *Gospel of Thomas*, suffered what he called "macro-level" alterations, whereas other texts, particularly those that early on acquired a scriptural status and usage, exhibit "micro-level" variants (i.e., smaller variation in such things as verb tense, presence/absence of the definite

---

2. In a very brief manner, I pointed to this factor myself in an essay published several years ago: Larry W. Hurtado, "The New Testament in the Second Century: Text, Collections and Canon," in *Transmission and Reception: New Testament Text-Critical and Exegetical Studies*, ed. J. W. Childers and D. C. Parker (Piscataway, NJ: Gorgias, 2006), 3–27. So I am happy to have now Wright's supporting analysis.

article, word order of small phrases, etc.).[3] Wright's emphasis on the role of the repeated communal reading of texts helps us to account for this. Those texts that were read out communally more frequently acquired a comparatively greater textual stability.

I do not wish to distract readers further from the rich feast of data and discussion in this book, so I shall conclude simply by reiterating that it is a study that anyone interested in the *realia* of early Christianity should note. I hope that Wright's study will quickly acquire the attention that it deserves. As others have noted, early Christianity was a particularly "bookish" religious movement, evidenced in the place given to the reading of texts and also in the production, copying, and trans-local circulation of texts.[4] Wright's valuable book illumines in specific ways the social dimension of that early Christian bookishness, and we are all thereby enabled to perceive better features of that remarkable religious movement.

Larry W. Hurtado

---

3. Michael W. Holmes, "Text and Transmission in the Second Century," in *The Reliability of the New Testament: Bart Ehrman and Daniel Wallace in Dialogue*, ed. Robert B. Stewart (Minneapolis: Fortress Press, 2011), 47–65.

4. E.g., see my discussion of this in *Destroyer of the Gods: The Distinctiveness of Early Christianity in the Roman World* (Waco: Baylor University Press, 2016), 105–41.

Preface

The fact that you are one of my readers is no small encouragement to
new work.

—Pliny, *Letters* 4.26.3 (ca. 61–113 CE)

One thing remains: please be equally honest about telling me if you
think there are any additions, alterations, or omissions to be made. [...]
It is more likely to be long-lived the more I can attain to truth and
beauty and accuracy in detail.

—Pliny, *Letters* 3.10.5–6 (ca. 61–113 CE)

My interest in this topic, in one sense, started in the fall of 2004, when
I was taking a Greek course under Daniel B. Wallace at Dallas Theological Seminary. During that course, we not only had to recognize
and memorize Koine Greek, but also had to compose it—meaning we were required to go both ways, from Greek to English and
from English to Greek. That, in turn, gave me a greater appreciation for, and interest in, the Greek language. From there, my interest
developed and transitioned into the transmission of the Greek New
Testament text as I was selected to participate in several specialized
academic internships. In fact, I spent the next six years immersing
myself as much as possible in the ripe field of New Testament textual criticism (NTTC). This even included such tangible experiences
as participating in multiple manuscript expeditions with the Center
for the Study of New Testament Manuscripts, prepping and handling
over 100 manuscripts in order to preserve them digitally, and personally discovering one manuscript in Meteora, Greece. My unique
introduction to the Greek language and subsequent work in the field
of NTTC naturally segued into my current interest in ancient read-

ing practices and book culture, especially and more specifically how they relate to the New Testament and Christian origins.

I am first indebted, then, to those on the DTS faculty who helped me along my ThM journey to my PhD studies, especially my thesis advisers, Dan Wallace, mentioned above, and Darrell L. Bock. In fact, my gratitude continues to this day, as they have remained accessible and interested in my academic progress.

Years later, when I began my PhD program at Ridley College in Melbourne, Australia, I remember starting with a host of assumptions related to this volume. For example, I would have told you that reading in the ancient world was largely an elitist phenomenon; texts played more of a symbolic role than utilitarian; around 90 percent of the population in antiquity was illiterate; a "professional" scribe was behind every document, unless proven otherwise; writing materials were expensive and in short supply; and some sort of "professional" reader was required whenever a manuscript was read, because *scriptio continua* (i.e., a text without spacing between words) was extremely difficult to read. My views on all of these and a number of others, however, changed during my PhD studies and are still developing today. That does not mean I now believe the pendulum should swing to the equal but opposite extreme. But I certainly see the evidence much differently than I once did. In my view, the examples I just mentioned are misdescriptions of the ancient context during the time of Jesus. Yet they still seem to be representative of what a large portion of biblical scholars assume. In fact, I do not think it would be an overstatement to say that each one is the consensus position right now.

Special thanks, then, also go to my PhD supervisors, Michael F. Bird and Scott D. Charlesworth, and external examiners, Eckhard J. Schnabel, E. Randolph Richards, and Ched Spellman. Each one of them, most notably Mike and Scott, provided critical feedback on much of the early research that went into this project. My only regret is that I was unable to pursue all the additional avenues they suggested. Of course, this study is still quite broad and thus open to many criticisms from specialists in the many fields touched upon. Nevertheless, the decision to pursue what I did, for better or worse, was solely mine, as are any errors.

Finally, and most importantly, I want to thank my wife, Daniella, and kids, Neriah, Zephaniah, and Jedidiah. Without them around, I would have had much more time to improve this study. But with them, it was all the more enjoyable and worthwhile.

Soli Deo Gloria

Abbreviations

The abbreviations used in this study follow those in *The SBL Handbook of Style for Biblical Studies and Related Disciplines* (2014), with the following additions:

AGRW   *Associations in the Greco-Roman World: A Sourcebook.* Richard S. Ascough, Philip A. Harland, and John S. Kloppenborg, eds. Waco, TX: Baylor University, 2012.

AJEC   Ancient Judaism and Early Christianity Series

ASNU   *Acta Seminarii Neotestamentici Upsaliensis*

BETL   Bibliotheca ephemeridum theologicarum lovaniensium

BHT   Beiträge zur historischen Theologie

BIS   Biblical Interpretation Series

CIL   *Corpus Inscriptionum Latinarum*

ECL   Early Christianity and Its Literature

FRLANT   Forschungen zur Religion und Literatur des Alten und Neuen Testaments

IE   Impact of Empire

IGUR   Moretti, L., ed. *Inscriptiones graecae urbis Romae*. Rome: Istituto Italiano per la storia antica, 1968–90.

JSJSup   Journal for the Study of Judaism Supplement Series

JSRC   Jerusalem Studies in Religion and Culture

LBS   Linguistic Biblical Studies

LHJS   Library of Historical Jesus Studies

LNTS   Library of New Testament Studies

LXX   *Septuaginta*. Edited by A. Rahlfs. 7th ed. 2 vols. Stuttgart: Württembergische Bibelanstalt, 1935.

LEH   Lust, J., E. Eynikel, and K. Hauspin. *A Greek-English Lexicon of the Septuagint*. Stuttgart: German Bible Society, 1992–96.

MnS   Mnemosyne Supplements

NAC   New American Commentary

NIDNTTE   Silva, Moisés, ed. *New International Dictionary of New Testament Theology and Exegesis*. Grand Rapids: Zondervan, 2014.

NovTSup   Supplements to Novum Testamentum

NTD   Neue Testament Deutsch

NTGJC   New Testament Gospels in Their Judaic Contexts

NTOA   Novum Testamentum et Orbis Antiquus

PAST   Pauline Studies

SBG   Studies in Biblical Greek

SCJ   Studies in Christianity and Judaism

SJSJ   Supplements to the Journal for the Study of Judaism

SNT   Studien zum Neuen Testament

SNTSMS   Society for New Testament Studies Monograph Series

SPA   Studies in Philo of Alexandria

STDJ   Studies on the Texts of the Desert of Judah

TDNT   *Theological Dictionary of the New Testament*. Edited by G. Kittel and G. Friedrich. 10 vols. Grand Rapids: Eerdmans, 1964–76.

TENTS   Texts and Editions for New Testament Study

TSAJ   Texte und Studien zum antiken Judentum

UBSGNT[5] United Bible Societies' *Greek New Testament*. 5th ed. Edited by Barbara Aland, Kurt Aland, Johannes Karavidopoulos, Carlo M. Martini, and Bruce Metzger. Stuttgart: Deutsche Bibelgesellschaft, 2014.

WBC   Word Biblical Commentary

WUNT   Wissenschaftliche Untersuchungen zum Neuen Testament

1.

Introducing a New Control Category

Seeing that all the populace, owing to its numbers, was unable to be present at the reading of the most sacred and most beneficent letter to the city, I have deemed it necessary to display the letter publicly in order that reading it one by one you may admire the majesty of our god Caesar and feel gratitude for his goodwill towards the city.
—*Letter of Claudius to the Alexandrians* (Nov. 10, 41 CE), in *Select Papyri, Volume II: Public Documents* (LCL 282, p79)

A lecturer sometimes brings upon the platform a huge work of research, written in the tiniest hand and very closely folded; after reading off a large portion, he says: "I shall stop, if you wish;" and a shout arises: "Read on, read on!" from the lips of those who are anxious for the speaker to hold his peace then and there.
—Seneca the Younger, *Letters* 3.95.2 (ca. 4 BCE–65 CE)

INTRODUCTION

During the first few centuries CE, literary traditions were often broadcast via communal reading and recitation events. These events, in part, help explain why many ancient authors note the importance and influence of them. Among Christian communities, the author of 1 Timothy instructs the recipient of his letter to prioritize the communal reading of Scripture: "Devote yourself to the communal reading of Scripture" (1 Tim 4:13). The author of the book of Revelation addresses both the reader and the ones who hear the reading: "Blessed is the one who reads aloud the words of the prophecy, and blessed are those who hear and who keep what is written in it" (Rev 1:3). The author of 2 Clement urges his community to listen to what is being read communally: "Therefore, brothers and sisters, following the God of truth I am reading you an exhortation to pay attention to what is written, in order that you may save both yourselves and your reader" (2 Clem. 19:1).[1] The author of the Shepherd of Hermas narrates an account of an elderly woman, who represents "the church" (8.1), holding a book (2.2), reading the book (3.3), allowing copies of the book to be made for other believers (5.3), and then making this request: "Therefore you will write two little books, and you will send one to Clement and one to Grapte. Then Clement will send it to the cities abroad, because that is his job. . . . But you yourself will read it to this city, along with the elders who preside over the church" (8.3).[2]

Among other groups, Pliny writes in his *Letters* with excitement about personally hearing literary works read or recited in community among young students (Sentius Augurinus in 4:27),[3] old teachers (Isaeus in 2:3),[4] and many others (Calpurnius Piso in 5:17). In his work *Progymnasmata*, Theon urges students to listen to good communal reading in order to improve their overall rhetorical skills (Theon 61–62).[5] Apuleius states that one of the mystery cults (*Pastophores*) reads directly from a book during their meetings: "Then from a lofty platform he read aloud from a book verbatim" (*Metam.* 11.17). Pausanias notes that the Persian Cult magicians even sing from a book: "Entering the chamber a magician piles dry wood upon the altar; he first places a tiara upon his head and then sings to some god or other an invocation in a foreign tongue unintelligible to Greeks, reciting the invocation from a book" (5.27.6). The first-

---

1. Michael W. Holmes, ed. and trans., *The Apostolic Fathers: Greek Texts and English Translations*, 3rd ed. (Grand Rapids: Baker, 2007), 162–63.

2. Holmes, *Apostolic Fathers*, 468–69. This passage is not the only one in the Shepherd of Hermas that has a command to write and read. For instance, the author writes elsewhere, "I am commanding you to write down first the commandments and parables so that you may read them at once and be able to keep them" (25.5; ibid., 502–3).

3. All references to classical texts will be from the digital Loeb Classical Library (LCL) unless noted otherwise, sometimes with only the volume number and facing page numbers noted, except when there is no facing page with a foreign language.

4. Cf. Juvenal, *Sat.* 3.74.

5. See George A. Kennedy, ed., *Progymnasmata: Greek Textbooks of Prose Composition and Rhetoric* (Atlanta: SBL, 2003), 5–6. Cf. the discussion of these terms in James R. Butts, "The *Progymnasmata* of Theon: A New Text with Translation and Commentary" (PhD diss., Claremont Graduate School, 1986), esp. 17–8, 38, 130.

century funerary monument of an eleven-year-old boy (Quintus Sulpicius Maximus) pictures him holding an open roll while publicly delivering his poem during the third Capitoline games shortly before his death in 94 CE (*CIL* VI, 33976).[6] As these selected examples demonstrate, reading and reciting texts promulgated literary traditions.

At the same time, only some literary traditions were shared, read aloud, or recited during certain communal gatherings. For example, Tertullian specifically mentions the communal reading of the books of God during Christian gatherings: "We meet to read the books of God" (*Apol.* 39:3). Bishop Serapion writes to the Church in Rhossus about the Gospel of Peter, advising them not to read it communally (*Hist. Eccl.* 6.12.2).[7] Pliny's reading group often promoted or rejected certain texts, authors, and participants for their events (Pompeius Saturninus in *Letters* 1.16). The Muratorian Fragment notes that some people are not willing to read the Apocalypse of Peter in church (72), and even though the Shepherd of Hermas should be read personally (77), "it cannot be read publicly to the people in church" (78).[8] Justin Martyr refers to the communal reading of the apostolic memoirs and the writings of the prophets on the Lord's Day: "On the day called Sunday, all who live in cities or in the country gather together to one place, and the memoirs of the apostles or the writings of the prophets are read, as long as time permits" (*1 Apol.* 1:67).[9] Gregory Snyder perceptively points out another important implication worth noting here. He states:

> In fact, nine of the thirteen references to the ἀπομνημονεύματα τῶν ἀποστόλων [memoirs of the apostles] involve some form of γράφω [writing]. Justin's conceptions about Gospel literature draw from him a manner of reference that acknowledges the textual and documentary character of the source. By contrast, the Books of Moses and the Prophets massively favor modes of reference that involve voice or

---

6. See also the first-century BCE funerary inscription of a fourteen-year-old girl who is memorialized as being educated and erudite in all the arts (*CIL* I, 2.1214).

7. For the entire portion of the Greek text and a further discussion about it, see Paul Foster, *The Gospel of Peter: Introduction, Critical Edition and Commentary*, TENTS 4, ed. Stanley E. Porter and Wendy J. Porter (Leiden: Brill, 2010), 105–8.

8. For a recent reproduction of Lietzmann's Latin text and Metzger's English translation, followed by an update on the current state of research on this fragment, see Eckhard J. Schnabel, "The Muratorian Fragment: The State of Research," *JETS* 57, no. 2 (2014): 231–64.

9. Alfred Walter Frank Blunt, ed., *The Apologies of Justin Martyr*, Cambridge Patristic Texts (Cambridge: Cambridge University Press, 1911), 100.

speech. Clearly, there is something about the *writtenness* of the Memoirs that is important.[10]

This sampling of evidence at least suggests the possibility that various traditions eagerly awaited acceptance or rejection from various communal reading events. Will the literary community read it communally? Will they endorse it? Will they actively make copies and circulate it? Will the god(s) accept this text? Will the god(s) answer our petition? Will they preserve it for future generations—via manuscripts, monuments, frescos, notebooks, etc.?

These types of evidence and questions led William Johnson, professor of classical studies at Duke University, to conclude, "Reading [among the elite] in this [High Roman Empire] society is tightly bound up in the construction of the community. Group reading and serious conversation devolving from reading are twin axes around which much of the elite man's community turns."[11] His book, however, focused solely on the High Roman Empire during the second to fourth centuries CE, and on elite people like Gellius, Galen, and Lucian. Many other individuals, centuries, and trajectories are left open for further academic inquiry and scrutiny.[12] In addition, Johnson's goal was merely to "redirect scholarly attention" to the fact that ancient reading was unlike "the reading-from-a-printed-book model familiar to us today." Furthermore, he only mentions "public reading" once in his entire book—and even then it is only a quote from someone else's work.

The problem, as I see it, is that this entire subject of communal reading events and their role in controlling literary traditions has been largely neglected in early Christian studies. By control, I simply mean a tendency to preserve the integrity of a tradition's propositional content, even while acknowledging that variation was inevitable, and local contingencies could shape the preservationist tendency itself.[13] For example, Tommy Wasserman points to a situ-

10. H. Gregory Snyder, "The Classroom in the Text: Exegetical Practices in Justin and Galen," in *Christians Origins and Greco-Roman Culture: Social and Literary Contexts for the New Testament*, ed. Stanley E. Porter and Andrew W. Pitts (Leiden: Brill, 2013), 663–85, here 673.

11. William A. Johnson, *Readers and Reading Culture in the High Roman Empire: A Study on Elite Communities* (New York: Oxford University Press, 2010), 39.

12. The author does recognize this when he states, "Further work along these lines could be profitably pursued also for the classical period (esp. Cicero) and for the context of early Christian writings" (ibid., n. 22).

13. Though it is outside the scope of our study, future research should compare this type of control with others in order to note further avenues or limitations. For example, eyewitnesses

ation recorded in a letter from Augustine to Jerome. According to Augustine, there was one word in Jerome's Latin translation (the Vulgate) of Jonah 4:6 that differed from what they had been hearing read communally for generations, and it caused an uproar in his congregation.[14] Academic literature even hinting at the fact that communal reading events were a means of controlling literary traditions is sporadic and implicit at best—often centuries removed from the traditions' inception.

Take Harry Gamble's remarkable study on books and readers in the early church, where one might expect to find such a treatment. Out of the 337 pages, only three pages specifically deal with "the public reading of Christian books," and another three on "the reading of Scripture in early Christian worship."[15] Yet he does not appear to argue for or against communal reading as a major control of the Christian tradition, nor does he attempt to determine whether communal reading events were widespread. He does, however, help actualize the importance of our discussion when he suggests that communal reading was "*probably* universal" by the middle of the *second* century, but that "it is still difficult to determine just *how early* this practice began or *how widely* it was followed."[16] And he does note in another publication that the "formation of the canon of scripture was nothing other than the church's retrospective recognition of its own reading habits."[17] More recently, Guy Stroumsa made a similar statement regarding reading practices in late antique Christianity when he said that "the public reading of Scriptures *had become* a major aspect of Christian ritual."[18] Again, the discussions often begin after

were not everywhere in the first century, and they died off by the second century. Thus, even though eyewitnesses were an essential type of quality control, they were necessarily limited in nature. On the other hand, if communal reading events were widespread in the first century and continued into subsequent centuries, then they demand more attention than they have previously received.

14. Tommy Wasserman, "The Early Text of Matthew," in *The Early Text of the New Testament*, ed. Charles E. Hill and Michael J. Kruger (New York: Oxford University Press, 2012), 106.

15. Harry Y. Gamble, *Books and Readers in the Early Church: A History of Early Christian Texts* (New Haven, CT: Yale University Press, 1995), 205–8 and 211–14, respectively.

16. Ibid., 205 and 206, respectively (italics added).

17. "Literacy, Liturgy, and the Shaping of the New Testament Canon," in *The Earliest Gospels: The Origins and Transmission of the Earliest Christian Gospels; The Contribution of the Chester Beatty Gospel Codex P45*, ed. Charles Horton (London: T&T Clark, 2004), 27–39, here 37.

18. "The New Self and Reading Practices in Late Antique Christianity," *CHRC* 95 (2015): 1–18, here 16, italics added.

the first century and insinuate that communal reading events were not always the norm.

Similarly, Lee Martin McDonald's academic work on the biblical canon does not deal with communal reading.[19] Although he does mention that Christian traditions and texts were originally and often transmitted orally, he does not appear to make specific mention of the impact communal reading events had on controlling the tradition or overall process of canonization.[20] In relation to both communal reading and canon studies, Peter Davids writes this in his critical commentary on the epistle of Jude: "It was the Christians who started asking two questions in the *second* century: (1) which works should be bound together in a codex (book)? And (2) which works should be read in church (since most people could not read and so were dependent upon what was read in church) as reflecting the rule of faith?"[21] His assumption that Christians "started" asking such a communal question in the "second" century further exposes the value of our topic at hand.

Narrowing the focus from academic works on more general topics to more specialized ones on specific topics, one should expect different results. Unfortunately, one arrives at the same dead end. Even more specialized works appear to have overlooked or dismissed communal reading as another distinct means of controlling the Christian tradition. Take Richard Bauckham's work, *Jesus and the Eyewitnesses*.[22] It has several fruitful sections dealing specifically with quality controls. While some controls are interwoven throughout his entire work, others are given a distinct section and subtitle. For example, "Controlling the Tradition: Memorization" (280), "Controlling the Tradition: Writing?" (286), and "Controlling the Tradition: Eyewitnesses and Gospels" (305) are dealt with individually. Thus, he approached the overall subject well, but he did not go far enough. One reason for this seems to be that no study has yet determined

19. Lee Martin McDonald, *The Biblical Canon: Its Origin, Transmission, and Authority* (Peabody, MA: Hendrickson, 2008). More recently, however, Bokedal does discuss communal reading as part of liturgical worship at a number of key points in his treatment on biblical canonicity. Tomas Bokedal, *The Formation and Significance of the Christian Biblical Canon: A Study in Text, Ritual and Interpretation* (London: T&T Clark, 2014).

20. For example, even though they did not discuss "canon(icity)" as scholars do today, their understanding of readability arguably foreshadowed it.

21. *The Letters of 2 Peter and Jude* (Grand Rapids: Eerdmans, 2006), 76 (italics added).

22. *Jesus and the Eyewitnesses: The Gospels as Eyewitness Testimony* (Grand Rapids: Eerdmans, 2006).

how widespread these events were in order to determine what role they played as a guardian of the tradition. In light of this neglect, and observing that communal reading events were no inconsequential matter, given the amount of ancient references to them, concerted attention is warranted for further illuminating the book culture of the early church.[23]

The same neglect can be seen in Petr Pokorný's 2013 monograph. After analyzing the role *oral* gospel traditions played in shaping the earliest *literary* Gospel (Mark) and the way Gospels as texts (re-)introduce Jesus traditions into Christian liturgy and literature, he concludes by discussing the origins of the idea of the Christian canon.[24] Yet "public reading" is only mentioned once (in order to highlight the fact that certain literary genres helped readers read the text communally),[25] and when the author does mention certain liturgical settings in which texts were read (though only about half a dozen times in 248 pages), he seems to suggest that they were merely an aid for memory.[26] Yet the formation of the Gospels—and entire Christian tradition—should be examined in light of both the oral culture and book culture.[27]

Larry Hurtado has also noticed this lack of familiarity among some biblical scholars regarding book culture in the first few centuries CE.[28] After noting several academic works by classicists on this topic

23. Communal reading as a quality control has remained unaddressed elsewhere, even though many other scholars have offered various critiques of Bauckham's work, and he has often responded in kind. Take Bauckham's response to the reviews of Samuel Byrskog, David Catchpole, Howard Marshall, Stephen Patterson, and Theodore Weeden in his article "In Response to My Respondents: *Jesus and the Eyewitnesses* in Review," *JSHJ* 6 (2008): 225–53, and to Jens Schröter and Craig Evans in "Eyewitnesses and Critical History: A Response to Jens Schröter and Craig Evans," *JSNT* 31, no. 2 (2008): 221–35.

24. Petr Pokorný, *From the Gospel to the Gospels: History, Theology and Impact of the Biblical Term 'euangelion,'* Beihefte zur Zeitschrift für die neutestamentliche Wissenschaft 195 (Boston: De Gruyter, 2013). See also the lack of treatment of this topic in Bart D. Ehrman, *Forgery and Counterforgery: The Use of Literary Deceit in Early Christian Polemics* (New York: Oxford University Press, 2013); and Francis Watson, *Gospel Writing: A Canonical Perspective* (Grand Rapids: Eerdmans, 2013).

25. Ibid., 108.

26. For example, see ibid., 127.

27. Several important works have approached the subject via performance and audience response, but not in the same sense that it will be addressed in this volume. See, among others, William D. Shiell, *Reading Acts: The Lector and the Early Christian Audience*, Biblical Interpretation Series 70 (Leiden: Brill Academic, 2004); idem., *Delivering from Memory: The Effect of Performance on the Early Christian Audience* (Eugene, OR: Wipf & Stock, 2011).

28. Larry W. Hurtado, "Oral Fixation and New Testament Studies? 'Orality', 'Performance' and Reading Texts in Early Christianity," *NTS* 60 (2014): 321–40.

that appear to have gone unnoticed or unchallenged, he points to several pertinent gaps that need filling by biblical scholars. For example, clarity on what scholars mean when referring to "performance" during communal reading events, and the need for greater attention to the physical properties of the earliest Christian manuscripts, which contain various "readers' aids." Hurtado also remains one of the few scholars to even note the likely effects repeated communal readings had as a stabilizing force in the textual transmission of certain texts.[29] Similarly, Craig Evans has acknowledged the possibility that communal reading events "may well have created something like a 'standardized' text and undoubtedly facilitated memorization, which would also have a stabilizing affect [sic] on the text."[30] But apart from raising the possibility, he does not develop this factor much further.

A NEW CONTROL CATEGORY:
COMMUNAL READING EVENTS

Over the past few decades, various scholars have argued for or against certain "quality controls" that must have been in place—consciously or unconsciously—in order to account for the transmission of the earliest Jesus movement. By successfully identifying one or more of these controls, it is thought, one can better account for the similarities and differences between the various Christian traditions, get closer to the earliest sources of the nascent Jesus movement, and ultimately understand the historical Jesus more accurately. For example, Richard Bauckham argues that "eyewitnesses" were a means of controlling the Christian tradition.[31] James Dunn proposes "communal memory."[32] Kenneth Bailey suggests "memorization."[33] Alan Millard puts forth

---

29. Idem., "The New Testament in the Second Century: Text, Collections and Canon," in *Transmission and Reception: New Testament Text-Critical and Exegetical Studies*, ed. J. W. Childers and D. C. Parker (Piscataway, NJ: Gorgias, 2006), 3–27.

30. "How Long Were Late Antique Books in Use? Possible Implications for New Testament Textual Criticism," *BBR* 25, no. 1 (2015): 23–37, here 36.

31. Bauckham, *Jesus and the Eyewitnesses*.

32. *Jesus Remembered: Christianity in the Making*, vol. 1 (Grand Rapids: Eerdmans, 2003). Note also his published presidential address from the 57th Annual Meeting of *Studiorum Novi Testamenti Societas* at the University of Durham, published as "Altering the Default Setting: Re-envisaging the Early Transmission of the Jesus Tradition," *NTS* 49 (2003): 139–75.

33. "Informal Controlled Oral Tradition and the Synoptic Gospels," *AJT* 5 (1991): 34–54.

"writing."[34] Samuel Byrskog proposes "performance."[35] Chris Keith advocates "Jesus-memory."[36] Mikael Tellbe points to "texts."[37] John Dominic Crossan stresses "mimetics."[38] Tommy Wasserman and Jennifer Knust highlight "liturgical singing."[39] Of course, one could list several others.[40]

The debates, however, do not end there. Additional disputes exist over the different levels of quality within each control category. Were they flexible, somewhat flexible, or totally flexible? Rudolph Bultmann seems to imply that the transmission of the earliest Jesus tradition was fluid (often labeled *informal and uncontrolled*).[41] Kenneth Bailey suggests that it was *informal but controlled* (i.e., the community exercised the control).[42] Birger Gerhardsson argues for a *formal con-*

---

34. *Reading and Writing in the Time of Jesus* (New York: New York University Press, 2000).

35. *Story as History—History As Story: The Gospel Tradition in the Context of Ancient Oral History*, WUNT 123 (Tübingen: Mohr-Siebeck, 2000).

36. *Jesus' Literacy: Scribal Culture and the Teacher from Galilee*, repr. ed., LNTS 413 / LHJS 8 (New York: T&T Clark, 2013).

37. *Christ-Believers in Ephesus*, WUNT 242 (Tübingen: Mohr Siebeck, 2009).

38. "Itinerants and Householders in the Earliest Jesus Movement," in *Whose Historical Jesus?*, ed. William E. Arnal and Michael R. Desjardins, SCJ 7 (Waterloo, ON: Wilfred Laurier University Press, 1997), 7–24.

39. "The Biblical Odes and the Text of the Christian Bible: A Reconsideration of the Impact of Liturgical Singing on the Transmission of the Gospel of Luke," *JBL* 133, no. 2 (2014): 341–65.

40. Michael Bird, for example, while including several of the usual categories just mentioned, like eyewitnesses, adds a few other viable controls as distinct categories, including "Pedagogical and Rhetorical Devices," "Teachers as Custodians," "Interest in Jesus," and "Aramaic Sources," in order to better determine "what factors or controls may have enabled that [Jesus] tradition to be preserved effectively." "The Purpose and Preservation of the Jesus Tradition: Moderate Evidence for a Conserving Force in Its Transmission," *BBR* 15, no. 2 (2005): 161–85. To a lesser and slightly different extent, but nonetheless suggestive of other avenues for consideration, "genre" is being discussed more frequently as a type of control. For instance, see the portion of Mark Goodacre's response to John S. Kloppenborg under "Genre" in "Did Thomas Know the Synoptic Gospels? A Response to Denzey Lewis, Kloppenborg, and Patterson," *JSNT* 36, no. 3 (2014): 282–93, here 287–88. Likewise, other societal controls have been written about—as when Robert A. Kaster describes the grammarians who teach the younger generations as "guardians of articulate utterance," in his book *Guardians of Language: The Grammarian and Society in Late Antiquity*, The Transformation of the Classical Heritage 11 (Los Angeles: University of California Press, 1988), 17—but they are not as directly involved with our present study.

41. Rudolph Bultmann, *Jesus and the Word* (New York: Scribners, 1934).

42. Bailey, "Informal Controlled Oral Tradition." See also Weeden's methodological critique of Bailey's theory, "Kenneth Bailey's Theory of Oral Tradition: A Theory Contested by Its Evidence," *JSNT* 7 (2009): 3–43, as well as Eric Eve's critical review of these types of scholarly discussions regarding oral tradition in *Behind the Gospels: Understanding the Oral Tradition* (Minneapolis: Fortress Press, 2014).

trolled tradition.[43] Richard Bauckham incorporates another transmission continuum for scholars to consider: *stability-flexibility.*[44]

While all of these controls and various degrees of each have their place in the overall picture—strengths and weaknesses aside for now—one control that has not been explicitly proposed or given sufficient academic scrutiny is communal reading events. The main goal for us in this volume, then, is to ask and answer the first of a series of important historical questions regarding communal reading, namely, what evidence exists that would suggest that communal reading events were a widespread phenomenon in the first century CE? Our goal is not to determine how many communal reading events took place at any given location, but to determine whether communal reading events were extensive geographically.

This is the first historical question that must be answered before a host of other important, related historical questions can be adequately addressed and which connect more specifically with various elements of control. For example, to what extent did communal reading events control the transmission of the Christian tradition in the first century CE? When did communal reading first become a means for discerning and determining the validity or invalidity of a text? Why was there such an emphasis on the communal reading of texts? Did communities notice, discuss, and/or react to reading or hearing amended traditions? What commonalities and differences are there between nonbiblical and biblical communal reading events?

While some examples of and partial answers to several of these questions will be noted throughout our examination, the main contention is that by examining evidence from the first century CE, it will be demonstrated that communal reading events were widespread. If shown, this will open up new vistas in the study of the formation of the Jesus tradition, the contours of book culture in early Christianity, and factors shaping the transmission of the text of the New Testament.

---

43. Birger Gerhardsson, *Memory and Manuscript: Oral Tradition and Written Transmission in Rabbinic Judaism and Early Christianity*, ASNU 22 (Lund: Munksgaard, 1961); more recently see idem., "The Secret of the Transmission of the Unwritten Jesus Tradition," *NTS* 51 (2005): 1–18.

44. Bauckham, *Jesus and the Eyewitnesses*, 257–60.

2.

Finding Communal Reading Events in the Time of Jesus

He is said to have read, written and declaimed every day. . . . To avoid
the danger of forgetting what he was to say, or wasting time in commit-
ting it to memory, he adopted the practice of reading everything from
a manuscript. Even his conversations with individuals and the more
important of those with his own wife Livia, he always wrote out and
read from a note-book.

—Suetonius, *Augustus* 84 (ca. 69–140 CE)

[Lycurgus introduced the law] that their tragedies be written out and
kept in a public depository, and that the clerk of the State read them to
the actors who were to perform their plays for comparison of the texts
and that it be unlawful to depart from the authorized text in acting.

—Plutarch, *Life of Lycugus* 841 (ca. 46–120 CE)

No doubt exists that communal reading events were part of the first-
century Greco-Roman socio-historical milieu. Identifying and locating such events, however, is complicated. There are many kinds of
evidence. The dating of such evidence is debatable. Provenances are
often difficult, if not impossible, to establish. The terminology varied
significantly among communities and individuals.

Before launching further into this study, then, these details need to
be addressed. Similarly, it should be said from the outset that the more
common "public reading," which is used in most modern translations
and academic works, will be avoided because of the confusion that

often comes (or may come) from the word *public*. The word *communal* is preferred because it both highlights the social aspect of reading and defines the reading event as one in which two or more persons are involved. In other words, "communal reading" can be public or private, but not individualistic.

REGISTERING A FEW CAUTIONS

The defined period I will be covering is the first century CE. Nevertheless, there must be some flexibility at both ends of the century, since not every author included in this study was limited to it. Strabo of Amaseia lived the majority of his life prior to the first century CE. Yet he will be included in chapter 5, since the selected text was probably written toward the end of his life, between 18 and 19 CE.

With that in mind, three broad categories will be highlighted here regarding the evidence: types, dating, and location. We will then look at some key terms that often refer explicitly to communal reading events.

TYPES OF EVIDENCE

The primary type of evidence we will examine is literary. The main reason for stating this upfront is to emphasize that our study is not exhaustive. Considerable amounts and various types of sources exist for just about every category of "writing" that could have been read communally (law, grammar, astronomy, astrology, religious, cooking, geography, farming, medicine, etc.). Further examination of other types of evidence, such as epigraphic and archaeological, ought to be pursued across ancient geographical landscapes in order to help balance the overall assessment of this study and to provide additional clarity on the proposed historical reconstruction.[1] To provide just one key example, there is a first-century funerary altar facing the Via Salaria that includes a niche with a two-foot statue of an eleven-year-old boy. The portrait represents the boy as an adult orator dressed in a toga. He stands in a pose as if delivering his poem, with an open roll in his left hand, the right hand placed over his chest, and the head

---

1. Williams Tabbernee notes various types of evidence across several geographical areas in his recent study, "Material Evidence for Early Christian Groups during the First Two Centuries C.E.," *ASE* 30, no. 2 (2013): 287–301.

turned slightly to the left and looking ahead. The Greek inscription on the left and the right of the niche consists of a brief introduction and the poem that the boy read communally during the third Capitoline games in 94 CE.[2]

In addition, we must recognize the caution that is required in drawing generalizations from any ancient evidence. Many studies advance strong conclusions based primarily or exclusively on one type of evidence (typically papyrus) or from one geographical area, and assume without qualification that it is representative of all sources and locations. Roger Bagnall, for instance, highlights how papyrus finds can be unrepresentative and notes the dangers of historical reconstructions based on generalizations from unrepresentative data.[3] Todd Hickey similarly states, "The papyri provide explicit testimony that cultural exchange occurred, but why it occurred is another question."[4] At the same time, if one type of evidence—in this case, literary—does reveal communal reading events across broad geographical terrains, then the probability necessarily increases that communal reading events were widespread and regular.

Moreover, several important matters will not receive extensive attention, given the main focus of our study. For example, we will not directly address why any author or community would have wished to preserve their tradition. We will not assess what motives may have led writers to have their works read publicly.[5] We will not deal with the ways various orality theories interact with the main thesis. We will not set out to compare the events or communities with one another. We will not ask how a given communal reading event helped form the group socially. We will not pursue the numerous and important implicit indicators of communal reading events, such as lectional signs found in certain manuscripts.[6] Likewise, we will

2. For more details concerning this monument, see my articles "Ancient Literacy in New Testament Research: Incorporating a Few More Lines of Enquiry," *TrinJ* 36, no. 2 (2015): 161–89; and "The First-Century Inscription of Quintus Sulpicius Maximus: An Initial Catalogue of Lexical Parallels with the New Testament," *BBR* 27.1 (2017): 53–63.

3. *Everyday Writing in the Graeco-Roman East* (Berkeley: University of California, 2011).

4. Todd M. Hickey, "Writing Histories from the Papyri," in *The Oxford Handbook of Papyrology*, ed. Roger S. Bagnall (Oxford: Oxford University Press, 2009), 495–520, here 506.

5. Bruce Metzger notes at least eight motives for why a work may get published under an assumed name: (1) financial gain, (2) pure malice, (3) love and respect, (4) modesty, (5) interests of dramatic composition, (6) production of spurious epistles, (7) accidents of copying, and (8) important/prestigious figures of antiquity. See "Literary Forgeries and Canonical Pseudepigrapha," *JBL* 91, no. 1 (1972): 3–24.

6. Different scholars use different terminology here (e.g., reader's aids, reading aids, aids for

not outline all the implications our investigation will have on many other disciplines and subdisciplines, such as canonicity, New Testament textual criticism, source criticism, orality, historical Jesus, social identity, and performance criticism. Again, our sole goal is to identify the locations of communal reading events in the first century in order to provide additional parameters for considering what controlled the earliest Christian tradition(s).

DATING THE EVIDENCE

Most ancient evidence is difficult to date precisely.[7] This is in part why scholars often work within a controlled range, establishing, if possible, a *terminus post quem* and *terminus ante quem*. Our study will follow this academic pattern when possible. Michael Holmes also rightly points out that the dating of a particular manuscript may not be as old as the text the manuscript contains.[8] This does not mean

reading, helps for the reader). For a helpful sampling of examples, see Dan Nässelqvist, *Public Reading in Early Christianity: Lectors, Manuscripts, and Sound in the Oral Delivery of John 1–4*, NovTSup 163 (Leiden: Brill, 2016), 23n17. In addition, for a study further examining and defining the physical manuscripts as either being produced primarily for public or private consumption, see Scott D. Charlesworth, "Public and Private: Second- and Third-Century Gospel Manuscripts," in *Jewish and Christian Scripture as Artifact and Canon*, ed. Craig A. Evans and H. Daniel Zacharias (London: T&T Clark, 2009): 148–75. Moreover, for further discussions regarding other physical features, see, among others, William A. Johnson, *Bookrolls and Scribes in Oxyrhynchus*, repr. paperback (Toronto: University of Toronto Press, 2013); Larry W. Hurtado, *The Earliest Christian Artifacts: Manuscripts and Christian Origins* (Grand Rapids: Eerdmans, 2006); Zeev Elizur, "The Book and the Holy: Chapters in the History of the Concept of Holy Book from the Second Temple Period to Late Antiquity" (PhD diss., Ben Gurion University, 2012 [Hebrew]); Jean-Marie Carrié, "Le livre comme objet d'usage, le livre comme valeur symbolique," *Antiquité Tardive* 18 (2010): 181–90.There are certainly other indicators as well, such as the possibility of what Stephen Young calls "markers of orality," such as mnemonic constructions, redundancy, and additive connectives. For more details, categories, and examples of such indicators, see, among others, Stephen E. Young, *Jesus Tradition in the Apostolic Fathers*, WUNT 311 (Tübingen: Mohr Siebeck, 2011), 81–97. At the same time, his underlining methodology is amiss, since he believes oral performances originated primarily without a written text. For a recent evaluation and critique of this methodology, see Larry W. Hurtado, "Oral Fixation and New Testament Studies? 'Orality', 'Performance' and Reading Texts in Early Christianity," *NTS* 60 (2014): 321–40.

7. This fact especially concerns literary papyri. See, among others, Pasquale Orsini and Willy Clarysse, "Early New Testament Manuscripts and Their Dates: A Critique of Theological Palaeography," *ETL* (2012): 443–74.

8. Michael W. Holmes, "Working with an Open Textual Tradition: Challenges in Theory and Practice," in *The Textual History of the Greek New Testament: Changing Views in Contemporary Research*, ed. Klaus Wachtel and Michael W. Holmes, Text-Critical Studies 8 (Atlanta: SBL, 2011), 65–78. See also Konrad Martin Heide's recent study comparing several papyri manuscripts dated prior to Constantine with several minuscule manuscripts dated after his reign,

the date—or other factors—of the manuscript does not matter, but that there are more layers of complexity to consider as the evidence is examined. One example of this is the *Didache*. Although the text is typically dated to the first or second century, there is no manuscript of it dated to either century. In fact, only two manuscripts of the *Didache* exist: One is the Byrennios manuscript (H), which is self-dated by the scribe Λέων νοτάριος καὶ ἀλείτης (= Leon the notary and sinner) as completed on Tuesday, June 11, 1056. The second is the P.Oxy. 1782 (P), which is likely from the fourth or fifth century CE. This is why citations of the *Didache* by early writers need to be incorporated in these dating discussions.[9]

Therefore, only when the dating of an author greatly affects the results of the main thesis, will there be further discussion, documentation, or justification for such dating. In addition, only if there seems to be a significant argument to be made between the text and manuscript will additional arguments and documentation be supplied. Put more simply, this study proceeds on a case-by-case basis with these considerations of dating in mind.

LOCATING THE EVIDENCE

Even if there is consistency across one type of evidence, and even if there is accurate dating, the general location still needs to be determined. The geographical scope of this study primarily focuses on the main areas in which Christianity was active in the first century, such as Palestine, Greece, Syria, and Asia Minor, as well as Italy, Gaul, and North Africa.

Whenever evidence is discovered in a particular geographic location, it does not necessarily mean that the artifact originated from there or was ever supposed to be there. Put more simply, the source of the tradition may be different from the find site. For example, a letter is often found at the recipient's location, not the author's. A strong

in order to better gauge the reliability of the New Testament text in comparison with the Shepherd of Hermas: "Labilität und Festigkeit des überlieferten Textes des Neuen Testaments und des *Pastor Hermae*: Demonstriert an wichtigen Textzeugen," *Sacra Scripta* 7, no. 1 (2009): 65–97.

9. For such history, sources, and dating of the *Didache*, see, among others, Kurt Niederwimmer, *The* Didache: *A Commentary*, trans. Linda M. Maloney (Minneapolis: Fortress Press, 1998), 19–20; Aaron Milavec, *The* Didache: *Faith, Hope, and Life of the Earliest Christian Communities, 50–70 CE* (New York: Newman, 2003), 3–5.

caution exists, then, not to automatically draw conclusions based on provenance. A prime example of this can be seen in the hotly debated area of Qumran.[10] No one doubts that archaeologists found scrolls there. But were the scrolls brought to Qumran from elsewhere?

For this study, the scholarly consensus will be followed where possible concerning the general region mentioned in or implied by the evidence. Only in cases where there seems to be no consensus or identifying signals will there be additional information provided regarding the provenance. No doubt, this approach comes with a higher degree of subjectivity. Nevertheless, this study is focusing more on how widespread the evidence is across large regions, such as Asia Minor, than on specific locations within those regions, such as the Lycus Valley.[11]

SOME KEY TERMINOLOGY

There is not a list of terms or phrases being investigated. There will be times throughout our study where there will be evidence that strongly suggests a communal reading event but that never uses explicit terminology to denote the event (and vice versa). For example, 3 Maccabees contains no explicit mention of reading, reciting, hearing, listening, or books. One may yet argue that many features, such as the appearance of "αμην" at the end of the book (7:23), do suggest that the book was read communally on the very festival that 3 Maccabees describes (similar to the public reading of Esther on Purim). Likewise, a communal reading event might have been scheduled to take place but never occurred, due to some extenuating circumstances. Appian writes about a text that would have been read communally were it not for the death of its author: "When the people heard these charges [regarding a man's mysterious death] they were

10. See, among others, Robert R. Cargill, "The State of the Archaeological Debate at Qumran," *CBR* 10, no. 1 (2011): 101–18. As for debates over the purpose and province of individual texts, see, among others, S. J. Hultgren, *From the Damascus Covenant to the Covenant of the Community: Literary, Historical, and Theological Studies in the Dead Sea Scrolls*, STDJ 66 (Leiden: Brill, 2007); Daniel Stökl Ben Ezra, "Old Caves and Young Caves: A Statistical Reevaluation of a Qumran Consensus," *DSD* 14, no. 3 (2007): 313–33; John J. Collins, "The Site of Qumran and the Sectarian Communities in the Dead Sea Scrolls," in *The World of Jesus and the Early Church: Identity and Interpretation in Early Communities of Faith*, ed. Craig A. Evans (Peabody, MA: Hendrickson, 2011), 9–22.

11. Ulrich Huttner, *Early Christianity in the Lycus Valley*, trans. David Green, AJEC 85 (Leiden: Brill, 2013).

in a state of alarm until Scipio, after placing near his couch at home one evening a tablet on which to write during the night the speech he intended to deliver before the people, was found dead in his bed without a wound" (*Hist. Rom.* 3.1.20). Examples such as these two offer a clue as to the types of contexts being assessed while also seeking to identify explicit terminology.[12]

At the same time, it will be easier to identify what is not being addressed: silent or individual reading.[13] Likewise, what some scholars are calling "secondary orality" (or re-oralization) will not be addressed. This study essentially agrees with Mark Goodacre and others who see this term as more confusing than helpful.[14] There was never a time in early Christianity that the transmission was exclusively oral. Moreover, Holt Parker writes, "There is no example known to me of any person who performed a Latin poem or a speech before a second person, who in turn transmitted it orally it [sic] to a third."[15] Written texts and oral traditions interacted in dynamic ways (2 Thess 2:15; see also Eccl 12:9–14). Both eyes and ears were involved. Both writer and speaker were heralds of God. In any case, the range of flexibility within both oral and written channels of

---

12. Again, other explicit terminology exists, especially the terms signifying the people hearing the texts—and not just the people reading the texts. In fact, at least one term could arguably be added to the list of designations given to certain people in the New Testament: ἀκροατής (e.g., in Rom 2:13; James 1:22–25). Cf., among others, the seven common self-designations noted in Paul Trebilco, *Self-Designations and Group Identity in the New Testament* (Cambridge: Cambridge University Press, 2012).

13. See, among others, Paul J. Achtemeier, "*Omne verbum sonat*: The New Testament and the Oral Environment of Late Western Antiquity," *JBL* 109 (1990): 3–27; G.L. Hendrickson, "Ancient Reading," *CJ* 25, no. 3 (1929): 182–96; Raymond J. Starr, "Reading Aloud: *Lectores* and Roman Reading," *CJ* 86, no. 4 (1991): 337–43; Frank D. Gilliard, "More Silent Reading in Antiquity: *Non Omne Verbum Sonabat*," *JBL* 112, no. 4 (1993): 689–96; A. K. Gavrilov, "Techniques of Reading in Classical Antiquity," *CQ* 47, no. 1 (1997): 56–73; William A. Johnson, "Toward a Sociology of Reading in Classical Antiquity," *AJP* 121, no. 4 (2000): 593–627.

14. Mark Goodacre initially expressed his opinions about secondary orality in his book *Thomas and the Gospels: The Making of an Apocryphal Text* (Grand Rapids: Eerdmans, 2012), 135–40. A couple of years later, John Kloppenborg (among others) challenged a number of points concerning Goodacre's book (and Simon Gathercole's book on the *Gospel of Thomas*), including his section on secondary orality. John S. Kloppenborg, "A New Synoptic Problem: Mark Goodacre and Simon Gathercole on *Thomas*," *JSNT* 36, no. 3 (2014): 199–239, see 201–5. In the same journal volume, Goodacre (as well as Gathercole) provided a response to Kloppenborg's (and the others') review of his book. Mark Goodacre, "Did Thomas Know the Synoptic Gospels? A Response to Denzey Lewis, Kloppenborg and Patterson," *JSNT* 36, no. 3 (2014): 282–93, see 286–87.

15. "Books and Reading Latin Poetry," in *Ancient Literacies: The Culture of Reading in Greece and Rome*, ed. William A. Johnson and Holt N. Parker (Oxford: Oxford University Press, 2009), 186–229, here 193.

any tradition essentially diminishes, and stability increases, when and where the two frequently touch.

Nevertheless, several terms are often common markers of communal reading events. The simplified definitions are not meant to be definitive or exhaustive, but rather are utilized simply as working definitions at the outset of our study. The parameters here have purposefully been broadened to include the first few centuries CE, so that a few more modern works that do not have as narrow of a time frame as ours can be incorporated.

ἈΝΑΓΙΝΏΣΚΩ

One of the most common and explicit Greek terms denoting a communal reading event is ἀναγινώσκω. This word had a long history prior to the first century AD. It was the word periodically chosen to translate the Hebrew word קרא in the LXX, as in Jeremiah 3:12: "Go, and read [ἀνάγνωθι] these words toward the north." One of its basic meanings appears to have remained unchanged: to read communally.[16] In fact, the noun form of this word is found in the "Theodotus inscription" from a synagogue in Jerusalem during the first-century AD: "Theodotus [. . .] rebuilt this synagogue for the reading [ἀνάγνωσιν] of the Law" (CIJ 1404).[17] Likewise, there is evidence of its usage in Greek MSS from Qumran.[18] Thus, ἀναγινώσκω is a common and significant term for the present study and often points directly to a communal reading event. At the same time, one must be cautious in assuming a communal setting even if translating the term(s) consistently. Donald Allan, who wrote one of the standard articles on the term ἀναγινώσκω and its cognates, warns the reader that "one must judge from the context whether reading to one or more other people, or private reading, is meant."[19]

16. LEH, 36; TDNT, 1.343–44; NIDNTTE, 278–79; BDAG 60; LSJ, s.v. "ἀναγινώσκω."

17. Regarding the possibility of a plurality of synagogues, see, among others, Matthew J. Martin, "Interpreting the Theodotos Inscription: Some Reflections on a First Century Jerusalem Synagogue Inscription and E.P. Sanders 'Common Judaism,'" ANES 39 (2002): 160–81.

18. See 8HevXIIgr 17:25 (Hab 2:2): [ὅπως τρέχ]ῃ ἀναγεινώσκων [ἐν αὐτῇ.

19. Donald J. Allan, "ΑΝΑΓΙΓΝΩΣΚΩ and Some Cognate Words," CQ 30, no. 1 (1980): 244–51, here 244. See also the similar warning by T. C. Skeat in "The Use of Dictation in Ancient Book-Production," Proceedings of the British Academy 42 (1956): 179–208, esp. 180, or the cautions given in William A. Johnson, "Toward a Sociology of Reading in Classical Antiquity," AJP 121, no. 4 (2000): 593–627. For another, more recent study of ἀναγινώσκω—even though several classic studies addressing the term are absent from her examination (as in Allan's article just referenced)—see Claire S. Smith, Pauline Communities as 'Scholastic Communities': A

In addition, this study will not define "reading" in such a broad way as to move beyond actual reading and mean merely hearing and listening.[20] Likewise, this study does not concur with those who seem to strip the textual aspect out of the reading and translate ἀναγινώσκω something like "to perform the Scriptures in public," with oral performance from memory in mind.[21]

RECITATIO

Recitatio is one of the most common and explicit Latin terms denoting a communal reading event. This word also had a rich history prior to the first century CE and maintained its most basic meaning: to read or recall from memory a written text communally.[22] Parker simply states, "Much that was written was not recited; nothing was recited that was not written."[23]

Communal recitations included written tragedies, comedies, elegies, histories, poems, and even less-formal, superficial writings, like certain personal letters. Sometimes a well-to-do author would read his own material communally (Horace), and other times, an author would hire a slave to read for communal entertainment (Cicero). Sometimes the event was private, and at others times, the event was

---

Study of the Vocabulary of 'Teaching' in 1 Corinthians, 1 and 2 Timothy and Titus, WUNT 335 (Tübingen: Mohr Siebeck, 2012), esp. 157–59.

20. Though not specifically discussing ἀναγινώσκω, Andrew McGowan states, "I use 'reading' in a rather loose sense, of course, since it may be assumed that many who used and heard these texts, in whatever ways, did not actually read them." Andrew Brian McGowan, "'Is There a Liturgical Text in This Gospel?': The Institution Narratives and Their Early Interpretive Communities," *JBL* 118, no. 1 (1999): 73–87, here 76n11.

21. See Richard F. Ward and David J. Trobisch, *Bringing the Word to Life: Engaging the New Testament through Performing It* (Grand Rapids: Eerdmans, 2013): xi.

22. Giovanni B. Funaioli, "Recitationes," in *Paulys Realencyclopädie der classischen Altertumswissenschaft* (Stuttgart: Druckenmüller, 1949), 435–46. Cf. *Brill's New Pauly* online platform; Michael Winterbottom, "Recitatio," in *The Oxford Classical Dictionary* (fourth edition; eds. Simon Hornblower, Antony Spawforth, and Esther Eidinow; Oxford: Oxford University Press, 2012), 1258. Though Winterbottom mistakenly repeats the error made by many other scholars that C. Asinius Pollio was the first Roman to recite what he had written to an invited audience. According to Suetonius (*De Grammaticis et Rhetoribus* 2), Crates introduced poetry reading in Rome in the second century BC. See among others A. Dalzell, "C. Asinius Pollio and the Early History of Public Recitation at Rome," *Hermathena* 86 (1955): 20–28.

23. "Books and Reading Latin Poetry," in *Ancient Literacies: The Culture of Reading in Greece and Rome* (eds. William A. Johnson and Holt N. Parker; Oxford: Oxford University Press, 2009), 186–229, here 217. See also Alessandro Vatri, "Ancient Greek Writing for Memory: Textual Features as Mnemonic Facilitators," *Mnemosyne* 68 (2015): 750–73.

public.[24] Without getting into all the specifics here, the fundamental point is that this term is also important to our study, is regularly linked to communal reading events, and "takes for granted the existence of a written text, which is to be read."[25]

’ΕΝΤΥΓΧΆΝΩ AND ’ΕΞΗΓΈΟΜΑΙ

These two terms will be grouped together, since they are not as common.[26] ’Εντυγχάνω normally means "to approach." However, it can periodically refer to reading "from the idea of 'coming across' or 'encountering' a book."[27] Examples of this usage can be seen in Plutarch, Philo, Josephus, Justin, et al. Here are three prime examples:

> 2 Macc 2:25 = We have aimed to please those who wish to read [ἀναγινώσκειν], to make it easy for those who are inclined to memorize [μνήμης] and to profit all those who happen to come across (i.e., read) [ἐντυγχάνουσιν] this.

> Jos. Ant. 1.15 = At the outset, then, I entreat those who will read [ἐντευξομένος] these volumes to fix their thoughts on God . . .

> Philo Spec. Laws 4.161 = Still after writing he must endeavor every day to read [ἐντυγχάνειν] and familiarize [ἀναγινώσκειν] himself with what he has written, so that he may have a constant and unbroken memory of ordinances so good and profitable to all.

’Εξηγέομαι usually means, "to report, explain, or describe," but can also be rendered "to expound [a written text]."[28] Examples of this usage can be found among soothsayers, Irenaeus, Justin, and so on. Two examples of this usage will suffice:

---

24. See among others, Florence Dupont, "*Recitatio* and the Space of Public Discourse," in *The Roman Cultural Revolution* (eds. T. Habinek and A. Schiesaro; Cambridge: Cambridge University Press, 1997), 44–59. Cf. José Miguel González, "*Rhapsōidos, Prophētēs,* and *Hypokritēs*: A Diachronic Study of the Performance of Homeric Poetry in Ancient Greece" (PhD diss., Harvard University, 2005).

25. Dupont, *Recitatio*, 52.

26. There are certainly other terms to consider, but many of them seem to require a complement term(s) before justifying the sense of "to read." See Dirk M. Schenkeveld, "Prose Usages of Ἀκούειν 'To Read'," *CQ* 42.1 (1992): 129–41, esp. 135.

27. LEH, 208; TDNT, 8.242–3; NIDNTTE, 207–11; BDAG 341; LSJ, s.v. "ἐντυγχάνω."

28. LEH, 214; *NIDNTTE*, 212–16; BDAG 349; LSJ, s.v. "ἐξηγέομαι."

Trypho 71 = But I am far from putting reliance in your teachers, who refuse to admit that the exposition (or interpretation) [ἐξηγεῖσθαι] made by the seventy elders who were with Ptolemy of the Egyptians is a correct one; and they attempt to expound [ἐξηγεῖσθαι] another.

Pilate 16:3 = And the rulers of the synagogue, and the priests and the Levites, said to themselves: "Come, let us send to Galilee for the three men that came and expounded [ἐξηγησαμένους] his teaching and his taking up, and let them tell us how they saw him taken up."

SUMMARY

This chapter has registered several cautions regarding types of evidence, dating, provenance, and terminology. While the dating, provenance, and terminology are not always clear or the same, there is no doubt evidence exists for communal reading events in the first-century Greco-Roman world. I also established that we will primarily examine select literary evidence from authors presumably writing in the first century CE. A controlled dating range will be provided on a case-by-case basis, and the main areas of focus will be those in which Christianity was active in the first century. The general province of each author and literary work will follow the scholarly consensus when possible, with larger regions being the focus. Our study will also move beyond merely identifying a set of terms or phrases, even though some terms and phrases do occur more often than others do. In the next few chapters, we will examine several key factors that would have either hindered or enabled widespread communal reading events.

3.

Economic and Political Factors

[Regulus] even collected a vast audience the other day to hear him read a memoir of his son—the life of a mere boy, but nevertheless he read it, and has had countless copies made to distribute throughout Italy and the provinces.

—Pliny, *Letters* 4.7.2 (ca. 61–113 CE)

Hordeonius read to the army copies of all the letters that he had dispatched throughout the Gauls, Britain, and the Spains asking for aid.

—Tacitus, *Histories* 4.25 (ca. 56–120 CE)

ECONOMIC REALITIES

For an economy to flourish, there ought to be growth in various areas. In modern terms, these areas would include such topics as jobs, government spending, infrastructure, aggregate demand, and progressive inventions.[1] Looking at the first few centuries CE,[2] then, there ought to be development in several of these types of categories if the core economy were stable to prospering.[3] In relation to our

1. Among recent estimates of Roman consumer markets and economic activity, see Walter Scheidel and Steven J. Friesen, "The Size of the Economy and the Distribution of Income in the Roman Empire," *JRS* 99 (2009): 61–91; David J. Downs, "Economics, Taxes, and Tithes," in *The World of the New Testament: Cultural, Social, and Historical Contexts*, ed. Joel B. Green and Lee Martin McDonald (Grand Rapids: Baker Academic, 2013), 156–68.

2. Not every study focuses exclusively on the first century. Thus, the first few centuries will be included in order to incorporate a wider range of studies.

3. It is important to register a caution in trying to establish or support one economy as if it represents "the" ancient economy. Certainly, there were various economies across the

present topic, if the core economy across multiple regions had been at least stable, then it makes sense that communal reading events would not have been greatly hindered by economic circumstances—arguably allowing them to be more widespread.[4] While it is still true that people read individually and communally during every era, irrespective of how well the economies were doing, the extent to which such events happened—individually or communally—has connections to the socioeconomic situation, such as disposable income, leisure time, and the production of materials. Likewise, even if a few specific locations remained outside the general socioeconomic norms across the Mediterranean world, those special cases would not radically negate the relative stability—and even prosperity—elsewhere. A few examples of this relative economic prosperity during the first few centuries CE ought to suffice. Again, our scope here is limited to a survey of studies in order to provide a general overview that may have implications for our study. The focus is especially on archaeological findings.

Recent studies are gradually modifying the state of ancient economies, not just in Rome, but also across the entire Mediterranean world. There is extensive evidence for increased infrastructure, such as roads and the sophisticated watermill systems;[5] aggregate demand, such as the high level of lead imports and exports; and progressive inventions, such as hydraulic mining. For instance, no one has overturned the research of David Dorsey, who persuasively argued that even rural locations such as Galilee had an elaborate network of roads and paths that connected them to other towns, villages, and

Mediterranean world. At the same time, identifying patterns of ancient economic developments across various regions can help historical reconstructions of a core economy in some significant—though not absolute—ways.

4. It is outside the scope of this study to examine the impact specific socioeconomic contexts had on communal reading events in general. Rather, we are casting a wide net and making broad observations on the core economy, since our main goal is to see how widespread communal reading events were in general.

5. The consensus among scholars was that water mills were probably part of the technology available in the first few centuries AD, but that water mills did not become widespread until the Middle Ages. The main reason for the consensus was the limited literary mention of water mills in the first few centuries and the more frequent mention of them in literary works of the Middle Ages. According to the Oxford Roman Economy Project (OREP), in 1984 the consensus ended with Örjan Wikander's study, which argued that literary evidence of water mills in the first few centuries should not be expected, given their typical genres. Since his work, the economic picture is even clearer. For all their latest information regarding the OREP project, see their frequently updated website, http://oxrep.classics.ox.ac.uk/home/ (accessed August 6, 2014).

provinces.[6] To be sure, less optimistic assessments have been made. David Fiensy's recent essay on Lower Galilee concludes, "If the reader had lived in Lower Galilee in the first century C.E., chances are he or she would have lived in a village of fewer than 2,000 inhabitants. The village would have consisted mostly of simply made houses, haphazardly planned, unpaved streets, perhaps a public building or two, and a few open areas used on market day or by nomadic persons for pitching their tents."[7] His study, however, was done prior to or without the benefit of many of the studies incorporated in this section, such as Bradley Root's recent study on Galilee in the first century. Root concludes, "Overall, the evidence suggests that Galilee was relatively prosperous and politically stable between Herod the Great's death and the outbreak of the Jewish Revolt. During this time, the region experienced the unusual combination of aggregate economic growth, urbanization, and significant population growth without suffering a concomitant decline in living standards."[8] Similarly, J. Andrew Overman and Ze'ev Safrai separately present recent data from their findings that indicate population growth and economic stability and vitality in and around both Galilee and Jerusalem.[9]

There is also widespread evidence of increased jobs and government spending. Jürgen Zangenberg reports:

In recent years large-scale excavations (such as in Tiberias and Magdala) produced important evidence for a high degree of Hellenization in the larger cities of the Galilee, at the same time chance discoveries (such as the synagogue in Magdala) or excavations in rural sites added important information on Jewish material culture in the first centuries CE, and—perhaps the most important new trend—renewed interest in rural Galilee helps fill in many 'blank areas' between towns and cities and

---

6. *The Roads and Highways of Ancient Israel* (Baltimore: John Hopkins University Press, 1991).

7. "The Galilean Village in the Late Second Temple and Mishnaic Periods," in *Galilee in the Late Second Temple and Mishnaic Periods*, vol. 1, *Life, Culture, and Society*, ed. David A. Fiensy and James Riley Strange (Minneapolis: Fortress Press, 2014), 177–207, here 201.

8. *First Century Galilee: A Fresh Examination of the Sources*, WUNT 2.378 (Tübingen: Mohr Siebeck, 2014), 182.

9. J. Andrew Overman, "The Destruction of the Temple and the Conformation of Judaism and Christianity," in *Jews and Christians in the First and Second Centuries: How to Write Their History*, ed. Peter J. Tomson and Joshua J. Schwartz, Compendia Rerum Iudaicarum ad Novum Testamentum 13 (Leiden: Brill, 2014), 251–77; Ze'ev Safrai, "Socio-Economic and Cultural Developments in the Galilee from the Late First to the Early Third Century CE," in Tomson and Schwartz, *Jews and Christians in the First and Second Centuries*, 278–310.

develop a more accurate picture of daily life in rural Galilean communities—a major factor in the earliest Jesus tradition.[10]

After discussing new building projects, such as the "massive Roman theater" in Tiberias begun around 19 CE, Zangenberg goes on to argue that the "massive redistribution and influx of capital (much of which must have come from outside of Galilee)" increased the local population, and settlements expanded.[11] He claims the same for Magdala: "It is entirely justified to see Magdala in the same category as the large Hellenistic cities in Greece or Asia Minor."[12] He even challenges the current consensus on rural villages: "Instead of seeing villages as traditionalistic and backwater, many of them actually were hotspots of cultural development."[13] This archeological picture would not make sense if all-out poverty had reigned, Zangenberg concludes. Stefano De Luca and Anna Lena draw similar conclusions from the archaeological context of Magdala by noting additional evidence: the well-structured thermal bath.[14]

Of course, contra these more recent treatments, others have argued that this was only as regards certain areas like Sepphoris and Tiberias, not elsewhere in Galilee.[15] Yet there does seem to be a similar picture developing with surrounding areas. Richard Bauckham and Stefano De Luca state:

> The importance of Magdala does not lie only in itself. We can now begin to build up a much clearer picture of the area around the North

10. Jürgen K. Zangenberg, "Archaeological News from the Galilee: Tiberias, Magdala and Rural Galilee," *EC* 1 (2010): 471–84. See also idem., "Jesus der Galiläer und die Archäologie: Beobachtungen zur Bedeutung der Archäologie für die historische Jesusforschung," *MTZ* 64, no. 2 (2013): 123–56; idem., "Climate, Droughts, Wars, and Famines in Galilee as a Background for Understanding the Historical Jesus," *JBL* 131, no. 2 (2012): 307–24; Uzi Leibner, *Settlement and History in Hellenistic, Roman, and Byzantine Galilee: An Archaeological Survey of the Eastern Galilee*, TSAJ 127 (Tübingen: Mohr Siebeck, 2009).

11. Zangenberg, "Archaeological News from the Galilee," 473–75.

12. Ibid., 475.

13. Ibid., 481.

14. Stefano De Luca and Anna Lena, "The Mosaic of the Thermal Bath Complex of Magdala Reconsidered: Archaeological Context, Epigraphy and Iconography," in *Knowledge and Wisdom: Archaeological and Historical Essays in Honour of Leah Di Segni*, ed. G. C. Bottini, L. D. Crupcala, and J. Patrich, SBF Collectio Maior 54 (Milan: Terra Santa, 2014), 1–33.

15. John Dominic Crossan and Jonathan L. Reed, *Excavating Jesus: Beneath the Stones, behind the Texts* (San Francisco: HarperCollins, 2001); Richard A. Horsley, *Archaeology, History and Society in Galilee: The Social Context of Jesus and the Rabbis* (Harrisburg, PA: Trinity Press International, 1996); Douglas E. Oakman, "Models and Archaeology in the Social Interpretation of Jesus," in *Social Scientific Models for Interpreting the Bible*, ed. John J. Pilch (Leiden: Brill, 2001), 102–31.

West shore of the lake of Galilee, from Magdala to Capernaum, including both the Wadi Hamam valley and the plain of Gennesaret. If we take into account, not only Magdala itself, but the settlements at Arbel, Khirbet Wadi Hamam, Abu Shusheh and Horvat Kur, as well as the indications of habitation suggested in Ken Dark's survey of the area north of Magdala, it is clear that *this whole area was heavily populated* in the time of Jesus, doubtless owing to the *famous fertility* of the plain of Gennesaret and to the *flourishing fishing industry* of which Magdala was the center and Capernaum a part. The *high population of the area* may be one of the reasons Jesus chose to make Capernaum his base.[16]

Bauckham, De Luca, Zangenberg, and Lena are also not alone. In 2006, Morten Jensen wrote, "It seems indisputable that the rural area [of Galilee] was able to sustain its livelihood and even expand it in this period."[17] In 2012, after reporting several more details from a number of excavations and surface surveys, he found further evidence for the same conclusion: "Taken together, the picture we get is of a thriving economic situation in the rural areas of Galilee that does not match earlier proposals of a devastating urban elite's exploitation of a uniformly poor peasant population."[18] The artistic, linguistic, and archaeological evidence points in the opposite direction of all-out poverty.

It also now appears that subsistence-level households formed a solid majority in urban settings—not just in Rome, for example, but elsewhere.[19] Take the Isauria region in southern Asia Minor. Noel Lenski suggests that the Romans finally established dominion over

16. "Magdala as We Know It," *EC* 6 (2015): 91–118, here 114–5 (italics added).

17. Morten Hørning Jensen, *Herod Antipas in Galilee: The Literary and Archaeological Sources on the Reign of Herod Antipas and Its Socio-economic Impact on Galilee*, WUNT 2.215 (Tübingen: Mohr Siebeck, 2006), 247.

18. Morten Hørning Jensen, "Antipas: The Herod Jesus Knew," *BAR* 38, no. 5 (2012): 42–46, here 45. See also idem., "Rural Galilee and Rapid Changes: An Investigation of the Socio-economic Dynamics and Developments in Roman Galilee," *Biblica* 93, no. 1 (2012): 43–67; K. R. Dark, "Archaeological Evidence for a Previously Unrecognised Roman Town Near the Sea of Galilee," *PEQ* 145, no. 3 (2013): 185–202; James H. Charlesworth and Mordechai Aviam, "Reconstructing First-Century Galilee: Reflections on Ten Major Problems," in *Jesus Research: New Methodologies and Perceptions*, ed. James H. Charlesworth and Brian Rhea, The Second Princeton-Prague Symposium on Jesus Research, Princeton 2007 (Grand Rapids: Eerdmans, 2014), 103–37.

19. P. Erdkamp, "Beyond the Limits of the 'Consumer City': A Model of the Urban and Rural Economy in the Roman World," *Historia* 50 (2001): 332–56. Cf. Edwin A. Judge, *The First Christians in the Roman World: Augustan and New Testament Essays*, ed. James R. Harrison, WUNT 229 (Tübingen: Mohr Siebeck, 2008); Wayne Meeks, *The First Urban Christians: The Social World of the Apostle Paul*, 2nd ed. (New Haven, CT: Yale University Press, 2003).

this region by the middle of the first century CE, and concludes, "Isauria witnessed a marked growth in urbanization and participation in Roman state structures which lasted until the mid-third century."[20] Similarly, the Lower City of Jerusalem has often been regarded as poor, since the area seemed to have lacked wealthy structures. More recent excavations, however, strongly challenge this notion. Doron Ben-Ami and Yana Tchekhanovets, for instance, conclude, "It thus appears that in the first century C.E., the Lower City experienced clear changes in its layout, with large-scale building activity which turned it into a vivid neighborhood. This phenomenon can be explained by the *general economic prosperity* of Jerusalem in this time, which was, in turn, a direct outcome of the expanding phenomenon of pilgrimage to the Temple."[21] Eyal Regev similarly concludes, "We have seen that the Jerusalem society during the early and mid-first century CE contained various social groups, schools, parties, religious perceptions, and charismatic figures. The economy flourished and Hebrew, Aramaic, Greek, and Latin were heard in the streets."[22] In addition, Jews minted their own coins during the First Jewish Revolt of 66–70 CE, something that would have been less likely if the majority of them were subject to mass poverty levels.[23]

In addition to those macro-level examples, there are micro-level examples that coincide with this picture. Strabo highlights the great wealth at Corinth, as well as the numerous people growing rich (*Geogr.* 8.6.20–23).[24] Pausanias talks about the displays of wealth he saw in the sanctuaries and towns in Greece during the second century CE.[25] Epictetus discusses people who read (ἀναγιγνώσκοντος) hypothetical arguments and goes on to speak about how it relates

20. "Assimilation and Revolt in the Territory of Isauria, from the 1st Century BC to the 6th Century AD," *JESHO* 42, no. 4 (1999): 413–65, here 455.

21. Doron Ben-Ami and Yana Tchekhanovets, "The Lower City of Jerusalem on the Eve of Its Destruction, 70 C.E.: A View from Hanyon Givati," *BASOR* 364 (2011): 81 (italics added).

22. "Flourishing before the Crisis: Mapping Judaean Society in the First Century CE," in *Jews and Christians in the First and Second Centuries*, 52–79, here 68.

23. R. Deutsch, "Roman Coins Boast 'Judaea Capta'," *BAR* 36, no. 1 (2010): 51–53.

24. George Guthrie surveys several studies on the city of Corinth in his recent commentary and underscores the impressive buildings, such as the synagogue, temples, and 15,000-seat theater, and displays of great wealth, as seen in such things as the amount and types of occupations, goods, and services available. Guthrie, *2 Corinthians* (Grand Rapids: Baker Academic, 2015), 11–14.

25. K. W. Arafat, "Treasure, Treasuries and Value in Pausanias," *CQ* 59, no. 2 (2009): 578–92. See also Elfriede R. Knauer, "Roman Wall Paintings from Boscotrecase: Three Studies in the Relationship between Writing and Painting," *Metropolitan Museum Journal* 28 (1993): 13–46.

to parents who are frustrated with how impractical philosophy is for their children:

> Only he can so speak who has applied himself to philosophy in such a spirit. But if a man reads [ἀναγιγνώσκει] upon the subject and resorts to the philosophers merely because he wants to make a display at a banquet of his knowledge of hypothetical arguments, what else is he doing but trying to win the admiration of some senator sitting by his side? For there in Rome are found in truth the great resources, while the riches of Nicopolis look to them like mere child's-play (Epict., *Diatr.* 1.26.8–10).

His point is that many people in Rome read such philosophers, in light of the vast literary resources available there,[26] in order to achieve a certain social status by later reciting them communally or referencing them during a communal reading. Peter White emphasizes this variety of available literary resources when he writes, "At Rome it was possible to purchase Greek books and Latin books, newly authored works and established titles, recently copied manuscripts and antiquarian ones, books written to order as well as books ready made, and by the time of Martial, codices as well as bookrolls."[27] Life in Nicopolis, in contrast, does not have the same enticement, as far as Epictetus is concerned.

These select examples are not meant to oversimplify the complex economic context. Yet they do reveal some macro- and microeconomic trends across several regions that support our general argument and offer a coherent and controlled conjecture of a stable-to-stronger economy.[28] The overly simplistic divide between "rich" and "poor"—or "elite" and "sub-elite"—seems to be amiss. There is more complexity within every level of the overall social pyramid scheme, even if the majority of the population was above poverty. This is why the attempts of scholars like Bruce Longenecker and Steven Friesen to construct economic strata scales beyond such simple divisions as mentioned above ought to be considered carefully,[29] even if nuanced

26. Florence Dupont writes, "By the end of the Republic, Rome is full of books." Dupont, "The Corrupted Boy and the Crowned Poet: or, The Material Reality and the Symbolic Status of the Literary Book at Rome," in *Ancient Literacies: The Culture of Reading in Greece and Rome*, ed. William A. Johnson and Holt N. Parker, trans. Holt N. Parker (Oxford: Oxford University Press, 2009), 143–63, here 144.

27. "Bookshops in the Literary Culture of Rome," in Johnson and Parker, *Ancient Literacies*, 268–87, here 271.

28. Certainly, the surviving evidence is not entirely representative. Yet this alone should not deter us from assessing the apparent contexts and attempting to gauge the historical settings.

29. Bruce Longenecker, "Exposing the Economic Middle: A Revised Economy Scale for the

further.[30] The main point here, however, is that across the empire, the core economy was at least stable and arguably prospering. Certainly, one can note exceptions to each of these categories and select some counterexamples. Besides Josephus, for instance, few Roman writers focused at all on various economies like Galilee. Nevertheless, such limitations, exceptions, and counter examples now seem more sporadic than consistent, and should no longer be viewed as the norm.

Although only a few factors have been canvassed here, where an increase in levels helps justify a strong economy, other factors also need to be incorporated into a more comprehensive discussion. One example that would be pertinent for our consideration would be the cost of materials associated with communal reading events, such as writing materials and manuscripts (Pliny, *Letters* 5.8). Yet again, recent studies are cautiously challenging previous assessments. Emanuel Tov states, "The peak years of scroll production, at least for those found at Qumran, were between 100 BCE and 50 CE, again in ever-increasing numbers."[31] Stanley Porter and Andrew Pitts argue, "Papyrus, the paper of the ancient world, was widely available and not expensive."[32] As for Christians specifically, Kim Hanes-Eitzen states, "There is no reason to suppose that literate Christians who wished for copies of literature had substantially different resources from those of other literate folk in the empire."[33]

In sum, the state of the economies in the Mediterranean world during the first two centuries CE can be seen as broadly flourishing, with stable-to-low inflation at both the local and imperial levels. Even where there are exceptions to this general description, as in some city-states or villages, it is easier to account for the exceptions than it would be the other way around, given the strength of the patterns noted previously. This relative prosperity does seem to wane close to

Study of Early Urban Christianity," *JSNT* 31, no. 3 (2013): 243–78; Steven Friesen, "Poverty in Pauline Studies: Beyond the So-Called New Consensus," *JSNT* 26 (2004): 323–61.

30. Peter Oakes, "Constructing Poverty Scales for Graeco-Roman Society: A Response to Steve Friesen's 'Poverty in Pauline Studies,'" *JSNT* 26, no. 3 (2004): 367–71.

31. *Textual Criticism of the Hebrew Bible, Qumran, Septuagint: Collected Essays,* VTSup 167 (Leiden: Brill, 2015), 3:61.

32. "Paul's Bible, His Education and His Access to the Scriptures of Israel," *JGRChJ* 5 (2008): 9–41, here 24.

33. *Guardians of Letters: Literacy, Power, and the Transmission of Early Christian Literature* (Oxford: Oxford University Press, 2000), 40. See also Jon W. Iddeng, "*Publica aut Peri! The Releasing and Distribution of Roman Books," *Symbolae Osloenses* 81 (2006): 58–84, esp. 72–73.

the late second century, though all of the factors leading to the third-century decline are still being debated.[34]

I differ, then, with scholars like Wolfgang Stegemann, who argues that "the great majority of the rural population in antiquity lived on the narrow margin between survival and hunger, . . . in constant anxiety about whether they could earn enough for basic sustenance."[35] At the same time, I fully sympathize with Stegemann when he notes that "every summary of this kind is subjective . . . [and] scholars can reach widely differing conclusions precisely in this field."[36] Granted that qualification, I cautiously maintain that a growing evidence is indicative of a core Mediterranean economy that was stronger than previously recognized. This overall economic context strengthens the possibility of widespread communal reading events, and leaves the main thesis of our study open to further investigation.

POLITICAL CLIMATE

Having considered the financial context and argued that the economy was at least strong enough to permit—if not enable—widespread communal reading events, we will now evaluate the political context. Once again, the scope of our investigation will be limited by only addressing two main topics related to the policital climate that help situate communal reading events across the Mediterranean world: (1) the *Pax Romana*, and (2) travel and mobility.

---

34. See, for example, Roger S, Bagnall's response to Walter Scheidel concerning the effects of the Antonine plague on the economic situation in parts of Egypt. Bagnall, "The Effects of Plague: Model and Evidence," *JRA* 15 (2002): 114–20.

35. Wolfgang Stegemann, "Background III: The Social and Political Climate in Which Jesus of Nazareth Preached," in *Handbook for the Study of the Historical Jesus: How to Study the Historical Jesus*, ed. Tom Holmén and Stanley E. Porter (Leiden: Brill, 2011), 3:2291–314, here 3:2312. For a recent assessment of previous economic models, such as Gerhard Lenski's seminal work, and more recent social stratification theories, see Lee A. Johnson, "Social Stratification," *BTB* 43, no. 3 (2013): 155–68.

36. Stegemann, "Background III," 2313. For a similar assessment regarding the wide range of studies and positions available that tend to emphasize either the economic hardships or economic growth, see Mark A. Chancey, "Disputed Issues in the Study of Cities, Villages, and the Economy in Jesus' Galilee," in *The World of Jesus and the Early Church: Identity and Interpretation in Early Communities of Faith*, ed. Craig A. Evans (Peabody, MA: Hendrickson, 2011), 53–68.

PAX ROMANA

Covering the entire timeframe of our investigation (ca. 31 BCE–180 CE) is a period often labeled and described by historians as the *Pax Romana*. The concept of the *Pax Romana* is not a purely modern invention, nor are the words. Both the concept and words occur in the famous monumental inscription of Augustus's self-aggrandizing record of his accomplishments, the *Res Gestae* (e.g., line 13). According to Michael Grant, it was the "*Pax Romana* or *Pax Augusta* that insured the survival and eventual transmission of the classical heritage, Greek and Roman alike, and made possible the diffusion of Christianity, of which the founder, Jesus, was born during this reign."[37]

For our purposes, the *Pax Romana* ushered in a unique opportunity for widespread communal reading events, as well as other performances and competitions. Anna Janzen summarizes it in this way: "The *Pax Romana* enjoyed an enormous amount of growth: The exchange of goods flourished, by enhancing the infrastructure and developing new areas, jobs were created, and by the conquest of the provinces flowed tax revenues into the treasury, and due to the expansion of the kingdom, land owners enlarged their lands."[38] Because of these and other prevailing factors, there was relative peace due to minimal military expansion by force. With this relative sociopolitical calmness and stability, it seems to be no mere coincidence that there was an increase in leisurely activities and entertainment—both public and private. Zeev Weiss writes, "The increased number of festival days in the Roman period, and especially the massive construction of theatres, hippodromes, and amphitheaters throughout the empire during the first three centuries of the Common Era, provide abundant evidence for their popularity. . . . By

37. Michael Grant, *History of Rome* (New York: Scribner's, 1978), 258. See also Eckhard J. Schnabel, *Early Christian Mission: Paul and the Early Church* (Downers Grove: InterVarsity, 2004), 2:1551, 1556, 1585.

38. "Die Pax Romana könnte ein enormes Wirtschaftswachstum verzeichnen: Der Warenumtausch florierte, durch die Aufbesserung der Infrastruktur und der Erschließung neuer Gebiete wurden Arbeitsplätze geschaffen, durch die Eroberung der Provinzen flössen Steuereinnahmen in die Staatskasse, und aufgrund der Erweiterung des Reiches konnten die Grundbesitzer ihre Ländereien vergrößern." Anna Janzen, "Der Friede im lukanischen Doppelwerk vor dem Hintergrund der Pax Romana" (PhD diss., Toronto School of Theology, 2001), 154. See especially her first section in chapter three (112–54) that discusses the economic and social conditions during the time period regarded as the *Pax Romana*.

the end of the first century CE, and especially during the second and third centuries CE, many buildings were constructed in Roman Palestine for the primary purpose of housing entertainment for the local populace." [39] In fact, one reference work specifically lists 28 *principal* public games mentioned by ancient writers—several of which were annually sponsored by the Roman state.[40]

Not only are there numerous references of actual events, but there is also evidence of entire associations established and honors given solely for those linked with these events, such as athletes,[41] performers,[42] singers,[43] officials,[44] sports lovers,[45] and the families of gladiators.[46] Not only were the games, associations, and honors mentioned far and wide in the ancient records during this time period, but also there are specific individuals often highlighted. Martial records Collinus (4.54) and Scaevus Memor (11.9–10) as the winners of Latin poetry at the Capitoline contests in 86 CE.[47] Or later in 106 CE, L. Valerius Pudens won, by a unanimous vote of judges, in Latin poetry at thirteen years old (*CIL* 9.2860). There is not just evidence of winners, however; there is also evidence about some losers. Statius, who won a literary competition at the Alban games in 90 CE, writes about how upset he was when he lost in a different set of literary contests that same year, the second Capitoline games.[48]

39. Zeev Weiss, "Theatres, Hippodromes, Amphitheaters, and Performances," in *The Oxford Handbook of Jewish Daily Life in Roman Palestine*, ed. Catherine Hezser (Oxford: Oxford University Press, 2010), 623–40, here 623.

40. Harry Thurston Peck, ed., *Harper's Dictionary of Classical Literature and Antiquities* (New York: Cooper Square, 1965), 972–79. Cf., among others, P. J. Davis, "Roman Games," in *The Oxford Encyclopedia of Ancient Greece & Rome*, ed. Michael Gagarin (Oxford: Oxford University Press, 2010), 3:264–71, esp. 268–69; Hartmut Leppin, "Between Marginality and Celebrity: Entertainers and Entertainments in Roman Society," in *Social Relations in the Roman World*, ed. Michael Peachin (Oxford: Oxford University Press, 2011), 660–78, esp. 668–72.

41. Letters from 46–47 CE and 69–79 CE collected in 194 CE in Upper Egypt: see AGRW, 188–89.

42. First to second century CE, Miletos area (ibid., 110).

43. 41–54 CE, Ephesus area (ibid., 100–101).

44. 128 CE, Galatia (ibid., 127–28).

45. Ca. 100–150 CE, Thessalonica (ibid., 49).

46. Early second century CE, Ephesus (ibid., 105).

47. J. P. Sullivan, *Martial: The Unexpected Classic* (Cambridge: Cambridge University Press, 1992), 146.

48. For brief discussion on background and dating, see Harm-Jan Van Dam, *P. Papinius Statius, Silvae, Book II: A Commentary* (Leiden: Brill, 1984), 14n16.

To clarify the main point and its relation to our study, the history of one prime example will be sketched here as a test case: the Capitoline games (*Ludi Capitolini*). According to Livy (5.50.4), the commencing of this specific tradition of public contests was after the defeat of the Gauls around 387 BCE—well before our study's time period. And although determining a precise date is not possible, these games appear to have died out within a generation or so and were relatively nonexistent until Domitian reinstituted them in 86 CE. Several details regarding its reestablishment can be found in the writings of Suetonius. He states, "He [Domitian] also established a quinquennial contest in honour of Jupiter Capitolinus of a threefold character, comprising music, riding, and gymnastics, and with considerably more prizes than are awarded nowadays. For there were competitions in prose declamation both in Greek and in Latin" (Sue., *Dom.* 8.4.4). As far as the available evidence goes, these games continued uninterrupted until around 389 CE, when Emperor Theodosius suppressed these types of games and festivals, including the most prestigious Olympic games.[49]

This one test case supports the primary point that, during this time period under the *Pax Romana*, conditions were right for the spread of communal reading events. Root states this concerning the *Pax Romana* and its impact on the Galilean economy: "The *Pax Romana* was one of the few periods in history in which a large, interregional economy enjoyed economic growth, population growth, and a rising standard of living."[50] Again, similar to the economic situation previously addressed, this does not mean that communal reading events did not exist before the *Pax Romana* or in other times or locations of uncertainty or conflict. Rather, due to the relative socio-political stability during the first century CE, there were necessarily more unhindered opportunities for communal reading events as a whole. In turn, this additional influence increases the prospects of our study's main thesis.

---

49. P. J. Davis, "Roman Games," in *The Oxford Encyclopedia of Ancient Greece and Rome*, ed. Michael Gagarin (Oxford: Oxford University Press, 2010), 3:269–70.

50. Root, *Galilee*, 155.

TRAVEL AND MOBILITY

In conjunction with the relatively strong economy and peaceful military times under the time period often termed the *Pax Romana*, travel was more frequent and easier than has often been thought. This aspect of "the rich evocation of travels"—especially among early Christians—has been "greatly neglected" in recent scholarship, according to François Bovon.[51] Paolo Siniscalco also points out that by the second century CE, "the web of communication and traffic reached its maximum level of extension and efficiency."[52] Moreover, using literary, epigraphic, and archaeological evidence, Rebecca Benefiel examines the region of Campania during the early Roman Empire. After assessing the social, cultural, and economic interactions among various elite and non-elite communities there, she concludes:

> We can therefore see how well integrated and mobile the population of Campania was during the first century AD. The geography of the region, a flat plain served by an extensive road network, aided short- and long-distance travel. Cities along the Bay of Naples were only a short boat ride away from each other. The density of urban settlement also facilitated interaction, since cities were located within manageable distances of each other. Within this framework, regional networks existed and facilitated the movement of goods, ideas, and people. Multiple market circuits connected the towns of the region, offering both producers and consumers the opportunity for exchange every 2–3 days. Networks for cultural entertainment also existed, which provided the sponsor with greater prestige and regional renown and the spectator with additional opportunities to attend popular sporting events.[53]

Increased travel and mobility increases the likelihood that literature, ideas, and reading materials would have accompanied the high levels of movement. This, in turn, would have increased communal readings, at least upon first delivery of a letter to a community, for example. Rachel Zelnick-Abramovitz even describes how historians,

---

51. François Bovon, "The Emergence of Christianity," *ASE* 24, no. 1 (2007): 13–29, here 23. Cf. Philip A. Harland, "Pausing at the Intersection of Religion and Travel," in *Travel and Religion in Antiquity*, ed. Philip A. Harland, SCJ 21 (Waterloo: Wilfrid Laurier University Press, 2011), 1–26.

52. Paolo Siniscalco, "Travel—Means of Communication," in *Encyclopedia of Ancient Christianity* (Downers Grove: InterVarsity, 2014), 3:831–82, here 831.

53. Rebecca R. Benefiel, *"Litora mundi hospita*: Mobility and Social Interaction in Roman Campania" (PhD diss., Harvard University, 2005), 188.

among others, traveled around the Greco-Roman world performing portions of their literary work(s) to wide-ranging audiences.[54] Her examination includes explicit statements found in primary texts such as Lucian: "My dearest wish was to become known to you all and to show off my works to as many in Macedonia as I could" (*Herodotus* 7).

Furthermore, both elite and non-elite authors affirm the probability of this type of widespread distribution by explicitly stating that their works were read far and wide. Propertius claims a worldwide reputation for his writings, "renown that has travelled to the wintry northlands." Pliny the Elder held that Marcus Varro wrote a book and "despatched it all over the world, enabling his subjects to be ubiquitous, like the gods." Martial, who was a non-elite, claims that his works are "famous throughout the world," read even among soldiers in distant border districts. Ovid claims to be read "wherever the world extends. . . . Across the land, across deep waters," even when he was exiled to the east. In fact, he asserts that because of the extent of his readership throughout the world, his fame will never die, even when he physically dies. Thus, he thanks all his readers: "But whether through favour or by very poetry I have gained this fame, 'tis right, kind reader, that I render thanks to thee" (Ovid, *Tristia* 4.130).

The picture these authors paint seems to fit well with the other evidence we have for travel and mobility. And if the scope of distribution was widespread, then the probabilities increase that communal reading events were widespread as well. In fact, these types of statements were not just from authors regarding their own renown. Pliny the Younger shares a story that would have only made sense in a world where literature was disseminated far and wide. He writes, "Have you never heard the story of the Spaniard from Gades? He was so stirred by the famous name of Livy that he came from his far corner of the earth to have one look at him and then went back again" (*Letters* 2.3.8).

Moreover, many scholars note the unrestrained spread of cults in part because of widespread travel and mobility.[55] The spread of ideas

---

54. "Look and Listen: History Performed and Inscribed," in *Between Orality and Literacy: Communication and Adaptation in Antiquity*, ed. Ruth Scodel, MnS 367 (Leiden: Brill, 2014), 10:175–96.

55. See, among others, *La Méditerranée d'une rive à l'autre: culture classique et cultures périphériques*, ed. André Laronde and Jean Leclant (Paris: Académie des Inscriptions et Belles-Lettres, 2007); *Settlement, Urbanisation and Population: Oxford Studies in the Roman Economy*, vol.

and religions necessarily reveals the movement of people and communities. As people traveled, so did literature and the opportunities for writing and reading it.[56] This is also why many studies are now emphasizing the vast social networking possible among the earliest churches, given the mobile social environments.[57] Timothy Marquis even attempts to identify a series of travel motifs in a portion of Pauline literature.[58]

Needless to say, not all movement was for positive reasons such as the expansion of ideas, economic opportunities, distribution of literature, social networking, or participation in communal reading events. Some people merely wanted to avoid military enrollment, run away from enslavement, or flee various local regulations. The two key points to highlight here, however, are that there is abundant evidence of travel and mobility among all demographics.[59] Widespread travel and mobility increase the odds that communal reading events could have been widespread enough to be a means of controlling traditions in the first few centuries CE.

SUMMARY

This chapter has laid out a few more factors to consider as we assess the overall context of the day. Broadly speaking, the economic and political contexts within which communal reading events occurred more than likely helped the spread of communal reading events in some unexpected ways. It was determined that the core economy across the ancient Mediterranean was stable to broadly flourishing until at least the late second century. This big-picture deduction

2, ed. A. K. Bowman and A. Wilson (Oxford: Oxford University Press, 2011); Simon Price, "Religious Mobility in the Roman Empire," *JRS* 102 (2012): 1–19; Anna Collar, *Religious Networks in the Roman Empire* (Cambridge: Cambridge University Press, 2013).

56. Ornella Rossi, "Letters from Far Away: Ancient Epistolary Travel Writing and the Case of Cicero's Correspondence" (PhD diss., Yale University, 2010).

57. Among others, see Michael B. Thompson, "The Holy Internet: Communication between Churches in the First Christian Generation," in *The Gospels for All Christians: Rethinking the Gospel Audiences*, ed. Richard Bauckham (Edinburgh: T&T Clark, 1998), 49–70. However, Reidar Hvalvik correctly suggested amending Thompson's terminology from "Internet" to "intranet." "All Those Who in Every Place Call on the Name of Our Lord Jesus Christ: The Unity of the Pauline Churches," in *The Formation of the Early Church*, ed. Jostein Ådna, WUNT 183 (Tübingen: Mohr Siebeck, 2005), 143.

58. "At Home or Away: Travel and Death in 2 Corinthians 1–9" (PhD diss., Yale University, 2008).

59. Agnes Choi, "Urban-Rural Interaction and the Economy of Lower Galilee" (PhD diss., University of St. Michael's College, 2010).

demonstrated in part that communal reading events probably were not hindered on a broad scale due to the core economy. Moreover, the general socio-political calmness and stability during the period of the *Pax Romana* and the increase in travel and mobility did not hinder the contention that communal reading events were widespread. The overall conditions, then, were favorable for the unhindered spread of communal reading events.

4.

Social Context

I am not just an admirer of comely beauty or of any woman who boasts illustrious ancestors: be it my delight to recite my verses in the lap of a scholar girl and have them approved by the pure taste of her ear.

—Propertius, *Elegies* 2.13 (ca. 48–15 BCE)

She is highly intelligent. . . . In addition, this love has given her an interest in literature: she keeps copies of my works to read again and again and even learn by heart. . . . If I am giving a reading she sits behind a curtain near by and greedily drinks in every word of appreciation.

—Pliny, *Letters* 4.19 (ca. 61–113 CE)

SURVEYING THE DYNAMIC ENVIRONMENT IN WHICH JESUS AND HIS FIRST FOLLOWERS OPERATED

French historian Jérôme Carcopino wrote one of the classic texts on ancient Roman life,[1] with an entire section devoted to communal reading and recitation events. His work, however, is often missing from such discussions in modern works.[2] This is unfortunate, since he still has much to offer. He writes about communal reading events as follows:

---

1. *La Vie quotidienne à Rome à l'apogée de l'Empire* (Paris: Hachette, 1939).
2. The same can be said regarding Ludwig Friedländer's work, *Roman Life and Manners under the Early Empire*, authorized translation of *Sittengeschichte Roms*, 7th ed., vol. 3, trans. J. H. Freese (New York: E. P. Dutton, 1910), which draws many of the same conclusions.

This practice [of Asinius Pollio reading his works before his friends] was too well suited to the conditions of writers and the desires of government not to become the fashion quickly. Thus the conjunction of omnipotent publishers and servile libraries gave birth to a monster, the public *recitatio*, which soon grew to be the curse of literature. The calculations of the politicians and the vanity of authors set the fashion. After that nothing could stop it.[3]

He goes on to say that communal reading events even crossed social boundaries: "Examining the contemporary literature, we soon get the impression that everyone was reading something, no matter what, aloud in public all the time, morning and evening, winter and summer."[4]

Overall, Carcopino complains that due to "the public-reading mania,"[5] which became "a chaos of deafening sound,"[6] these events eventually ate away at the moral and intellectual fabric of the empire. He even concludes that communal reading events became cancer-like: "When there were as many writers as listeners, or, as we should say, as many authors as readers, and the two roles were indistinguishable, literature suffered from an incurable, malignant tumour."[7]

At first blush, Carcopino may seem extreme. Yet he is merely summarizing the sentiments of numerous Roman authors who felt crushed by the sheer volume of communal reading events. He is also not alone in describing these types of communal reading events as "the trend of the day."[8] Pliny writes to Sosius Senecio, "This year has raised a fine crop of poets; there was scarcely a day throughout the month of April when someone was not giving a public reading" (*Letters* 1.13.1). Later in the same work, after discussing the great pleasure he received from having friends come to listen to him read for several days, Pliny reflects, "Am I to look upon this as a tribute to myself or to the art of oratory? I hope the latter, as it is now enjoying a revival

3. Jérôme Carcopino, *Daily Life in Ancient Rome: The People and the City at the Height of the Empire*, ed. Henry T. Rowell, trans. E. O. Lorimer (Mitchham, Victoria, Australia: Penguin, 1956), 197. See also Keith Bradley's perceptive critiques regarding the recent multiauthored handbook *The Oxford Handbook of Social Relations in the Roman World*, in Keith Bradley, "Roman Society: A Review," *CJ* 107, no. 2 (2011): 230–36.

4. Carcopino, *Daily Life*, 199.

5. Ibid., 203.

6. Ibid., 201.

7. Ibid., 203.

8. Zelnick-Abramovitz, "Look and Listen," 183. She arrives at this conclusion by examining still other primay texts not included in Carcopino, such as Lucian, *Quomodo Historia Conscribenda Sit*, 5–51, esp. 7.

after almost dying out" (*Letters* 3.18.5–6). He goes on to share that his ultimate audience is the mass population: "I have not forgotten that only a few friends have heard me read what I have written for the *general public*; but even so, my delight in their keen attentiveness makes me hopeful that *popular opinion* will coincide with theirs" (*Letters* 3.18.9; italics added).[9] In *Satyrica*, Petronius writes this about a bad poet:

> Some of the people who were walking in the colonnades threw stones at Eumolpus as he recited. . . . [He later told me] 'Whenever I go into the theatre to recite anything, this is the sort of come-if-you-wish gathering with which the house usually welcomes me'. . . . We left Eumolpus behind—for he was reciting a poem in the bathroom . . . [he found us later and explained] 'Why, I was nearly flogged while I was washing,' he cried, 'because I tried to go round the bath and recite poetry to the people sitting in it, and when I was thrown out of the bathroom as if it were the theatre, I proceeded to look round all the corners, and shouted for Encolpius in a loud voice'. (*Sat.* 90–92)

Martial tries explaining to a man, Ligurinus, why no one wants to spend time with him, and why the people even leave when they see Ligurinus coming: "You are not too much of a poet," Martial states, yet "you read to me while I am standing, and read to me when I am sitting; while I am running you read to me, and read to me while I am shitting" (*Epi.* 1.3.44). Ironically, some authors during this time period, like Galen, suggest that certain people were not permitted to speak in public (e.g., *On the Therapeutic Method* 1.2.3). Yet the context of Galen's remarks (i.e., complaining about a below-par physician who became publicly popular) seems to support Carcopino's appraisal even more. Galen is simply jealous of a rival and attempts to belittle him with a statement that has no real justification. In other words, communal readings were rampant, and even unqualified people were doing it to such an extent that some elites were responding to it via their writings.

According to Carcopino, the multiplication of libraries and the rise of publishers provided the early impetus to these communal reading events. From there, certain celebrities—and their rivals—were created. Once book merchants, with their team of scribal slaves, capitalized on

---

9. On reading aloud to popular audiences, see also Timothy P. Wiseman, "Practice and Theory in Roman Historiography," in *Roman Studies: Literary and Historical,* vol. 1 of *Collected Classical Papers* (Liverpool: Francis Cairns, 1987), 244–62, esp. 253–56.

the profits, then publishers and authors grew quickly—though most authors remained in relative poverty. It was only a matter of time that those *not* qualified would also seize the opportunities, financially and socially. He summarizes and concludes as follows:

> When once the public reading became an established fashion in Rome, and was recognised as the main and almost exclusive occupation of people of letters, literature lost all dignity and all serious purpose. The fashionable world adopted a currency which became more and more alloyed as the circle of amateurs was enlarged. Those who were invited wished to be the inviters in their turn, and when everybody mounted the dais in rotation, it ended by every listener becoming an author. This was in appearance the triumph of literature. But it was a Pyrrhic victory, an insensate inflation which foreshadowed bankruptcy.[10]

If Carcopino's interpretation is generally accurate—and I think it is—then it also helps scholars better understand and interpret certain ancient texts. Lucian's *Rhetorum Praeceptor* may well be a reaction to the students of his day wanting to bypass the traditional education system by finding new and faster ways to gain enough rhetorical abilities to participate in the reading craze.[11]

There are still many factors beyond merely the *quantity* of communal reading events. Therefore, instead of relying solely on Carcopino's interpretation, and before embarking on the more extensive treatments in chapters 5 and 6, here are a few provisional considerations from primary evidence beyond that which Carcopino cites. What follows is merely a sampling, with no commentary or qualifications provided.[12] Instead, the examples are designed to help situate and actualize the social context as it relates to ancient book culture and communal reading events.[13]

---

10. Carcopino, *Daily Life*, 203.

11. Though he does not mention Carcopino or communal reading events, see the recent work on this text and topic in Craig Gibson, "How (Not) to Learn Rhetoric: Lucian's *Rhetorum Praeceptor* as Rebuttal of a School Exercise," *GRBS* 52 (2012): 89–110.

12. I drew several of these sample texts from Donka D. Markus's outstanding study, "Performing the Book: The Recital of Epic in First-Century C.E. Rome," *Classical Antiquity* 19, no. 1 (2000): 138–79. For an extended treatment on many of them, consult her work.

13. For more specific details regarding the ancient book culture, see, among others, Frederic G. Kenyon, *Book and Readers in Ancient Greece and Rome* (Chicago: Ares, 1980); Edward J. Kenney, "Books and Readers in the Roman World," in *The Cambridge History of Classical Literature*, vol. 2, *Latin Literature, Part 1: The Early Republic*, ed. W. V. Clausen and E. J. Kenney (Cambridge: Cambridge University Press, 1983), 3–31; Raymond J. Starr, "The Circulation of Literary Texts in the Roman World," *CQ* 37 (1987): 213–23; Harry Y. Gamble, "The Book

Communal reading events in the context of ancient book culture were instrumental in social networking (Pliny, *Letters* 1.13). Invitations were sent out (P.Oxy. 2592). Children were involved (Fronto, *Ad M. Caes.* 1.7.2). Women were involved (P.Oxy. VIII 1148/1149). Literary contests existed (Martial, *Epi.* 4.54; *CIL* IX 2860). Certain authors criticized communal reading events as nothing more than popular pandering (Persius, *Satires* 1.13–23). Other authors defended the aristocratic nature of these communal reading events (Statius, *Silv.* 5.3.215). Some authors felt completely cut off from society when they were not reading communally (Ovid, *Ex Ponto* 4.25). Other authors were content to send representatives to read their works to others (Lucian, *Symp.* 21).[14] Still other writers roamed around mocking communal reading events (Juvenal, *Sat.* 1.1–14). Satirists criticized communal reading events (Persius, *Sat.* 1.67–70). Notaries attempted to write down everything they heard (Seneca, *Apoc.* 9.1).[15] Local publications discussed communal reading events (*Acta Diurna*). There were "ghostwriting" services available (dating all the way back to Antiphon). There were "historical reporters" (Dionysius, *Roman Antiquities* 1.1.4). There were artistic representations of communal reading events (*IGUR* 1228). There were times when participants (re-)wrote their text on the spot during communal reading events (Suet. *Poet. Vir.* 34; cf. Tacitus, *Ann.* 13:15). There were other individual controls over texts before being performed or published (Tertullian, *Marc.* 1:1). There were scripts sold to actors (Juvenal, *Sat.*

Trade in the Roman Empire," in *The Early Text of the New Testament*, ed. Charles E. Hill and Michael J. Kruger (New York: Oxford University Press, 2012), 23–36; idem., *Books and Readers in the Early Church: A History of Early Christian Texts* (New Haven: Yale University Press, 1995); Michael J. Kruger, "Manuscripts, Scribes, and Book Production within Early Christianity," in *Christian Origins and Classical Culture: Social and Literacy Contexts for the New Testament*, ed. Stanley E. Porter and Andrew W. Pitts (Leiden: Brill, 2012), 15–40; Loveday Alexander, "Ancient Book Production and the Circulation of the Gospels," in *The Gospels for All Christians: Rethinking the Gospel Audiences*, ed. Richard Bauckham (Grand Rapids: Eerdmans, 1998), 71–112, including photos.

14. In this account, a man, Hetoemocles, sends his slave to a symposium of his friends to read the small tablet he sent with his slave: "You see, a servant came into the midst of us, saying that he was from Hetoemocles the Stoic and carrying a paper (γραμματίδιον) which he said his master had told him to read in public, so that everybody would hear, and then to go back again. On getting the consent of Aristaenetus, he went up to the lamp and began to read."

15. It is also interesting to note that some authors, such as the one noted here, assumed it was normal to have a written report to examine after a discourse. Seneca the Younger states, "He made an eloquent harangue, because his life was passed in the forum, but a harangue too fast for the notary to take down. That is why I give no full report of it, for I don't want to change the words he used" (*Apol.* 9).

7.87). Some events circulated as pamphlets (Lysias, *Eratosthenes* 12). There were times when members of the audience would take notes and attempt to plagiarize the work of the presenter after the event (Quintilian, *Inst.* 1.7–8). Forgeries existed (Lucian, *Pseud.* 30). Book dealers existed (P.Oxy 2192). Bookstores existed (Catullus, *Carm.* 14:17–20). Authors generated various kinds of reading lists for people and requested others (Quintilian, *Inst.* 1.8.2; Lucian, *Ind.* 27). Bibliographies were provided upon request (Pliny, *Letters* 3.5). Prepublication drafts were delivered at certain gatherings with editorial purposes in mind (Horace, *Ars* 438). There were grammar books (a first-century schoolteacher, Quintus Remmius Palaemon, wrote one noted grammar; Juvenal, *Sat.* 6.452) and lexicons (Aelius Dionysius and Pausanias) to assist readers. Various kinds of public libraries existed, both ancient and modern (Suet., *Dom.* 8.20). Substantial personal libraries existed (Strabo, *Geogr.* 13.1.54). Books were often given to friends as gifts (Martial, *Epigrams* 14.183–96). Elite members of society sometimes pretended they were more highly educated than they really were (Seneca, *Epi.* 27.5–7). Some people thought memorizing was a waste of time because they had written texts (Suet. *Aug.* 84).

This list could go on, but the real debates are not over these statements, especially with only one example given of each. Rather, the debates exist over the extent and qualifications of each one. No one disputes that libraries existed, but to what extent did libraries exist?[16] No one argues against the fact that communal reading events existed, but can the events be reconciled with statements such as the one from Seneca, who said there were only three events that popularized people's views (Cic. *Sest.* 106)?[17] Ancient writers often withheld the very details now needed to increase the accuracy of modern histor-

---

16. Marshall argues, "By the end of the first century of our era, the number of authors to be consulted in the common store of literature was enormous and ever growing. The importance of finding access to sizable collections of books could only increase." Anthony J. Marshall, "Library Resources and Creative Writing at Rome," *Phoenix* 30, no. 3 (1976): 252–64, here 264. See, among others, the more specialized discussions of them in ibid.; Christopher Jones, "Books and Libraries in a Newly-Discovered Treatise of Galen," *JRA* 22 (2009): 390–97; Matthew C. Nicholls, "Galen and Libraries in the *Peri Alupias*," *JRS* 101 (2011): 123–42.

17. For a recent discussion of this question, see Gesine Manuwald, "The Speeches to the People in Cicero's Oratorical Corpora," *Rhetorica* 30, no. 2 (2012): 153–75. Cf. Anthony L. Hollingsworth, "Recitation and the Stage: The Performance of Senecan Tragedy" (PhD diss., Brown University, 1998).

ical reconstructions.[18] At the same time, by underscoring the social context as it relates to ancient book culture and communal reading events, we are in a better position to propose that communal reading events were deeply embedded within the social fabric of society, and we can no longer (or so easily) claim that any evidence of them is the exception to the rule.

One additional point that has yet not been specifically addressed is relevant here. For whom were communal reading events held? Though the answer is not simple, nor is it the focus of our investigation, it seems that many texts and events were produced and held not solely for the elite, but also for popular consumption, because their appeal was broad (see chapters 5 and 6 of this study for some examples).[19] Granted, much evidence comes from elites. They were certainly able to utilize the events more than most people, since they could hire multiple slaves to read, take dictation, or both. Nicholas Horsfall, after noting many examples, puts the matter this way: "*Lector* and *notarius* mean that twenty-four hours per day are available for work, if their owner so wishes."[20] Furthermore, not much has been written on non-elites in ancient or modern sources. Ancient literary sources only seem to mention the lower classes when they become a public nuisance[21] or are needed for some specific task, such as reading literature. Ovid writes, "You too, plebeian hands, receive, if you may,

18. See, among others, David E. Aune, "Prolegomena to the Study of Oral Tradition in the Hellenistic World," in *Jesus, Gospel Tradition and Paul in the Context of Jewish and Greco-Roman Antiquity*, WUNT 303 (Tübingen: Mohr Siebeck, 2013), 220–55.

19. By popular culture, I essentially agree with Jerry Toner's simple definition: "Popular culture is probably best defined in a negative way as the culture of the non-elite [i.e., peasants, craftsmen and artisans, laborers, healers, fortune-tellers, storytellers and entertainers, shopkeepers, and traders, slaves, and most women and children]." *Popular Culture in Ancient Rome* (Cambridge: Polity, 2009), 1. In other words, it consists of all the have-nots of Roman society.

20. Nicholas Horsfall, "Rome without Spectacles," *Greece and Rome* 42, no. 1 (1995): 49–56, here 54.

21. "Two Athenian slaves in the Piraeus—either because they favoured the Romans or were looking out for their own safety in an emergency—wrote down everything that took place there, inscribed on leaden balls, and shot them at the Romans with slings" (Appian, *Rom. Hist.* 12.5.31). See also Seneca *Epi.* 56:2 and Martial 12:57. For earlier illustrations, including Aristophanes, Menander, Plautus, and Terence, see, among others, Erin Kristine Moodie, "Metatheater, Pretense Disruption, and Social Class in Greek and Roman Comedy" (PhD diss., University of Pennsylvania, 2007). See also the two-part series by James C. Scott, who discusses both "little" and "great" traditions and concludes, "The little tradition achieves historical visibility only at those moments when it becomes mobilized into dissident movements which pose a direct threat to ruling elites." "Protest and Profanation: Agrarian Revolt and the Little Tradition, Part I," *Theory and Society* 4, no. 1 (1977): 1–38; "Protest and Profanation: Agrarian Revolt and the Little Tradition, Part II," *Theory and Society* 4, no. 2 (1977): 211–46, here 240.

our verses dismayed by the shame of their rejection" (Ovid, *Tristia* 1.1.82). Since some local libraries appear to have rejected Ovid's work (the temple of Apollo, the porticus Octavia, and the temple of Liberty), he appeals to "plebeian hands" to pick up and read his book. Even if this type of readership is rarely petitioned or acknowledged by the "elite" literary culture, evidence like this confirms it existed in a quantity enough to petition.

What remains may merely be "the 'bestseller list' of late antiquity"[22] or works primarily written by only a segment of society, neither of which provide a representative picture.[23] But that does not negate popular culture's involvement. For instance, although surviving evidence written by or about ancient women is minimal, Kim Haines-Eitzen notes, "Women were (occasionally? rarely? sometimes?) involved in the many and various stages of the production, reproduction, and dissemination of early Christian literature. . . . And the combined documentary, epigraphic, and literary evidence surely suggests we must rethink the ancient book world as being entirely male."[24] Or even more simplistically regarding a smaller portion of women in antiquity, one can infer that prostitutes would not have put their profession on their tombstones. But surviving evidence shows that prostitutes existed by the graffiti they wrote on the walls with their own hands as advertisements in Pompeii (4.1969, 4.4023, 4.4150, 4.4439, 4.2450, 4.5203, 4.5127, 4.2193, et al.). In fact, after noting the vast amount of graffiti in Pompeii, which included about ten thousand political advertisements on top of all the other categories, such as ads for sex trade, real estate, and gladiatorial games, Ben Witherington reasoned, "There seems to have been more writings on the wall than

22. Daniel Stökl Ben Ezra uses this phrase when discussing the abundant Christian papyri from Egypt drawn from the "13,058 Greek, Latin, Coptic, and Demotic literary texts" found in the Leuven Database of Ancient Books. Daniel Stökl Ben Ezra, "Canonization—a Non-Linear Process? Observing the Process of Canonization through the Christian (and Jewish) Papyri from Egypt," *ZAC* 12 (2008): 193–214, here 194. See also Gregory Goswell, "Titles without Texts: What the Lost Books of the Bible Tell Us about the Books We Have," *Colloq* 41, no. 1 (2009): 73–93.

23. A similar, general conclusion was drawn by Neville Morley regarding his study of ancient women and specifically stories about women in the Apocryphal Acts by Prema Vakayil. Morley, *Theories, Models and Concepts in Ancient History* (London: Routledge, 2004), 90; Vakayil, "'Go and Teach the Word of God': Paul's Missionary Command to Thecla," *Indian Theological Studies* 49 (2012): 23–29.

24. Kim Haines-Eitzen, *The Gendered Palimpsest: Women, Writing, and Representation in Early Christianity* (Oxford: Oxford University Press, 2012), 37–38.

inhabitants within them . . . [which] may suggest a higher level of literacy than previously suspected in the Greco-Roman world."[25]

And on top of all these examples, the words of Ramsey MacMullen still ring broadly true regarding modern pursuits of evidence: "Archeology fails us [regarding non-elites], for no one has sought fame through the excavation of a slum."[26] Putting all this still another way, historical reconstructions are more often drawn from texts popular enough, copied enough, and circulated enough. The societal elite necessarily would have had the resources to make that happen.

SETTINGS

David Rhoads lists many possible locations where communal reading events took place: "a village market place, an assembly hall, a reception hall, a synagogue, a theater, the house of a poor person, the house of an elite person, an urban tenement building, or out in an open space between villages."[27] Likewise, if one were to consider the impact of communal reading events in these settings on individuals, communities, and regions, then many other avenues for further inquiry would be opened.[28] While neither settings nor "effectual history" (*Wirkungsgeschichte*) are the primary focus of our study, there are still elements worth noting here in order to better understand the social context and extent of communal reading groups.

William Shiell lists seven social settings—in addition to the popular *symposia*, which he argues most closely represent the early Christian setting—for communal reading events in the Greco-Roman world: reception of a letter, private performance, revision of the composition, public competition, an author's nondramatic performance, a professional lector's public performance, and an author's dramatic

---

25. "Graffiti at the SBL!" Ben Witherington's untitled blog, December 16, 2008, http://ben-witherington.blogspot.com/2008/12/graffiti-at-sbl.html.

26. Ramsey MacMullen, *Roman Social Relations: 50 B.C. to A.D. 284* (New Haven: Yale University Press, 1974), 93. Among works on non-elites, see Peter O'Neill, "A Culture of Sociability: Popular Speech in Ancient Rome" (PhD diss., University of California, 2001); Robert Knapp, *Invisible Romans: Prostitutes, Outlaws, Slaves, Gladiators, Ordinary Men and Women . . . the Romans That History Forgot* (London: Profile, 2011).

27. David Rhoads, "Performance Events in Early Christianity: New Testament Writings in an Oral Context," in *The Interface of Orality and Writing*, ed. Annette Weissenrieder and Robert B. Coote, WUNT 260 (Tübingen: Mohr Siebeck, 2010), 188.

28. For a recent study on the proactive influence Jewish and Christian communities probably had on the elite in the Hellenistic-Roman world, see Johann Maier, "Jüdisch-christliches Milieu als Magnet für Intellektuelle in der Antike," *ThPQ* 158, no. 1 (2010): 39–49.

performance.[29] Although we will not repeat or address each one of Shiell's categories, the main point is that the settings varied, with each venue being governed by its own set of codes and rules—implied, written, or assumed. In turn, this is pertinent because the extensive variation further supports our main contention that communal reading events were a frequent occurrence in every city of the ancient world, as evinced in both private and public settings from archaeological, epigraphic, and literary evidence. A few prevalent examples will be provided to illustrate the variety of settings in which communal reading events took place.

Indoor

As far as inside communal reading events are concerned, the usual point of congregation was a private home—often around a meal, which was typically dinner. In fact, these events were embedded in many social and family structures. Pliny often notes the context of his communal readings, and the events are typically indoors. "I chose the most suitable time and place," Pliny explains, "and to accustom them from now onwards to being received by a leisured audience in the dining-room, I gathered my friends together in the month of July (which is usually a quiet time in the law courts) and settled them with chairs in front of the couches" (*Letters* 8.21.2–3).

More generally, there were many other indoor places used for communal reading events, such as rented lecture halls, city council chambers, atria, extra rooms, ancestral shrines, workshops, theaters, temples, and baths. Take the New Testament writings. There is evidence of communal reading events in lecture halls (Acts 19:9) and private homes (Luke 1:40). Yet without providing an extended list here, the main point is that the likelihood of demonstrating that communal reading events were widespread is increased, given the wide-ranging evidence for indoor locations that attest these types of events.

Outdoor

At the other end of the spectrum, there were many places in antiquity where people could congregate outdoors in order to have a commu-

---

29. Shiell, *Reading Acts: The Lector and the Early Christian Audience*, Biblical Interpretation Series 70 (Leiden: Brill, 2004), 116–17n36.

nal reading event. Juvenal complains about his boredom in listening to the "continual recitations" from all sorts of people, "poets at every corner" (*Sat.* 1:1–21). There were also other locations established for meeting outdoors. In the New Testament writings, there were outdoor venues such as marketplaces (Acts 17:17). Edward Adams suggests these four specific outside locations—at least for Christians—as the most probable meeting areas: "gardens, waterside, urban open space and tombsides."[30] He does not provide an exhaustive list, nor will we, but the fact that there is ample evidence of outdoor venues that attest communal reading groups—not just by number, but by variation—necessarily increases the probability that communal reading events were widespread.

Nonsacred

During Ovid's exile at the edge of the Black Sea, he shares one of his anxieties: not being able to read communally. This problem, according to Ovid, is a matter of social deterioration. He even draws a stark analogy when he says, "To dance in the dark and to write a poem that you may read to no one is the same thing."[31] This corresponds well with what other authors say about the social (and literary) importance of communal reading events. Plutarch discusses various ways people form friendships, and one of the ways is "reading books with the scholarly" (φιλολόγοις συναναγιγνώσκοντος; *Mor.* 97).

Additionally, the amount of time that many ancient authors spent on rhetoric and editing their works strongly suggests how much they cared about their reputation and the opinions of those who would receive their work—orally, textually, or both. Michele Kennerly examines the explicit editorial vocabulary in several sections of

---

30. Edward Adams, *The Earliest Christian Meeting Places: Almost Exclusively Houses?*, LNTS 450 (London: T&T Clark, 2013), 196. Adams does not seem to consider at any great length, however, the impact persecutions had on his topic and the search for evidence, given the underground and illegal status of many Christian communities during their formative years. See also idem., "Placing the Corinthian Communal Meal," in *Text, Image, and Christians in the Graeco-Roman World: A Festschrift in Honor of David Lee Balch*, ed. Aliou Cissé Niang and Carolyn Osiek, PTMS 176 (Eugene, OR: Wipf and Stock, 2012), 22–37; the collection of essays in *Contested Spaces: Houses and Temples in Roman Antiquity and the New Testament*, ed. David L. Balch and Annette Weissenrieder, WUNT 285 (Tübingen: Mohr Siebeck, 2012); Peter Richardson, "Towards a Typology of Levantine/Palestinian Houses," *JSNT* 27, no. 1 (2004): 47–68.

31. For more details, context, and texts, see Benjamin Stevens, "*Per gestum res est significanda mihi*: Ovid and Language in Exile," *CP* 104, no. 2 (2009): 162–83, here 180.

four well-known, ancient authors in order to determine their editorial processes. Her work supports this claim given the statements of several ancient authors. She concludes, "Isocrates, Catullus, Horace, and Ovid expose their editorial labors for various reasons, but they all stake a claim for the superior staying power of the well-tidied text."[32]

Sacred

Nonsacred communal reading events were not the only ones occurring in the first few centuries CE. There were also sacred events, both Christian and non-Christian. A few samples of each will be provided in this segment of the study.

Sacred non-Christian communal reading events could be either public, like the Delphic Oracles,[33] or private, such as the broad category of mystery religions.[34] For this portion of our study, several relevant examples of the sacred non-Christian category will be noted by simply highlighting Matthias Klinghardt's study on ancient public prayers.[35] He essentially examines the use and function of communally recited prayers across different religions, such as in the Greek magical papyri. One may quickly notice, even though he does not use the same terminology as this study, that Klinghardt's examples are widespread and often acted as a control over the tradition. Communal prayers had to be recited correctly, including proper pronunciation, if the prayers were going to be effective. He points to texts such as Livy, *Hist. Rom.* 8.9.4. In this text, Decius asks a religious figure

32. Michele Jean Kennerly, "Editorial Bodies in Ancient Roman Rhetorical Culture" (PhD diss., University of Pittsburgh, 2010), 186. Cf. Sean Gurd, *Work in Progress: Literary Revision as Social Performance in Ancient Rome* (Oxford: Oxford University Press, 2012), esp. 49 and 105; J. Mira Seo, "Plagiarism and Poetic Identity in Martial," *AJP* 130, no. 4 (2009): 567–93.

33. See, among others, Ferguson, *Backgrounds*, 166–71; Joseph Fontenrose, *The Delphic Oracle: Its Responses and Operations, with a Catalogue of Respsonses* (Berkeley: University of California Press, 1978); Herbert B. Huffmon, "The Oracular Process: Delphi and the Near East," *VT* 57 (2007): 449–90.

34. Jan N. Bremmer, *Initiation into the Mysteries of the Ancient World* (Berlin: De Gruyter, 2014), 96, 105, 112, 113, 119, etc.

35. Matthias Klinghardt, "Prayer Formularies for Public Recitation: Their Use and Function in Ancient Religion," *Numen* 46 (1999): 1–52. Cf. Daniela Averna, "La suasoria nelle preghiere agli dei: percorso diacronico dalla commedia alla tragedia," *Rhetorica* 27, no. 1 (2009): 19–46; Peter T. Struck, "Reading Symbols: Traces of the Gods in the Ancient Greek-Speaking World" (PhD diss., University of Chicago, 1997); Richard Lynn Phillips, "Invisibility Spells in the Greek Magical Papyri: Prolegomena, Texts, and Commentaries" (PhD diss., University of Illinois at Urbana-Champaign, 2002); Gerald Septimus, "On the Boundaries of Prayer: Talmudic Ritual Texts with Addressees Other than God" (PhD diss., Yale University, 2008).

to recite a prayer to the army and state. What is all the more power-
ful about this example is that Decius's son recycled the same prayer a
generation later in a similar situation (Livy, *Hist. Rom.* 10.28.14). This
is not merely Klinghardt's keen observation, however. He correctly
points out that these events were noticed and discussed by later writers.[36] Another example was when Licinius's officers handed out copies
of a formulary prayer to their soldiers, and everyone together had to
read the prayer three times for it to work (Lact., *Mort.* 46.10; cf. Plut.
Cam. 21; Suet. *Claud.* 22; Tacitus *Hist.* 1.50.3; 2 Macc 1:23–30).

Robyn Gillam makes similar observations and comments regarding
performances in ancient Egypt. At one point in his study, he states,
"As noted above, the performative, that is, magical force of the texts
ensured their effectiveness in the next world."[37] He later concludes,
"What is clear is that performances, both formal and informal, both
social and religious, occupied a central position in Egyptian culture
and society for the duration of its existence."[38]

Though there are certainly more examples and details that could
be mentioned, those given ought to suffice to make this main point:
there were sacred non-Christian communal reading events throughout the Mediterranean world. This additional category further
increases the probabilities that communal reading events were ubiquitous.

With regard to Christianity, François Bovon states, "Faith always
was and still is expressed in a social context."[39] Part of that social context, as already mentioned, was communal reading events. There is
no doubt that early Christianity was deeply invested in communal
reading. And while church elders had substantial discretion about *how*
to do it, they had no discretion about *whether* to do it. Consider 1
Timothy 4:13: "Until I arrive, give attention to the public reading
of scripture, to exhorting, to teaching."[40] That was true not just of

---

36. E.g., Seneca *Epi.* 67.9; Cicero *Nat. d.* 2.10; Pliny *Nat. hist.* 28.12.

37. *Performance and Drama in Ancient Egypt* (London: Duckworth, 2005), 66.

38. Ibid., 155.

39. François Bovon, "The Emergence of Christianity," *ASE* 24, no. 1 (2007): 13–29, here 14.
The social context may be another reason why Christians were often called "the people" of the
book. Of course, the centrality of sacred texts within a community does not necessarily prove
the widespread communal reading of them as we seek to determine. For a few recent works
discussing the broader aspects of the Christian community and the Bible, see Rudolf Voderholzer, "Liest Du noch oder glaubst Du schon? Überlegungen zur Benennung des Christentums als 'Buchreligion'," *TTZ* 2 (2012): 101–11; José Manuel Sánchez Caro, "La Biblia, libro de
la Iglesia, libro de la Humanidad," *Salm* 59 (2012): 15–39.

40. Suffice it to say here that I acknowledge the extreme difficulty in distinguishing precisely

Scripture from the Hebrew Bible, but also of apostolic letters and gospels. The author of 1 Thessalonians gives this directive to the church: "I put you under oath before the Lord to have this letter read to all the brothers" (5:27). The author of Colossians takes for granted the practice of communal reading when he states, "And when this letter has been read among you, have it read also in the church of the Laodiceans; and see that you read also the letter from Laodicea" (4:16). The author of 2 Clem. exhorts his congregation, "Therefore, brothers and sisters, following the God of truth I am reading you an exhortation to pay attention to what is written, in order that you may save both yourselves and your reader" (19:1).[41]

AUDIENCES

Although a complete understanding of audiences and their entire range of responses is outside our present purview, it is worth noting that audiences and their responses played a major role in both communal reading events and the preservation of the various traditions presented. Shiell persuasively argues that audiences often played as much of a role in controlling the performance as the reader.[42] The audience could at times, especially if the story was well known to them, correct what was read or recited. According to Ovid, one storyteller (Pylian Nestor) omits part of a story he shares with an audience. The moment the reciter is done, a person in the audience chastises him for leaving out a detail in the story that the audience member recalls their father frequently sharing (*Meta.* 12.539, entire 536–579). At least three points are worth highlighting here. First, the account reveals that at least part of one's education took place in the home and included communal recitations (i.e., the alleged father supposedly repeated the tale enough times for this person to remember precise details). Second, hearing the same story told multiple times in an apparently consistent way increased the likelihood that the audience—or at least someone in it—could recall a particular version of the story in great detail. Third, this account suggests that at least some

---

between teaching, preaching, and evangelizing in the New Testament writings. Likewise, certain phrases can also remain undefined, such as "word of God" or "word of the Lord." Therefore, chapter 6 will note a few passages affected by this uncertainty.

41. Cf. Justin, *1 Apol.* 66–67; Tertullian, *Praescr.* 36.5.

42. Shiell, *Reading Acts.* See also idem., *Delivering from Memory: The Effect of Performance on the Early Christian Audience* (Eugene, OR: Pickwick, 2011).

people believed they could recognize *the* version, not merely *a* version, of a story. What is more, Ovid's account mentions no one disagreeing with the respondent's corrected version of the story.[43] In turn, these events acted as a conserving force over the transmission of the tradition.

In addition, a significant reason that there is much evidence today is that audiences continued sharing, rereading, and preserving certain traditions given to them via communal reading events. There was a symbiotic relationship between the audiences and the traditions,[44] and the audiences helped promote or destroy the long-term potential of the traditions.

Finally, although the primary focus is going to be on the immediate audience throughout our study,[45] there was often also an understanding of a future audience. Thucydides writes in *History of the Peloponnesian War* about the struggle between Sparta and Athens around 431 BCE and explicitly states, "My work is not a piece of writing designed to meet the taste of an immediate public, but was done to last forever" (1.22.4). Closer to our time period, in the pastoral *Daphnis and Chloe*, Longus hopes his four books will be "a delightful possession for all mankind" (*Prologue* 3). In other words, his works were not just for some specific audience or people in his present day, but to all people and future audiences. He continues with the hope these are works "that will heal the sick and encourage the depressed, that will stir memories in those experienced in love and for the inexperienced will be a lesson for the future" (*Prologue* 3). He even goes on to ask god for help to write it, and while writing to keep his mind attentive while writing. Philo writes about the longevity of literary works in this way: "The flame of their virtues is kept alive by

43. Though she is discussing an author and writing prior to our time period, Greta Hawes provides several examples of this type of mind-set and even states, "Local informants thus serve as the guardians of a repository of authentic records about the past with the power to counter the mistakes and exaggerations current elsewhere." "Story Time at the Library: Palaephatus and the Emergence of Highly Literate Mythology," in *Between Orality and Literacy: Communication and Adaptation in Antiquity*, ed. Ruth Scodel, MnS 367 (Leiden: Brill, 2014), 10:125–47, here 137.

44. It seems that Stanley Stowers misunderstands this as he attempts to critique Bauckham's and others' understanding of how social contexts formed. "The Concept of 'Community' and the History of Early Christianity," *MTSR* 23 (2011): 238–56.

45. Among the recent studies evaluating the intended audience of various first- and second-century works, see the collection of essays in Edward W. Klink III, ed., *The Audience of the Gospels: The Origin and Function of the Gospels in Early Christianity*, LNTS 353 (London: T&T Clark, 2010).

the written records which have survived them in poetry or in prose and serve to promote the growth of goodness in the soul" (*Abr.* 23). To put these examples yet another way, even if a reader and audience shared the same address, the same friends, and the same context, even the same reading habits, only part of the event belongs to that particular society, and the other to perpetuity.

BACKGROUND IN JUDAISM

If history shows that Jewish communal reading events were not a new phenomenon in the first century CE, and they were not irregular or limited to certain areas across the Mediterranean world, then such evidence would necessarily increase the probability that communal reading events were widespread in the first century CE.[46]

JEWISH COMMUNAL READING EVENTS

The first mention of a communal reading event in the Old Testament is found in Exodus 17:14–16. In this passage, Moses is told to write down the events that just occurred, and then read the written account to/with Joshua.[47] From there, numerous examples of communal reading events exist in the Old Testament, often involving larger groups of people than just two (e.g., Josh 8:30–35; Jer 36:6). In fact, communal reading events are often the point of emphasis at key historical moments: at the conclusion of the Torah (Deut 31:11–12), the return of the exilic community in Nehemiah (8:7–8), and a community turning to God during the reign of Josiah (2 Chron 34:18, 30). Given that the Old Testament portrays several ideal scenes of the Torah being read before larger groups and assemblies of Israelites at key

46. Though absent from several more recent monographs on synagogues, including Levine's and Duncan's mentioned below, Stephen Spence's work has additional considerations worth exploring, especially regarding "the parting of ways" between the church and synagogue. Stephen Spence, "The Separation of the Church and the Synagogue in First-Century Rome" (PhD diss., Fuller Theological Seminary, 2001), esp. 379–406.

47. Contra several scholars who state that Exod 24:1–18 is the first communal reading event, since it is the first time קרא is used with a written text as its direct object. Ronald Bloomfield lists forty-six occurrences of קרא (thirty-nine in Hebrew and seven in Aramaic) in twenty passages that directly relate to communal reading events. "Reading Sacred Texts Aloud in the Old Testament" (ThM thesis, Southern Baptist Theological Seminary, 1991). This further accentuates the methodological parameters we outlined earlier, as it relates to the importance of not merely searching for terms or phrases, since there are other explicit terms and entire contexts to consider.

moments in Israel's sacred history, Jewish communal reading events are pre-rabbinic, pre-Christian, and pre-Qumran.[48]

SYNAGOGUES

Several recent studies have questioned a strong continuity between early Christian communal reading events and Jewish communal reading events. Both Henk Jan de Jonge and Valeriy Alikin propose that there is no evidence of Christians reading the Law communally prior to the third century CE,[49] whereas for the Jews, the primary characteristic of Jewish worship was the communal reading of the law. These types of claims will be examined more closely in chapter 6, but for the moment, it is worth noting that Alikin does not seem to consider—since he does not include—several key New Testament texts that suggest a strong connection or even an adapted liturgical parallel. Consider [τὰ] ἱερὰ γράμματα in 2 Timothy 3:15, which is the only time this terminology is used in the New Testament in order to authenticate the gospel both prophetically and scripturally via the Old Testament.[50] The main point here is that regardless of what or when texts were read communally, no serious doubt exists that the term *synagogue* was often used explicitly in connection with communal reading events in the first century CE, as an assembly of people more generally or as a meeting place more specifically. Synagogues as structures were in active use during the first century CE (with the main one being Jerusalem, where the Great Council was).[51] One can

48. For a few examples of the communal reading of Scripture in synagogues before 70 CE, see, among others, Charles Perrot, "The Reading of the Bible in the Ancient Synagogue," in *Mikra: Text, Translation, Reading and Interpretation of the Hebrew Bible in Ancient Judaism and Early Christianity*, ed. Martin Jan Mulder (Assen, Netherlands: Van Gorcum, 1988), 137–59. Cf. Matthew Barahal Schwartz, "Torah Reading in the Ancient Synagogues" (PhD diss., Wayne State University, 1975), esp. 117–259; Lawrence H. Schiffman, "The Early History of Public Reading of the Torah," in *Jews, Christians, and Polytheists in the Ancient Synagogue: Cultural Interaction during the Greco-Roman Period*, ed. Steven Fine (London: T&T Clark, 1999), 44–56.

49. Henk Jan de Jonge, "The Use of the Old Testament in Scripture Readings in Early Christian Assemblies," in *The Scriptures of Israel in Jewish and Christian Tradition: Essays in Honour of Maarten J. J. Menken*, ed. Steve Moyise, Bart J. Koet, and Joseph Verheyden, SNT 148 (Leiden: Brill, 2013), 376–92, specifically 392; Valeriy A. Alikin, *The Earliest History of the Christian Gathering: Origin, Development and Content of the Christian Gathering in the First to Third Centuries* (Leiden: Brill, 2010), 182.

50. See, among others, Hans-Jürgen van der Minde, *Schrift und Tradition bei Paulus* (Paderborn: Schöningh, 1976), 39.

51. James T. Burtchaell, *From Synagogue to Church: Public Services and Offices in the Earliest Christian Communities* (Cambridge: Cambridge University Press, 1992), 217; Michael Rand,

find literary references to them in Philo, Josephus, Christian writings, pagan writings, inscriptions, papyri, Dead Sea scrolls, and rabbinical documents. Moreover, no less than seven first-century synagogues have been uncovered archeologically (Masada, Herodium, Gamla, Herodian Jericho, Qiryat Sefer, Modi'in, and Magdala),[52] with an eighth already receiving more academic attention.[53]

Synagogues were (most) often a place of communal reading, though debate continues over what form(s) the readings took—sermons, homilies, etc.[54] This picture is consistent with archeological excavations. Emanuel Tov suggests the strong possibility of communal reading, given the burial of a couple of damaged scrolls underneath a synagogue floor:

> The only solid piece of identifying information is that two biblical scrolls were buried under the floor of the synagogue, in two separate *genizot*, namely scrolls of Deuteronomy and Ezekiel. Why these specific scrolls, and not others, were buried there remains unknown since only fragments of the scrolls have been preserved. However, it stands to reason that these scrolls, or segments of them, had been damaged at an earlier stage, making them unfit for public reading, so that religious storage in a special burial place (*genizah*) became mandatory.[55]

"Fundamentals of the Study of Piyyut," in *Literature or Liturgy? Early Christian Hymns and Prayers in Their Literary and Liturgical Context in Antiquity*, ed. Clemens Leonhard and Hermut Lohr, WUNT 2.363 (Tübingen: Mohr Siebeck, 2014), esp. 107–9. Cf. Gerard A. M. Rouwhorst, "The Reading of Scripture in Early Christian Liturgy," in *What Athens Has to Do with Jerusalem: Essays on Classical, Jewish, and Early Christian Art and Archaeology in Honor of Gideon Foerster*, ed. Leonard V. Rutgers (Leuven: Peeters, 2002), 305–31; Daniel K. Falk, *Daily, Sabbath, and Festival Prayers in the Dead Sea Scrolls*, ed. F. García Martínez and A. S. van der Woude, STDJ 27 (Leiden: Brill, 1998), esp. 46–57.

52. Joey Corbett, "New Synagogue Excavations in Israel and Beyond," *BAR* 37, no. 4 (2011): 52–59. Cf. Anders Runesson, Donald D. Binder, and Birger Olsson, *The Ancient Synagogue from Its Origins to 200 C.E.: A Source Book* (Leiden: Brill, 2010).

53. Peter Richardson, in his published book review of *Alexander to Constantine: Archaeology of the Land of the Bible* (*BASOR* 370 [2013]: 242–44, here 243), notes Khirbet Qana as another likely first-century synagogue that was excavated by the late Douglas Edwards. This evidence is confirmed by Lee Levine's most recent count: "Solid archaeological evidence for the first-century synagogue is attested at eight sites in Judea." Levine, "The Synagogues of Galilee," in *Galilee in the Late Second Temple and Mishnaic Periods*, vol. 1, *Life, Culture, and Society*, ed. David A. Fiensy and James Riley Strange (Minneapolis: Fortress Press, 2014), 129–50, here 130.

54. For a well-argued critique of such distinctions, though not in direct relation to synagogues, see James A. Kelhoffer, "If *Second Clement* Really Were a 'Sermon,' How Would We Know, and Why Would We Care? Prolegomena to Analyses of the Writing's Genre and Community," in *Early Christian Communities between Ideal and Reality*, ed. Mark Grundeken and Joseph Verheyden, WUNT 342 (Tübingen: Mohr Siebeck, 2015), 83–108.

55. Emanuel Tov, "A Qumran Origin for the Masada Non-biblical Texts?," *DSD* 7, no. 1 (2000): 58–63.

Major articles have appeared regarding the decorated stone from a synagogue at Migdal. Among them, Mordechai Aviam argues well that the stone served as a base for a lectern on which Jewish scripture was read communally.[56] More recently, Richard Bauckham and Stefano De Luca agree with Aviam's general point here and add, "What the stone would have done was make constantly visible to the people assembled in the synagogue the connection of what they were doing with the Temple in Jerusalem. For this reason it makes a hugely important new contribution to discussion of early synagogues in Palestine."[57] In addition, Eric Meyers points to the continued focus on communal reading in everyday Jewish life, even after the two Jewish revolts in 70 and 135 CE.[58]

The editors of *A Comparative Handbook to the Gospel of Mark* state, "Although the implements of the Temple were later associated with synagogues, the ark for the scrolls of the law is attested as early as Caesar's edict as quoted by Josephus (*Antiquities* XVI § 164). The centrality of reading and interpreting the law is also conveyed in the scene of Nehemiah 8, which the Rabbis of Talmud later associated with reciting the scripture and giving its interpretation in Aramaic (see b. Megillah 3a; b. Nedarim 37b)."[59]

These pictures of "a type of ethnic reading-house"[60] are also consistent with what is seen in the New Testament.[61] Jesus reads in the synagogue in Luke 4:16.[62] Luke relates how Paul stood up and

---

56. "The Decorated Stone from the Synagogue at Migdal: A Holistic Interpretation and a Glimpse into the Life of Galilean Jews at the Time of Jesus," *NovT* 55 (2013): 205–20.

57. "Magdala as We Know It," *EC* 6 (2015): 91–118, here 111.

58. Eric M. Meyers, "Early and Late Synagogues at Nabratein in Upper Galilee: Regional and Other Considerations," in *A Wandering Galilean: Essays in Honour of Seán Freyne*, ed. Zuleika Rodgers, Margaret Daly-Denton, and Anne Fitzpatrick McKinley, SJSJ 132 (Leiden: Brill, 2009), 257–78, here 271.

59. Bruce Chilton, Darrell Bock, Daniel M. Gurtner, Jacob Neusner, Lawrence H. Schiffman, and Daniel Oden, eds., *A Comparative Handbook to the Gospel of Mark: Comparisons with Pseudepigrapha, the Qumran Scrolls, and Rabbinic Literature*, NTGJC 1 (Leiden: Brill, 2010), 570.

60. Paula Fredriksen, "How Later Contexts Affect Pauline Content, or: Retrospect is the Mother of Anachronism," in *Jews and Christians in the First and Second Centuries* (Leiden: Brill, 2015), 17–51, here 23.

61. James Dunn defends the notion that Jesus grew up attending Second Temple synagogues. See "Did Jesus Attend the Synagogue?," in *Jesus and Archaeology*, ed. James H. Charlesworth (Grand Rapids: Eerdmans, 2006), 206–22.

62. For a discussion on the main texts referring to synagogue(s) during Jesus' public ministry, see, among others, Herold Weiss, "The Sabbath in the Synoptic Gospels," *JSNT* 38 (1990): 13–27; idem., "The Sabbath in the Fourth Gospel," *JBL* 110, no. 2 (1991): 311–21; Christopher Tuckett, "Jesus and the Sabbath," in *Jesus in Continuum*, ed. Tom Holmén, WUNT 289 (Tübingen: Mohr Siebeck, 2012), 411–42, here 442; John P. Meier, "Jesus and the Sabbath," in *A Mar-*

addressed the congregation in Antioch after the leaders read in the synagogue (Acts 13:14–16). Luke also writes that James told the church in Jerusalem that Moses was still read communally every Sabbath (Acts 15:21). The author of the book of James uses both συναγωγή (2:2) and ἐκκλησία (5:14) without appearing to differentiate between the two. Some scholars suggest that the phrase used at the end of Acts 18:7 is significant in regards to Christians and the synagogue (i.e., οὗ ἡ οἰκία ἦν συνομοροῦσα τῇ συναγωγῇ).[63] Martin Hengel, while discussing communal reading in early Christian communities, concludes:

> From the end of the first century we can presuppose the reading of letters of Paul in numerous communities. The prescripts and endings of Paul's letters are deliberately formulated for liturgical use. The 'holy kiss' at the end of the letter . . . marks the transition to the Supper at the end of the reading of the letter. . . . I would say that in its basic form primitive Christian worship was more uniform than is usually assumed today.[64]

Simply put, the "Jesus movement was born and nurtured in Second Temple synagogues,"[65] and it inherited, at least in part, its practices in regard to its book culture, reading communities, and literary prac-

ginal Jew: Rethinking the Historical Jesus, vol. 4, *Law and Love* (New Haven: Yale University Press, 2009), 235–341.

63. David Peterson writes, "It must have also been very disturbing for the synagogue to have the rival Christian meeting taking place in the house next door." David G. Peterson, *The Acts of the Apostles* (Grand Rapids: Eerdmans, 2009), 512.

64. Martin Hengel, *Studies in the Gospel of Mark* (London: SCM, 1985), 176–77n80. Cf. Harry Y. Gamble, "The Book Trade in the Roman Empire," in *The Early Text of the New Testament,* ed. Charles E. Hill and Michael J. Kruger (New York: Oxford University Press, 2012), 23–36, esp. 34n38.

65. Carl Mosser, "Torah Instruction, Discussion, and Prophecy in First-Century Synagogues," in *Christian Origins and Hellenistic Judaism: Social and Literary Contexts for the New Testament,* ed. Stanley E. Porter and Wendy J. Porter (Leiden: Brill, 2013), 2:523–51, here 523. This does not mean "only" or even "most often" nurtured in synagogues. Many studies still seem to agree with three general stages set out in the five-volume series of *Corpus Basilicarum Christianarum Romae* (Rome: Pontifical Gregorian Institute, 1937–77). Cf. also Graham Twelftree, "Jesus and Synagogue," in *Handbook for the Study of the Historical Jesus: How to Study the Historical Jesus,* ed. Tom Holmén and Stanley E. Porter (Leiden: Brill, 2011), 3:3105–34; Michael Graves, "The Public Reading of Scripture in Early Judaism," *JETS* 50, no. 3 (2007): 467–87; Mayer Gruber, "Review Essay: The Tannaitic Synagogue Revisted," *RRJ* 5, no. 1 (2002): 113–25; Edward Adams, *The Earliest Christian Meeting Places: Almost Exclusively Houses?* LNTS 450 (London: T&T Clark, 2013); David Horrell, "Domestic Space and Christian Meetings at Corinth: Imagining New Contexts and the Buildings East of the Theatre," *NTS* 50 (2004): 349–69; Carmelo Pappalardo, "Synagogue," in *Encyclopedia of Ancient Christianity* (Downers Grove: InterVarsity, 2014), 3:670–78.

tices, even if early Christian communities modified them or transformed them in diverse ways.

SUMMARY

Surveying the social context, especially in relation to communal reading events, it would be no exaggeration to state that virtually all literature during this time period was composed to be read communally. We found out that communal reading events crossed social boundaries. They involved numerous segments of the population—and most importantly, not just the elite. They took place in many different indoor and outdoor settings. Communal reading events could be sacred or nonsacred, Christian or non-Christian. Given that such events had the ability to attract people, they had the potential to create an intellectual and textual community.

In addition, the background of Judaism was considered a relevant source for better understanding the large portion of this study devoted specifically to Christian communal reading events (see chapter 6). In the least, it was shown that Christian communal reading events were not a new sacred phenomenon. It appears most likely that the early Christian movement largely inherited the book culture, reading communities, and literary practices of Judaism, even if early Christian communities modified or transformed them in diverse ways. A main factor suggesting this was the role that synagogues played in early Christian origins. Despite the reality that synagogues were not exclusively for Jewish communal reading events, or even Jewish by necessity, it was shown that they were most often associated with communal reading events in Jewish traditions. This picture coincides with what we read about Jesus in the Gospel accounts.

The main conclusion here is that communal reading events existed in many different contexts and could have been an available conserving force within literary traditions in the first century CE. This conclusion still leaves open the task of investigating how widespread the events were. We will take up this investigative task in chapters 5 and 6.

5.

Communal Reading Events in the First Century: Selected Authors and Texts

At long last, Faustinus, give your little books to the public.
      – Martial, *Epigrams* 1.1.25 (ca. 40–102 CE)

Some dramatists write for the common people, and others for the few, but it is not easy to say which of them all is capable of adapting his work to both classes.
      – Plutarch, *Moralia* 854b (ca. 46–120 CE)

It was written for the common herd, the mob of farmers and of artizans, and after them for students who have nothing else to occupy their time.
      – Pliny, *Natural History* Preface 6 (ca. 61–113 CE)

Now that we have established some parameters while surveying and defining communal reading events, let us examine a selective and specifically targeted set of literary evidence in order to identify where there is enough evidence to find a plausible context for communal reading events in the Greco-Roman world apart from the New Testament writings. It is acknowledged that this selectivity necessarily excludes valuable information from other evidence. Nevertheless, due to the scope of our study, such selectivity is necessary. Not included are many authors writing around the beginning and the end of the first century CE, such as Pliny the Younger, Tacitus, Horace, Livy, and Suetonius. Another key author is Plutarch. He lived most of his life in the first century (ca. 45–120 CE). He wrote more than almost any other author did about communal reading events.[1] He traveled extensively over Greece and visited many other places, such as Asia Minor, Egypt, and Italy. Nevertheless, he is not going to be included in our study, because most of his works were actually written after 96 CE. Christopher Jones concludes, "The only works that can be placed with certainty before that date on historical grounds are the *Lives of the Caesars* [of which, only Galba and Otho survive] and the *consolatio ad uxorem*."[2]

Whether the account is direct or indirect, the aim here is to offer a survey of instances that probably involved communal reading events, in order to better gauge how widespread they were in the first century CE. Each passage is examined on its own terms and with due regard for its historical context. The overall result is a series of case studies from Greek and Roman authors, as well as some Jewish sources.[3]

By identifying such specific locations where there is enough evidence to find a plausible context for communal reading events in the Greco-Roman world, we will provide a (necessarily limited) geographical mapping of reading communities in the first century. Ultimately, the scope of these events will help us determine the extent to which communal reading events were a viable quality control.

1. LCL 46: 514–15; LCL 80: 306–7; LCL 87: 270–71; LCL 98: 28–29, 68–69, 354–55; LCL 99: 4–7, 16–17, 26–29, 90–91, 380–81, 444–45; LCL 100: 224–27; LCL 197: 188–89; LCL 222: 332–33; LCL 306:186–87; LCL 321: 86–87, 116–19, 380–83, 392–93, 468–69; LCL 405: 60–61, 64–65; LCL 406: 318–19; LCL 425: 20–21.

2. "Towards a Chronology of Plutarch's Works," *JRS* 56, nos. 1–2 (1966): 61–74, here 73. The main reason for this silence and the delay in writing, as was the case with many other writers during this era (e.g., Tacitus), is the reign of Domitian.

3. We will generally rely on three standard volumes for background information on classical authors and texts: Harry Thurston Peck, ed., *Harper's Dictionary of Classical Literature and Antiquities* (New York: Cooper Square, 1965); Simon Hornblower and Antony Spawforth, eds., *The Oxford Classical Dictionary*, 4th ed. (Oxford: Oxford University Press, 2012); and the Loeb Classical Library (LCL).

GREEK AND ROMAN AUTHORS

EPICTETUS (CA. 55–135 CE)

Epictetus was born a slave at Hierapolis, Phrygia (present-day Pamukkale, Turkey), and lived many years as a slave. He died in exile in Nicopolis in northwestern Greece, where he resided for the last years of his life with other philosophers who were exiled by Domitian in 89 CE. Epictetus set up a school there, and Arrian, one of his students, wrote down and published his discourses. William Oldfather concludes, "That Arrian's report is a stenographic record of the *ipsissima verba* of the master there can be no doubt."[4]

For our interest, Epictetus's first discourse is about people who focus solely on obtaining a promotion or office in Rome. It is addressed to his students in order to encourage them to use philosophy for better ends than solely business or contemplation. Rather, philosophy should be productive and put into action. During this discourse, Epictetus specifies how he prepares for the classes he teaches: "[A]s soon as day breaks I call to mind briefly what author I must read over" (*Diatr.* 1.10.8). Presumably, after reviewing the designated text, he would be better prepared to instruct the students once they had finished reading and interpreting it on their own. However, Epictetus goes on to say, "Yet what difference does it really make to me how so-and-so reads [ἀναγνῷ]? The first thing is that I get my sleep" (*Diatr.* 1.10.9).

One pertinent aspect to note here is that this episode provides a clue to the book culture and pedagogy that took place in Epictetus's school.[5] Apparently, the students had their own matching copies of the text, and regularly read and expounded texts in a communal

---

4. LCL 131: xii–xiii.

5. For stages of education, see Raffaella Cribiore, "Education in the Papyri," in *The Oxford Handbook of Papyrology*, ed. Roger S. Bagnall (Oxford: Oxford University Press, 2009), 320–37. She writes, "The aims of the first stage were to teach basic reading, writing, and numeracy. The second-level teacher, the grammarian, trained students to read literary texts (particularly the poets) fluently, and reinforced grammatical and orthographical knowledge of the language. In schools of rhetoric, young men of the elite read prose (the orators and historians in particular), continued to study some poetry, and perfected their oral and written expression. These three stages formed what the ancients called the *enkyklios paideia*, that is, the 'complete education,' which enveloped those privileged young men who had access to it until the end" (p. 321). See also Raffaella Cribiore, *Gymnastics of the Mind: Greek Education in Hellenistic and Roman Egypt* (Princeton, NJ: Princeton University Press, 2001).

fashion and setting (see Fronto, *De Eloq.* 5.4; Gellius, *Attic Nights* 17.20; Lucian, *Hermot.*).⁶ This communal reading aspect is expanded upon in other texts, such as when Arrian writes, "Once when he had disconcerted the student who was reading [ἀναγιγνώσκοντα] the hypothetical arguments, and the one who had set the other the passage to read [ἀνάγνωσιν] laughed at him, Epictetus said to the latter, "You are laughing at yourself. You did not give the young man a preliminary training, nor discover whether he was able to follow these arguments, but you treat him merely as a reader [ἀναγνώστῃ]" (*Diatr.* 1.26.13–4). This account reveals that various readers read at different levels, and that sometimes one student might preside over what was to be read (maybe as the teacher's assistant). It also shows what Epicetetus thought was a major problem regarding this communal reading: the lack of quality control. He chastises the presiding student for not scrutinizing the quality of what was being read. The presiding student simply laughed at the way the other student read, without regard to the content of what was being read. Another noteworthy point is that there were probably many of these types of communal reading events to prepare the students for courses of study. Dobbin comments, "[Epictetus] wanted his school to provide a supportative setting where one could face up to one's deficiencies without fear of derision."⁷ This training was to prepare students for far greater challenges and opportunities, as will be seen below.

The next discourse, which is about how to interact with tyrants, takes place in Nicopolis, where Epictetus taught. It is important to note from the outset that most Greek and Roman formal documents were read aloud in the presence of people. In this case, one of the signatories is a priest of Augustus.⁸ This account, then, presents another venue where texts were read communally: the reading of a deed of sale. Consequently, Epictetus ends this discourse with a dialogue between Augustus and a man aspiring to be one of Augustus's priests. Arrian writes:

> To-day a man was talking to me about a priesthood of Augustus. I say to him, "Man, drop the matter; you will be spending a great deal to no

6. Robert F. Dobbin, *Epictetus, Discourses Book I: Translated with an Introduction and Commentary* (Oxford: Oxford University Press, 1998), 130.

7. Dobbin, *Epictetus*, 213.

8. W. A. Oldfather, *Epictetus: The Discourses as Reported by Arrian, the Manual, and Fragments* (London: Heinemann, 1925), 1:136–37.

purpose." "But," says he, "those who draw up deeds of sale will inscribe my name." "Do you really expect, then, to be present when the deeds are read [ἀναγιγνώσκουσι] and say, 'That is my name they have written?' And even supposing you are now able to be present whenever anyone reads them, what will you do if you die?" "My name will remain after me." "Inscribe it on a stone (λίθον) and it will remain after you. Come now, who will remember you outside of Nicopolis?" (*Diatr.* 1.19.26–29)

Besides Epictetus's belief that these deeds are read aloud in the presence of others, he expects that these communal readings are often done on more than one occasion, "whenever anyone reads them."

The next discourse argues that caution and confidence should work together in the life of a philosopher. In the middle of his discourse, there is an interruption from a student, who says, "But have I not read to you [ἀνέγνων], and do you not know what I am doing?" (*Diatr.* 2.1.31). This statement refers to the student's own composition that he read aloud to Epictetus. The main reason to understand his statement this way is that a dialogue ensues regarding the writing habits of philosophers. At one point, Epictetus responds to the student, "Trifling phrases! Keep your trifling phrases! . . . Will you go off and make an exhibition of your compositions, and give a reading [ἀναγνώσῃ] from them, and boast, 'See, how I write dialogues?'" (*Diatr.* 2.1.31–35). He therefore chastises the student who would even consider this, especially since the quality of the student's work did not merit attention, according to Epictetus. Rather, one should seek the higher road of modesty and wait until one has something excellent to read. Anthony Long further links communal reading events and quality controls with performances when he writes, "[Epictetus] regularly exhorts his students to 'reveal' themselves, not in the sense of parading or showing off, but of publicly revealing their progress and education. . . . His pedagogy is aimed at their performances."[9]

Another communal reading event happens in a discourse about the learning process of becoming a philosopher. The account reads, "Once when a certain Roman citizen accompanied by his son had come in and was listening to one of his readings [ἀναγνώσματος], Epictetus said: This is the style of my teaching, and then lapsed into silence" (*Diatr.* 2.14.1–2). Epictetus goes on to state that most people will think the process of learning to be a philosopher is boring if they just come and listen to the readings, but the same could be said,

---

9. *Epictetus: A Stoic and Socratic Guide to Life* (Oxford: Oxford University Press, 2002), 242.

he argues, if someone sat around and watched a shoemaker, artist, or carpenter work.

In the next discourse, Epictetus addresses the concept of presuppositions, the quality of content being read, and the audience's ability to identify writing styles via readings. One example he gives relates to terminology. Just as physicians have a preconceived idea of what the term *healthy* means, so it is with everyone, including philosophers. As the discourse continues, Epictetus states, "With sorrow you will read [ἀναγνώσῃ] the whole treatise [of Chrysippus on *The Liar*], and with trembling you will talk about it to others. This is the way you also, my hearers, behave. You say: 'Shall I read aloud [ἀναγνῶ] to you, brother, and you to me?' 'Man, you write wonderfully.' And again, 'You have a great gift for writing in the style of Xenophon,' 'You for that of Plato,' 'You for that of Antisthenes'" (*Diatr.* 2.17.35).

Shortly afterward, Epictetus discusses some problems that happen when people study the philosophers merely to be able to talk about them. In turn, he addresses how someone can tell the sect of the philosophers to which he or she belongs:

> Observe yourselves thus in your actions and you will find out to what sect of the philosophers you belong. You will find that most of you are Epicureans, some few Peripatetics, but these without any backbone; for wherein do you in fact show that you consider virtue equal to all things else, or even superior? But as for a Stoic, show me one if you can! Where, or how? Nay, but you can show me thousands [μυρίους] who recite the petty arguments of the Stoics. Yes, but do these same men recite the petty arguments of the Epicureans any less well? Do they not handle with the same precision the petty arguments of the Peripatetics also? Who, then, is a Stoic? (Epict., *Diatr.* 2.19.20–23)

An argument could be made here that numerous people could recite arguments they heard or read with some degree of precision. Of course, this assumes a type of quality control if someone can gauge the precision and reliability in what is quoted. Here, Epictetus declares that the recited arguments are petty, but they must have been at least somewhat representative of each group. In addition, the translation "thousands" is from the word μυρίος, which means "numberless, countless, infinite" (cf. 1 Cor 4:15; 14:19).[10] Even though there is no doubt a level of exaggeration, there must be some relation to

---

10. BDAG, 661.

reality for his statement and argument to be conceivable. The implication is that there were many people who were able to and did recite their own composition(s) at communal reading events while referencing various philosophers.

The last passage included here comes from a different volume, namely, the *Encheiridion*. This work is basically Arrian's compilation from the *Discourses*, so even though it is probably a later work written in the first couple of decades of the second century CE, it is based upon Epictetus's previous discourses, most of which were delivered in the first century CE. The specific section that this excerpt comes from is dealing with all the literary entertainment in the surrounding culture. In short, Epictetus recommends that people, especially his students, do not go to all of the events. "It is not necessary, for the most part, to go to the public [τὰ θέατρα] shows [ἀναγκαῖον]" (*Ench.* 33.10). Of course, if they must go for some reason or discuss the event with someone, then he offers some additional advice, such as asking themselves, "'What would Socrates or Zeno have done under these circumstances?' and then you will not be at a loss to make proper use of the occasion" (*Ench.* 33.12–13). He then states more specifically, "Do not go rashly or readily to people's public readings [ἀκροάσεις], but when you do go, maintain your own dignity and gravity, and at the same time be careful not to make yourself disagreeable" (*Ench.* 33.11).

According to Epictetus, communal reading events were one of the main ways people would introduce their new literary work(s) to the public. That does not mean they were worth attending, but it is possible that reputable authors would be present. Therefore, he was not advising people to never attend them, but for our purposes, he certainly attests to their prevalence for better or worse.

STRABO (CA. 64/63 BCE–24 CE)

Strabo was from Amaseia (in northern Turkey, above the Black Sea). He traveled extensively during his life, as demonstrated in his seventeen-volume work, *Geography*, probably written ca. 18/19 CE. [11]

---

11. "He lived during the whole of the reign of Augustus, and during the early part, at least, of the reign of Tiberius. He is supposed to have died after A.D. 21" Peck, *Harper's Dictionary*, 1500. Cf. Sarah Pothecary, "Strabo, the Tiberian Author: Past, Present and Silence in Strabo's *Geography*," *Mnemosyne* 55, no. 4 (2002): 387–438.

"Strabo is so well-known as a geographer," Horace Jones notes, "that it is often forgotten that he was a historian before he was a geographer."[12] Scholars still debate when and where Strabo wrote his volumes,[13] but that should not delay us here.

One key passage from this volume will be examined in our study, for several reasons. Strabo argues at length regarding the specificity or lack thereof of what poets recite communally. In fact, he laments the inconsistency of what they wrote and even how they spelled; he devotes a long section to textual inconsistencies and his desire for more consistency.

Strabo sets out to compare and contrast different versions of their recited texts. "As for me," Strabo writes at one point, "let me place his assumption and those of the other critics side by side with my own and consider them" (*Geogr.* 5.12.20). He stresses how many audiences automatically grant the performer a level of authority from the simple fact that they appear learned. In one particular instance, he has a long section devoted to numerous textual differences between what writings poets recite, both past and present. He seems to consider this as important because of the authority audiences often give to poets.

The focus here will be on his statements about textual differences in order to highlight the control he thinks should be in place when audiences hear poets read their works. Strabo writes, "Some change the text and make it read 'Alazones', others 'Araazones', and for the words 'from Alybê' they read 'from Alopê', or 'from Alobê'" (*Geogr.* 5.12.21). He then states, "[Ephorus'] change of the text, with innovations so contrary to the evidence of the early manuscripts, looks like rashness" (*Geogr.* 5.12.22). Strabo explains, "One should spell the name with two l's he says, but on account of the metre the poet spells it with only one. . . . How, then, can the opinions of these men deserve approval? . . . [T]hese men also disturb the early text . . . some things are arbitrarily inserted in the text" (*Geogr.* 5.12.22). Strabo continues pointing out examples from the writings and recitations of poets of how they should be faulted at times, but at other times they should not:[14]

12. LCL 49: xxviii. Cf. Duane W. Roller, *The* Geography *of Strabo: An English Translation, with Introduction and Notes* (Cambridge: Cambridge University Press, 2014).

13. LCL 49: xxvi.

14. For arguments regarding Strabo's correct understanding of the geography here, see Walter Leaf, ed., *Strabo on the Troad, Book XIII, Cap. 1* (Cambridge: Cambridge University Press, 1923), 208–10.

From all these facts it is clear that every man who judges from the poet's failure to mention anything that he is ignorant of that thing uses faulty evidence. And it is necessary to set forth several examples to prove that it is faulty, for many use such evidence to a great extent. We must therefore rebuke them when they bring forward such evidences, even though in so doing I shall be repeating previous argument (*Geogr.* 5.12.27).

Apparently, people brought forth evidence to prove that a poet was wrong because the poet might not mention a certain place, like a river. But Strabo also argues against this illogical attack.

In sum, he counsels that discernment is required, and that listeners ought to assess the quality of the work they are hearing read to them. Strabo was certainly not alone in holding precision in high regard: "My uncle, who was also my father by adoption, was a historian of scrupulous accuracy" (Pliny, *Letters* 5.8). But even the quality of the literary tradition being recited is diminished and the truth threatened by a lackluster performance.

VALERIUS MAXIMUS (1ST CENT. CE)

Valerius Maximus wrote *Memorable Words and Deeds* during the reign of Tiberius, to whom the work is dedicated. "He had culled some thousand anecdotes from Greek and Roman history," Hans -Friedrich Mueller writes, "and arranged them in nine books."[15] Thus, not only was Valerius writing in the first century CE, but as Robert Hodgson Jr. points out, he "offers a rich dossier of texts for reconstructing the social world of early Christianity."[16] Though Valerius accompanied the proconsul Sextus Pompeius to Asia ca. 27 CE, he probably composed this work upon his return to Rome. Pompeius was the center of a literary circle to which Ovid belonged; he was also an intimate friend of the most learned prince of the imperial family, Germanicus. Nothing is known of Valerius's life except that his family was poor and undistinguished. The author's chief sources are Cicero and Livy, though his treatment of his material is known to

15. *Roman Religion in Valerius Maximus* (London: Routledge, 2002), 2. For an extensive survey and critique of the possible sources, see chapter 3 in W. Martin Bloomer, *Valerius Maximus and the Rhetoric of the New Nobility* (Chapel Hill: University of North Carolina Press, 1992), 59–146.

16. "Valerius Maximus and the Social World of the New Testament," *CBQ* 51 (1989): 683–93, here 693. Cf. Henry John Walker, *Valerius Maximus: Memorable Deeds and Sayings; One Thousand Tales from Ancient Rome* (Cambridge: Hackett, 2004), xiii–xxiv.

be careless. Also noteworthy is that this work already experienced a level of success in the first century CE, as it is referred to by Pliny the Elder, Plutarch, and others.

While it is probably true that the work, *Memorable Words and Deeds*, was not intended to be read at a communal reading event,[17] there are still two passages that concern us here, since they illuminate ancient reading practices. The first takes place inside private homes. "At dinners the elders used to recite poems [*carmine comprehensa peragebant*] to the flute on the noble deeds of their forbears to make the young more eager to imitate them," writes Valerius, "What Athens, what school of philosophy, what alien-born studies should I prefer to this domestic discipline?" (2.1.10). Whether Cicero or Varro influenced Valerius here is not important.[18] The main point is obvious, even if somewhat embellished: communal reading events at home are compared to even the most distinguished types of formal education. The picture of elders delivering a number of written poems in front of younger generations resembles some of the most prestigious types of schooling and is meant to inspire the youth to imitate the elders. The whole episode is also referred to as a domestic discipline, which suggests that was customary, not random; habitual, not ad hoc. Walker confirms, "Older men used to write songs that dealt with the famous deeds of men before their time, and they sang them at parties to the sound of the flute."[19] This form of in-house, educational entertainment may also be the primary way in which Valerius Maximus learned, especially given that his family was poor.

The second passage depicts a scene outside of the home, and beyond Rome and Athens. Maximus writes:

> After his judicial humiliation he [Aeschines] left Athens and went to Rhodes, where, at the request of the community [*civitatis*] he recited first his own speech against Ctesiphon, then that of Demosthenes on behalf of the same in very loud and melodious tones. Everyone admired the eloquence of both works, but that of Demosthenes somewhat the more of the two. "What if you had heard himself?" said Aeschines. So great an orator and recently so bitter an adversary, he had so high an esteem for his enemy's oratorical force and ardour as to declare himself ill qualified

17. Clive Skidmore argues that this work was intended for private study but was also no doubt read communally at dinner parties. *Practical Ethics for Roman Gentlemen: The Work of Valerius Maximus* (Liverpool: Liverpool University Press, 1996), 107–12.

18. Bloomer, *Valerius Maximus*, 123.

19. Walker, *Valerius Maximus*, 45.

[*parum idoneum*] to read his writings aloud [*lectorem esse praedicaret*]. He had experienced the piercing force of the eyes, the formidable gravity of the countenance, the timbre of the voice accommodated to the several words, the arresting movements of the body. So although nothing can be added to his work, yet a great part of Demosthenes is absent in Demosthenes because he is read [*legitur*], not heard [*auditur*] (2.8.10).

Many points are important here, but only three will be highlighted. First, when discussing orators, Maximus tells a story about a community making the request for a specific recitation. This assumes that even a distant audience has already experienced these types of events and judged them accordingly—in this case, positively. Second, even though Aeschines was talented and had the ability to read, he declared himself ill qualified to read Demosthenes's writings aloud because he could not provide what was lacking because of Demosthenes's physical absence. Third, there seems to be an expectation—and even assumption—that there is some level of stability to his literary work when Maximus contrasts how "nothing can be added to his work," even though the audience is missing out on certain things since they only get to hear his works read by others and not directly by himself.

CHARITON (25 BCE–50 CE)

The author of this novel begins his work by naming himself, Chariton, and his city, Aphrodisias (modern Geyre). Regarding dating, Ewen Bowie concludes, "Papyri date Chariton not later than the mid-2nd cent. AD, but . . . dates are canvassed between the 1st cent. BC and Hadrian's reign."[20] The introduction to the Loeb edition has this further remark: "Thus the range 25 B.C.–A.D. 50 would seem to fix more reliably, if imprecisely, the period within which Callirhoe is to be placed."[21]

The five passages included here all pertain to a dispute at Artaxerxes's court between Mithradates and Dionysius. The exact details and dating of the legal battle are moot for our investigation. Our

---

20. *OCD*, 306.

21. LCL 481: 2–3. Cf. also Adrian Smith's more recent discussion on dating in *The Representation of Speech Events in Chariton's* Callirhoe *and the Acts of the Apostles*, LBS 10 (Leiden: Brill, 2014), 198–202; Consuelo R. Ruiz-Montero, "Chariton von Aphrodisias: Ein Überblick," *ANRW* 2.34.2 (1994): 1006–54.

interest lies in the general depiction of reading communally in a court setting and the public interest surrounding such a trial.

As opposing sides plead their cases, letters are read, and the audience periodically responds. Chariton writes:

> Dionysius followed after him [Mithridates], dressed in Greek fashion with a Milesian mantle and holding the letters in his hand. On being ushered in, they knelt in homage. Then the king ordered the clerk [τὸν γραμματέα] to read [ἀναγνῶναι] the letters, both that of Pharnaces and the one which he himself had written in reply, so that his fellow judges might know how the case had come about. After his letter had been read out [ἀναγνωσθείσης], there came a loud burst of applause from those who admired the restraint and justice of the king (*Chaer*. 5.4.7–8).

The court adjourned for the day. When it resumed, Chariton notes, "In the morning a jostling crowd gathered about the palace, and the streets were thronged to the city limits. Everyone flocked together, ostensibly to listen to the trial, but really to see Callirhoe" (*Chaer*. 5.5.8–9). After laying out his case, Dionysius says, "I conclude by reading [ἀναγνούς] the letter which he [Mithridates] sent from Caria to Miletus by the hands of his own servants. Take the letter and read [he instructs the clerk]" (Char. *Chaer*. 5.6.10). Shortly thereafter, in response to these accusations, and more specifically the letters he read, Mithridates states, "Let him [Dionysius] first read [ἀναγνώτω] to you the certificate of her emancipation and then let him talk of marriage. . . . He reads us irrelevant letters [ἀναγινώσκει γράμματια κενά]. Yet the laws exact punishment only for actual deeds. You produce a letter. I could say, 'I did not write it. That is not my handwriting' [ἐδυνάμην εἰπεῖν 'οὐ γέγραφα· χεῖρα ἐμὴν οὐκ ἔχεις]" (*Chaer*. 5.7.4–6). Finally, with everything that took place in the entire court scene, and all the emotions that were conveyed, Chariton concludes, "What reporter could do justice to the scene in that courtroom?" (*Chaer*. 5.8.2).

In this one account, a gathered audience displays interest in a court case by their attendance as well as their responses. Multiple letters, written by multiple people, are read communally. At one point, after hearing a letter read aloud, Mithridates suggests that it would be easy to deny having written a letter if one were to actually examine the handwriting. Granted, one could dismiss this evidence based on the fact that the source is a romance novel. Nevertheless, as with almost any literary work, there must be enough elements in the story that are based to some extent on reality for it to have the rhetorical impact the author desires for his audience. Given the probability that real court cases did include such aspects from this fictitious novel—such as a judge, clerk, opponents, audience, and legal documents—it is not difficult to imagine that literary evidence would have been read communally in such situations.

OVID (CA. 43 BCE–17 CE)

Ovid was born at Sulmo in the Abruzzi (central Italy). He studied at Athens, taught at Rome, but ultimately died at Tomis on the Black Sea about a decade after Augustus exiled him in 8 CE. The reason for his expulsion was in large part an erotic poem he authored called the *Ars Amatoria*. It gained the notoriety of a teaching handbook on the subject and became "so popular with his 'host of readers'"[22] that it was "expelled from the public libraries and placed under a ban."[23]

He is the author of numerous works, but the focus here will be on two works he wrote during his exile, since they were written in the first century CE: *Tristia* from 8–12 CE and *Ex Ponto* from 12–16 CE.[24] Lutz Doering points out that in "the Graeco-Roman world, letters could be used for '*networking*'. Thus, Ovid's letters from his exile at the Black Sea [*Ex Ponto* and *Tristia*] . . . can thus be seen as letters constituting a reading community that is to be influenced and co-opted, although as open letters they do so in a socially rather loose form."[25] Though it is outside the scope of our study, Ovid's letter to his daughter, Perilla, has many other important links to our study worth at least mentioning. For example, his stress on the importance of reading and being read, his assumption of her access to literary resources, his knowledge of her talents as a writer, his memory of reading to/with her communally, his quoting of her writings, etc.[26]

22. LCL 151: xxiv.

23. LCL 151: xx.

24. It is often noted that Ovid does not supply the names of his friends and patrons in *Tristia*, but he frequently does in *Ex Ponto*. Besides observing this lack of specificity in *Tristia*, it does not significantly affect the overall aim of our study.

25. *Ancient Jewish Letters and the Beginnings of Christian Epistolography*, WUNT 298 (Tübingen: Mohr Siebeck, 2012), 388–89. For a recent study on Ovid's literary quality, see Christy N. Wise, "Banished to the Black Sea: Ovid's Poetic Transformations in *Tristia* 1:1" (PhD diss., Georgetown University, 2014).

26. For more information on this important correspondence, see Holly Lynn Murphy,

Given that we do not know many of the details surrounding the passages in *Tristia*, we will simply look at several key texts related to communal reading events. It should also be noted that *Tristia* was written during his journey to Tomis, as he sailed to Corinth and then to Samothrace, before ultimately proceeding by land up the Thracian coast.[27]

> Alas! harsh was he and too cruelly an enemy of mine, who read [*legit*] to thee my playful verse, when other poems from my oeuvre doing thee homage might have been read [*legi*] with fairer judgment (*Tristia* 2.77–9).

> Yet think not all my work trivial; oft have I set grand sails upon my bark. Six books of Fasti and as many more have I written, each containing its own month. This work did I recently compose, Caesar, under thy name, dedicated to thee, but my fate has broken it off. . . . Would that thou mightest recall thy temper awhile from wrath and bid a few lines of this be read [*legi*] to thee when thou art at leisure . . . not [sic] letter of mine is dipped in poisoned jest. Amid all the myriads of our people, many as are my writings, I am the only one whom my own Calliope [i.e., the Muse of heroic poetry] has injured (*Tristia* 2.547–70).

> There is none to whom I may read [*recitem*] my verses, none whose ears can comprehend Latin words. I write for myself—what else can I do?—and I read [*legoque*] to myself, and my writing is secure in its own criticism. Yet have I often said, "For whom this careful toil? Will the Sauromatae and the Getae read [*legent*] my writings?" Often too my tears have flowed as I wrote, my writing has been moistened by my weeping, my heart feels the old wounds as if they were fresh, and sorrow's rain glides down upon my breast (*Tristia* 4.88–98).

> Ofttimes Macer, already advanced in years, read [*legit*] to me of the birds he loved, of noxious snakes and healing plants. Ofttimes Propertius would declaim [*recitare*] his flaming verse by right of the comradeship that joined him to me. Ponticus famed in epic, Bassus also, famed in iambics, were pleasant members of that friendly circle. And Horace of

"Reconstructing Home in Exile: Ovid's *Tristia*" (MA thesis, University of Kansas, 2012), esp. 47–50.

27. For some important observations regarding his physical journey into exile, as well as how Ovid metaphorically returns to Rome via his poetry, see Samuel Jonathan Huskey, "Ovid's *Tristia* I and III: An Intertextual Katabasis" (PhD diss., University of Iowa, 2002); Matthew M. McGowan, *Ovid in Exile: Power and Poetic Redress in the* Tristia *and* Epistulae Ex Ponto, MnS 309 (Leiden: Brill, 2009).

the many rhythms held in thrall our ears while he attuned his fine-wrought songs to the Ausonian lyre. Vergil I only saw, and to Tibullus greedy fate gave no time for friendship with me (Tibullus was thy successor, Gallus, and Propertius his; after them came I, fourth in order of time). And as I reverenced older poets so was I reverenced by the younger, for my Thalia was not slow to become renowned. When first I read [*legi*] my youthful songs in public, my beard had been cut but once or twice. My genius had been stirred by her who was sung throughout the city, whom I called, not by a real name, Corinna. Much did I write, but what I thought defective I gave in person to the flames for their revision. Even when I was setting forth into exile I burned certain verse that would have found favour, for I was angry with my calling and with my songs [*studio carminibusque*] (*Tristia* 4.42–64).

These selected texts show that communal reading events were common and assumed throughout Ovid's life. On the one hand, he shares his frustration about someone else reading the emperor one of his erotic works. Of all his writings that are read communally, which were numerous, he feels it is unfair for the emperor to view only one work as representative of him. On the other hand, now that he is in exile, he is disappointed that he cannot read his own literary works to people around him, since they do not know Latin. It is almost unimaginable to him to write anything that will not be read communally, even though that does not stop him.[28] We even find out that he was driven to learn additional languages in order to be able to read his writings communally: "He even wrote a poem in Getic [one of the two native languages of Tomis]."[29] Moreover, he speaks about what many older poets would read to him communally, and relates those experiences with what he does for younger generations. So long has he been reading communally that he recalls his first event being when he only started shaving after puberty.

Moving on to Ovin's second work relevant to our study, the results are identical. Many different communal reading events are mentioned. At times, he references people reading to each other. At other times, he is the one reading—or desiring to do so—communally. Here are several instances:

---

28. For several helpful reflections on Ovid's persistence in continuing to write (according to *Tristia* 4), see Deborah Beth Shaw, "The Power of Assumptions and the Power of Poetry: A Reading of Ovid's *Tristia* 4" (PhD diss., University of California at Berkeley, 1994).

29. LCL 151: xxvii.

I am he who led Hymenaeus to your wedding torches and sang a lay worthy of your propitious union, whose books, I remember, you used to praise with the exception of those which harmed their master; who used to admire the writings that you sometimes read [*legebas*] to him, to whom a bride was given from your household (*Pont.* 1.129–34).

He who revered your house from his earliest years, Naso, the exile on Euxine's left-hand shore, sends to you, Messalinus, from the land of the unconquered Getae this greeting which he used to offer face to face. Alas! if at the reading [*lecto*] of his name you have not the countenance you had of old and hesitate to read [*perlegere*] what remains. Yet read to the end [*perlege*], nor banish my words along with myself; my verses are permitted to dwell in your city (*Pont.* 2.2.1–9).[30]

But tell me, my youthful friend, you who are inspired with my own studies, if these very studies bring you any remembrance of me. Whenever you read [*recitas*] to your friends a poem newly composed or, as you are often wont to do, urge them to read [*recitent*], do you miss me so that at times your mind, though forgetful of what is lacking, yet feels at least some part of it is gone? As you used to talk often of me in my presence, is Naso's name now also on your lips? (*Pont.* 3.3.37–43).

That which you are reading [*legis*], Severus, mightiest bard of mighty kings, comes all the way from the land of the unshorn Getae, and that as yet my books have made no mention of your name—if you will permit me to speak the truth—brings me shame. Yet letters not in metre have never ceased to go on their mission of friendship between us. Verse alone, bearing witness to your thoughtful care, I have not given you; why should I give what you yourself compose? Who would give honey to Aristaeus, Falernian wine to Bacchus, grain to Triptolemus, fruit to Alcinous? You have a productive heart; of those who cultivate Helicon, none displays a richer crop. To send verse to such a one were to add leaves to the forest: this has caused my delay, Severus. Yet my talent does not answer the call as of old, for I am furrowing a barren shore with an ineffective plough. Surely just as clogging silt jams channels and the outraged water halts in the choked fountain, so my mind has been injured by the silt of misfortune, and my verse flows with a scantier vein. If anyone had set in this land Homer himself, let me assure you, even he would have become a Getan. Pardon one who confesses, but in my pursuit I have relaxed the rein, my fingers rarely trace a letter. That inspired

---

30. Martin Helzle notes the heightened importance of this *Wortspiel* (play on words): "Wer nicht durchliest (*perlegere*), relegiert (*perlege*) Ovids Schreiben mit seinem Autor." *Ovids* Epistulae ex Ponto: *Buch I–II Kommentar* (Heidelberg: Universitätsverlag C. Winter, 2002), 270.

impulse, the nurse of poets' thoughts, which once was mine, is gone. My Muse scarce takes her part, and when I have taken up my tablets scarce does she lay upon them an inert hand, almost under coercion. I have little pleasure, or none at all, in writing, no zest in joining words to metre, whether it is that I have so reaped from it no profit that this very thing is the source of my misfortune, or that making rhythmic gestures in the dark and composing a poem which you may read [legas] to nobody are one and the same thing. A hearer rouses zeal, excellence increases with praise, and renown possesses a mighty spur. In this place who is there to whom I can read [recitem] my compositions except the yellow-haired Coralli, or the other tribes of the wild Hister? But what shall I do in my loneliness, with what occupation shall I pass my ill-starred leisure and beguile the day? For since neither wine nor treacherous dice attract me, which oft cause time to steal quietly away, nor—although I should like it if fierce war permitted—can I take pleasure in renewing the earth by cultivation, what remains except the Pierians, a cold solace,—the goddesses who have not deserved well of me? But you, who quaff more happily the Aonian spring, continue your love for the pursuit which yields you profit; worship as is right the cult of the Muses and for my reading [legamus] send hither some work over which you have recently toiled (Pont. 4.2).

These accounts are some of the last words Ovid wrote. Yet, as McGowan persuasively argues, "Ovid lays claim to the immortalizing power of poetry over against the exiling power of the princeps."[31] There seems to be no doubt in Ovid's mind that communal readings events still occur, and will continue occurring, wherever there is literature—in exile or Rome.

MARTIAL (CA. 40–102 CE)

Martial was born, and probably died, at Bilbilis in Spain. He was extremely poor most of his life, relying on the sale of his writings in order to have means of support. The literary form he employs is that of epigram. As an epigrammatist, Martial "develops fully articulated fictional scenarios depicting the nature of his writing and its role in society."[32] According to Luke Roman, "Epigram is an ephemeral

31. McGowan, Ovid in Exile, 203.

32. Luke Roman, "The Representation of Literary Materiality in Martial's Epigrams," JRS 91 (2001): 113–45, here 113. See also Roman's important observations and implications about the codex form of Martial's book (p. 127).

form of literature embedded in specific, social contexts, and dedicated to immediate uses. . . . Most statements made within epigram fall within the category of joking to some degree, but this does not mean that these jokes cannot also have serious content."[33] As a whole, "[Martial] is apt to deal in ostensibly typical characters and situations, portraying the life around him."[34] William Fitzgerald similarly remarks, "I hope to show that the book has a coherence (though not a unity), which emerges from the overlapping themes of the book as they constellate in their shifting configuration."[35] Martial is being included under Italy, since he lived in Rome for about thirty-four years and most of his epigrams either were written from there or specifically addressed life in and around Rome.

The first two epigrams included here are close together and address the same person:

> Rumor has it, Fidentinus, that you recite [recitare] my little books [libellos] in public [populo] just like your own. If you want the poems called mine, I'll send you them for nothing. If you want them called yours, buy out my ownership (Epig. 1.1.29).

> The little book you are reciting [recitas], Fidentinus, belongs to me. But when you recite [recitas] it badly, it begins to belong to you (Epig. 1.1.38).

In both of these texts, Martial addresses a plagiarist, Fidentinus, who is reciting Martial's works to a gathering of people (cf. 1.52, 53, 66, 72). Given the frequency with which Martial addresses plagiarism in book 1, compared with how rarely he mentions it in later works, there is a suggestion that Martial was publishing his works and people were reading them soon after publication.[36] Moreover, Martial suggests here that his copyist (see further below) makes enough additional copies for Martial to give away free, beyond what the copyist presumably sells or provides for the booksellers.

Fidentinus is apparently not the only person whom Martial knows is reading his works. Martial continues, "You ask me to recite [recitem] my epigrams for your benefit. Not I. You don't want to lis-

---

33. Ibid., 113 and 117–18, respectively.

34. LCL 94: 4–5.

35. *Martial: The World of the Epigram* (Chicago: University of Chicago Press, 2007), 69.

36. Peter Howell, *A Commentary on Book One of the Epigrams of Martial* (London: Athlone, 1980), 168.

ten, Celer, you want to recite [*recitare*]" (*Epig.* 1.1.63). It is possible to understand the last phrase as if Celer wants to read his own works to Martial, but it is more likely that he wants to use Martial's works as his own, especially given other similar references by Martial in the same work. Moreover, Martial is aware that people do the same thing with other authors' works, not just his. A prime example is Epigram 66:

> You are mistaken, greedy purloiner [*fur*] of my books, in thinking that it costs no more to become a poet than the price of copying and a cheap length of papyrus [*scriptura quanti constet et tomus vilis*]. Applause is not to be had for six or ten sesterces. You must look for private, unpublished work, poems known only to the parent of the virgin sheet [*virginis pater chartae*], which he keeps sealed up in his book-box [*scrinioque*], work not rubbed rough by hard chins [while being rolled up]. A well-known book cannot change author. But if you find one whose face is not yet smoothed by the pumice stone [*pumicata*], one not embellished with bosses and parchment cover [*membrana*], buy it. I have such, and nobody will be the wiser. Whoever recites [*recitat*] other men's productions and seeks fame thereby, ought to buy—not a book, but silence (*Epig.* 1.1.66).

In this next epigram, Martial makes fun of his book's length. On the one hand, he could have written three times as much, but it would deter readers. On the other hand, readers may get bored if it is too short. Either way, Patricia Larash states, "Martial makes it clear [here and elsewhere] that an author prefers his work to be read, and to be read completely, not just skimmed through."[37] Moreover, Martial notes one realistic context for such communal readings: banquet settings. Ruurd Nauta emphasizes this communal aspect when he states, "The symposiast will not read the book in silence, but will recite it out loud to his drinking companions."[38] Martial writes:

> You could bear three hundred epigrams, but who would bear with you and read you through [*perlegeretque*], my book? And now let me tell you the virtues of a compact little book [*libelli*]. The first is that I use up less paper [*charta*]. The second is that the copyist gets through this stuff in a single hour and will not spend all his time on my trifles. The third

37. "Martial's *Lector*, the Practice of Reading, and the Emergence of the General Reader in Flavian Rome" (PhD diss., University of California at Berkeley, 2004), 181n432.

38. *Poetry for Patrons: Literary Communications in the Age of Domitian* (Leiden: Brill, 2002), 93.

thing is that if you happen to get read [*legeris*] to somebody, you may be thoroughly bad but you won't be a bore. The diner [*te conviva*] will read [*leget*] you when his five measures have been mixed, but before the cup set down begins to cool. Do you suppose you are protected by such brevity? Ah me, how many will think you long even so! (*Epig.* 1.2.1).

In yet another epigram, Martial addresses the reading of his own writings. "What lies behind the epigram's final point," Craig Williams points out, "is that Martial sees through Caecilianus' practice: he is reading from Marsus and Catullus not to pay Martial a compliment but rather so that the latter's verse may suffer by comparison."[39] The account reads:

> None kinder than you, Caecilianus. I have noticed that if ever I read [*lego*] a few couplets from my work, you at once recite [*recitas*] something of Marsus or Catullus. Is this a favor to me, as though you were reading [*legas*] inferior productions so that mine may the better please by comparison? I believe that. However, I'd rather you read [*recites*] your own, Caecilianus (*Epig.* 1.2.71).

In a very short epigram later on, Martial states that everything written is meant to be read. "Cinna is reported to write verses against me," he states. "Nobody writes, whose poems nobody reads [*legit*]" (*Epig.* 1.3.9). So frequent were such poems read communally that Martial then shares about the annoying communal reading habits of a man named Ligurinus. He writes at more length:

> Do you wish to know why it is, Ligurinus, that nobody is glad to meet you, that, wherever you go, there is flight and a vast solitude around you? You are too much of a poet. This is a very dangerous fault. A tigress roused by the theft of her cubs is not feared so much, nor yet a viper burnt by the midday sun, nor yet a vicious scorpion. For I ask you, who would endure such trials? You read to me as I stand, you read to me as I sit, you read to me as I run, you read to me as I shit. I flee to the baths: you boom in my ear. I head for the pool: I'm not allowed to swim. I hurry to dinner: you stop me in my tracks. I arrive at dinner: you drive me away as I eat. Tired out, I take a nap: you rouse me as I lie. Do you care to see how much damage you do? A just man, upright and innocent, you are feared. (*Epig.* 1.3.44).

---

39. Craig A. Williams, ed., *Martial,* Epigrams, *Book Two* (Oxford: Oxford University Press, 2004), 227.

In fact, so bad was Ligurinus's reputation of reading to everyone everywhere that the epigram directly following this one depicts the following:

> Whether Phoebus fled Thyestes' dinner table or not, I don't know; but we flee yours, Ligurinus. Elegant indeed it is, furnished with lordly repasts, but nothing in the world gives pleasure when you are reciting [*recitante*]. I don't want you to serve me turbot or a two-pounder mullet, nor do I want mushrooms, oysters I don't want: shut up [*tace*] (*Epig.* 1.3.45).

And if those two accounts were not enough, Martial writes yet another epigram chastising Ligurinus for the communal reading events he hosts:

> This and no other is the reason why you invite me to dinner, Ligurinus: to recite [*recites*] your verses. I take my slippers off: immediately a bulky [*ingens*] volume is brought in among the lettuces and the sharp sauce. Another is read [*perlegitur*] through while the first course hangs fire. There's a third, and the dessert is not yet come. And you recite [*recitas*] a fourth and finally a fifth roll [*librum*]. If you serve me boar this often, it stinks. But if you don't consign your damnable poems to the mackerel, Ligurinus, in future you will dine at home by yourself (*Epig.* 1.3.50).

In another volume, Martial alleges that he receives a report that his works are being read by everyone, even young women in front of their husbands. More importantly for our study is that it pertains to a faraway location beyond Rome: Vienne on the Rhone River. He writes, "Fair Vienna is said, if report speak true, to hold my little books in high favor. Everybody there reads [*legit*] me—old man, young man, boy, and virtuous young woman in front of her straight-laced husband" (*Epig.* 2.7.88).

This report may not be entirely accurate, as Martial indicates. It is also true that Martial is known to use hyperbole in his writings. But even within joking there can be elements of truth and seriousness. For example, here are four distinct epigrams that refer to his claimed scope of distribution:

> If you know Caesius Sabinus well, little book, Caesius the ornament of hilly Umbria, fellow townsman of my friend Aulus Pudens, you will give him these, even if he be busy. Though a thousand cares press and

beset him, yet he will have time for my verses. For he loves me and reads me next to Turnus' famous little volumes [*libellis*]. Oh, what renown is in the making for you! Oh, what glory! What a multitude of fans! The dinner tables, the Forum, the houses, the crossroads, the colonnades, the shops will utter you. You are sent to one, you will be read by all (*Epig.* 2.7.97).

A certain person, dearest Julius, is bursting with envy because Rome reads me—bursting with envy (*Epig.* 2.9.97).

In the time I escort you out and bring you back home, in the time I lend an ear to your chatter and praise whatever you say or do, how many verses, Labullus, could have come into being! Do you think it no loss that what Rome reads and strangers demand, what knights do not scorn, senators know by heart, barristers praise, poets criticize, goes to waste because of you? Is this fair, Labullus? Would anyone stand for it? So that the number of your little clients be larger, should the number of my books be smaller? In almost thirty days I have finished scarce a page [*pagina*]. So it goes when a poet does not want to dine at home (*Epig.* 3.11.24).

If perchance (though this can scarce be hoped for) he has time to spare, ask him to hand my verses personally to the Leader and commend my timid, brief little book with only four words: "This your Rome reads" (*Epig.* 3.12.11).

It is difficult to gauge how accurate these complaints are, but Martial at least goes so far as to say that his daily life has prevented him from writing more, and he assumes his writings could have been widespread. Even if he is exaggerating to some extent, each of these epigrams hints at the broader point that his works could have been included in communal reading events. Putting this another way, his entire assumption in several epigrams is that people can purchase his writings; that they are relatively easy to read, carry, and recite; and that people are reading them communally.

PERSIUS (CA. 34–62 CE)

Persius was born at Volaterrae in Etruria (central Italy) and moved to Rome when he was around twelve years old. The sole passage included in our study is the "programmatic poem placed at the start of

the book"[40] (Satire 1), which opens his only extant work. The introduction to the Loeb edition of Persius's work highlights his attitude
toward literary activity in this satire, "where he appears to be content with a small or nonexistent audience" and "starts by rejecting the
conventional standards of assessing poetry."[41] This rejection is dealt
with in various portions of the poem, as he creates a dialogue between
a poet and a fictitious interlocutor. Although the entire account is
important for consideration, our study will survey just the opening,
where "he depicts a poetry recitation as if it were a sex show in which
the audience are brought to orgasm" and "their reading matter is
advertising hype for popular entertainments and romantic novels."[42]
Persius writes:

> We shut ourselves away and write some grand stuff, one in verse,
> another in prose, stuff which only a generous lung of breath can gasp
> out. And of course that's what you will finally read to the public from
> your seat on the platform, neatly combed and in your fresh toga, all
> dressed in white and wearing your birthday ring of sardonyx, after you
> have rinsed your supple throat with a liquid warble, in a state of enerva-
> tion with your orgasmic eye. Then, as the poetry enters their backsides
> and as their inmost parts are tickled by verse vibrations, you can see huge
> Tituses quivering, both their respectable manner and their calm voice
> gone. . . . But it's splendid to be pointed out and to hear people say:
> "That's him!" Is it worth nothing to you to be the dictation text [*dictata*]
> of a hundred curly-headed boys? (*Sat.* 1.13–30).

Guy Lee and William Barr comment, "The bulk of the Satire (vv.
13–106) is used by Persius in order to cast a jaundiced eye over
the current literary scene at Rome."[43] There is no doubt this literary
scene assumes widespread communal reading events, which Persius
views negatively. In the picture he portrays, "Everyone is writing and
reciting. Audiences squirm with depraved appreciation of salacious
rubbish."[44] This is somewhat similar to Juvenal's first satire, where
he mocks the volume of public recitations and complains that it is
one of the worst aspects of living at Rome (cf. also Juvenal's seventh satire).[45] Moreover, the additional elements related to communal

40. LCL 91: 46.
41. LCL 91: 46.
42. LCL 91: 47.
43. *The Satires of Persius* (Liverpool: Francis Cairns, 1987), 66.
44. Ibid., 69.
45. Regarding the author's use of *dictata*, Oleg Nikitinski writes, "dictata (plurale tantum)

reading events, such as the mention of a toga, vocal preparations, and high seat, all underscore the point of recitations and how crowds are so easily aroused and gratified by the reciters.[46] The main point here, however, is that he writes about how pervasive communal reading events were in his day.

DIO CHRYSOSTOM (CA. 40/50–110/120 CE)

The precise dating of all his works is not certain, but Dio Chrysostom is still included in our study because he was writing in the first century and some of his works, such as *Discourse* 44, can be assigned to the first century with reasonable certainty.[47] Furthermore, Christopher Fuhrmann argues, "Some orations may have suffered unauthorized publication by audience members who took liberties with the text (see *Or.* 42.4–5). The author himself likely revised most texts for publication. . . . Nevertheless, I think it safe overall to proceed as if most of the texts under discussion here are decent approximations of what was said on a particular occasion."[48]

Dio Chrysostom discusses what it is like to attend a symposium. The focus here will be on the first group of people he identifies: the people who come just to drink a lot and socialize. The people in this category, he writes, "feeling that they have got their table-companions for an audience, recite [διατίθενται] stupid and tedious speeches" (*Or.* 27.3).

In another episode, Dio Chrysostom describes why it is better to read communally instead of individually. In fact, he deduces that reading works to oneself is a careless way of reading, thus increasing the focus on and promoting the practice of reading communally. He writes:

sunt omnia (ut theses, praecepta, carmina, orationes etc.) quae magistri discipulis scribenda ediscendaque tradunt." *A. Persius Flaccus Saturae: accedunt varia de Persio iudicia saec. XIV–XX* (München: K. G. Saur, 2002), 65. Cf. R. A. Harvey, *A Commentary on Persius* (Leiden: Brill, 1981), 26.

46. For more points of parallel with communal reading events, see Harvey, *A Commentary on Persius*, 16–23.

47. "Internal evidence makes it fairly certain that this Discourse was delivered in the winter of A.D. 96–97." LCL 376: 189.

48. "Dio Chrysostom as a Local Politician: A Critical Reappraisal," in Aspects of Ancient Institutions and Geography, ed. Lee L. Brice and Daniëlle Slootjes, IE 19 (Leiden, Brill, 2015), 161–76, here 161–62.

So let us consider the poets: I would counsel you to read [ἐντυγχάνειν] Menander of the writers of Comedy quite carefully, and Euripides of the writers of Tragedy, and to do so, not casually by reading [ἀναγιγνώσκοντα] them to yourself, but by having them read to you by others, preferably by men who know how to render [ἐπισταμένων] the lines pleasurably, but at any rate so as not to offend [ἀλύπως ὑποκρίνασθαι]. For the effect is enhanced when one is relieved of the preoccupation of reading [ἀναγιγνώσκειν] (Or. 18.6–7).

He goes on to state one reason why he did not mention works more advanced than Menander's plays: "For physicians do not prescribe the most costly diet for their patients, but that which is salutary" (Or. 18.7). This illustration seems to indicate that sometimes it is more important that someone is getting food then how expensive the food is. In relation to reading, he seems to be arguing that even lesser works can be enjoyed, especially when performed well communally. It is also interesting to see his choice of terms. The first term noted above seems to indicate that someone is personally going through a text, but he prefers someone else to be reading it to another person or persons. Certainly, it is preferable to have someone who is well versed in a work to be the one reading it, but it seems to be more of a preference than a necessity. Moreover, it seems to be more than just reading in a pleasurable way, that is, to be reading a text without causing pain, as seen in the combination of ἀλύπως ὑποκρίνασθαι.

In Dio Chrysostom's so-called "Eighteenth Discourse: On Training for Public Speaking," he again discusses the reading of different texts and their application to reading communally. While discussing some significant points regarding Xenophon's treatise (that is, the *Anabasis* or *Journey Inland*), he recommends that his audience ambitiously read (φιλοτίμως ἐντυγχάνοις) Xenophon's work. What follows are a few comments regarding his preference for dictating a public address to someone else instead of writing it down himself. From there, he mentions that the recipient of his writing—presumably a young man, especially given that his analogies are in the context of young wrestlers and young artists—probably knows more than he is suggesting. In turn, Dio concludes that they should get together so that they can read some of the ancient writers together and discuss them in order to grow in their disciplines. He writes:

Just as it is not enough to say to painters and to sculptors that their colours should be just so and that their lines should be just so, but they derive the greatest help if the critic can see them at work, painting or modelling; and just as it is not sufficient for the gymnastic masters to name the different holds in wrestling, but they must go on and demonstrate them to the youth who wishes to learn: so too in consultations like this, the help would be greater if one were to see the man who has given the advice in action himself. I declare for my part that even if I had to read aloud [ἀναγιγνώσκειν] to you while you listened, for the sake of helping you I should not hesitate, since I both love you and admire you for your ambition, and am grateful for the honour you have shown me (*Or.* 18.21).

Moving on to Dio Chrysostom's thirty-third discourse, it appears that he has been invited to speak at a communal reading event in Tarsus. He begins his discourse (διαλέγεσθαι) by asking many rhetorical questions as to why they would have invited him. He assumes that they have had many communal reading events before this one, but he assures them that he is not there to give "a eulogy of your land," since "that sort of performance requires ample [μεγάλης] preparation [παρασκευῆς]" before one is able to "mount the platform [ἰόντων ἐπὶ τοὺς λόγους]" (*Or.* 33.2–3).

He goes on to state that the people who have frequently presented before them claim to and seem like they know everything, because they offer to speak on any topic the audience wants, and "the speaker starts from there and pours forth a steady and copious flood of speech, like some abundant river that has been dammed up within him." Consequently, the audience is deceived and never critically judges what they recite and quote:

> Then, as you listen, the thought of testing his several statements or of distrusting such a learned man seems to you to be shabby treatment and inopportune, nay, you are heedlessly elated by the power and the speed of his delivery and are very happy, as, without a pause for breath, he strings together such a multitude of phrases, and you are affected very much as are those who gaze at horses running at a gallop—though not at all benefited by the experience, still you are full of admiration and exclaim, "What a marvellous thing to own!" And yet in the case of the horses it is frequently not the owners who may be seen handling the reins, but rather some worthless slave (*Or.* 33.5).

He goes on to state that this is somewhat similar to what false physicians do in order to get clientele. They speak about all that they know regarding the physical body, whereas the real physician just prescribes what needs to be done. Furthermore, he argues that many bad poets have been able to present their works before the masses because it sounds so sweet and pleasurable, but in the end have infected the city "with effrontery and gibes and ribald jests" (*Or.* 33.10).

Dio Chrysostom's thirty-sixth discourse has a dialogue about poets. The response of one of the men is important for our consideration:

> And he laughed and said, "Why, as for myself, I do not even know the other poet's name, and I suppose that none of these men does, either. For we do not believe in any other poet than Homer. But as for Homer, you might say that no man alive is ignorant of him. For Homer is the only one whom their poets recall in their compositions, and it is their habit to recite his verses on many an occasion, but invariably they employ his poetry to inspire their troops when about to enter battle, just as the songs of Tyrtaeus used to be employed in Lacedaemon. Moreover, all these poets are blind, and they do not believe it possible for any one to become a poet otherwise" (*Or.* 36.10).

There is no doubt everyone has heard of Homer,[49] especially because poets recite his works at "many" communal reading events. Not just that, but in order to be a poet, one must be familiar enough with Homer to recite his writings, which must have functioned somewhat like a canonical text, at communal reading events.[50]

Dio Chrysostom's forty-fourth discourse has another passing comment regarding communal reading events. This time, it is in his concluding remarks, when he announces to the audience that he is going to read some letters between himself and the emperor, Nerva. He states, "But that you may know my opinion from another source as well, I will read [ἀναγνώσομαι] you a letter which I myself sent to the Emperor in answer to his invitation to visit him, because in that letter I begged to be excused in favour of you, and also the letter which he wrote in reply" (*Or.* 44.12).

In another short composition, Dio Chrysostom makes some spe-

---

49. See Maren R. Niehoff, "Why Compare Homer's Readers to Biblical Readers?," in *Homer and the Bible in the Eyes of Ancient Interpreters*, ed. Maren R. Niehoff, JSRC 16 (Leiden: Brill, 2012), 3–14. See also G. H. R. Horsley, *Homer in Pisidia: Degrees of Literateness in a Backwoods Province of the Roman Empire* (New South Wales, Australia: University of New England, 1999); Catherine Hezser, "The Torah versus Homer: Jewish and Greco-Roman Education in Late Roman Palestine," in *Ancient Education and Early Christianity*, ed. Matthew Ryan Hauge and Andrew W. Pitts (London: T&T Clark, 2016), 5–24.

50. For more insights into this entire discourse, see D. A. Russell, *Dio Chrysostom: Orations VII, XII, and XXXVI* (Cambridge: Cambridge University Press, 1992), 211–47, esp. 216–18.

cific remarks concerning the manuscript that contained his writing. He states, "There is no need to unroll the parchment [ἐξελίττειν τὸ βιβλίον]; instead I will recite [ἐρῶ] the speech myself. For in fact it does not contain many lines [πολύστιχόν]; yet it is a polished composition, and its beauty lingers in my memory, so that not even if I wished to do so could I forget."[51] Dio's *Encomium on Hair* runs for several pages and concludes, "There you have the words of Dio."[52]

When the narrator of the *Testimonia* identifies Dio Chrysostom as a sophist, he writes, "After publishing [ἐξενηνοχώς] among the Greeks treatises [συγγράμματα] worthy of a philosopher's serious attention, he became so enslaved to the reputation of a sophist as to repent, as he grew older, of the solemnity that marked his prime and to knock for admission to the theatres [θέατρα] of Magna Graecia and Asia, entering into competitions in declamation [μελέταις ἐναγωνιζόμενον]."[53] A couple of points are worth mentioning here. First, he published many treatises. Second, he entered into many competitions that involved reciting his works. Third, the locations of these events appear to have been in well-known theaters in southern Italy and Asia.

The narrator provides various details about many other speeches and discourses by Dio, ones that a "superficial reader [παρέργως ἐντυγχάνοντι]" may not understand. He recalls many speeches not extant, such as one work "consisting of eighty speeches."[54] The most important details concerning our study are the locations and terminology. As for the locations where they were delivered, he names no less than Athens, Alexandria, Celaenae in Phrygia, Prusa, Rhodes, Corinth, between Nicaea and Nicomedia, etc. Though he does not always use explicit terminology, he does at times. For instance, he writes, "The title of the nineteenth [discourse] reveals that it had been delivered in Borysthenes [by the Black Sea], but that it was given as a public reading [ἀναγνωσθῆναι] in Dio's native city."[55]

51. LCL 385: 336–37.
52. LCL 385: 342–43.
53. LCL 385: 368–69.
54. LCL 385: 386–87.
55. LCL 385: 396–97.

STATIUS (CA. 45–96 CE)

Statius was born in the Greek city of Naples around 45 CE, but lived most of his life between there and Rome until he died around 96 CE. He competed in various literary competitions, most notably the poetry divisions at the Alban and Capitoline Games in 90 CE. The following text is taken from his work *Silvae*, which is essentially a collection of thirty-two short poems. "With the *Silvae* the poet participates wholeheartedly in the epideictic tradition," writes Donka Markus, "a highly popular genre of public performance at the time."[56]

The short text germane to our study reveals one of Statius's assumptions: the younger generation—including girls—had ample access to the literary work he references. "As for his polished verses, what youths, what girls [*puellae*] in all Rome do not have them by heart [*didicere*]?" (*Silv.* 1.2.172–3). As seen elsewhere, there is certainly a level of exaggeration in this comment. Likewise, it is doubtful that he is implying that everyone had their own copy of this work. Rather, and especially in light of our study, it is likely that Statius's impromptu comment does reflect an element of truth that communal reading events were widespread enough to have provided adequate venues for youths to have heard this work read multiple times, and thus know it well.

QUINTUS CURTIUS RUFUS (1ST CENT. CE)

Quintus Curtius Rufus was a rhetorician and historian. The preferred dating of his works is during the reign of Tiberius.[57] Both texts included in our study are from his work *Historiae*, specifically about the life of Alexander the Great. This may initially appear to be beyond the scope of our study. He is certainly writing about alleged events that preceded the first century CE. At the same time, John Rolfe notes, "The *Historiae* seem to be the work of a rhetorician rather than of an historian. One of his principle [sic] aims was to insert in his work brilliant speeches and romantic incidents."[58] Therefore, since the work itself was composed in the first century, and he

56. "The Politics of Entertainment: Tradition and Romanization in Statius' *Thebaid*" (PhD diss., University of Michigan, 1997), 3.
57. *OCD*, 400. Cf. LCL 368: xviii–xxii.
58. LCL 368: xx–xxi.

does contribute at times to the longevity and extent of communal reading events, this work is being included in our study. Among other literary features—including the rhetorical outlines, verbal coloring, syntax, and vocabulary—it has also been well argued that Curtius made a systematic use of other written works, such as the writings of Livy, Vergil, and Horace.[59]

The first episode takes place somewhere in Mesopotamia, between the Tigris River and Gordyaean Mountains (present-day Armenia). He writes, "Then letters of Darius were intercepted, in which the Greek soldiers were tempted either to kill or to betray their king, and Alexander was in doubt whether to read [*recitaret*] them before an assembly, since he thoroughly trusted the goodwill and loyalty towards him of the Greek troops also. But Parmenion dissuaded him, declaring that the ears of the soldiers ought not to be infected by such promises" (1.4.16–17). Alexander accepted the advice, never read the letters before the whole army, and left camp. Even though he never read the letters in front of all the soldiers, the narrative reveals that letters were circulating; soldiers could intercept, read, and discuss them together; and Alexander had the option of reading them in front of more people.

Much later in his work, during some different military campaigns, this time in Macedonia, there is again the picture of multiple letters circulating, communal reading events occurring, and decisions being made. In the middle of this, a man named Polydamas read two letters written to him by the king. While he was reading the second letter, a man named Cleander killed him. Shortly after the murder, Curtius recounts, "Cleander ordered their leaders to be admitted, and read [*recitat*] to the soldiers the letters which the king had written, in which were contained an account of the plots of Parmenion against the king and Alexander's prayers that they should avenge him" (2.7.30–31). Following this chaotic episode, all the soldiers were asked to write letters to their people in Macedonia, telling them about their experiences. Alexander had these letters intercepted and read, and ultimately withdrew the soldiers who wrote unfavorably about the circumstances.

---

59. R. B. Steele, "Quintus Curtius Rufus," *AJP* 36, no. 4 (1915): 402–23.

QUINTILIAN (CA. 35–90S CE)

Quintilian was born at Calagurris in Spain and lived during most of the first century CE. He spent most of his life in both Rome and Spain. He is also the first known rhetorician to receive a salary from public funds at Rome (under Vespasian). Several key texts from his volume on oratorical training (*Institutio Oratoria*), which covers childhood training through the peak of an orator's career, ought to suffice to demonstrate from another author that these types of events were well known and widespread in the first century CE.

In volume 1 of *Institutio Oratoria*, Quintilian provides some guidelines for schooling young children. Martin Bloomer writes that, according to Quintilian, "The training of the child is a well-directed encounter with, and gradual approximation, to texts. . . . The child's development becomes assimilated with the texts he reads, recites, annotates, and composes in a graduated and supervised routine."[60] This does not mean just any of the numerous texts circulating during this time. As Quintilian states, "For the present I will only say that I do not want young men to think their education complete when they have mastered one of the small text-books [*artis libellum*] of which so many are in circulation [*plerumque circumferuntur*]" (*Inst.* 2.13.15). Moreover, Quintilian acknowledges that some teachers do not have the time to supervise each student's individual reading. At the same time, it is essential that each student be given a chance to read communally so that the teacher can point out any mistakes while also preparing the student for "speaking in public" (*Inst.* 2.5.7). With these larger communal reading events in mind, he goes on to suggest, "It can also be useful sometimes to read aloud bad or faulty speeches, but of the kind that many admire out of bad taste, and to point out what a lot of expressions in these are inexact, obscure, turgid, low, mean, extravagant, or effeminate. These expressions are not only praised by many people but, what is worse, praised just for their badness" (*Inst.* 2.5.10–11).

Several points are significant here. First, for the purposes of assessment, there is a preference for communal reading instead of individual reading. This coincides with what Bloomer argues elsewhere: "For Quintilian, learning necessarily takes place within the context

60. "Quintilian on the Child as Learning Subject," *Classical World* 105, no. 1 (2011): 109–37, here 111.

of a social community," and "no good education will arise from tutor and student alone. Rhetorical training and oratorical performance demand an audience."[61] Second, reading communally in one venue—a small class, in this case—is sometimes done with other venues in mind. Peter Lampe even discusses the emphasis and importance Quintilian places on visual memory, such as always using the same wax tablet, in preparing for the delivery of a written speech. For Quintilian, visualizations are far more significant than relying on acoustic memory, as he explicitly states here: "If we attempt to learn by heart from another person reading aloud, . . . the process of learning will be slower, because the perception of the eye adheres more [in the memory] than that of the ear."[62] Third, even bad and faulty speeches are apparently available for further communal reading. Fourth, in order for an audience to judge speeches as bad or faulty, there must have been a standard among reading communities, especially in educational settings. Fifth, many people are said to attend these speeches, even though they are deemed unacceptable.

In volume 3 of *Institutio Oratoria*, Quintilian names some of his authoritative sources. In the process, he discusses multiple speeches, books, and readers. In one scene, he recounts one of Cicero's stories about how Lucius Crassus handled a situation involving a man named Brutus, though the details of the case are unknown. He writes, "Brutus, in his accusation of Gnaeus Plancus, had produced two readers [*duobus lectoribus*] to show that Plancus' advocate, Crassus, in his speech [*oratione*] on the colony of Narbo, had urged measures contrary to those which he had urged when speaking of the Lex Servilia. Crassus thereupon produced three readers [*tris lectores*], and gave them the Dialogues of Brutus' father to read out [*legendos*]" (*Inst.* 6.3.44). The main point in relation to our study is that multiple readers are called, in order to build a case about what was presented at a communal reading event.

In volume 4 of *Institutio Oratoria*, Quintilian deals with style, and provides many examples from various authors and literary works. He also explains how students should hone their skills by reading, writing, and imitating good exemplars. One example provides a unique window into how easy it is to provide examples and how common

61. Bloomer, "Quintilian on the Child," 111 and 120, respectively.

62. Peter Lampe, "Quintilian's Psychological Insights in His *Institutio Oratoria*," in *Paul and Rhetoric*, ed. J. Paul Sampley and Peter Lampe (London: T&T Clark, 2010), 180–99, here 196. See also *Inst.* 11.2.32; 11.2.10.

communal reading events were. To illustrate the difference between judgments concerning people and arguments based on things, he writes, "There is surely no difference between asking 'Should Cornelius, tribune of the plebs [*tribunus plebis*], be put on trial for reading out [*legerit*] his proposed law?' and asking 'Is it breach of maiestas if a magistrate himself reads [*recitarit*] his proposal to the people [*populo*]?'" (*Inst.* 10.5.13).

Quintilian's final two books on oratorical training form volume 5 of *Institutio Oratoria*. In these two final books, he discusses memory, delivery, dress, and gestures; presenting in the end, the epitome of an accomplished orator. In chapter 3, he discusses why an orator needs to know "so many things on which society is chiefly based" (*Inst.* 12.3.1), such as civil law, customs, and religious practices. If he does not, Quintilian compares him to professional readers who merely read the works of others at performances. "He will be almost like those people who give readings from the poets! In fact, in a sense, he will just be a transmitter of instructions, relying on the good faith of others" (*Inst.* 12.3.2). In turn, he will be viewed as a fool. More specifically, it is better that some people do not become orators, since "every certain point of law depends either on a written text or on custom" (*Inst.* 12.3.6–7). He goes on to argue that what people need the most is reading [*lectioni*], which fortunately "is the least laborious kind of study" (*Inst.* 12.3.9).

SENECA THE ELDER (CA. 55 BCE–41 CE)

Seneca the Elder was born at Corduba in Spain, but he spent substantial time in Rome until he died. Especially important to highlight for our study is that all the extracts in his literary collection of rhetorical exercises are purportedly from communal reading events he had experienced firsthand. The following selected texts are drawn from this work, which consists of *controversiae* (debates) and *suasoriae* (speeches of advice).[63] The date of composition for these two works is typically assigned to the period between 37 and 41 CE.[64]

In this first account, Seneca has been discussing many different

63. For more information about the first-century oratorical context of *controversiae* and *suasoriae*, see Erica Melanie Bexley, "Performing Oratory in Early Imperial Rome: Courtroom, Schoolroom, Stage" (PhD diss., Cornell University, 2013).

64. Lewis A. Sussman, *The Elder Seneca* (Leiden: Brill, 1978), 91–93.

book burnings when he reaches a man named Labienus.[65] He writes, "I remember that once, when he was reciting [*recitaret*] his history, Labienus rolled up a good deal of the book, saying: 'The parts I pass over will be read [*legentur*] after my death'" (*Controv.* 2.10.8). So bad were the book burnings, that Labienus's enemy, Cassius Severus, states this: "I ought to be burnt alive now—I have those books by heart" (*Controv.* 2.10.8). His point—albeit rhetorical hyperbole—is that if the Senate wants to extinguish the contents of all the works, they must also start burning the people who know them. Moreover, bold statements such as these circulated and motivated other literary works. "Here is a nice book for you to ask for from your friend Gallio: he read out [*recitavit*] once a reply to Labienus on behalf of Bathyllus, Maecenas' freedman, a speech in which you will admire the spirit of a youth prepared to provoke those teeth to bite" (*Controv.* 2.10.8).

In the second episode, Seneca provides an example of communal reading events producing fictitious information. One argument he gives for knowing this information is false is eyewitness testimony from people present during the communal reading event:

> [Schoolmen] often declaim on the theme: "Cicero deliberates whether to burn his speeches on Antony's promising him his life." Anyone must realise that this is a crude fiction. Pollio wants to make us think it the truth. For this is what he said in his published speech for Lamia: "Thus Cicero never hesitated to go back on his passionate outpourings against Antony; he promised to produce, more carefully, many times more speeches in the opposite sense, and even to recite [*recitare*] them personally at a public meeting [*contione*]." This together with other things much more shabby: from which it was quite clear that the whole was false—in fact even Pollio himself did not venture to find a place for it in his history. Indeed eye-witnesses of his speech for Lamia assert that he didn't say these things, not being prepared to lie when the triumvirs could show him up, but composed them later (*Suas.* 6.14–15).

---

65. Many ancient authors discuss book burnings. Tacitus recounts, "The Fathers ordered his books to be burned by the aediles; but copies remained, hidden and afterwards published: a fact which moves us the more to deride the folly of those who believe that by an act of despotism in the present there can be extinguished also the memory of a succeeding age" (*Ann.* 4.35). For more examples of book burnings, see Daniel Christopher Sarefield, "'Burning Knowledge': Studies of Bookburning in Ancient Rome" (PhD diss., Ohio State University, 2004); cf. also Dirk Rohmann, *Christianity, Book-Burning and Censorship in Late Antiquity*, Arbeiten zur Kirchengeschichte 135 (Berlin: De Gruyter, 2016).

The third and final scene included in our study involves a man named Sextilius Ena, who had a distinct foreign accent and was not well received by Asinius Pollio. He writes:

> Proposing to recite [*recitaturus*] on the subject of this same proscription in the house of Messala Corvinus, he had invited Asinius Pollio. And he started his recital [*recitavit*] with a line that was greeted with some applause: "I must lament Cicero and the silence of the Latin tongue."
>
> Asinius Pollio did not take this lying down. He said: "Messala, you can decide for yourself what goes on in your own house; I do not propose to listen to someone who thinks I am dumb"—and he immediately got up. I know that Cornelius Severus was also present at Ena's recitation [*recitationi*]; and it's obvious that he didn't dislike the line as much as Pollio, seeing that he composed a similar, though better, line himself (*Suas.* 6.27).

There are a few points to highlight here. First, this communal reading event took place in a private home in Italy, presumably at Rome. Second, at least four separate composers are noted, and knowledge of their work(s) assumed: Ena, Pollio, Severus, and Seneca. Third, there were books discussing the compositions from communal reading events. Fourth, there is comparison between the works read at various communal reading events.

CELSUS (CA. 15 BCE–50 CE)

Aulus Cornelius Celsus wrote during the reign of Tiberius (14–37 CE). He was a noted physician, probably from Rome or Verona. The two passages surveyed here are from his only surviving works on medicine. Early in this work, he discusses several possible cures for "anyone" (*quis*) who experiences stomach pains (1.1.8). The first remedy listed is reading aloud [*legere clare*]. Granted, this does not mean it has to be communally, but the next passage below (3.18.11–12) certainly allows it. It is also very suggestive that a physician assumes anyone with a stomachache could do this—having both access to books and the ability to read them aloud. Moreover, Celsus places it first in his list of possible treatments, right before exercise and hot wine. This emphasis, along with its placement alongside activities such as exercising and drinking, may suggest that reading and reading materials were more widespread and assumed than is often acknowledged.

Much later in the same work, he brings up the topic of reading again when discussing remedies for other issues, such as fever or sleeplessness. This time, however, he introduces the concept of a person's mind being distracted by hearing a book read to them that is not pleasing to them. Moreover, he recommends reciting any literary works they can recall. Celsus writes:

> At times also his interest should be awakened; as may be done in the case of men fond [*studiosis*] of literature [*litterarum*], to whom a book [*liber*] may be read [*legitur*], correctly when they are pleased by it, or incorrectly if that very thing annoys them; for by making corrections [*emendando*] they begin to divert their mind. Moreover, they should be pressed to recite [*recitare*] anything they can remember. Some who did not want to eat were induced to do so, by being placed on couches between other diners (3.18.11–12).

PETRONIUS (CA. 27–66 CE)

Petronius was Nero's courtier and is often identified as the author of *Satyricon*. Although this identification is not certain,[66] there is no doubt that the work itself was written during the Neronian period, and thus it will be included in our study.

The first of three passages is about a young boy reading aloud the names of the guests so that they can receive their presents. What he is reading is a small leaf or parchment containing a riddle. The parody depends on the connection between the riddles and the names of the guests in attendance. Once the riddles are matched with recipients, the guests are given their specific present (*apophoreta*) to carry off with them as they leave the event. Petronius—who is, in the words of DeSmidt, thereby "turning his [Trimalchio's] *convivium* into *convicium*"[67]—writes "He was just throwing the philosophers out of work, when tickets [*pittacia*] were carried round in a cup, and a boy [*puerque*] who was entrusted with this duty read aloud [*recitavit*] the names of the presents for the guests" (*Sat.* 56). As for the presents, one

---

66. For a recent argument against this view, see Dirk Rohmann and Thomas Völker, "*Praenomen Petronii*: The Date and Author of the *Satyricon* Reconsidered," *CQ* 61, no. 2 (2011): 660–76.

67. David Benjamin DeSmidt, "The Declamatory Origin of Petronius' *Satyrica*" (PhD diss., Columbia University, 2006), 172.

of the guests received "a piece of meat and note-books [*tabulas*]" (*Sat.* 56).

For Petronius's parody to be effective, it has to resemble reality to some extent. The games that are played, the presents that are received, and the picture of a young boy reading riddles in front of a group (cf. Suet., *Aug.* 75) seem to suffice.

In talking about slaves, Petronius also mentions communal reading. He writes, "They all went on to thank their master for his kindness, when he turned serious, and had a copy of the will [*testamenti*] brought in, which he read aloud [*recitavit*] from beginning to end, while the slaves moaned and groaned" (*Sat.* 71). Edward Courtney notes, "All this is clearly written in relation to Seneca, *Ep.* 47, in which Seneca commends Lucilius for his treatment of slaves."[68] For our purposes, however, the main point is that Petronius chooses to provide another communal reading event as his illustration.

The next episode does not speak explicitly to communal reading events, but rather the extent to which literary works were produced and their influence on people. In her description of it, Elaine Fantham states, "After a singularly unedifying story of pederastic seduction, he shifts gears to present a critical introduction to the problems of composing poetry. . . . The miniature manual is less than a hundred words, but each sentence is replete with imagery and implications."[69] Petronius writes:

> "Yes, my young friends," said Eumolpus, "poetry has led many astray. As soon as a man has shaped his verse in feet and woven into it a more delicate meaning with an ingenious circumlocution, he thinks that forthwith he has scaled Helicon. In this fashion people who are tired out with forensic oratory often take refuge in the calm of poetry as in some happier haven, supposing that a poem is easier to construct than a declamation adorned with quivering epigrams. But nobler souls love wholesomeness, and the mind cannot conceive or bring forth its fruit unless it is steeped in the vast flood of literature [*ingenti flumine litterarum inundata*]. One must flee away from all diction that is, so to speak, cheap, and choose words divorced from popular [*plebe*] use, putting into practice, 'I hate the common herd and hold it afar.' Besides, one must take care that the thoughts do not stand out from the body of the speech: they must shine with a brilliancy that is woven into the material.

68. *A Companion to Petronius*, repr. ed. (Oxford: Oxford University Press, 2010), 113.

69. *Roman Literary Culture: From Plautus to Macrobius*, 2nd ed, (Baltimore, MD: Johns Hopkins University Press, 2013), 168.

Homer proves this, and the lyric poets, and Roman Virgil, and the studied felicity of Horace. The others either did not see the path that leads to poetry, or saw it and were afraid to walk in it. For instance, anyone who attempts the vast theme of the civil war will sink under the burden unless he is full of literature [*plenus litteris*]. It is not a question of recording real events in verse; historians can do that far better (*Sat.* 118).

One problem with Eumolpus is that he is better at seeing other poets' faults than his own. Of course, the reader is left to wonder whether these are Petronius's views on literature or simply his characterization of Eumolpus.[70] Either way, there is probably a connection to reality.

SENECA THE YOUNGER (CA. 4 BCE–65 CE)

Seneca the Younger was born at Corduba in Spain, but he spent most of his life in Rome. He committed suicide around 65 CE after allegedly conspiring to assassinate Nero, who Seneca had tutored as a boy.[71] Several of the texts included in this section come from his work *Epistles*. These letters are all addressed to a man named Lucilius, located in southern Italy (Campania, Pompeii, or Naples), and were written toward the end of Seneca's life in Rome.

In this letter, Seneca mentions why crowds should be avoided. In one paragraph specifically, he writes, "There is no reason why pride in advertising your abilities should lure you into publicity, so that you should desire to recite [*recitare*] or harangue [*disputare*] before the general public" (*Epi.* 1.7.9). This is another example of someone who disdains some of the communal reading events.

In another letter, Seneca makes it clear that he would rather read and examine a book then merely hear it read to him. He states, "I shall discuss the book more fully after a second perusal; meantime, my judgment is somewhat unsettled, just as if I had heard it read aloud [*audierim*], and had not read [*legerim*] it myself. You must allow me to examine [*inquirere*] it also" (*Epi.* 1.46.3).

70. For further discussion of Eumolpus's literary theory, see Courtney, *A Companion to Petronius*, 181–84. For a creative proposal on the characterization of Eumolpus in *Satyricon*, see Michael Norman Sham, "Characterization in Petronius' *Satyricon*" (PhD diss., University of New York at Buffalo, 1994), 169–99.

71. For more details about Seneca's life and works, see Susanna Braund, "Seneca *Multiplex*: The Phases (and Phrases) of Seneca's Life and Works," in *The Cambridge Companion to Seneca*, ed. Shadi Bartsch and Alessandro Schiesaro (Cambridge: Cambridge University Press, 2015), 15–28.

In this next letter, Seneca discusses a communal reading event at a banquet. He writes, "Our talk ran on various themes, as is natural at a dinner [*convivio*]; it pursued no chain of thought to the end, but jumped from one topic to another. We then had read [*lectus*] to us a book by Quintus Sextius the Elder" (*Epi.* 1.64.2). While his opinion of this philosopher's writings is high, he does not think other philosophical writings compare as well. He states, "This is not the case with all philosophers; there are some men of illustrious name whose writings are sapless. They lay down rules, they argue, and they quibble; they do not infuse spirit simply because they have no spirit. But when you come to read [*legeris*] Sextius, you will say: 'He is alive; he is strong; he is free; he is more than a man; he fills me with a mighty confidence before I close his book'" (*Epi.* 1.64.3).

In another letter, Seneca addresses the way darkness is used to cover up evil. One such way concerns communal reading events. Many people would use nightfall as an excuse to leave a bad communal reading event. But before he gives a few examples of that, he states:

> Julius Montanus was once reading a poem aloud [*recitabat*]; he was a middling good poet, noted for his friendship with Tiberius, as well as his fall from favour. He always used to fill his poems with a generous sprinkling of sunrises and sunsets. Hence, when a certain person was complaining that Montanus had read [*recitasse*] all day long, and declared that no man should attend any of his readings [*recitationes*], Natta Pinariusa remarked: "I couldn't make a fairer bargain than this: I am ready to listen to him from sunrise to sunset!" Montanus was reading [*recitasset*], and had reached the words. . . " (*Epi.* 3.122.11).

After he quotes a couple of lines from the recitation, he states how a person responded that it was getting late and bedtime had arrived.[72]

In this next account, Seneca discusses some reasons that people get angry.[73] One of them pertains to the quality of the manuscript they receive to read. He writes, "Our anger is stirred [when we receive] certain inanimate things, such as the manuscript [*liber*] which we often hurl from us [*proiecimus*] because it is written in too small a

72. To better understand how this section, especially its theme and terminology, connects with the wider work of Seneca, see Brad Inwood, trans., *Seneca: Selected Philosophical Letters* (Oxford: Oxford University Press, 2007), 346–54.

73. For more information regarding Seneca's use of anger in relation to this passage, see William E. Wycislo, "The *De Ira*: Seneca's Satire of Roman Law" (PhD diss., University of Chicago, 1996), 205–52, esp. 227–30.

script [*minutioribus litteris scriptum*] or tear up because it is full of mistakes [*mendosum*]" (*Ira* 2.26.3). He does not discuss what types of mistakes. They could include grammar or spelling. They could be errors in quoting source material. But regardless of what types of mistakes they were, there seems to be a common notion among this community that books must meet a certain standard. If they don't meet this quality control, they are discarded, or thrown away (*proiecimus*). This indicates yet another community that has a high regard for written texts.

Still on the topic of anger, Seneca discusses a historian who made some disparaging remarks against Augustus and his family. In the end, even though he was banned from Caesar's palace, he was invited to hold communal reading events in houses all over the city and used these opportunities to disseminate his views. Seneca writes, "After this, Timagenes lived to old age in the house of Asinius Pollio, and was lionized by the whole city. Though Caesar had excluded him from the palace, he was debarred from no other door. He gave readings [*recitavit*] of the history which he had written after the incident, and the books which contained the doings of Augustus Caesar he put in the fire and burned" (*Ira* 3.23.5–7). Seneca's point is that he found a wider audience that accepted him throughout the rest of his life.

JEWISH SOURCES

4 MACCABEES (1ST CENT. CE)

Written in the first person singular, 4 Maccabees is widely regarded as a philosophical discourse written by a Jew for Jews, and it is, according to Jan Willem van Henten, "the oldest Jewish text which is devoted to martyrdom in its entirety."[74] Hugh Anderson argues that a composition date between 18 and 55 CE "must be deemed a very

---

74. *The Maccabean Martyrs as Saviours of the Jewish People: A Study of 2 and 4 Maccabees,* JSJ-Sup 57 (Leiden: Brill, 1997), 58.

plausible hypothesis."[75] As for provenance, the consensus is that it was written somewhere in the coastal lands of Asia Minor.

Regardless of whether 4 Maccabees was a synagogue sermon, an encomium for the Antiochene martyrs read at a commemorative festival, or some other communal address, one key passage is pertinent here. There is a scene toward the end of the book where a mother addresses her seven sons about their deceased father. Over the course of her speech (18:10–18), she focuses exclusively on what their father read, taught, and sang at home: the Jewish Scriptures. By citing various scriptural passages, the mother also presumably hopes to comfort her sons:

> And he used to teach [ἐδίδασκεν] you, when yet with you, the law and the prophets. He use to read [ἀνεγίνωσκεν] to you the slaying of Abel by Cain, and the offering up of Isaac, and the imprisonment of Joseph. And he used to tell you of the zealous Phinehas; and informed [ἐδίδασκεν] you of Ananias and Azarias, and Misael in the fire. And he used to glorify Daniel, who was in the den of lions, and pronounce him blessed. And he used to put you in mind [ὑπεμίμνησκεν] of the scripture of Esaias, which says, Even if you pass through the fire, it will not burn you. He chanted [ἐμελῴδει] to you David, the hymn-writer, who says, Many are the afflictions of the just. He declared [ἐπαροιμίαζεν] the proverbs of Solomon, who says, He is a tree of life to all those who do His will. He used to verify [ἐπιστοποιεῖτο] Ezekiel, who said, will these dry bones live? For he did not forget the song which Moses taught [ἐδίδαξεν], proclaiming [διδάσκουσαν], I will kill, and I will make to live.

Though the terms and scriptural allusions that the author deploys vary, there is no doubt that this family of at least nine members is meant to be viewed as one that held many communal reading events as a family (cf. 4 Macc 5:22–24, 34; 9:2). The departed father thus fulfilled his obligation to the Torah by training his family in it at home (Deut 4:9). As we have seen elsewhere, it is possible this is a fictitious story painting an idealized portrait of the pious Jewish family who are literate and learned in their sacred texts.[76] But again, that should not

---

75. "4 Maccabees: A New Translation and Introduction," in *The Old Testament Pseudepigrapha*, ed. James H. Charlesworth (Peabody, MA: Hendrickson, 2009), 2:531–64, here 534. Cf. David J. Elliott, "4 Maccabees," in *The Apocrypha*, ed. Martin Goodman (Oxford: Oxford University Press, 2012), 239–42; David A. deSilva, *4 Maccabees* (Sheffield: Sheffield Academic, 1998), 12–18.

76. For a brief discussion on the possible influence this martyrdom story of a mother and her

distract us here from the fact that the author does present such an idealized scene of what was probably a well-known practice, as well as his assumption that his audience will identify with them. Therefore, it should not be automatically dismissed as a priori improbable.

PHILO (CA. 20 BCE–50 CE)

Philo is one of the most prominent figures in Hellenistic Jewish literature. Though his writings are extensive, references to communal reading events numerous,[77] and discussions of synagogues frequent, we will only highlight two passages from two distinct works, in order to support the contention that communal reading events were commonplace in Alexandria, Egypt.[78] It is also worth underscoring one key place at this location for people to access literary works: the Alexandrian library. According to Mireille Hadas-Lebel, "Without doubt the library of Alexandria was the richest collection in all antiquity and 'the largest library the world ever knew prior to the invention of printing'."[79]

The first passage is simply one that highlights continual Sabbath observances, where literary works are read communally, in order to defend such traditional Jewish events.[80] Dulcinea Boesenberg summarizes, "In seven of his works, Philo describes Jewish Sabbath practice as he knows it. Some of these descriptions are longer and fuller

---

seven sons had on subsequent literature, such as Rabbinic and Christian literature, see Moses Hadas, ed. and trans., *The Third and Fourth Books of Maccabees* (New York: Harper & Brothers, 1953), 123–35.

77. *Dreams* 2.127; *Creation* 128; *Abraham* 22-23; *Alleg. Interp.* 156; *Spec. Laws* 2.61; *Moses* 2.216; *Contempl. Life* 31.

78. For more information related to Philo and Alexandria on schooling and education, as well as their relation to local synagogues, see Otto Kaiser, *Philo von Alexandrien: Denkender Glaube—eine Einführung* (Göttingen: Vandenhoeck & Ruprecht, 2015), esp. 62–66.

79. *Philo of Alexandria: A Thinker in the Jewish Diaspora*, trans. Robyn Fréchet, SPA 7 (Leiden: Brill, 2012), 13–14. Cf. James R. Royse, "Did Philo Publish His Works?," *Studia Philonica Annual* 25 (2013): 75–100; David Lincicum, "Philo's Library," *Studia Philonica Annual* 26 (2014): 99–114.

80. Gregory E. Sterling, "The *Hypothetica*: Introduction," *Studia Philonica Annual* 20 (2008): 139–42. In a later article Sterling also highlights a lacuna in Philonic scholarship regarding the reception of Philo among pagan readers. "Philo's Ancient Readers: Introduction," *Studia Philonica Annual* 25 (2013): 69–73, esp. 72, It is important to note the lacuna in relation to our study, in that Philo is often describing and defending Jewish communal reading events, as opposed to pagan ones.

than others, but all provide a general outline of what the Jews do on the Sabbath."[81] In this account, Philo writes:

> For that day has been set apart to be kept holy and on it they abstain from all other work and proceed to sacred spots which they call synagogues [συναγωγαί]. There, arranged in rows according to their ages, the younger below the elder, they sit decorously as befits the occasion with attentive ears. Then one takes the books [τὰς βίβλους] and reads aloud [ἀναγινώσκει] and another [ἕτερος] of especial proficiency [τῶν ἐμπειροτάτων] comes forward and expounds [ἀναδιδάσκει] what is not understood (*Good Person* 81–82).

Not only does Philo describe them as meeting in places called synagogues, but he also describes a scene where everyone was attentive. Someone took and read books, while someone else explained them communally.

The second passage is from Philo's *Hypothetica*, a work that is categorized as a "non-biblical" treatise, in that it is not interpreting scripture,[82] even though the portion of the passage here pertains to the Sabbath and the sabbatical year. George Carras examined this passage alongside Josephus's *Contra Apionem* in order to determine whether they had a common source or if one might have used the work of the other. He concludes, "Many of the traditions used were part of a common Judaism that consisted of a wide variety of Jewish witnesses and influences, which are attributed to different locations within the diaspora; Alexandria and Rome, as well as Palestine. The fact that Josephus writing in Rome and Philo in Alexandria appeal to similar ideas suggests the presence of a common Judaism that was not tied to a single location or to a single synagogue."[83] The relevance of Carras's comparative conclusion here is that communal reading events were another common custom uniting Judaism across a wide-ranging geographical area. Scholars have also highlighted the fact that

---

81. "Philo's Descriptions of Jewish Sabbath Practice," *Studia Philonica Annual* 22 (2010): 143–63, here 145.

82. Samuel Sandmel, "Philo Judaeus: An Introduction to the Man, His Writings, and His Significance," *ANRW* 2.21.1 (1984): 3–46, here 6.

83. "Dependence or Common Tradition in Philo *Hypothetica* VIII 6.10–7.20 and Josephus *Contra Apionem* 2.190–219," *Studia Philonica Annual* 5 (1993): 24–47, here 47. Cf. Naomi G. Cohen, *Philo's Scriptures: Citations from the Prophets and Writings, Evidence for a* Haftarah *Cycle in Second Temple Judaism* (JSJSup 123; Leiden: Brill, 2007).

Philo refers to synagogues as significant places of education and communal reading events, both sacred and nonsacred.[84]
Philo writes:

> And indeed [δῆτα] they do always [μὲν αἰεί] assemble and sit together, most of them in silence except when it is the practice [νομίζεται] to add something to signify approval [προσεπευφημῆσαι] of what is read [ἀναγινωσκομένοις]. But some priest who is present or one of the elders reads [ἀναγινώσκει] the holy laws to them and expounds [ἐξηγεῖται] them point by point till about the late afternoon, when they depart having gained both expert knowledge of the holy laws and considerable advance in piety (*Hypothetica* 7.13).

Even though Philo does not rely directly on the Jewish scriptures or Josephus, Carras points out that "it is here [*Hypoth.* 7.13] that the *Hypothetica* supports the view of the OT and Josephus."[85] In other words, children, as well as adults, are to learn and obey the readings they hear at Jewish communal reading events. This picture somewhat resembles a school setting with teachers and students.[86] In addition, "elders" in the passage could mean experienced synagogue preachers and teachers.

Philo uses many words to emphasize how customary and consistent these gatherings were. The picture he paints is one of an audience being silent except when it is time to approve what is read. The word used for signifying the audience's approval is προσεπευφημῆσαι, which can carry the meaning of shouting with applause. Apparently, this was a normal practice, as signified by the word *practice*. This episode confirms the presence of a quality control within communal reading events, even if they are simply signaling assent.

---

84. See Valentin Nikiprowetzky, *Le commentaire de l'écriture chez Philon d'Alexandrie: Son caractère et sa portée, observations philologiques* (Leiden: Brill, 1977), esp. 174–80.

85. "Dependence or Common Tradition in Philo *Hypothetica*," 41.

86. Christian Noack, *Gottesbewußtsein: Exegetische Studien zur Soteriologie und Mystik bei Philo von Alexandria*, WUNT 2.116 (Tübingen: Mohr Siebeck, 2000), 28.

PSEUDO-PHILO (1ST CENT. CE)

Frederick Murphy's assessment regarding the dating of Pseudo-Philo still appears correct: "Few doubt that the *Biblical Antiquities* was written in the first century C.E."[87] At the same time, he goes on to state, "No arguments will convince all parties."[88] A similar statement could be made regarding provenance. Most scholars accept a Palestinian provenance, but there are still a few dissenters. The consensus on both issues is followed here.

"In a context loosely based on Joshua 8:30–35," states Bruce Fisk,[89] the author of Pseudo-Philo draws attention to a communal reading event. The author writes, "And he [Joshua] gathered all the people together [*congregavit omnem populum*] and read out loud before them [*legit in aures eorum*] all the words of the Law" (21.7–10).[90] For the author, this event provides a context for the audience's direct response, which they later deliver.

The author of this work maintains certain scriptural elements. However, the narrator modifies, expands, and omits other features from the scriptural account. In Joshua 8:30–35, Joshua simply reads to the people. In Pseudo-Philo, Joshua also later pronounces a blessing over them. In the Joshua passage, writes Christopher Begg, "The people are passive, silent witnesses of the proceedings. Pseudo-Philo, by contrast, represents them as 'singing many praises', playing musical instruments and acknowledging the fulfillment of the Lord's past promises."[91] Beyond such differences, though, lies the central focus of the communal reading event. This type of reading event is meant to be reflective of current practices to some extent, even if it is in a modified form, which helps the author connect with his audience as he recasts the accounts according to his purposes.

---

87. *Pseudo-Philo: Rewriting the Bible* (New York: Oxford University Press, 1993), 6.

88. Ibid.

89. "Retelling Israel's Story: Scripture, Exegesis and Transformation in Pseudo-Philo's *Liber Antiquitatum Biblicarum* 12–24" (PhD diss., Duke University, 1997), 196.

90. For the Latin text of this verse, see Howard Jacobson, *A Commentary on Pseudo-Philo's* Liber Antiquitatum Biblicarum *with Latin Text and English Translation* (Leiden: Brill, 1996), 2:688.

91. "Josephus' and Pseudo-Philo's Rewritings of the Book of Joshua," in *The Book of Joshua*, ed. Ed Noort, BETL 250 (Leuven: Peeters, 2012), 555–88, here 573.

JOSEPHUS (CA. 37–100 CE)

Along with Philo, Josephus is a well-known author of Jewish Hellenistic literature.[92] He was born in Jerusalem but died at Rome.[93] The passages selected are by no means exhaustive as regards mention of communal reading events.[94] Nevertheless, they are representative and support the notion that these events were both widespread and well established during the first century CE.

In one episode, Josephus addresses an embassy at Gabaroth. Part of the focus of this address is the written correspondences between Josephus and a few others. Josephus even pulls out and displays the letters to everyone, lest anyone reject a purely oral presentation. He writes, "I then began by reminding Jonathan and his colleagues of their letter [τῆς ἐπιστολῆς τούς], how they had written [γράψειαν] that they had been commissioned by the general assembly at Jerusalem to settle my quarrels with John and how they had desired me to visit them. While relating these facts I held out the letter [τὴν ἐπιστολήν] for all to see, to prevent any possibility of denial, the document [τῶν γραμμάτων] being there to convict them" (*Life* 49). He then proceeds to read the letters to the audience. "I then read aloud [παρανεγίνωσκον] to the Galilaeans two of the letters [ἐπιστολῶν] dispatched by Jonathan, which had been intercepted and forwarded to me by the scouts whom I had picketed on the roads" (*Life* 50). By reading the contents of the letters to the Galileans, explains Steve Mason, "Josephus shows clemency and diverts the furious mob to Sogane."[95]

In another instance, Josephus writes about the communal reading of the Torah. Especially interesting in this account is that all ages are present and the audience is called to respond:

And so, after the woman had prophesied, they came and reported her words to the king. Thereupon he sent round to all parts, commanding

92. For a recent and concise survey of scholarship assessing the historicity of Josephus's work, see David W. Chapman and Eckhard J. Schnabel, *The Trial and Crucifixion of Jesus: Texts and Commentary*, WUNT 344 (Tübingen: Mohr Siebeck, 2015), 5–6.

93. Scholarly enquiry into Josephus' social life in the city of Rome still provides very few details. See William den Hollander, *Josephus, the Emperors, and the City of Rome: From Hostage to Historian*, AJEC 86 (Leiden: Brill, 2014).

94. *Ap.* 2.175; *Vita* 276–82; *Ant.* 16:43–44.

95. *Flavius Josephus: Translation and Commentary*, vol. 9, *Life of Josephus* (Leiden: Brill, 2001), 118.

the people to gather in Jerusalem, as also the priests and Levites, and ordering those of every age to be present. When these had been assembled, he first read [ἀνέγνω] them the sacred books [τὰς ἱερὰς βίβλους] and then, standing on the tribune in the midst of the people, he compelled them to take an oath and pledge that they would truly worship God and keep the laws of Moses. And they eagerly assented and undertook to do what the king urged upon them, and straightway sacrificed and, while singing the sacred hymns [καλλιεροῦντες], supplicated God to be favourable and gracious to them (*Ant.* 10.4.3).

This is a clear example of a communal reading event that Josephus seems to assume his audience would understand and probably have experienced.

In a third account, Josephus writes about Ptolemy learning why the Jewish law has remained unknown to Greeks. Ptolemy learns this because someone reads the texts to him. Josephus writes, "Especially did he rejoice when the laws were read [ἀναγνωσθέντων] to him, and he was amazed at the depth of mind and wisdom of the lawgiver; and he began to discuss with Demetrius how it was that though this legislation was so admirable none of the historians or poets had made mention of it" (*Ant.* 12.2.14).

Josephus later addresses Agrippa about the violation of the rights of Jewish people in Ionia. He writes, "Moreover, we could read [ἀναγινώσκειν] to you many decrees [δόγματα] of the Senate and tablets [δέλτους] deposited in the Capitol to the same effect, which were obviously published after you had received proof of our loyalty to you and would be valid even if you had granted them in the absence of any such condition" (*Ant.* 16.2.4). It is also worth noting that decrees such as this one were first read in the Senate before reading them to the general population. Gensine Manuwald writes, "While it is true that, because of the organization of political procedures at Rome, speeches in the Senate always preceded speeches before the People on the same issue, and senatorial speeches were more important for initiating immediate action in the form of decrees, it should be noted that the speeches before the People also had a significant, though more indirect political effect."[96] This assessment necessarily increases the amount and types of communal reading events available in the first century CE.

---

96. "The Speeches to the People in Cicero's Oratorical Corpora," *Rhetorica* 30, no. 2 (2012): 153–75, here 154n4.

In the next account, after mentioning several literary correspondences involving Augustus, Herod, and council members, Josephus describes Herod accusing his sons before the council of Roman officials that numbered 150 men:

> He did not permit the members of the council to examine the proofs but offered arguments in advocacy of these that were a disgrace for a father to use against his sons. When he read aloud [ἀναγινώσκων] the letters written by them, there was no plot or any notion of filial disloyalty mentioned in them, only that they were planning to flee, and some offensive remarks about Herod that included reproaches for his ill-will toward them. When he came to these passages, he cried out even more loudly and exaggerated their excessive language into a confession of a plot formed against him by his sons, swearing that he would much rather lose his life than hear such words as these (*Ant.* 16.11.2).

As he is reading, it is noticeable that he changed his tone in order to emphasize and rhetorically influence the audience.

Later in the same work, Josephus details Herod's funeral:

> By now the death of the king had become public knowledge, and Salome and Alexas assembled the army in the amphitheatre at Jericho and first read aloud [ἀνέγνωσαν] the letter [ἐπιστολήν] that Herod had written to the soldiers to thank them for their faithfulness and goodwill to him and to ask them to give the same support to his son Archelaus, whom he had appointed king. The next thing was that Ptolemy, who had been entrusted with the king's seal, read aloud [ἀνέλεγεν] his will, but this was not to become effective until Caesar had examined [ἐντυχόντος] it (*Ant.* 16.11.2).

There are several important features to highlight here. First, a large group was assembled in an amphitheater. Second, after the letter was read communally, so was the will, but not with the typical terminology, but rather ἀνέλεγεν, which can carry the meaning "to read through." Third, Caesar had to read through it, again, with a term used less frequently, ἐντυχόντος (see chapter 2).

This next episode recounts an edict (διάταγμα) that was sent to Alexandria by Tiberius on behalf of the Jews. According to Josephus, the edict read as follows: "It is my will that the ruling bodies of the cities and colonies and municipia in Italy and outside Italy, and the kings and other authorities through their own ambassadors, shall cause this edict of mine to be inscribed [ἐγγράψασθαι], and keep it posted [ἐκκείμενόν] for not less than thirty days in a place where it can plainly be read [ἀναγνωσθῆναι] from the ground [ἐπιπέδου]" (*Ant.* 19.5.3).

These types of edicts, Josephus further states, would have also been sent "to the world at large" (τὴν οἰκουμένην πᾶσαν) (*Ant.* 19.6.1). There must have been at least some expectation that many people could read it, and that in the majority of places, there was someone to inscribe the message and post it somewhere visible for all to see. Moreover, since the edict was inscribed for viewing, those who heard it read could verify it by checking the written form. This was a frequent practice according to many ancient sources. For example, an edict in 41 CE reads, "Seeing that all the populace, owing to its numbers, was unable to be present at the reading of the most sacred and most beneficent letter to the city, I have deemed it necessary to display the letter publicly in order that reading it one by one you may admire the majesty of our god Caesar and feel gratitude for his goodwill towards the city."[97]

Contradictions with other sources aside, Josephus describes another very detailed scene about a national Jewish communal reading event:

> When the multitude hath assembled in the holy city for the sacrifices, every seven years at the season of the feast of tabernacles, let the high priest, standing upon a raised platform [ἐπὶ βήματος ὑψηλοῦ] from which he may be heard, recite [ἀναγινωσκέτω] the laws to the whole assembly; and let neither woman nor child be excluded from this audience, nay nor yet the slaves. For it is good that these laws should be so graven on their hearts and stored in the memory that they can never be effaced (*Ant.* 4.8.12).

This event was most likely in Jerusalem, given the references to the holy city, sacrifices, Feast of Tabernacles, and high priest.[98] Josephus goes on to state that children should be learning these laws, people should be inscribing them on physical structures around them, and people should be binding the written instructions on their body. In

---

97. LCL 282: 78–79. Christians also noted this convention in their writings. For example, Justin Martyr wrote, "I command this my edict to be published in the Forum of Trajan, in order that it may be read. The prefect Vitrasius Pollio will see that it be transmitted to all the provinces round about, and that no one who wishes to make use of or to possess it be hindered from obtaining a copy from the document I now publish" (1.71).

98. Arie van der Kooij, "The Public Reading of Scriptures at Feasts," in *Feasts and Festivals*, ed. Christopher Tuckett, CBET 53 (Leuven: Peeters, 2009), 27–44, esp. 33–34.

other words, these written words were to be on display for everyone to read, learn from, and obey.

4 EZRA (1ST CENT. CE)

The last decade of the first century CE is the most probable date for the composition of 4 Ezra.[99] This Jewish writing, then, is an example of a text written after the destruction of the temple that speaks of God commanding the writing of more books for communal reading. The main passage explicitly stating this is found in the final (seventh) vision given to Ezra, as recorded in 4 Ezra 14.1–48, especially verses 37–48. Here are just the last few lines:

> The Most High spoke to me, saying, 'Make public the twenty-four books that you wrote first and let the worthy and the unworthy read them; but keep the seventy that were written last, in order to give them to the wise among your people. For in them is the spring of understanding, the fountain of wisdom, and the river of knowledge. And I did so.[100]

As elsewhere, Ezra's final vision has both a public and private aspect to it—this time in relation to books made public and private. One important feature to note is that in order for the author to imitate figures such as Moses and Ezra, who both read texts communally, the author transforms earlier written traditions and creates new "Ezra-produced texts."[101] After five scribes copy out the ninety-four books mentioned back in 12.42, two sets of books are divided here. Twenty-four books are meant for the public, which are certainly the twenty-four books of the Hebrew Bible, while seventy are to be read only by the wise, though we can only speculate what they were or

---

99. Michael E. Stone and Matthias Henze, *4 Ezra and 2 Baruch: Translations, Introductions, and Notes* (Minneapolis: Fortress Press, 2013), 2–3. Cf. Jonathan A. Moo, *Creation, Nature and Hope in 4 Ezra*, FRLANT 237 (Göttingen: Vandenhoeck & Ruprecht, 2011), 9–10.

100. Bruce M. Metzger, "The Fourth Book of Ezra: A New Translation and Introduction," in *The Old Testament Pseudepigrapha*, vol. 1, *Apocalyptic Literature and Testaments*, ed. James H. Charlesworth (Peabody, MA: Hendrickson, 2009), 517–59, here 555. Cf. also Matthias Henze, "4 Ezra and 2 Baruch: Literary Composition and Oral Performance in First-Century Apocalyptic Literature," *JBL* 131, no. 1 (2012): 181–200.

101. Hindy Najman, "How Should We Contextualize Pseudepigrapha? Imitation and Emulation in 4 Ezra," in *Flores Florentino: Dead Sea Scrolls and Other Early Jewish Studies in Honour of Florentino García Martínez*, ed. Anthony Hilhorst, Émile Puech, and Eibert Tigchelaar, JSJSup 122 (Leiden: Brill, 2007), 529–36, esp. 534–36. For more discussion on the overall flow of the episodes, see Alexander E. Stewart, "Narrative World, Rhetorical Logic, and the Voice of the Author in 4 Ezra," *JBL* 132, no. 2 (2013): 373–91.

represented.[102] This so-called Ezra confirms that he has accomplished all the Most High has required of him.

SUMMARY

We investigated a number of select passages that related to communal reading by various authors who wrote in the first century CE. More specifically, we explored the writings of twenty first-century authors. Not all of the authors were social elites. Some authors were born slaves, like Epictetus; others came from very poor families, like Valerius Maximus; and still others remained poor most of their lives, such as Martial.

The locations experiencing some level of exposure to communal reading events were widespread and too systematic to be accidental. Well over a dozen specific locations were identified: Asia, Aphrodisias, Rhodes, Gabaroth, Athens, Nicopolis, Tomis, Jerusalem, Alexandria, Celaenae in Phrygia, Prusa, Rhodes, Vienne, Corinth, Borysthenes, Tarsus, Narbo, Rome, Tyana, Jericho, Magna Graecia, Spain, and Umbria. Several general areas were also cited, such as the area between Nicaea and Nicomedia, the coastal land of Asia Minor, southern Italy, and the Lacedaemon province in Greece. At the geographical extremes, some level of exposure to communal reading events can be claimed as far east as Jericho, as far west as Spain, as far north as Prusa, and as far south as Alexandria.

It was demonstrated that people read texts in community, and such events were indeed a frequent activity and widespread across the Roman Empire. The reading of different types of texts often made for different venues. The various types of texts included satire, poetry, legal documents, epigrams, letters, novels, geographical works, discourses, decrees, edicts, medical works, treatises, declamations, speeches, philosophical compositions, wills, tribunes, laws, disputations, historical works, epideictic oratory, dictation texts, and hymns. The numerous settings and occasions included courtrooms, private homes, dinners, schools, synagogues, theaters, festivals, competitions, funerals, amphitheaters, symposia, recitations, public meetings,

---

102. The identity of these books does not concern our study. Nevertheless, there may be some additional similarities worth exploring regarding the sealing of these books and the sealing of books mentioned in the books of Daniel and Revelation. For a brief survey of scholarly opinions regarding the identity of the books, see Karina M. Hogan, *Theologies in Conflict in 4 Ezra: Wisdom Debate and Apocalyptic Solution*, JSJSup 130 (Leiden: Brill, 2008), 214–17.

forums, crossroads, colonnades, shops, and open-air fields. Moreover, the variety of texts and events revealed a wide range of materials and terminology. The table provides a representative—not exhaustive—list of the types of material and differing terminology the selected authors explicitly mentioned or used.

Sampling of Terms

English Translation	Greek Term or Phrase	Latin Term or Phrase	Author or Work
Book		*liber*	Celsus
Book-box		*scrinioque*	Martial
Books	τὰς βίβλους		Philo
Bulky volume		*ingens*	Martial
Certificate of emancipation	τὸ γραμμάτιον τῆς ἀπελευθερώσεως		Chariton
Cheap length of papyrus		*scriptura quanti constet et tomus vilis*	Martial
Compact little book		*libelli*	Martial
Compositions	τοῖς ποιήμασιν		Dio Chrysostom
Couplets		*disticha*	Martial
Decrees	δόγματα		Josephus
Deeds of sale	τὰς ὠνάς		Epictetus
Dialogues	διαλόγους		Epictetus
Dictation text		*dictata*	Persius
Documents	τῶν γραμμάτων		Josephus
Edict	διάταγμα		Josephus
Epigrams		*epigrammata*	Martial
Letters	ἐπιστολῶν		Josephus
Lines	πολύστιχόν		Dio Chrysostom
Literature		*litterarum*	Celsus

English Translation	Greek Term or Phrase	Latin Term or Phrase	Author or Work
Note-books		*tabulas*	Petronius
Page		*pagina*	Martial
Paper		*charta*	Martial
Parchment cover		*membrana*	Martial
Poems		*carmine*	Valerius Maximus
Pumice stones		*pumicata*	Martial
Rolls		*librum*	Martial
Small scripted manuscript		*minutioribus litteris scriptum*	Seneca
Small text-books		*artis libellum*	Quintilian
Stone	λίθον		Epictetus
Tablets	δέλτους		Josephus
The law and the prophets	τὸν νόμον καὶ τοὺς προφήτας		4 Maccabees
The sacred books	τὰς ἱερὰς βίβλους		Josephus
Thief (i.e., forger of literary work)		*fur*	Martial
Tickets		*pittacia*	Petronius
Transcribed text	μεταγράφουσιν		Strabo
Treatises	συγγράμματα		Dio Chrysostom
Unrolled parchment	ἐξελίττειν τὸ βιβλίον		Dio Chrysostom
Verses		*versibus*	Ovid
Virgin sheet		*virginis chartae*	Martial
Volumes		*libellis*	Martial
Wax tablet		*cera*	Quintilian
Will		*testamenti*	Petronius
Writings		*scripta*	Ovid

It was also shown that the readers of these texts included clerks, emperors, students, young boys, politicians, scribes, fathers, lectors, magistrates, plagiarists, old men, and young women. Likewise, the hearers of these texts comprised emperors, children, men, women, slaves, students, plebs, assemblies, soldiers, Roman officials, invited guests, and crowds. These events occurred in big cities like Rome, as well as faraway places of exile such as Tomis. According to these selected authors, people heard readings while standing, sitting, running, bathing, eating, dining, and swimming.

It is also worth noting four additional observations that we gleaned, even though none of them were the focus of this chapter or study. First, there were various levels of reading needs and capabilities. The various terms and phrases used to distinguish this range of needs and capabilities included the following: ample preparation, superficial reader, especial proficiency, to examine, to expound, to read through, to skim, to select portions, to read line by line, to read correctly, to read incorrectly, to render the lines pleasurably, to not read offensively, and to be ill qualified to read (even though the author himself certainly possessed the actual abilities to do so). Likewise, some authors, including Dio Chrysostom, state that excellent reading abilities were more of a preference than a necessity. Other authors, such as Seneca the Elder, note hearing someone with a foreign accent read. Texts such as these directly challenge the assumptions of scholars who argue that communal reading events could only occur if there was a reader with notable proficiency available and that everyone could understand.

Second, various quality controls were identified, even though no author was attempting to write about communal reading events per se or quality controls linked to them. Several of the quality controls we detected were eyewitnesses (Seneca Elder), examining differing manuscripts (Strabo), disposing of manuscripts with errors (Seneca), public posting of read edicts (Josephus), comparing authors (Seneca Elder), comparing lines (Martial), authorship (Martial regarding plagiarists), audiences (Chariton), labeling via terminology (Dio Chrysostom), peer pressure (Epictetus, laughing), and making corrections (Celsus). Also equally important were the remarks from several authors, such as Persius and Dio Chrysostom, about their disdain for communal reading events when no quality controls were implemented.

Third, there were many different impressions of and reactions to communal reading events. Martial, for example, states that one person ought to "shut up." Seneca the Younger says that some people made excuses in order to leave these reading events early, such as stating how late it was in the day. Chariton narrates a loud burst of applause from the audience after hearing a letter read.

Fourth, even in spite of the radical suppression of literature at certain times during the first century, such as the exiles, book burnings, and bans during the reign of Domitian (81–96 CE), there was still a "vast flood of literature," to use one of Petronius's phrases; "thousands who recite," as Epictetus states; and opportunities for "advertising your abilities" before "a multitude of fans" at communal reading events, according to Seneca the Younger and Martial, respectively.

The prevalence of literary works and activities associated with them in the first century CE suggests a world carefully shaped and controlled by a book culture typified by commonly held, albeit highly diverse, communal reading events. Active engagement with literary works seems to be a base expectation of many authors, with no indication that such activity would decrease or cease. This future expectation was especially seen from authors, such as Ovid, explicitly addressing or mentioning that future audiences of varying kinds would be able to continue reading their works communally.

This chapter has established with a high degree of probability that communal reading events were widespread in the first century CE according to numerous authors in the Roman Empire. Chapter 6 will take up the task of determining whether the same can be said according to the New Testament authors during the same era.

6.

Communal Reading Events in the First Century: The New Testament Corpus

I put you all under oath before the Lord to have this letter read aloud to all the brothers.

—1 Thess 5:27

Devote yourself to the communal reading of Scripture.

—1 Tim 4:13

After this letter has been read aloud to you all, make sure that it is also read communally in the church of the Laodiceans. Make sure that you also read communally the letter from Laodicea.

—Col 4:16

Christ-believing communities were much like other scholastic communities in that they focused on the reading and interpretation of texts.[1] In over three hundred passages, the New Testament includes 317 direct quotes of the Old Testament.[2] If allusions and verbal paral-

---

1. As noted in chapter 4, it is not difficult to find first-century Jewish sources that provide ample background for the communal reading of Scripture in synagogues. Several of the best-known sources are Philo, Josephus, and the Dead Sea Scrolls (4Q266 5.2; 1QS 6.7–8; 7.1; 4Q397 14–21; 1QSa 1.4–5). It is also not difficult to find this trajectory continuing after the first century. For example, Justin Martyr bases his polemic against Crescens, a Cynic philosopher, upon his encounter with written teachings: "For if he runs us down without having read the teachings of Christ, he is thoroughly evil" (2 Apol. 3.3).

2. UBS[5], 860–63.

lels are included, there are another 2,310 Old Testament references.[3] When comparing the formulas introducing Scriptural quotations in the New Testament corpus with other literature, such as the Mishnah, Bruce Metzger notes that "in the NT the frequency of this type [of formulas involving a verb of saying] is more evenly balanced by the type containing a reference to the written record."[4]

With that in mind, I seek to demonstrate here that communal reading events according to the New Testament involve a broad range of venues, participants, and cultures. They were widespread socially, as well as geographically. Even more specifically, Christian communities are depicted as communally reading more than just the Jewish scriptures or apostolic writings.

In modern terms, activities in these communities included reading, preaching, teaching, words of exhortation, catechesis, apologetics, and proclamation.[5] In light of the previous chapter, readers or reciters often operated under the assumption that the audience had intimate knowledge of other communal reading events. A speaker often assumes that what he or she shares regarding a written text faithfully represents what others have already heard communally and that they would be able to recognize it as such; even if the quotes or allusions are not exact in all the particulars, they are in principle.

Still other features enhance the notion that the earliest Christian communities were didactic: office of teacher, gift of teaching, commands to teach, traditions passed on, and communal teaching. The picture more often than not is of a didactic community that used texts. In fact, many outsiders attended and imitated Christian communal reading events.

Whereas the previous chapter examined certain literary evidence from the first century CE in order to identify and map communal reading events in the Greco-Roman world, now we want to determine how widespread these events were according to the New Tes-

---

3. UBS[5], 864–82.

4. Bruce M. Metzger, "The Formulas Introducing Quotations of Scripture in the NT and the Mishnah," JBL 70, no. 4 (1951): 297–307, here 305.

5. There are certainly various levels of overlap between some of these phrases, such as proclamation, teaching, and preaching. For example, proclamation can be directly linked to teaching that is associated with the Hebrew Scriptures, as in Matt 4:23. The point here, however, is simply that various forms of learning, often text based, were involved during Christian communal reading events.

tament authors.[6] To accomplish this, we will identify and categorize several geographically and culturally separated locations in the Roman Empire in order to draw overall conclusions from the individual writings examined within each locale. Gauging the basic geographical framework of communal reading events in various first-century communities will better equip scholars to determine the extent to which these types of events controlled and shaped the New Testament tradition in the first century CE. The goal is not, then, to determine *how many* communal reading events occurred at any given location or how they collectively shaped the Christian tradition, but rather to determine *where* geographically there is enough evidence to find a plausible context for communal reading events according to the New Testament.

Excursus: Notes, Excerpts, and Compilations

[He left] me 160 notebooks of selected passages, written in a minute hand on both sides of the page, so that their number is really doubled.
—Pliny, *Letters* 3.5.17 (ca. 61–113 CE)

However, other comic poets too, if you do not read them too critically, contain passages you can excerpt.
—Quintilian, *Inst.* 10.1.72 (ca. 35–90s CE)

People took notes in the first century CE. This fact is confirmed by Jewish, Christian, and Greco-Roman sources.[1] Just a sampling of such available evidence makes clear that there was a broad spectrum of note-taking practices. This diversity is readily seen by the variety of terminology used, writing materials utilized, and explicit statements made by authors writing in the first century.

It is reasonable to argue, then, that as many people as there were who could take notes, there were as many different ways in which people could and did write them. The main reason this is being emphasized here is that many passages examined in this chapter either indicate or insinuate that someone was reading or reciting from some form of abridged notes derived from a longer literary work or collection of works. Thus, we should not expect or imagine that every time

---

6. Decisions on authorship are not essential to the overall argument of our study. Nevertheless, a brief footnote will be provided at the beginning of several works in order to give a general sense of where our study stands in relation to some of these debates.

a person is reading or reciting a text, they had the complete work or that it was solely from memory without any written text.

While none of these note-taking practices automatically rule out the possibility that on certain occasions, there was a complete scroll or literary work present or directly accessed,[2] it seems more probable and practical from the available evidence that more often than not, people read or recited from some condensed form of a particular text(s). Although some scholars have attempted to be more specific regarding the exact contents of some of the abridged notes, excerpts, and/or compilations, such as an anthology of prooftexts from the Jewish Scriptures to show that Jesus is the Christ,[3] I accept and underscore the more general case that people in the first century CE, such as the apostles and disciples, were using excerpts, notes, and incipient testimonia, especially during many communal reading events, or at least according to the author's portrayal of them.

The main point being stressed here is that even if the assumption is correct that orality dominated the earliest proclamation, it does not mean that was always the case. The use of notes, excerpts, and compilations was already happening in Christian communal reading events in the first century, as we seek to demonstrate, with some use of rolls of the Jewish Scriptures and written gospels likely as well. The precise way in which and the extent to which a text was used, however, is beyond the scope of our purposes here.

---

1. Some note takers even published books without an author's permission. For several examples and an excellent discussion, see Michael Winterbottom, ed., *The Minor Declamations Ascribed to Quintilian* (Berlin: De Gruyter, 1984).

2. David Lincicum, "Paul and the *Testimonia*: Quo Vademus?," *JETS* 51, no. 2 (2008): 297–308, esp. 305.

3. For a concise overview of the so-called *testimonia* hypothesis, as well as a few case studies, see Martin C. Albl, "The Testimonia Hypothesis and Composite Citations," in *Composite Citations in Antiquity*, vol. 1, *Jewish, Graeco-Roman, and Early Christian Uses*, ed. Sean A. Adams and Seth M. Ehorn, LNTS 525 (London: T&T Clark, 2015).

"The most difficult question to answer in working on an ancient Jewish or Christian document," James Charlesworth writes, "is its provenance."[7] While acknowledging and agreeing with this diffi-

7. *The Old Testament Pseudepigrapha*, ed. James H. Charlesworth (Peabody, MA: Hendrickson, 2009), 2:727.

culty, it needs to be emphasized here that we are *not* attempting to identify the provenance of any New Testament writing. Rather, the writings discussed in this chapter will be categorized based solely on the author(s) stated or implied reference(s) to communal reading events.

THE GOSPELS AND ACTS

MATTHEW, MARK, AND JOHN

Jesus is universally described as quoting from Scripture, making scriptural allusions, and directing people to consider what they have read in the Scripture. The overwhelming depiction of Jesus as a teacher in all of the gospel traditions (including apocryphal gospels) and non-Christian sources depicts a didactic movement focused on the transmission of written traditions, prophecies, exhortations, and Scripture.[8] The further depiction of Jesus reading, teaching, and speaking in formal venues like synagogues and temple, reveals, at the very least, that the evangelists included such events because they knew about and perhaps even shared in similar reading communities themselves irrespective of the provenance of each gospel. Therefore, as just mentioned, we are not arguing or assuming that the compilation or destination of the four canonical gospels was Palestine. Rather, the events they narrate are primarily in that location, and their intended message is not specifically focused on or limited to the local Christian community out of which they emerged.[9]

8. See Rainer Riesner, *Jesus als Lehrer: Eine Untersuchung zum Ursprung der Evangelien-Überlieferung*, WUNT 2.7 (Tübingen: Mohr Siebeck, 1988). More recently, see Michael F. Bird, *The Gospel of the Lord: How the Early Church Wrote the Story of Jesus* (Grand Rapids: Eerdmans, 2014).

9. See Richard Bauckham, "For Whom Were Gospels Written?," *HTS* 55, no. 4 (1999): 865–82. Compare also the recent study by Richard Last, who argues that the social setting of gospel writers and their literary works reveal a broader range of social activities, "less fully situated in 'Christianity', than is often assumed." "The Social Relationships of Gospel Writers: New Insights from Inscriptions Commending Greek Historiographers," *JSNT* 37, no. 3 (2015): 223–52, here 227. His more recent study, however, barely improves upon his previous work, which overemphasizes certain correlations with other ancient writing communities, often confuses the lines between emic and etic representations (as defined in Mike Morris, ed., *Concise Dictionary of Social and Cultural Anthropology* [Oxford: Wiley-Blackwell, 2012]), and does not adequately address a host of issues, such as genre, motives, and tradition. "Communities That Write: Christ-Groups, Associations, and Gospel Communities," *NTS* 58 (2012): 173–98. For a satisfactory corrective to Last's view on the social and historical setting of gospel literature,

Comparably, the author of Luke's Gospel narrates most vividly the actual reading events that took place at the various venues mentioned in the fourfold Gospels. For that reason, and due to the limitations of our study, the Gospel of Luke will be the focus. This selectivity, however, will not greatly jeopardize the final results of this examination, since the main locations are the same. The author of Matthew mentions four places in relation to communal reading events: Capernaum, Nazareth, Jerusalem, and the broader region of Galilee. The places where Mark explicitly discusses venues for communal reading events are as follows: Capernaum, Galilee, Nazareth, Jerusalem, and the broader areas of Galilee and Nazareth. As for specific locations in the Gospel of John where there would have been some degree of exposure to communal reading events, there are at least two: a synagogue in Capernaum (6:59–60), and the temple courtyards (7:14, 28; 8:20; cf. 12:34) and synagogues (9:22; 12:42; 16:2; 18:20) in Jerusalem.[10] All these locations are also included in Luke's account.

In addition, there are many features provided by the other three canonical gospel authors that are related to our study but that will not receive the same extended examination the Gospel of Luke will receive. A prime example is their consistent emphasis on written traditions.[11] The Matthean Jesus is depicted as quoting, referencing, and alluding to written texts everywhere he goes geographically, and with every person he meets socially. He references written texts to scribes (8:20), disciples (8:22), and bystanders alike (19:18–19). He tells the Pharisees to go back and learn what the Scriptures really mean (9:13).[12] When scribes and Pharisees together asked for a physical sign, he pointed them back to the physical Scriptures (12:38–42). When John the Baptist is questioning Jesus' ministry, Jesus tells John's disciples to go back and quote him Scripture (11:4–6). The narrator

though not specifically addressing Last or only Gospel communities, see Udo Schnelle, "Das frühe Christentum und die Bildung," *NTS* 61, no. 2 (2015): 113–43.

10. Regarding the unique use of ἀποσυνάγωγος in John's Gospel, see Jonathan Bernier, *Aposynagōgos and the Historical Jesus in John: Rethinking the Historicity of the Johannine Expulsion Passages*, BIS 122 (Leiden: Brill, 2013).

11. Santiago Guijarro Oporto even argues that the cluster of quotations at the beginnings of Matthew and Mark perform several rhetorical functions for the reading and readers of each Gospel. "'Como está escrito': Las citas de la escritura en los comienzos de los evangelios," *Salmanticensis* 61, no. 1 (2014): 91–115. Cf. also Michel Berder, "'Ne soyez pas comme…', 'Ne faites pas comme…': Étude des formules rhétoriques de demarcation attribuées à Jésus dans l'Évangile de Matthieu," *Transversalités* 129 (2014): 61–75.

12. According to David Hill, this phrase does not mean that they need to read what they do not know, but that they need to understand the sense of Scripture. "On the Use and Meaning of Hosea 6:6 in Matthew's Gospel," *NTS* 24, no. 1 (1977): 107–19, esp. 111.

has Jesus referencing Scripture when discussing John's ministry with the crowd (11:10, 13). He does this within places of communal reading, like synagogues (9:37–8), and in open meeting places, as for the Sermon on the Mount (7:12). He even sings certain written texts with his disciples (26:30; Hallel, Pss. 113–18).

The author of Mark's Gospel highlights that audiences often seemed prepared to critically evaluate someone who read, recited, or mentioned texts communally—especially sacred texts—and how they responded in various ways.[13] For example, in 6:2–3, some people were amazed by the teaching in the synagogue, while others took offense. Other times, Mark reveals that the teacher was assuming the audience had already heard the text(s) he read, recited, or mentioned, as in 10:19 ("you know the commandments"). The assumption also suggests that whatever copy of the Scriptures they have read or heard is similar and stable enough to permit such a statement,[14] and it assumes they know it well enough to recall it either from reading or hearing it enough times. Moreover, depending on the familiarity the teacher expected the audience to have with the text(s), there is necessarily a correlation between the number of times an audience would have had to hear the particular text(s) read aloud for such familiarity—especially if illiteracy was pervasive.

In the Gospel of John, there seems to be a sustained effort to picture at least Jesus and his audiences as familiar with writings.[15] According to the author, during Jesus' public ministry around the Lake of

13. Broad access to, and even ownership of, sacred texts should not be automatically dismissed. There were many ways individuals and synagogues could obtain copies of Scripture, and the same can be argued for subsequent Christian communities. For a survey of numerous options for early Christians, see Roy E. Ciampa, *The Presence and Function of Scripture in Galatians 1 and 2*, WUNT 2, book 102 (Tübingen: Mohr Siebeck, 1998), 256–70.

14. Although our study is not seeking to answer questions of textual stability, it is worth noting that the studies of some textual critics, such as Emanuel Tov, demonstrate that certain sacred texts were selected by scribes to receive extraordinary care. Tov writes, "Almost all biblical scrolls (all: proto-Masoretic) from sites in the Judean Desert other than Qumran were copied carefully [i.e., exhibit a low degree of scribal intervention]." *Scribal Practices and Approaches Reflected in the Texts Found in the Judean Desert*, STDJ 54 (Leiden, Brill, 2004], 254. Over a decade later, Tov writes again concerning the transmission of proto-Masoretic texts, "These scrolls must have been used everywhere in Israel, for public reading as well as for instruction, public and private." *Textual Criticism of the Hebrew Bible, Qumran, Septuagint: Collected Essays*, VTSup 167 (Leiden: Brill, 2015), 3:320.

15. At the same time, this does not mean that every time the author writes that a group responds to or reads something written, it is a communal reading event as defined by our study. In 19:19–20, the author of John narrates that many people read (ἀνέγνωσαν) an inscription at the same time and in the same place, yet the event would not be considered a communal reading event.

Galilee, it was the crowd—not the religious leaders, scribes, or other so-called social elites—who recalled and recited what had been written (6:31). Many commentaries note the uniqueness of this account. J. Ramsey Michaels, for example, states, "Nowhere else in the Gospel of John do we find anyone but Jesus or the gospel writer quoting Scripture in this manner. The crowd's chosen text, 'He gave them bread from heaven to eat,' echoing both Exodus 16 and Psalm 78, seems to have been quoted from memory."[16] Yet this account is not unique in the broader cultural context (see previous chapters), and even if the exact words are not used, there are other occasions when the crowd does attempt to exercise control over what they presumably had heard read communally, by stating it aloud. For example, as the crowd continues to increase throughout John's Gospel (even including Greeks; 12:20), they periodically speak in unison about written texts they have heard read communally, such as the law (= Torah). In one case, it is over one verb in one subordinate clause (ὑψωθῶ; 12:32–34).

One other common characteristic worth mentioning here is that these canonical gospel authors seem to envision their own literary works being read communally. In fact, Gordon Lathrop detects consistency on this from all four canonical gospels when he states, "The Gospels presume the Christian assembly and include it within their reference. They seem to have been intended for communities, for reading or orally reciting the story of Jesus in those communities. These meetings existed before the Gospels did. So did the stories and sayings of Jesus. But the Gospels gathered those stories and those sayings into an intentional form and made that form available to those meetings."[17] One example from the Gospel of Matthew, Gospel of Mark, and Gospel of John will be briefly noted here.

Beyond the Markan Jesus' use of the formula "have you not read" (12:3, 5; 19:4; 21:16; 21:42; 22:31; cf. 12:7),[18] one key indication that

---

16. *The Gospel of John* (Grand Rapids: Eerdmans, 2010), 368.

17. *The Four Gospels on Sunday: The New Testament and the Reform of Christian Worship* (Minneapolis: Fortress Press, 2011), 5.

18. The Matthean Jesus seems to assume that a prerequisite for theological discussion was the intensive reading of Scripture (*NIDNTTE* 279). Moreover, the dialogues regarding these texts display a certain type of quality control that was assumed and called for during Matthew's narrative of Jesus' communal teaching ministry. In fact, Cedric Vine uses Matthew's expansion of the Markan Jesus' use of this formula to argue, "Matthew represents a more literary work that, while often imitating orality, calls for an emphasis on reading rather than performance." *The Audience of Matthew: An Appraisal of the Local Audience Thesis*, LNTS (London: T&T Clark, 2014), 131.

the author of Matthew assumes his gospel will be read communally is found in 24:15.[19] In a reference to the book of Daniel, there is an editorial note: "Let the reader [ὁ ἀναγινώσκων] understand." Some commentators, including William Davies and Dale Allison, suggest it is referring to the reader of Daniel and therefore not an editorial aside for the reader of Matthew's Gospel, but then they provide no justification or further explanation for their interpretation.[20] I follow the more traditional understanding that the phrase is more than merely an editorial note. It is probably an invitation to the reader of Matthew to provide an interpretation to the audience(s) to whom he is reading the gospel aloud, or perhaps that "this text speaks of something that its readers well remember, some perhaps even as eyewitnesses."[21] Either of these editorial interpretations would make better sense, given the normal New Testament usage of ὁ ἀναγινώσκων and Mark's similar usage of these editorial notes.[22]

In the Gospel of Mark, one indication that the author meant for his work to be read communally is in 13:14, when Mark uses the phrase "let the reader understand" (see 2:10; 3:30; 7:3–4, 19). While it is possible that this phrase was part of the recorded speech, in that the audience was referred to the book of Daniel, it is unlikely. "The clause is better taken as an aside from the evangelist," Adela Collins writes, "to the individual who read the Gospel aloud to a group of assembled followers of Jesus (directly) and to his audience (indirectly), a hypothesis supported by the concluding statement in v. 37, which makes clear that the speech is directed to a broader audience than the four disciples named in v. 3."[23] Another indication is when Mark describes an event in which Jesus assumes—and expects—an incident during his public ministry to be included in all future communal

19. Another feature to consider would include the introduction and conclusion of the book. The author starts by referring to a written account (1:1) and ends with Jesus commanding everyone to teach all that he has taught (28:20)—presumably as recorded by the author in this work. While this provides another conceptual *inclusio* to consider, it is also a strong implicit indication that the author of Matthew assumes his gospel will be read communally—especially via Jesus' command to teach what he taught.

20. *A Critical and Exegetical Commentary on the Gospel According to Saint Matthew*, vol. 3, *Commentary on Matthew XIX–XXVIII* (Edinburgh: T&T Clark, 1997), 346.

21. Ulrich Luz, *Matthew 21–28: A Commentary*, ed. Helmut Koester, trans. James E. Crouch (Minneapolis: Fortress Press, 2005), 196.

22. *Contra* Larry Perkins, who argues that it is an authentic statement of Jesus meant to correct the disciples' misunderstanding of the phrase "abomination of desolation." "'Let the Reader Understand': A Contextual Interpretation of Mark 13:14," *BBR* 16 (2006): 95–104.

23. Collins, *Mark: A Commentary*, ed. Harold W. Attridge (Minneapolis: Fortress Press, 2007), 608. Cf. Robert H. Stein, *Mark* (Grand Rapids: Baker Academic, 2008), 602–3.

gospel presentations in the whole world (14:9). His statement, therefore, assumes future communal events (see, by way of comparison 2
Tim 4:2: "preach the word"), events "in which the Gospel was read
aloud and expounded, that is, in a social context of reoralization."[24]
Moreover, Richard France observes an important shift in meaning
from the earlier use of "the gospel" in 13:10, which "denoted the message preached by Jesus," to a new meaning that "has now become a
message about Jesus" in 14:9.[25] Therefore, Mark's depiction of Jesus's
proclamation is that it is not just for people in Galilee, but to "all
the nations." France goes on to note, "That Mark should have such a
view of the future worldwide proclamation of the gospel is not surprising, but that he should attribute such an expectation to Jesus in
the days immediately before his death . . . is more remarkable. He
wants his readers to understand that Jesus does not view the death
which he has been so insistently predicting as the end of his life's
work."[26] Mark's initial expectation that his gospel will be read communally, then, is not difficult to imagine, especially when Mark also
recounts Jesus' prediction that places of communal reading events
(synagogues in general) will be one of the places his disciples will be
beaten in the future (13:9).

The writer of John's Gospel draws attention to the written nature
of his gospel and clearly references his audience.[27] Whether they are
Jews or Gentiles, he writes for all who believe in Jesus, even if they
were not part of his public ministry or did not experience any of the
events firsthand. In 20:29, for example, John writes that Jesus made
permanent the application of the passage to any future reader or audi-

---

24. Ibid., 644.

25. France, *The Gospel of Mark* (Grand Rapids, MI: Eerdmans, 2002), 555.

26. Ibid.

27. Another indication that John assumes a future audience will hear his gospel read communally is the incident between Jesus and some Jewish authorities in 7:35–36. The leaders are
wondering where Jesus is going to go if he is not going to be with them much longer, as he
just stated (7:33–34). One of their guesses is that Jesus plans to leave Judea in order to have a
teaching ministry to the Gentile world. The reader of John's Gospel will probably know this
ministry has already begun in the work of the disciples (see 17:18; 20:21). In 7:40–44, after Jesus
teaches the people about the Spirit by alluding to many Jewish writings, the crowd is explicitly
said to have heard these words with various reactions. In the midst of their various responses,
some quickly say, "Did not the Scripture say?" (7:42). This immediate reaction to recall, recite,
or quote what they have heard read communally suggests the controlling influence of communal reading events. In other words, the question raised by Jesus' appeal to Scripture centers on
how the readers of the gospel are meant to view it. Do they agree with it or not? Given that
several Jewish scriptures reflect these words (e.g., Isa 44:3; 55:1; 58:11; Zech 14:8) and that Jesus
has already told them Scripture cannot be broken (10:35), "they are hardly free to disagree"
(Michaels, *The Gospel of John*, 470), yet they still do.

ence (cf. 17:20, where John recounts another statement by Jesus, this time from a prayer, which includes anyone invited to respond to what they hear from the disciples—in this case, John—even if they were not present with Jesus during his earthly ministry). Likewise, he states that his purpose for writing is so that everyone will believe (20:30–31). Looking earlier in the same chapter, Francis Moloney uses 20:9 to argue that the verse is part of the author's longer narrative and theological strategy to present John's Gospel as Scripture. Thus, whenever future readers have the Gospel of John in their hand, they presumably are those who have not seen (v. 29) yet have access to a Scripture "having been written" (γέγραπται; v. 31) so that they may go on believing.[28]

LUKE

More than any other canonical gospel, Luke's account emphasizes the actual reading events that took place at various venues. Not only does his gospel begin and end with communal reading events, but he also provides arguably the most explicit examples of the communal reading of Scripture. This ought to be especially surprising for at least two reasons. First, Luke was probably a non-Jew, assuming he is the same Luke mentioned in Colossians 4:14, making his two volumes (Luke-Acts) the only books in the New Testament written by a non-Jew. Second, the Gospel of Luke is the only canonical gospel that does not provide explicit notes to readers, probably because his stated audience is one person, Theophilus (though see the extended discussion on Theophilus in the next section, which examines Acts). However, this emphasis is not that surprising when factoring in Luke's use of Scripture.[29]

Nevertheless, there are still a few indications that Luke assumed a broader audience, and even that he would have expected his gospel to be read communally from the beginning. A few of these features will be noted at the end of this discussion, but first, the communal reading events in this gospel will be located and mapped, along with mentions of a few implicit indicators.

28. "'For as Yet They Did Not Know the Scripture' (John 20:9): A Study in Narrative Time," *IrTheolQuart* 79, no. 2 (2014): 97–111.

29. For a survey of scholarly positions, see Peter Mallen, *The Reading and Transformation of Isaiah in Luke-Acts*, ed. Mark Goodacre, LNTS 367 (London: T&T Clark, 2008), 4–9.

The first communal reading event is not in a temple, synagogue, or out in the open air. It is in someone's home in a town in Judah (1:39; cf. 1:65).[30] Inside his own home in the countryside, a local priest, Zechariah,[31] wrote four words on a writing tablet in order for a group of common people to read it communally (1:63). While it is possible that everyone read what he wrote individually and silently, it is more probable that someone was able to read it aloud to everyone, especially since Luke states they were collectively amazed.

The next location to examine is found in Luke 2. When Jesus was twelve years old, he was in the Jerusalem temple courts with the teachers (2:46). Luke recounts that everyone was amazed at his understanding (2:47), but understanding of what? The prior verse suggests that it was his understanding of what the Jewish rabbis were discussing. Given the location, terminology, and context of this episode, it seems safe to say that written sources would have been included. The type of questioning and answering was typical in Jewish dialogues, such as Jesus' dialogue with an expert in the law where Jesus asks for scriptural support in 10:26 ("What is written in the Law? What do you read there?"), or his final two questions and citing of Psalms in 20:41–44.[32] In fact, regarding the latter passage, Camille Focant argues that in the parallel account in the Gospel of Mark (12:35–44), "the Jewish halakah with question and counter question" moves into a private scene at the end of the pericope with the disciples that "has the appearances of a Christian halakah."[33] Either way, this typical question-and-answer pattern is often based on physical texts, whether present or recited.

In chapter 4, Jesus is back in Galilee. The text says he was teaching in their synagogues in Galilee, and everyone praised him (4:15). It does not matter for our purposes whether it was a literal building

30. This report is also chronologically the first instance of writing in the New Testament. See Alan Millard, "Zechariah Wrote (Luke 1:63)," in *The New Testament in Its First Century Setting: Essays on Context and Background in Honour of B. W. Winter on His 65th Birthday*, ed. P. J. Williams et al. (Grand Rapids: Eerdmans, 2004), 46–55, here 46.

31. In light of Gerhard Lenski's social stratification model, Esa Autero places Zechariah among the non-elite (or common people), since he "was probably poor and lived perhaps at the subsistence level much of the time, except perhaps when he was on duty in the Jerusalem Temple." "Social Status in Luke's Infancy Narrative: Zechariah the Priest," *BTB* 41, no. 1 (2011): 36–45, here 44.

32. This does not mean to suggest that people—in this case, lawyers—were carrying around scrolls or physical texts, but rather that the reading and reciting of written sources is assumed.

33. *The Gospel According to Mark: A Commentary*, trans. Leslie Robert Keylock (Eugene, OR: Wipf and Stock, 2012), 398. See also his discussion on the architectural code of the temple in Mark in *Marc, un évangile étonnant: Recueil d'essais*, BETL 194 (Leuven: Peeters, 2006), 286–69.

or structure. Just mentioning a Jewish assembly at a synagogue is enough to point to an opportunity for a communal reading event, since it is safe to assume that Jewish synagogue services included the reading of Scripture, whether or not Jesus would have performed such a task on each or any occasion he attended. The mere mention of these Jewish assemblies implies that communal reading took place there. Furthermore, Jesus' intimate knowledge of the Scriptures—implied here and stated elsewhere—assumes his exposure to many communal reading events, as they would certainly have been a contributor to his knowledge of Scripture, with some scholars even arguing that, since Jesus was illiterate, these types of communal events would have been the only source.[34] Bovon identifies two other significant points here in relation to our study. First, Jesus' teaching should be understood "in terms of the Jewish interpretation of Scripture."[35] Second, he writes, "The content of Jesus' teaching remains open in this verse, [sic] because Luke does not want to anticipate the representative sample of Jesus' teaching that follows, that is, his preaching in Nazareth, and thus diminish its effect."[36]

Following this brief statement in 4:15 is the most explicit account in all of the canonical gospels of Jesus reading (ἀναγνῶναι) communally, and it is in a synagogue in Nazareth (4:16–30). Lee Levine quotes this entire passage when he remarks, "The importance of Luke's narrative cannot be overestimated for our understanding of the first-century Galilean synagogue. . . . The positioning of this tradition is clearly significant for Luke's agenda, as he apparently intended to use Jesus's 'inaugural address' in Nazareth to set forth some main themes of both his Gospel and his companion volume, Acts."[37] Among these main themes, Levine underscores that Jesus' message is rooted in Jewish tradition, given the synagogue setting, reading from Scriptures, and preaching. This incident is so important to Luke's developing narrative that many scholars identify the passage as "programmatic."[38]

---

34. Chris Keith, *Jesus against the Scribal Elite: The Origins of the Conflict* (Grand Rapids: Baker Academic, 2014).

35. Bovon, *Luke 1: A Commentary on the Gospel of Luke 1:1–9:50* (Minneapolis: Fortress Press, 2002), 152.

36. Ibid., 152.

37. "The Synagogues of Galilee," in *Galilee in the Late Second Temple and Mishnaic Periods*, vol. 1, *Life, Culture, and Society*, ed. David A. Fiensy and James Riley Strange (Minneapolis: Fortress Press, 2014), 129–50, here 131.

38. See, for example, the survey of secondary literature in C. J. Schreck, "The Nazareth Peri-

According to Luke, Jesus states that the same Scripture he just read has been fulfilled in their hearing (4:21). "There is thus a clear literary trail," writes Mallen, "from Jesus' baptism to his inaugural sermon."[39] During Jesus' teaching, he also states that the audience "will" quote him some literary traditions: the two proverbs in verse 23. Both these sayings were known in Judaism and the Greek world.[40] At the end of the episode, in verse 28, the crowd apparently controlled the outcome of the event, physically driving him out of town and planning to throw him off a cliff (v. 29).

The next location to consider is on the Sabbath in a synagogue at Capernaum (4:31–37). Regarding this synagogue, Richard France notes, "[Capernaum] was a significant lakeside settlement, sufficiently important to have a detachment of Roman troops (Mt. 8:5–13), a customs post (2:14), and a resident official described as βασιλικός (Jn. 4:46). Its population at the time could have been as high as 10,000; its συναγωγή . . . would therefore have held a considerable Sabbath congregation."[41] Population estimates are difficult to gauge,[42] however, and even first-century writers like Josephus cannot automatically be trusted.[43] At the same time, France's general assessment is not far off from the most recent scholarship on first century Galilee. Bradley Root writes, "The settlement patterns established in the Late Hellenistic Period [ca. 100–50 BCE] continued throughout the Early

---

cope: Luke 4:16–30 in Recent Study," in *L'Évangile de Luc – The Gospel of Luke*, ed. F. Neirynck, BETL 32 (Leuven: Leuven University Press, 1989), 399–471.

39. Mallen, *Isaiah in Luke Acts*, 75.

40. For a sampling of literary references to the first proverb, "Physician, heal yourself," going back at least as early as Homer, see John Nolland, "Classical and Rabbinic Parallels to 'Physician, Heal Yourself' (Lk. IV 23)," *NovT* 21, no. 3 (1979): 193–209. Cf. Gos. Thom. 31.

41. *The Gospel of Mark* (Grand Rapids: Eerdmans, 2002), 101.

42. Jonathan L. Reed, *Archaeology and the Galilean Jesus: A Re-examination of the Evidence* (Harrisburg, PA: Trinity Press International, 2000), esp. 69–99. "Unfortunately," Sharon Mattila writes, "Reed's characterization of the Capernaum site is very misleading, as are those of other New Testament scholars such as Richard A. Horsley, Seán Freyne, and James H. Charlesworth. This is despite the fact that a sufficient number of detailed reports have been published on the site to make possible the kind of close analysis I present here in *refutation* of such characterizations. The time has come for these misleading characterizations of Jesus' Capernaum to be set aside." "Revisiting Jesus' Capernaum: A Village of Only Subsistence-Level Fishers and Farmers?," in *The Galilean Economy in the Time of Jesus*, ed. David A. Fiensy and Ralph K. Hawkins (Atlanta: SBL, 2013), 75–138, here 76.

43. Anthony Byatt, "Josephus and Population Numbers in First Century Palestine," *PEQ* 105 (1973): 51–60. Cf. Jürgen Zangenberg, "Das Galiläa des Josephus und das Galiläa der Archäologie: Tendenzen und Probleme der neueren Forschung," in *Josephus und das Neue Testament: Wechselseitige Wahrnehmungen, II. Internationales Symposium zum Corpus Judaeo-Hellenisticum, 25–28, Mai 2006, Greifswald*, WUNT 209 (Tübingen: Mohr Siebeck, 2007), 265–94.

Roman Period as Galilee's population grew rapidly. The population reached a zenith sometime in the early first century CE, when it contained roughly twice as many people as it had in the mid second century BCE."[44]

More generally, "The focus of Jesus' ministry in Jewish synagogues," writes James Edwards, "indicates he is not an itinerant Greco-Roman philosopher, a wandering Cynic sage, a Qumran rigorist, or even a hermetic moral reformer like John. Jesus proclaims the good news of God's reign in practicing communities of Jewish faith to signify that his message and mission are the fulfillment of God's revelatory history in Israel."[45] These types of events caused the news about Jesus to spread even further. The chapter concludes with Jesus continuing to participate in the synagogues of Judea (44). "By 'Judea'," François Bovon writes, "Luke seems to mean not only the southern part but the entire country."[46]

In chapter 5, there is another communal event to consider, but this time, it is not in a synagogue. Luke narrates that a crowd of people gathered around Jesus by the Lake of Gennesaret in order to listen to the word of God (5:1). This type of open-air teaching was not novel to Jesus, but there is not always the emphasis on the word of God. Granted, "the word of God" does not always refer to Scripture, as in John 10:35, but Luke can and does use the phrase at times as divine revelation to Israel as recorded in books (Acts 6:2; 18:11).[47] This interpretation does not mean to imply that Jesus would have been carrying scrolls of the Jewish scriptures around on his person, as discussed in

44. *First Century Galilee: A Fresh Examination of the Sources*, WUNT 2.378 (Tübingen: Mohr Siebeck, 2014), 99–100. Cf. Milton Moreland, "The Inhabitants of Galilee in the Hellenistic and Early Roman Periods: Probes into the Archaeological and Literary Evidence," in *Religion, Ethnicity, and Identity in Ancient Galilee: A Region in Transition*, ed. Jürgen Zangenberg, Harold W. Attridge, and Dale B. Martin, WUNT 210 (Tübingen: Mohr Siebeck, 2007), 133–59.

45. *The Gospel according to Luke* (Grand Rapids: Eerdmans, 2015), 150.

46. Bovon, *Luke 1: A Commentary on the Gospel of Luke 1:1–9:50* (Minneapolis, MN: Fortress Press, 2002), 165. It is also worth pointing out that Luke notes a broader geography here than Mark or Matthew.

47. *Contra* Ben Witherington III, who argues that "the phrase 'Word of God' in the NT *never once* refers to a text." "'Almost Thou Persuadest Me . . .': The Importance of Greco-Roman Rhetoric for the Understanding of the Text and Context of the NT," *JETS* 58, no. 1 (2015): 63–88, here 69. It is also worth noting up front that there is often an overlap and difficulty in distinguishing between the phrases "word of God" and "word of the Lord." Sometimes "word of God" refers to written texts (Mark 7:13; John 10:35; Acts 18:11), but other times, it is less clear (Luke 8:11, 13, 15, 21; 11:28; Acts 4:31; 11:1). The main point in this is that neither phrase should be automatically placed in one category to the exclusion of the other. See Stanley E. Porter and Bryan R. Dyer, "Oral Texts? A Reassessment of the Oral and Rhetorical Nature of Paul's Letters in Light of Recent Studies," *JETS* 55, no. 2 (2012): 323–41.

the excursus (pp. 119–20, above). He could have simply been reciting written texts from memory or using some form of abridged notes. Moreover, as David Pao perceptively argues, examining the phrase "word of God" needs to include other theological emphases in Luke-Acts and should not be based on a purely synchronic reading.[48] This phrase, for example, is one of the important features that link Luke-Acts with Old Testament historiography.[49] Nevertheless, there does not seem to be even support here to regard this episode as a communal reading event.

In 6:6–11, Luke states that Jesus is once again in the synagogue around Galilee teaching with scribes present. Based on what Luke has already described in chapter 4 regarding Jesus reading at Nazareth, reading is conceivable again. In 7:5, though this is certainly not an example of a communal reading event, it is still worth noting here, because Luke states that the synagogue in Capernaum was built by a Gentile. This is not a novel idea. There is precedent for this. A mid-first-century CE inscription in Phrygia (*CIJ* 2.766) mentions a Roman priestess who donates a house to a Jewish synagogue.[50] But the reason for noting it is that it reveals broader societal support and involvement in places that held communal reading events—regardless of motives.

In 13:10, Jesus is teaching on his way to Jerusalem in "one of the synagogues" on Sabbath for the last time in Luke's Gospel. This qualification (μιᾷ) is rare, but what is more interesting is that "the leader of synagogue" rebukes Jesus' healing—not his teaching (13:14). The main reason for the rebuke, however, according to the ruler of the synagogue, is that the written Torah is the ultimate authority and Jesus has violated it. Moreover, the synagogue leader chooses to address the congregation instead of Jesus, the teacher. The quality control here is not specifically on what Jesus read or taught per se,

---

48. *Acts and the Isaianic New Exodus* (Grand Rapids: Baker Academic, 2000), 147–80, esp. 149.

49. See Scott Shauf, "The 'Word of God' and Retribution Theology in Luke-Acts," in *Scripture and Traditions: Essays on Early Judaism and Christianity in Honor of Carl R. Holladay*, ed. Patrick Gray and Gail R. O'Day (NovTSup 129 (Leiden: Brill, 2008), 173–91. See also Hans Klein, *Das Lukasevangelium: übersetzt und erklärt* (Göttingen: Vandenhoeck & Ruprecht, 2006), 207; John L. McKenzie, "The Word of God in the Old Testament," *TS* 21 (1960): 183–206; Samuel S. H. Chan, "The Preached Gospel as the Word of God: An Old Question Revisited with Special Reference to Speech Act Theory" (PhD diss., Trinity Evangelical Divinity School, 2006), 100–216.

50. For additional examples see, among others, Darrell L. Bock, *Luke*, vol. 2, *9:51–24:53* (Grand Rapids: Baker, 1996), 638.

but that his actions seemed contrary to their written tradition that they supposedly knew well enough to judge accordingly. This quality control, then, is linked to the communal reading event as a whole: teacher, leader, people attending, written tradition, and an arbitrated response according to their written tradition. Jesus' reply also suggests an emphasis on the entire gathering. Jesus uses the plural form of *hypocrites* when he responds (13:15). Therefore, he responds not just to the synagogue leader but also to everyone. The result is a division among the audience of the event. Some people rejoiced, and others sided with the synagogue leader. According to Luke, Jesus even supersedes the written Torah.

In 19:47, Jesus is teaching daily in the Jerusalem temple courts. It is worth noting that the leaders (chief priests, scribes, lawyers, elders) with all their power and positions were not able to silence Jesus, because of his popularity among the crowds. Therefore, the greater control over the teaching ministry of Jesus, at least here, appears to be the community over against the noted leaders. This emphasis on his daily teaching in the Jerusalem temple courts occurs again in 20:1 and 21:37–38. All people came to hear him, along with leaders asking him questions regarding what "Moses wrote for us" (20:28). Shortly after this, in 24:19, the author says that Jesus was known for being "mighty in word." Given that there are strong connections—both here and elsewhere—to Moses, who gave the people the Torah, the author likely has the written word in the background of many contexts such as this one, even where the written word is not present or read (as opposed to its reading and hearing in the synagogues meant that it was "present").

Luke's Gospel ends with a non-synagogue communal reading event. In 24:32, on the road to a village called Emmaus, located about eight miles out from Jerusalem, Jesus opens up (διήνοιγεν) the Scriptures. Luke does not state from where they get or in what form they have the Scriptures, but apparently his reader(s) would not have a problem assuming that there was some form of access to them. Of course, this verb can also be rendered figuratively, thus having the idea that Jesus merely helped them understand the Scriptures they hopefully had already heard and remembered. This interpretation is less probable, though, for at least five reasons. First, the language here emphasizes the comprehensiveness of his teaching. He continually speaks of "all."[51] Again, this does not mean Jesus had complete physical scrolls of all the Scriptures, but rather implies some sort of *testimonia* or abridged compilation. Second, he states in 24:44, all that was written was fulfilled. Third, in 24:45, their minds were opened to understand the Scriptures, not merely what he told them about himself or the Scriptures. Fourth, the same verb (διήνοιγεν) is used elsewhere in Luke's writings during a communal reading event explicitly referring to the opening of the literal Scriptures in a Jewish synagogue (Acts 17:2–3). Fifth, there are a number of literary parallels between this account and Luke's narrative between Philip and the Eunuch in Acts 8, which included the literal Scriptures (see discussion of Acts in the next section). It seems most probable, then, that there would have been some type of literal text(s) Jesus was able to use in order to show these men about himself.

There are a few additional indicators worth noting here that people—whether they were the ones reading or hearing the text(s)—had ample access to communal reading events. Jesus assumes all the Pharisees collectively had read certain texts (6:3). Jesus states that his true "mother and brothers" are those who hear God's word and put it into practice (8:21). If there is consistency to how Luke is using this phrase, he is probably referring to hearing the Scriptures via a communal reading event and not solely extemporaneous oral proclamation (cf. Barn. 9). The Lukan Jesus is also able to identify a κεραία in a Torah scroll and use it as an example in his communal teaching. Jesus tells his audience that not one tiny stroke of the letter of the law will disappear, and he assumes his audience will be able to visualize his imagery (16:17). Moreover, the author of Luke is not the only person to narrate this detail. The Matthean parallel (5:18) is even more emphatic, with an additional textual symbol (ἰῶτα) followed by a double negative (οὐ μή). Even more, Edwards argues, Luke is reminding his readers that the written Scriptures, namely, the Law and the Prophets, "provide the indispensable pretext and context for the gospel."[52]

Next, Jesus gives a parable about a rich man in Hades who wants his five brothers who are still living on earth to be warned about the place of torment. The response the rich man gets from Abraham is

51. Bock, *Luke*, 2:1917. Bock goes on to note that this is a traditional phrase found in "1QS 1.3; 4Q504 [= 4QDibHama] 3:12; Matt. 11:13; John 1:45 [and] this figure (called zeugma) describes the discussions scope: he went through the entire Scripture, front to back."

52. Edwards, *Luke*, 464.

essentially that his brothers can all hear about it wherever they are by attending a communal reading event where Scripture is being read (16:29). Though it is a parable, Jesus seems to connect it with reality. There is no indication that the brothers would not have access to listen to God's word read communally wherever they might be. Again, this reveals that the Lukan Jesus operates under the assumption that communal reading events were widespread.

In addition to noting geographical locations as places for communal reading events, highlighting people's grasp of literary works, and narrating an actual reading event, Luke's Gospel includes a few implicit indicators that communal reading events were pervasive in the first century. Like all the other canonical gospels,[53] Luke notes that Jesus was often called "teacher"; people who do this include Simon (7:40), someone from the ruler's house (8:49), a man from a crowd (9:38), a scribe (10:25), experts (11:45), a bystander (12:13), a ruler (18:18), spies (20:21), Sadducees (20:37), experts (20:39), a crowd (21:7), and Jesus himself (21:11). Not only did many people call Jesus a teacher, but Jesus assumed many people had already heard texts read communally. Jesus automatically assumes an unidentified leper knows what Moses commanded (5:14). Both of these implicit indicators suggest that embedded in the culture are people's familiarity with and ability to identify those who teach communally, as well as an assumption that various texts were read widely enough that most people would have known them well. It is also particularly important to realize the broad range of people that Jesus assumes would have heard certain texts read communally: crowds in general, a leper specifically, family, all of the religious leaders, etc. This strengthens my thesis that communal reading events were widespread, given the broad range of stated and assumed participants.

In addition, Luke's own emphasis on Scripture—especially "as it is written in the law of the Lord" in chapter 2—and his emphasis on Jesus' economically poor parents knowing Scripture well (2:39), sug-

---

53. The author of the Gospel of Mark references more people and groups identifying Jesus as a teacher or rabbi than any other gospel (including Luke, since Luke does not include "rabbi" as one of the ascribed titles). If one only considers the term *teacher* in the Synoptic Gospels, here are the statistics of how many times it refers to Jesus: eleven of seventeen in Luke, eight of twelve in Matthew, and seven of eleven in Mark. As for the Gospel of John, Jesus is called rabbi or teacher by the following people: John the Baptist's disciples (1:38), Nathaniel (1:49), Nicodemus the Pharisee (3:2), his disciples (4:31; 9:2; 11:8), certain crowds (6:25), Martha (11:28), and Jesus himself (13:13–14). See John Yueh-Han Yieh, "One Teacher: Jesus' Teaching Role in Matthew's Gospel" (PhD diss., Yale University, 2003); Arthur F. Graudin, "Mark's Portrait of Jesus as Teacher" (PhD diss., Claremont, 1972).

gests a broad range of people being exposed to texts—most likely via communal reading events. In fact, even where no texts are explicitly mentioned, there often seem to be texts implied in the backdrop. For example, John Levison states this idea strongly regarding Simeon's short speech in Luke 2:28–32: "This exclamation, though it seems extemporaneous and unplanned, is actually deliberate and drenched in the dream of Isaiah 40–55."[54] He goes on to argue that Simeon's ability to know what to say in the moment was not due to ecstatic impulses, unaided by learning; nor to the spontaneity of the moment, void of preparation; nor to an emotional tizzy, stripped of his intellectual faculties. Rather, it reveals that Simeon was vigilant in his studies of the written Scriptures, specifically here the prophetic vision of Isaiah 40–55, which he applies to this young Galilean boy, who offers salvation to everyone (cf. Acts 15:14). To put all this in another way, even if Simeon is not holding a manuscript in his hand at the moment of his speech, it is as if he is reading a phantom one. There are textual reference points and no need for him to say something like, "Go see this or that specific scroll or codex in this or that specific location or synagogue." The speaker assumes that what he shares faithfully represents what others have already heard communally and that they would be able to recognize it as such. Even if the allusions are not exact in all the particulars, they certainly were in principle—at least here.

Now that the specific locations have been mapped and considered, and a few additional indicators mentioned, it is time to discuss whether the author of Luke meant for his gospel to be read communally from the beginning. To assess this, I will identify a few features throughout Luke's gospel that may indicate a broader audience than merely Theophilus, assuming for just a moment that he only represented one real individual.

The opening verses of Luke's gospel (1:1–4) show that Luke did not write in a vacuum. In fact, Luke-Acts is a literary work written by one who does research and claims to work as an ancient historian. Here, he explicitly states that there were already "many compiled accounts" (1:1). This suggests an intense interest in recording and

54. John R. Levison, "The Spirit, Simeon, and the Songs of the Servant," in *The Spirit and Christ in the New Testament and Christian Theology*, ed. I. Howard Marshall, Volker Rabens, and Cornelis Bennema (Grand Rapids: Eerdmans, 2012), 18–34, here 21. Cf. Collin Blake Bullard, *Jesus and the Thoughts of Many Hearts: Implicit Christology and Jesus' Knowledge in the Gospel of Luke*, LNTS 530 (London: T&T Clark, 2015), 65–81.

sharing what had taken place with others. Throughout the entire book, Luke also refers to other works to confirm his teaching (3:4), which means he is assuming his audience cares or that citing other sources has some rhetorical effect. Given that he did not write in a vacuum, there can be a similar expectation that he did not expect his writings to be read in one either. Though it was probably not in Luke's mind at the time, France observes that the verb translated "taught" in Luke 1:4 later became a designation in Christian usage of the "catechesis," formal instruction in the faith, which often preceded baptism.[55] He further states, "[Theophilus] is normally understood to be Luke's literary patron; such an address to a prominent figure was a recognized mode of launching a literary work, with no intention that the work was for his use alone."[56] In addition, Loveday Alexander concludes, "Whether Luke and Acts are treated as separate works or as a two-volume set, their prefaces belong to the same literary code."[57]

Still within these opening verses, there is another important phrase to consider in relation to our study. In 1:2, Luke states that there are not only eyewitnesses but also "servants of the word." Although he is not the first person to propose this, Thomas O'Loughlin is the most recent person to argue that "the servants of the word" refers to specific administrators in the church "whose task it was to preserve and guard each church's 'library'."[58] This would be *contra* commentators like Joseph Fitzmyer, who argue that the article οἱ governs the whole construction and points to one group of eyewitnesses who eventually became ministers of the word.[59] O'Loughlin goes on to state:

> Given the importance attached to them [i.e., the Scriptures] by Luke (e.g. in the Emmaus story at Luke 24:27, 32 and 45) and the way he imagines them being used by Peter and Paul (Acts 2:14–36; 17:2 and 11; 18:24 and 28), we must assume that having a copy of 'the scriptures' was a *desideratum* of each community. This is paralleled in the writing of the

---

55. R. T. France, *Luke*, ed. Mark L. Strauss and John H. Walton (Grand Rapids: Baker, 2013), 1.

56. Ibid.

57. *Acts in Its Ancient Literary Context: A Classicist Looks at the Acts of the Apostles*, LNTS 298 (London: T&T Clark, 2005), 42.

58. "Ὑπηρέται . . . τοῦ λόγου: Does Luke 1:2 Throw Light on to the Book Practices of the Late First-Century Churches?," in *Early Readers, Scholars and Editors of the New Testament*, ed. H. A. G. Houghton (Piscataway, NJ: Gorgias, 2014), 17–32. Cf. Daniel B. Wallace, *Granville Sharp's Canon and Its Kin: Semantics and Significance*, SBG 14 (New York: Peter Lang, 2008), 142.

59. *The Gospel according to Luke I–IX* (New York: Doubleday, 1981), 294.

other evangelists. In the time of Paul, the need would have been supplied in the synagogue; but by the end of the century—with groups gradually separating into different religions, and an increasing division upon linguistic lines—if a church wished to read 'the scriptures' (and all the evidence points to the fact that they did), then they had to have them for themselves. Obtaining and maintaining such a collection may have been the most demanding task facing the ὑπηρέται. Moreover, if we think of them having to look after both 'the scriptures' and the new texts of their own movement, then the designation ὑπηρέται τοῦ λόγου makes all the more sense. In this case, 'the word' would not simply refer to the Christian message—as most commentators on Luke assume—but to 'the word of God' implying the whole event of revelation to Israel as recorded in books.[60]

If he is correct, this does imply that Luke envisioned his gospel being read communally, and not merely by Theophilus. This would also increase the force of his statement to Theophilus that "you may know the certainty of the things you've been taught" (1:4).

Shortly after this introduction, Luke begins his Gospel with worship in the temple (1:8–25), a location in which Jesus so frequently taught when he was in Jerusalem. He then ends his Gospel with Jesus' followers being in the same spot, presumably to proclaim and teach all that Jesus commanded (24:52b–53). These accounts form a conceptual *inclusio* similar to the Gospel of Matthew. Nevertheless, as appealing as this interpretation is in light of these arguments and especially in light of our study, additional evidence and argumentation are needed to overturn the traditional understanding, so my study does not concur with O'Loughlin.

ACTS

Like the Gospel of Luke, the book of Acts is replete with examples of communal reading events and venues associated with them. While it is true that no scholar doubts that Jews read Scripture in the synagogues and that Christ followers such as Paul often argued with

---

60. O'Loughlin, "Ὑπηρέται . . . τοῦ λόγου.'" There are, however, textual variations in the manuscript tradition: in the almost three dozen times the phrases "word of the Lord" and "word of God" occur in Luke-Acts, "word of God" is more frequently attested. Further details and passages can be seen in Dom Jacques Dupont, "Notes sur les Actes des Apôtres," *RB* 66 (1955): 45–59; esp. 47–49.

them about it, it is important to identify all the possible locations and outline what probably took place at various events. Doing so makes it possible to map the geographical landscape of communal reading events, make additional connections, and evaluate the extent to which Christian communities from inception were controlled by such events. Likewise, each account will be mentioned in order to further highlight the scribal, literate, and communal nature of these earliest communities. For purposes of our study, though, the focus will on the various locations and venues.

The events recorded in Acts begin in Jerusalem. In fact, Jerusalem is the main location of the first eight chapters. Within these chapters, there are multiple references to places where communal reading events might have taken place, such as the temple courts (2:46), Solomon's Colonnade (3:11), privates houses (5:42), and synagogues (6:9). Jerusalem is also the only location in Acts where Luke provides the name of a rabbi, Gamaliel (5:34; 22:3), who would have read at Jewish communal reading events. Beyond the explicit mention of places that were available for holding communal reading events, and of specific individuals who would have led them beyond just Christ's followers, there are also a few features worth summarizing here that suggest that the author of Luke assumed these events were widespread in Jerusalem.

First, Luke has Peter addressing a group of believers with Jewish scripture that "had to be fulfilled," since it is God's word (1:16). During Peter's address, he either reads or recites several scriptural passages. Peter uses Judas's betrayal as another opportunity to offer to his crowd additional scriptural connections between the recent events and the Jewish scriptures. In fact, Darrell Bock notes that of the twenty-five times Luke uses the verb "to fulfill" in his two volumes, this is one of the only two times he combines Scripture with this verb.[61] The only other time is in Luke 4:21, when Jesus is at a communal reading event doing the same thing. Granted, beyond this rare combination of terms and Lukan parallel, the text does not explicitly state whether Peter cites his passages loosely from memory or via text (Pss. 69:25; 109:8). Nevertheless—given that Peter begins with a typical early-church introductory formula "it is written," he uncharacteristically names the book of Psalms directly, they are in Jerusalem, and

---

61. *Acts* (Grand Rapids, MI: Baker, 2007), 81.

the group is predominantly Jewish—reading some form of abridged notes is possible, though not defensible.

In addition, as Luke's narrative continues, not only does Peter read or recite an extended scriptural passage to his fellow Jews (2:14) from the book of Joel (2:16–21), but Luke's use of "this is" (τοῦτό ἐστιν) "for connecting Scripture in the NT is rare," following the typical pesher-style scriptural defense and interpretation (cf. CD 10:16).[62] This at least suggests that the Jewish Scriptures that are read weekly during Jewish communal reading events are and will remain the "indispensable foundation" of the early church.[63]

Before moving beyond Jerusalem, Luke mentions several other phrases ("the word of God continued to grow" in 6:7; "we have heard him speak blasphemous words against Moses and God" in 6:11), places ("the synagogue" in 6:9), and people (Stephen in 6:8) that communal reading events would have influenced or that would support the notion of the ongoing nature of communal teaching via reading events. In fact, Carl Mosser notes several important parallels between Luke's account of Stephen in Acts 6 and Jesus in Luke 4—parallels suggesting "that the dispute between Stephen and his opponents also took place within synagogues and the ἀνίστημι here [in 6:9] refers to people standing up in the synagogues to oppose Stephen's message."[64]

Luke adds a couple of other regions to his account of the widening preaching of the word: Judea and Samaria (8:1). In this brief section, the author states that everyone except the apostles left Jerusalem and preached the word. There is not enough evidence in these accounts, however, to support the idea that communal reading events took place in these locations according to Luke.

Between Gaza and Jerusalem, Luke narrates an event involving a non-apostle and a eunuch from Ethiopia.[65] In this account, the eunuch is reading (ἀνεγίνωσκεν) from Isaiah on his journey to

---

62. Ibid., 111.

63. C. K. Barrett, *A Critical and Exegetical Commentary on the Acts of the Apostles* (New York: T&T Clark, 2004), 1:135.

64. "Torah Instruction, Discussion, and Prophecy in First-Century Synagogues," in *Christian Origins and Hellenistic Judaism: Social and Literary Contexts for the New Testament*, ed. Stanley E. Porter and Wendy J. Porter (Leiden: Brill, 2013), 2:523–51, here 543. On the possibility of multiple synagogues around this location, see Craig Keener, *Acts: An Exegetical Commentary*, vol. 2, *3:1–14:28* (Grand Rapids: Baker Academic, 2013), 1298–1310.

65. Brittany E. Wilson argues that Luke is probably *not* portraying the Ethiopian eunuch as an elite, even though he is designated as an official, has certain access to political power and wealth via the queen of the Ethiopians, is able to read, and speaks well, given his use of the optative. This widespread assumption in Acts' scholarship, Wilson emphasizes, overlooks the mul-

Jerusalem (8:28). Philip hears him reading (ἀναγινώσκοντος) and asks if the eunuch understands what he is reading (ἀναγινώσκεις).[66] Part of Philip's assumption with his question is that there can be a difference between reading and understanding a religious text such as Isaiah. When the eunuch answers, he uses a word that can refer to a more formal communal reading event: ὁδηγέω, which BDAG defines as "to assist someone in acquiring information or knowledge" (8:31; cf. John 16:13).[67] Moreover, he asks Philip to come up into his chariot and sit beside him, presumably with the Isaiah scroll still open. After Luke cites the passage of Scripture the eunuch was reading, he states that "beginning with this scripture" Philip preached to him the good news about Jesus (8:35). "Beginning with" assumes that those six lines of Isaiah Luke mentions were not the only ones they read and discussed together communally, not to mention that the eunuch's request to get baptized suggests that they continued reading (8:36). Ernst Haenchen states, "Philip's witness to Christ is not limited to Isaiah 53.7f., which is here added to the passages adduced as Christological proofs."[68] Either way, however, this explicit communal reading event took place outside a typical venue and on a journey between Gaza and Jerusalem. Moreover, Craig Keener identifies no less than twelve parallels with Jesus' scriptural exposition in Luke 24:13–35 to consider.[69]

In Acts 9, there is an interesting exchange between Saul and the high priest. Saul asks the high priest for letters to bring to the synagogues in Damascus. The purpose of these letters was to be read communally in the synagogues at least with the synagogue elders whenever Saul found followers of Christ, so that he would have the authority to take them back to Jerusalem as prisoners (9:1–2; cf. 1 Macc 15:15–24). Though Luke does not detail what exactly the letters contained or stated, they demonstrate that writing, reading, and networking probably took place among places of communal reading events, such as synagogues. Keener is probably right to surmise

---

tifaceted connection between status, gender, and ethnicity. "'Neither Male nor Female': The Ethiopian Eunuch in Acts 8.26-40," *NTS* 60 (2014): 403–22.

66. Peter Müller uses Philip's question here to launch his study on certain reading practices in the New Testament and early Christianity, especially as they relate to Greco-Roman culture and ancient Judaism. *Verstehst du auch, was du liest? Lesen und Verstehen im Neuen Testament* (Darmstadt: Wissenschaftliche Buchgesellschaft, 1994).

67. Cf. *TDNT*, 5:97–102; *NIDNTTE*, 451–60.

68. *The Acts of the Apostles: A Commentary* (Philadelphia: Westminster, 1971), 312.

69. Keener, *Acts: An Exegetical Commentary*, 2:1536.

that these letters "may have asked local synagogues' cooperation in assisting Jerusalemites' discipline of errant members."[70] Regardless of what the letters stated, however, Damascus should be counted as another location where communal reading events took place given the synagogues there. This is further emphasized when Luke states that Paul—instead of reading the letters from the high priest in the synagogues—began "proving" to the Jews living in Damascus that Jesus is the Messiah (9:22) in the synagogues there (9:20). "The arguments," writes Barrett, "were no doubt Scriptural."[71] It is safe to suggest, then, that one method he probably used to persuade Jews in the synagogues was reading and discussing the Jewish Scriptures. In fact, the primary way Christ followers attempted to prove that Jesus is the Messiah to the Jews was via the written Jewish Scriptures. The reliance on this method provides a strong evidential basis that the earliest Christian gatherings were textually based.

While in Caesarea, Peter went inside the house of a Gentile, Cornelius. There was already a large crowd of people, mostly the relatives and close friends of Cornelius. In the midst of this communal meeting, Peter assumes that these Gentiles are "well aware" of the Jewish written law (10:28) and already know about the word God sent to Israel (10:36). It is important to note here that the "word" (λόγος) is never personified in Acts, so it should be read as a message, whether oral or written. After Peter mentions that all the prophets testify to what he has been sharing (10:43), everyone who heard the message received the Holy Spirit (10:44). And in 11:1, the apostles and believers throughout Judea heard a report about the Gentiles receiving the word of God. Again, it is not clear what the exact reference to "the word of God" is referring to, but the language is very similar to other places where Luke is talking about Scripture, like Luke 8:13 (cf. 1 Thess 1:6–7). In addition, Luke often mentions that the prophetic testimony found in the Jewish scriptures is fulfilled in Christ and being taught communally. Nevertheless, there is not enough clear evidence to suggest that the author was aware of communal reading events in this location.

Paul's first missionary journey (13:1–14:28) included at least four locations worth noting for purposes of our study. The first location

---

70. Ibid., 2:1619. Keener goes on to state that "Damascus had a massive Jewish community" (1674).

71. Barrett, *A Critical and Exegetical Commentary*, 1:465.

is Cyprus. In Cyprus, Luke briefly states that Barnabas and Saul pro-claimed the word of God in the Jewish synagogues there (13:4–5).

The second location is Pisidian Antioch. Once again, Luke narrates a communal reading event that took place in a synagogue (13:14), and given the extant evidence from this area, there is no reason to doubt "that there was a substantial Jewish population."[72] This time, however, he provides more details. In fact, this is arguably the most developed communal reading event involving Paul in the book of Acts, and there seems to be no mere coincidence that several aspects parallel Jesus' synagogue appearance in Luke 4. Paul sits down (13:14), listens to the reading (ἀνάγνωσιν) from the law and the prophets (13:15), stands up to deliver an exhortatory address that the synagogue leaders requested (13:16), and after referencing many other passages of Scripture, he emphasizes that the same Scriptures that are read (ἀναγινωσκομένας) communally every Sabbath in Jew-ish synagogues have been fulfilled in Jesus Christ (13:27). He goes on to read or recite more Scripture before the service ends, and the Jews and God-fearing proselytes urge them to come back to the syn-agogue the following Sabbath (13:43).

Persuaded by them, Paul and Barnabas came back the following week, and "the whole city gathered to heard the word of the Lord" (13:44). There are indications here that the people came to hear Paul's and Barnabas's reading and interpretation of the word of God, as opposed to the reading and discussion they had already been hearing every Sabbath, as was just mentioned. Both Paul and Barnabas con-firm that it was necessary to speak the word of God to the Jews first (even if they would experience severe discipline while in Jewish syn-agogues; 2 Cor 11:24), and they read or recite what the Lord com-manded through the prophet Isaiah (13:46–47). Moreover, Keener is right to note here, "Many synagogues must have also expounded Torah readings even before 70 C.E.; Luke is unlikely to have inad-vertently invented a custom that coincidentally became dominant over a wide geographical range later (Luke 4:16–20)."[73]

The third location is Iconium. And the first place Paul and Barn-abas went was to the Jewish synagogue there. According to Luke, this type of synagogue teaching is their typical pattern (κατὰ τὸ αὐτό; 14:1). Not only that, but they stayed there for a long time, and Luke

---

72. Ibid., 627. Notice also that Luke uses the plural "leaders" of the synagogue in 13:15, which suggests a large Jewish community there.

73. Keener, *Acts: An Exegetical Commentary*, 2:2048.

states that the Lord bore witness "to the word of his grace" (14:3). The episode ends by suggesting that there was continued consistency in their proclaiming the gospel (14:7).[74] There is no indication—here or elsewhere—that they greatly varied their approach.

The fourth location is Jerusalem. This time, however, there is an internal debate between believers (15:1–2). As would be expected, one of the leaders, James, reads or recites from the prophets in order to come to a solution (15:15–19). His conclusion is to write the solution down and send it to the churches, which suggests a normal means of communicating to a group: write correspondence that will be read during a communal reading event (15:20; cf. Heb 13:22). One stated reason for this conclusion is that Moses has been read (ἀναγινωσκόμενος) communally in synagogues every Sabbath from ancient times (15:21). Indeed, "Throughout the Empire, and beyond, wherever there were Jews the words of Moses were heard every week."[75] There seems to be an assumption among the leaders in Jerusalem that, just as there are communal reading events every week wherever there are Jews (cf. Jos. *Apion* 2.175), Christians are likewise gathering together and hearing texts read aloud. This finds further support when Judas and Silas are sent to "tell you these things," i.e., what is written in this letter (15:27), and then they read (ἀναγνόντες) the letter to the entire church in Antioch, and everyone rejoices (15:31).

During Paul's second missionary journey (15:36–18:23), there are eight locations to highlight in relation to our study. The first two locations are Derbe and Lystra (16:1). As Timothy, Paul, and Silas go through the towns, Luke mentions that they also continue to "deliver" the decree from the Council of Elders in Jerusalem to the churches (16:4). If the way they did it in Antioch is any indication of how they go about passing on the decree in other locations, then it is communally read in the churches. Bock adds, "The language of handing over . . . the decrees refers to passing on tradition, a more technical use than other instances in Acts. . . . These churches fall outside the addressed areas of the decree in the letters. Reading the letters to them shows that the intention was to issue a decision that extends

---

74. For a discussion on how early the term *gospel* may have designated written material(s), see James A. Kelhoffer, "'How Soon a Book' Revisited: ΕΥΑΓΓΕΛΙΟΝ as a Reference to 'Gospel' Materials in the First Half of the Second Century," *ZNW* 95 (2004): 1–34.

75. Barrett, *A Critical and Exegetical Commentary*, 2:737.

beyond the original region of the dispute."[76] This also suggests that what is appropriate to read in one church communally is also open and applicable to all churches.

The third location is Philippi, the leading city of the Macedonian district (16:12). In Philippi, Paul delivers a message at a "place of prayer" (16:13). Regardless of the physical details surrounding the group, the location served the same function as a synagogue, even though it was a less formal gathering, especially for Jews in the Diaspora during this period.[77] Even without any explicit features, then, the possibility of this being a communal reading event cannot be automatically rejected. The communal nature ("the women who had gathered there"), location (Jewish place of prayer), person speaking (Paul the Jew), and terminology used ("Sabbath," "prayer," "assembled," "heard," etc.), together open up the possibility. However, it is not certain. Therefore, this is another location that should not be included in a map of places where the author of Luke was probably aware of communal reading events.

The fourth location is Thessalonica. According to Barrett, this is "the most significant stop made by Paul and Silas in Macedonia, after leaving Philippi."[78] It is not just significant for their overall mission, though; it is also significant in relation to our study, due to Luke's sustained effort to reveal the influence communal reading events had on their mission. Luke explicitly states that the reason Paul and Silas stop there is that there was a Jewish synagogue (17:1). The lack of article with *synagogue* probably also suggests that there were other Jewish synagogues in Thessalonica.[79] Given that this was such a large city, it is most likely that at least some synagogues here would have owned their own Scripture scrolls. Moreover, the way Luke communicates the reason for their stop here implies that there were other places, such as Amphipolis and Apollonia, at which they did not stop because they did not readily see or know of any communal reading event locations, such as a Jewish synagogue.

Immediately after they arrive, Paul goes into the synagogue (17:2). Luke states, rather obviously by now, that Paul customarily went

76. Bock, *Acts*, 523–24.

77. See Susan Haber, "Common Judaism, Common Synagogue? Purity, Holiness, and Sacred Space at the Turn of the Common Era," in *Common Judaism: Explorations in Second-Temple Judaism*, ed. Wayne O. McCready and Adele Reinhartz (Minneapolis: Fortress Press, 2008), 69–71.

78. Barrett, *A Critical and Exegetical Commentary*, 2:807.

79. Barrett, *A Critical and Exegetical Commentary*, 2:809.

to the location of Jewish communal reading events—namely, synagogues. Interpreting Paul's actions there, Jacob Jervell states that Luke's use of "argue" (διελέξατο) "refers to didactic lectures and preaching."[80] While at these synagogue services for at least three Sabbaths, Paul "argued with them from the scriptures." Not only are some of the same phrases used in the accounts of Jesus entering the synagogues, such as "as was his custom" in Luke 4:16 (cf. 24:32, 46), but many other features are similar, such as reading and expounding the Jewish Scriptures and the divided response from the audience (cf. 1 Thess 2:15). Whether Luke intended these specific parallels, there seems to be no doubt that Jewish communal reading events were essential locations for Paul and Silas to wield influence in relation to their widespread mission.[81]

The fifth location is Berea, and once again Paul and Silas waste no time finding a Jewish synagogue in order to participate in the Jewish communal reading events held there (17:10). As they proclaimed the word of God in order to assure them that the Jewish scriptures affirm that Jesus is the Messiah, the Jews in this synagogue examined the Scriptures daily in order to determine whether they should accept or deny these claims. One detail of particular interest is the use of *examined* here. This verb is "nowhere else in the NT used of the study of Scripture; it suggests rather the legal examination of witnesses. . . . And this is in fact the sense in which it is used here. Paul has set up the Scriptures as witnesses: does their testimony, when tested, prove his case?"[82] Thus, beyond this merely being another location where communal reading events took place, there is a stated quality control regarding everything read and taught from Scripture.

The sixth location is Athens. Instead of just addressing people in the synagogue here, Paul also addresses them daily in the marketplace (17:17). No matter where he addresses them, though, he is reading or reciting texts that he assumes they already know. Even when he is outside of the synagogue, Luke notes that Paul reads or recites a passage to the audience, this time Aratus's *Phaenomena* (17:28). Regardless of when, where, or how Paul came to know this text,[83] he assumes

---

80. "Bezieht sich auf lehrhafte vorträge und predigten." Jacob Jervell, *Die Apostelgeschichte: Übersetzt und erklärt* (Göttingen: Vandenhoeck & Ruprecht, 1998), 433.

81. Ernst Haenchen, *The Acts of the Apostles: A Commentary* (Philadelphia: Westminster, 1971), 506–7.

82. Barrett, *A Critical and Exegetical Commentary*, 2:818.

83. Regarding Paul's education, Ryan Schellenberg reasonably concludes that Paul may have had some training in rhetoric, but not enough to be considered a specialist. Instead, he argues,

his audience is familiar enough with it for them to understand his argument. Paul's assumption seems to imply at least one of three things: there was a significant number of people in the marketplace who had (1) individually read this text, (2) communally heard this text, or (3) both. Assuming it was probably one of the latter two, this provides further evidence of a cultural assumption that there were widespread communal reading events, regardless of religious connections.

The seventh location is Corinth. While Paul was there, Luke says, he addressed both Jews and Greeks in the synagogue every Sabbath in order to persuade them (18:4). The synagogue, however, was not the only place in Corinth where Paul held communal reading events. When he left the synagogue, he would enter a house, where many Corinthians had the opportunity to hear him proclaim the word of God, believe the message, and be baptized (18:7–11). Luke states that he stayed there for one year and six months, teaching the word of God (18:11).

The eighth location is Ephesus (18:19). And even though this is not a new location or venue in Acts or in the ministry of Paul, Luke again recounts that Paul went into the synagogue and addressed the Jews. There is nothing in this account that suggests he was debating them via Scripture, but the author does explicitly mention the synagogue here.

During his time there, Luke also states that the Jews brought him before "the tribunal" because he was persuading people to worship God in a way contrary to the law (18:12–13). Two brief points are worth noting here. First, regardless of its exact location in Corinth or whether it has been excavated or not, "the tribunal" (τὸ βῆμα) would have been another place known for public recitations. Second, the charge brought against Paul is his mishandling of the law. Apparently, even Gallio, the proconsul of Achaia, was able to identify this disagreement as something pertaining to small textual matters ("words and names and your own law"; 18:15) that should be resolved between them without his intervention.[84] Of the seven oral or writ-

---

"Informal rhetorical socialization provides a far more credible explanation than does formal education for the nature of Paul's rhetoric." *Rethinking Paul's Rhetorical Education: Comparative Rhetoric and 2 Corinthians 10–13*, ECL 10 (Atlanta: SBL, 2013), 310.

84. For several examples of such arguments among ancient intellectuals over words, grammar, and style, see Craig Keener, *Acts: An Exegetical Commentary,* vol. 3, *15:1–23:35* (Grand Rapids: Baker Academic, 2014), 2771–72.

ten speeches of non-Christians in Acts,[85] this one comes the closest to identifying that communal reading events operated as a control over traditions.[86] Because Gallio will not settle the matter and puts the problem back into the hands of the Jewish accusers, Luke states that "the official of the synagogue," Sosthenes, who either replaced or joined Crispus, the other synagogue leader in Corinth (18:8), was beaten (18:17).

Paul's third missionary journey (18:24–21:16) includes three locations for our purposes here: Ephesus, Achaia, and Miletus. The first of these four locations, Ephesus, is Paul's "longest sustained ministry in one area in Acts, showing what a mission in a given locale might look like."[87] If his time in this area truly does provide the reader with insights into what his ministry might have typically looked like, then it will be all the more important to determine what Luke emphasizes during Paul's time there. As will be shown, one emphasis is communal reading events, which coincides well with other New Testament writings referring to Ephesus (such as the explicit mention of a synagogue at this location in 18:19, the circular letter to Ephesus, or the church in Ephesus that is addressed in Revelation).

Acts 18:24 starts with a Jew named Apollos. Luke states that Apollos is a native of Alexandria, a learned man (ἀνὴρ λόγιος),[88] and "well-versed in the scriptures" (18:24), suggesting he is well able to preach, teach, and debate. Apparently, though, his abilities were unable to mask his content. While in the synagogue, a couple in the audience, Priscilla and Aquila, hear his teaching and determine it is not wholly accurate. They proceed to correct his theology after he is done (18:26). This clearly demonstrates a quality control in relation to a communal reading event.

Before arriving at the second location, Achaia, one group of "brothers" in Ephesus wrote a letter to a group of "disciples" in Achaia so that they will welcome Apollos (18:27). "There are Christians in Ephesus besides Priscilla and Aquila," writes Jervell, "who

---

85. The other six speeches are as follows: Gamaliel (5:35–39), Demetrius (19:25–27), the Ephesian town clerk (19:35–40), Claudius Lysias (23:26–30), Tertullus (24:2–8), and Festus (25:24–27).

86. For a discussion on the speeches in Acts, and the clear indication that the author worked within ancient conventions by consulting existing material for his compositions, see Keener, *Acts: An Exegetical Commentary,* 1:87–98.

87. Bock, *Acts,* 596.

88. BDAG 598. Cf. Patrick L. Dickerson, "Apollos in Acts and First Corinthians" (PhD diss., University of Virginia, 1998), 130–32.

apparently also belonged to the synagogue. In a sense, a Christian congregation."[89] This is thus another example of how groups encouraged other communities: written correspondence intended to be read aloud communally (cf. 2 Cor 3:1–3; Rom 16:1–2; Col 4:10; Pliny *Epi.* 1.24.1–2).[90] Once Apollos arrives, Luke emphasizes the influence of communal reading events by stating, "for he powerfully refuted the Jews in public, showing by the scriptures that the Messiah is Jesus" (18:28). Even if Luke did not explicitly state that it was from the Scriptures, the context certainly suggests it, such as Luke's use of "public" to emphasize the communal nature of the event. In addition, being able to construct plausible arguments in public debates with Jews necessitates Scripture. This is another reason why I have argued elsewhere in our study that Luke often seems to assume texts were being read and recited more than he explicitly states it.

Continuing his ministry in Ephesus for another three months, Paul participates in communal reading events again in the local synagogue (19:8). Francis Watson argues convincingly that Paul must have been able to make solid arguments from Scripture to convince the Jews that he was reading the law and the prophets accurately.[91] But besides "reasoning" (cf. 17:2; 18:19) and "persuading" them in the synagogue, he meets with a group of disciples in "the lecture hall of Tyrannus" for two years, and teaches them every day. Given that Ephesus was a focal point for rhetorical training, hosted numerous Sophist luminaries, and had at least one designated "lecture hall," Keener considers several key points that are also germane to our study:

- "Securing use of an official lecture hall meant that Paul no longer played the role of a street corner Cynic . . . , user of public buildings, or lecturer at banquets; he was now a recognized teacher of philosophy in Ephesus, with his own students, listen-

---

89. "Es gibt also Christen in Ephesus ausser Priszilla und Aquila die offenbar auch zur Synagoge gehören. In dem Sinne also eine christliche Gemeinde." Jervell, *Die Apostelgeschichte*, 471.

90. For a list of frequent letter and letter-writing terms in Greek, see chapter 4 of M. Luther Stirewalt Jr., "Greek Terms for Letter and Letter-Writing from Homer through the Second Century C.E.," in *Studies in Ancient Greek Epistolography*, ed. Marvin A. Sweeney (Atlanta: Scholars, 1993), 67–87. For letters of recommendation, see Stanley K. Stowers, *Letter Writing in Greco-Roman Antiquity*, ed. Wayne A. Meeks (Philadelphia: Westminster, 1986), 153–65. Although the New Testament does not contain a pure letter of recommendation, passages such as this one confirm their existence. See Hans-Josef Klauck, *Ancient Letters and the New Testament: A Guide to Context and Exegesis* (Waco, TX: Baylor University Press, 2006), 72–77, esp. 76.

91. *Paul and the Hermeneutics of Faith* (London: T&T Clark, 2004).

ers, and patrons."[92]

- "Christianity's common goals as a teaching movement in a Mediterranean context would lead to its appearing like a philosophic school."[93]

- "Both Luke and Paul lead us to expect that Paul would have used the Scriptures for texts."[94]

Combining these observations with those of our study further supports the broader idea that Christians were involved in a didactic movement that relied heavily on the use of texts. More specifically, a cumulative argument can be made from this verse in favor of the reading and use of texts in this particular location. In addition, the multiplication of gatherings and further publicity allowed "all" in the province of Asia—"both Jews and Greeks"—to come hear "the word of the Lord" that Paul addressed them with, most likely from physical texts (19:9–10).

In addition to the many communal events at various locations in Ephesus, Luke describes two other details worth our consideration. First, some itinerant Jewish exorcists had apparently heard one or more communal reading events that Paul led in order to attempt an exorcism by mentioning Jesus, whom Paul preaches (19:13). Paul's success in the local communal reading and teaching/preaching events prompted this group to imitate him. This same type of imitation is pervasive in Greco-Roman communal reading events (see chapters 4 and 5),[95] and it seems to counter claims that "there is almost no evidence of outsiders paying attention to Christian social formation until the early second century CE."[96] Second, not only did these men attend events of Paul, there seems to be no doubt that they conducted their own communal reading events. This is stated most explicitly in

92. Keener, *Acts: An Exegetical Commentary*, 3:2831.

93. Ibid., 3:2831–32. See also Knut Backhaus's study on how Luke uses the Tyrannus lecture hall in order to further support Luke's view that the gospel is penetrating the pluralistic, non-Christian marketplace of ideas. "Im Hörsaal des Tyrannus (Apg 19.9): Von der Langlebigkeit des Evangeliums in kurzatmiger Zeit," *ThGl* 91, no. 1 (2001): 4–23.

94. Keener, *Acts: An Exegetical Commentary*, 3:2833.

95. Although he does not link communal reading events with how many authors would have been able to borrow from (or plagiarize) other literary works, see Winrich Löhr, "The Theft of the Greeks: Christian Self Definition in the Age of the Schools," *Revue d'histoire ecclésiastique* 95 (2000): 403–26.

96. Robert M. Royalty, "Don't Touch *This* Book! Revelation 22:18–19 and the Rhetoric of Reading (in) the Apocalypse of John," *BibInt* 12, no. 3 (2004): 282–99, here 286.

verse 19, where Luke states that a large number of people collected their books and burned them in the presence of everyone. This public demonstration is not the only significant point here. The verse gives a monetary calculation for the magic books alone that were burned, which was worth 50,000 silver coins.[97] Besides revealing the demise of a significant amount of texts written down and available for communal readings,[98] it further helps define what Luke states in verse 20 in relation to the Christian movement. Whereas these magic books decreased, "in this way" the word of the Lord increased and prevailed. The "word of the Lord" here probably refers to written texts and not merely oral proclamation, in light of this explicit comparison.

The third, and final, location is Miletus. From this place, Paul writes a letter to be read communally by the elders in Ephesus (20:17). When they arrive, Paul delivers the only speech made to an exclusively Christian audience in Luke's account. In this speech, Paul explicitly states that he had consistently taught in public and private everywhere he went, and will continue to do so in the future, with Jerusalem being his next stop (20:20–22). He has modeled, therefore, a pattern for the leaders to emulate. And since Paul still knows that some people will still teach perversions of the truth (20:30), he exhorts them to exercise a quality control (20:31) over the message he entrusts to them (20:32).

The author of Luke ends his second volume in Rome. For our purposes, four verses will be highlighted. First, as people gathered together at Paul's "lodgings" in Rome, Luke states that he tried to "convince" them from the Law, Moses, and the Prophets (28:23). Again, his communal gatherings are necessarily rooted in the Jewish scriptures. It is not difficult to suspect that Paul might even be reading Isa 6:9 to them in 28:26–27, according to Luke, especially given that the words are "substantially as they appear in the LXX."[99] This substantial agreement suggests that Paul was reading. Either way, for two years, Paul continues meeting with people (28:30), preaching and teaching communally (28:31), and there is little doubt he did this

97. Cf. Suetonius *Octavian* 31.

98. See Andrew T. Wilburn, Materia Magica: *The Archaeology of Magic in Roman Egypt, Cyprus, and Spain: New Texts from Ancient Cultures* (Ann Arbor: University of Michigan Press, 2013); idem., *The Greek Magical Papyri in Translation, Including the Demotic Spells*, ed. Hans Dieter Betz (Chicago: University of Chicago Press, 1986).

99. Barrett, *A Critical and Exegetical Commentary*, 2:1244.

in the same way as elsewhere via communal teaching and reading events.

Beyond locating and mapping communal reading events in Acts, there are also a number of indicators that Acts itself was written to be read communally. Three of them will be addressed here. First, Luke's two volumes are arguably focused more on communal reading events than are any other writings in the New Testament, which would suggest that the author expects his work to also be read communally. Luke is well aware that people were compiling these types of accounts and reading them communally—as his writings show more than any other New Testament writings.

Second, the opening verse (1:1) points to Luke's first volume, which he presumably meant to be read and understood communally (see my discussion of the Gospel of Luke). One solution regarding the stated audience of both works is that Luke's implied audience is anyone like Theophilus. Another option is that Theophilus was merely the most important reader to mention. Bede understands the name as functioning for an implied reader.[100] Loveday Alexander imagines, "If this scene [in Acts 28] is a window into the real intended audience of Luke's work (as I am increasingly inclined to think it may be), then we might see Luke's relation to Theophilus as a humbler parallel to Josephus' relations with the Herodian family in Rome in the 80s and 90s."[101] Richard Pervo states that Theophilus's name "readily yields to a symbolic interpretation," especially since there are no other details provided.[102] Moreover, even if he were not a symbolic figure, our study would strengthen the theory that he had a background in Judaism in the synagogue, since Luke was a non-Jew yet his account is saturated with references to the Jewish Scriptures and to communal reading events.

Third, Luke seems to assume that many details can be filled in by the reader(s) of his account. For example, Barrett notes regarding 2:22, "It is assumed that the hearers (from personal knowledge)—and equally the readers (from Luke's first volume?)—can fill in the details for themselves (καθὼς αὐτοὶ οἴδατε)."[103] He likewise states as regards

100. "Theophilus interpretatur dei amator uel a deo amatus. Quicumque ergo dei amator est ad se scriptum credat, suae hic animae quia. Lucas medicus scripsit inueniat salutem." Bede, *Expositio Actuum Apostolorum*, ed. Max L. W. Laistner (Brepols: Turnholt, 1983), 6.

101. "What if Luke Had Never Met Theophilus?," *BibInt* 8 (2000): 161–70, here 165.

102. *Acts*, ed. Harold W. Attridge (Minneapolis: Fortress Press, 2009), 35. Cf. Diogn. 1.

103. Barrett, *Acts*, 1.130–31.

20:30, "Strictly, ὑμεῖς should refer to the Ephesian elders, who are being addressed, but Luke is probably now thinking of the church at large."[104]

THE PAULINE CORPUS

ROMANS

There is no doubt that Paul's letter to the Romans was written to multiple Christian communities in Rome ("To all God's beloved in Rome, who are called to be saints"; 1:7)—whether they be Jew, Gentile, or both.[105] In fact, at the close of the letter, Paul instructs the church in Rome to greet numerous individuals, house churches, and families (16:3–16).[106] While there are probably many reasons why Paul did this, Douglas Moo mentions one in particular that specifically pertains to our study: "A public recognition—the request for greetings were probably read aloud to the assembled church—of those Christians in Rome whom Paul already knows would encourage them to think favorably of him and remind the church as a whole of the number of 'supporters' he already has."[107] This implies a significant Christian network just in Rome that would probably have had the opportunity (and obligation) to read Paul's letter communally.

Bypassing any attempt to determine a specific or general makeup of the congregation(s) or purpose(s) of the letter, then, it can be assumed with a high degree of certainty that this letter was written to be read communally in churches throughout Rome, whether by Phoebe or someone else.[108] Nevertheless, several key indicators will

104. Ibid., 979.

105. See also the use of second-person plural pronouns and verbs throughout the letter, for example, in 15:15.

106. For the view that Paul wrote to a much wider audience than the Roman Church alone, see, among others, Peter Lampe, *From Paul to Valentinus: Christians at Rome in the First Two Centuries*, ed. Marshall D. Johnson, trans. Michael Steinhauser (Minneapolis: Fortress Press, 2003); Brevard S. Childs, *The Church's Guide to Reading Paul: The Canonical Shape of the Pauline Corpus* (Grand Rapids: Eerdmans, 2008), esp. 65–69.

107. *The Epistle to the Romans* (Grand Rapids: Eerdmans, 1996), 918.

108. Many creative solutions have been offered to account for how Paul's letter to the Romans would have been originally delivered and received, such as Allan Chapple, "Getting *Romans* to the Right Romans: Phoebe and the Delivery of Paul's Letter," *TynBull* 62, no. 2 (2011): 195–214. That debate, however, is outside the scope of our study. The only importance for our study is the one that seems to be agreed upon by all scholars: Romans was read communally.

be noted here to further strengthen the communal reading event links with other works noted in our study.

Paul especially seems to stress (and assume) people's exposure to communal reading events in chapters 2 and 3. For example, one major difference Paul chooses to feature between Jews and Gentiles is their attendance at specific communal reading events, namely, Jewish ones that included the law. In 2:13, he states that Gentiles, not hearing the law read communally, demonstrate by their actions that they are following the law because it is written on their hearts. Paul uses this analogy to make a stronger point in the following verses: reading the law in their communal reading events weekly instructs the Jews (2:18). Moo writes, "The Jews' knowledge of God's will and their approval of the things that mattered the most came through their exposure to the instruction of the law in the synagogue and elsewhere."[109] Not only have they been given "the written code" (2:27) and "entrusted with the oracles of God" (3:2), but they get to hear it read communally every week. Again, Paul highlights here that one of the greatest benefits and distinctions the Jews had is that God has given them the Scriptures, which they read and hear communally every week. And because of it, after providing a series of quotations from the Jewish Scriptures (3:10–18), Paul assumes his audience already knows (οἴδαμεν) whatever the written law says, and when it speaks, every mouth will be silent (3:19; cf. 7:1, 7). Regardless of what Paul specifically means by "the law" here, we can be sure that one of the implications of his remarks is that the Jews understand what it means to live in the sphere of a text that is read communally.

Now some scholars have argued that the New Testament writers, and characters included in their discourses, have misjudged their audiences' capabilities or even fabricated them. For example, with regard to the apostle Paul, Christopher Stanley argues that scholars "need a realistic set of assumptions concerning the literary capabilities of Paul's first-century audience."[110] True as that statement is, and despite the many who have taken issue with his stance,[111] he barely

109. Moo, *The Epistle to the Romans*, 161.

110. "'Pearls before Swine': Did Paul's Audiences Understand His Biblical Quotations?," *NovT* 41, no. 2 (1999): 124–44, here 144.

111. See Brian J. Abasciano, "Diamonds in the Rough: A Reply to Christopher Stanley Concerning the Reader Competency of Paul's Original Audiences," *NovT* 49 (2007): 153–83. See also the more recent critiques and insights by Matthew S. Harmon, "Letter Carriers and Paul's Use of Scripture," *JSPL* 4, no. 2 (2014): 129–48, esp. 130–31; Christopher Seitz, "Jewish Scripture for Gentile Churches: Human Destiny and the Future of the Pauline Correspondence, Part

mentions the influence of communal reading events anywhere among the ten assumptions he offers and critiques. Moreover, when he does mention them, he seems to downplay them significantly in order to promote his belief that because very few people would have had access to texts or the literate ability to use them, Paul must have assumed too much from the recipients of his letters and implied readers. As our study seeks to demonstrate, communal reading events were widespread enough to suggest that the writers of what later became the New Testament and characters included in their discourses probably did not underestimate their audiences' abilities to be familiar with literary works—especially sacred texts. "Yet even if most of the members of Paul's original audiences were ignorant of Scripture," argues Abasciano, "corporate realities and processes surrounding Scripture and his letters in his churches would effectively offset this factor."[112] At a bare minimum, it is not difficult to imagine that there would have been different levels of recognition within any given audience, yielding different levels of rhetorical impact.

With that in mind, a proper understanding of the first-century background of communal reading events is one reason why it was natural for Paul to ask certain questions in this letter, such as "What does the Scripture say?" (4:3). Paul seems to have a realistic expectation for the churches, similar to ones he would have for Jewish congregations. For example, in chapter 10, Paul mentions that they have heard the message of the gospel (vv. 8, 14, 15), and even had the opportunity of hearing the actual voices of some of its messengers (14, 17, 18). Someone must preach the message. "But a preacher is nothing more than a herald," writes Moo, "a person entrusted by another with a message."[113] The discussion here about a preacher and a report is especially important for our study for at least two reasons. First, even though Paul is quoting scripture, "The quotation of this same text in John 12:38 suggests that it may have been a common early Christian 'testimonium' used to explain and justify in Scripture the Jews' unbelief."[114] If that is the case, then it helps explain why Paul mentions that the gospel has been proclaimed to the whole world (=

1: Romans," *ProEccl* 23, no. 3 (2014): 294–308; Bruce N. Fisk, "Synagogue Influence and Scriptural Knowledge among the Christians of Rome," in *As It Is Written: Studying Paul's Use of Scripture*, ed. Stanley E. Porter and Christopher D. Stanley (Atlanta: SBL, 2008), 157–85.

112. Abasciano, "Diamonds in the Rough," 183.

113. Moo, *The Epistle to the Romans*, 663.

114. Ibid., 665n23.

Roman Empire). Even with a level of exaggeration assumed, Paul is asserting that the whole world has had an opportunity to hear the gospel because Christian communal reading events were widespread (even by the time he is writing this letter in the 50s). This would further strengthen Moo's argument that "it cannot be lack of opportunity, then, that explains why so few Jews have come to experience the salvation God offers in Christ."[115] Just as the Jews have always had the opportunity to hear the Law of Moses read every week, they now also have the opportunity to hear Paul's gospel read every week.[116]

Another significant point to consider is the concept of the office of teaching that this letter mentions (12:7). Paul references the teacher, rather than the gift of teaching. As Moo notes, "Teaching . . . involves the passing on of the truth of the gospel as it has been preserved in the church."[117] Part of this specific type of ministry is the public reading of Scriptures. This element is especially evident in several places in the New Testament, most explicitly in 1 Timothy 4:13. For our purposes, Romans 12:7 is another passage suggesting that the office of teaching emerged relatively quickly, and part of teaching is the ability to read and interpret texts for the community.

Within Christian communities, Paul still feels that "everything that was written in former times" (15:4) was written for them. G. K. Beale and D. A. Carson write, "The writers of the NT books saw themselves not (in some Marcionite fashion) as originators who could cheerfully dispense with whatever they wanted from the OT, but as those who stood under the authority of those documents even as they promulgated fresh interpretations of those documents."[118] In other words, Paul does not reject Jewish writings that have been read communally throughout the centuries, but rather maintains their central role in the life of Christian communities. In fact, this is probably one reason why Paul considers them competent enough to instruct one another (15:14). It is not difficult to demonstrate that many of these writings were still being read communally during the gatherings of the early church, even if we cannot determine exactly what and how much they did. A similar idea can be found in 1 Maccabees 12:9:

115. Ibid., 667.
116. "When Paul refers to 'my gospel,' he does not mean a particular form of teaching peculiar to him, but the gospel, common to all Christians, which has been entrusted by God to Paul for his preservation and proclamation (cf. 1:1)." Ibid., 155.
117. Ibid., 767.
118. G. K. Beale and D. A. Carson, eds., *Commentary on the New Testament Use of the Old Testament* (Grand Rapids: Baker Academic, 2007), vii.

"Therefore, though we have no need of these things, since we have as encouragement the holy books that are in our hands."

All of these verses together suggest and assume ample exposure to both the written law and apostolic teaching in synagogues and elsewhere in Rome. Likewise, there is little doubt that Paul was under the impression that his letter to the Romans would be read communally in Rome.

1 CORINTHIANS

The first letter in the New Testament to the church of God in Corinth states that it is from two people (1:1) and is meant for both the church in Corinth and those everywhere who call on the name of our Lord Jesus Christ (1:2). The communal nature of this letter is also evident throughout it. As seen in other letters, Paul uses second-person plural language. Moreover, he speaks of multiple communities (1:11),[119] various leaders (1:12), and previously written communication between them (5:1, 11; 7:1). In fact, this letter assumes multiple written correspondences that would offer examples of nonscriptural texts being read communally (1 Cor 5:9; cf. 2 Cor 2:1–4)—a point further underscoring that literature, Scripture, and letters were widely used.

Paul also seems to stress that his letter is to act as a control, in the sense that he can explicitly state, "Nothing beyond what is written" (4:6). Regardless of what writing(s) he is referring to,[120] the reference is clearly to a written text that this community is meant to judge others according to. This is why he states in 4:14 that he is writing these things and not just passing them on orally. It can be inferred that Paul is writing to the people in his churches, even calling them his children, so that his letters will be read communally and words heeded. One of the strongest terms he uses for this type of control is found in the next verse, 4:15. He emphasizes their relationship in familial terms by using the term *guardian*. By doing so, he softens the blunt-

119. For more information on the social distinctions within the Corinthian congregations and how many communities there probably were, see Gerd Theissen, *The Social Setting of Pauline Christianity: Essays on Corinth*, trans. John H. Schultz (Philadelphia: Fortress Press, 1982).

120. Although he opts for "Scripture" being the best interpretation, see several other interpretative proposals, such as a public document the Corinth church adapted for their purposes, listed by Joseph A. Fitzmyer, *First Corinthians: A New Translation with Introduction and Commentary* (New Haven: Yale University Press, 2008), 215–16.

ness that comes next, essentially saying, "I want to remind you of my teaching, which is similar to everywhere" (4:17). Gordon Fee notes that Paul "expects the letter also to take the place of his presence . . . to remind them that what he and Timothy have taught them is in keeping with what is taught in the church universally, at least in all the Pauline churches."[121] This written letter, then, also functions as a reference point that can be used to verify the content of what is being taught.

A few chapters later, in 11:2, Paul mentions the traditions he delivered to them. Claire Smith specifically refers to this passage when discussing how communities—not any one community or individual—were called to "preserve the integrity of the content, ensure its perpetuity . . . and continue to be instructed by it."[122] Such educational activities associated with texts, traditions, and the guarding and keeping of the apostolic deposit played a significant role in early Christian communities, such as those in Corinth. The traditions Paul has in mind are probably drawn from the Jewish scriptures and some of the common written Christian tradition. By recalling what he has already taught them, he reinforces his consistency. Still, several interpretive options are available regarding what he is referring to here. Is he referring to traditions like that in 11:23? Does he mean teachings like that in 15:3? Is he simply being sarcastic, since there is not one example in the letter to indicate that the Corinthians have followed anything he has said? One solution that has not, to my knowledge, been proposed makes even greater sense here: they are keeping in their possession what he has written to them. There is no evidence that they have disregarded or changed the writings they have received. According to BDAG, κατέχω can be rendered with the idea of possessing or holding something tangible, like land (Ezek 33:24), goods (1 Cor 7:30), another person (Luke 4:42), or writing tablets (Eup. 4:4).[123] Furthermore, later in the same chapter (11:23), Paul speaks of a formal process of handing on the Jesus tradition, one that requires his readers to suppose that it already existed and was transmitted.

Following this discussion of traditions, he speaks for the first time in his extant letters of the ministry of teachers (12:28–29). Though

---

121. *The First Epistle to the Corinthians* (Grand Rapids: Eerdmans, 1987), 189.

122. *Pauline Communities as 'Scholastic Communities,'* WUNT 335 (Tübingen: Mohr Siebeck, 2012), 161–62.

123. Cf. *TDNT* 2.829–30.

there is no way to be sure what exactly he meant by it, or how it ought to be manifested, the fact that teaching developed in communities this early suggests that it emerged relatively quickly for reasons of quality control. This needs to be held in tension with reading and interpreting the Scriptures, which was a primary focus in the early church.

One example of this communal control can be seen in chapter 14. According to 14:26, the exhortation is to do everything in view of the edification of the church. Take, then, the assumption that everybody should and could bring a Psalm. It is unlikely that they composed their own psalms. The more natural reading and better option, then, seems to be that they would have chosen to bring with them one of the many Old Testament Psalms, either literally or figuratively.[124] In other words, this would not have been a viable assumption on Paul's part if these communities did not hear texts read communally, did not have access to them at an individual level, or both. My position is that the churches in those days had no more difficulty getting writing material or literary works than the surrounding culture. A problem New Testament writers address periodically is that certain members of the communities do not demonstrate having great skills of discernment between bad and good interpretations and claims based upon various literary works.

Moreover, as opposed to a written lesson to the church, if someone gives a purely oral one (either as prophecy or in tongues), then there must be someone to interpret or "weigh" it (14:27–33). Moreover, anyone who thinks he or she is a prophet or spiritual must acknowledge the writings of Paul that are read communally (14:37–38). In other words, the members of the church had to evaluate all messages communally to discern if they were from God, and something that was purely oral—with no referent point or written text behind it—was to be questioned. Incidentally, this type of instruction is for *all* congregations (14:33). The reasoning seems to be that if God is the one who brings good order and harmony to community worship, then there ought to be some consistency and overlap. In other words, if the edification of the church is the key, as the preceding verses suggest, then there ought to be orderliness to it so that everyone can discern, learn, and be encouraged.

---

124. For the major role communal reading and singing of the corpus of Psalms played, see Douglas Burton-Christie, *The Word in the Desert: Scripture and the Quest for Holiness in Early Christian Monasticism* (Oxford: Oxford University Press, 1993).

This letter not only is meant to be read communally, but also includes arguably one of the earliest creeds found in the New Testament writings. For our purposes, there is an apparent assumption that the audience has already heard this hymn or creed read or recited communally,[125] and Paul notes that it is "in accordance with the scriptures" (1 Cor 15:3, 4).

Finally yet importantly, even his indirect commands, such as in 16:11 are expected to be obeyed by everyone in the church. Thus, if Paul expects everyone in the whole community to obey, he expects everyone in the whole community to know what he has written. One way this is accomplished is by reading it communally. In his final greetings, which require a communal reading to be effective, he mentions multiple churches (those in the province of Asia, the church that meets at Aquila and Priscilla's house, and those with Paul) that send their greetings along with Paul's letter. This assumes that they also know about this correspondence(s), and Paul ends by stating he is writing it with his own hand (16:21; cf. Gal 6:11; Phlm 19; Col 4:18; 2 Thess 3:17). Jeffery Weima observes that such a declared shift in handwriting could have been an oral device for communal reading, since it would not have been evident to the audience.[126] Even more, Paul concludes with a curse, which would have had to be read aloud to have a rhetorical impact (16:22). This is significant for our purposes for at least two interconnected reasons. First, it adds yet another rhetorical dimension to a letter already filled with such devices. As John Fotopoulos writes, "In the letter itself the apostle has used almost every persuasive technique he could muster to change their behavior [e.g., proofs, exhortation, exempla, earlier traditions, logia of Jesus, the witness of Scripture, praise, shame, irony, imminent eschatology, threats, and fear]."[127] Second, and in light of all these techniques, it is most probable that Paul ends with this specific form of argument because it casts the widest net over his audience(s), both immediate and future. As Fotopoulos further notes, "There is widespread evidence from throughout the Greco-Roman world that people of

---

125. On the prevalent reading and reciting of ancient Greek hymns and formulaic phrasings, including some at the location of Corinth, see Yuriy Lozynsky, "Ancient Greek Cult Hymns: Poets, Performers and Rituals" (PhD diss., University of Toronto, 2014).

126. "Sincerely, Paul: The Significance of the Pauline Letter Closings," in *Paul and the Ancient Letter Form*, ed. Stanley E. Porter and Sean A. Adams, PAST 6 (Leiden: Brill Academic, 2010), 307–45.

127. "Paul's Curse of Corinthians: Restraining Rivals with Fear and *Voces Mysticae* (1 Cor 16:22)," *NovT* 56 (2014): 275–309, here 302.

all social statuses fear the power of curses" (cf. Pliny the Elder, *Nat.* 28.4.19).[128]

2 CORINTHIANS

Murray Harris rightly notes, "Paul's letters were 'read aloud' *to* all the believers in particular localities . . . but not *by* them all."[129] As with Paul's first letter to the church in Corinth, his second letter is also from two people to one community (1:1). Though this would not have been a true circular letter, the combination of "all" and "whole" (similar to 1 Thess 4:10) suggests a substantial number of believers in Achaia beyond Corinth who probably would have had access to Paul's letter via the church in Corinth.[130] In 1:13, he does write that they might all read it (ἀναγινώσκετε)—not just one person. Paul seems to state that in none of his previous letters to the church did they need to seek a meaning beyond what was written. All the church needed to do was read his letter communally, since there were no hidden meanings to discern.

Also similar to his first letter is the identification of multiple written correspondences. In 2:3, he refers to a correspondence that is lost, and there were presumably others (10:9).[131] There were also letters from the church (3:1), and given all of their written correspondences, he uses them in an analogy in 3:2. The figurative letter he writes about is meant to be known and read by all (ἀναγινωσκομένη). The living letter he has in mind is the one Paul helped to write: the indisputable living testimony, not the contestable written testimony. In this social context, it seems that everyone would figuratively read their metaphorical letter (i.e., living testimony) publicly just as this real letter is literally being read communally. Even more, the word order "known and read" is unique. Harris looks at lexical, logical, and stylistic explanations (i.e., a letter would have been inspected and rec-

---

128. Ibid., 289.

129. Murray J. Harris, *The Second Epistle to the Corinthians* (Grand Rapids: Eerdmans, 2005), 187. See the same Pauline terminology in 2 Cor 3:2, 15; Eph 3:4; Col 4:16; 1 Thess 5:27.

130. Ibid., 134. Cf. George H. Guthrie, *2 Corinthians* (Grand Rapids: Baker Academic, 2015), 58–60.

131. In fact, Paul wrote probably many unpreserved letters. "Indeed," Harris writes, "we may safely assume that the majority of his letters to churches or individuals have not been preserved (cf. 2 Thess. 3:17; 2 Pet 3:15–16)." Harris, *The Second Epistle to the Corinthians*, 8.

ognized before read) but concludes that the overall point is that the "letter" was permanently open for universal examination.[132]

This verse has even more importance in light of our study. If communal reading events were widespread, his statement comes across more powerfully in that the members of the community ought to be a walking communal reading event for everyone at all times. Guthrie hints at this when he speaks about the "public platform" the church is playing on before the entire world.[133] This interpretation also fits well with the way he compares Jewish reading practices in the following verses (ἀναγνώσει [. . .] ἀναγινώσκηται; 3:14, 15, respectively). Paul's point here is that the Jews failed to recognize the real purpose of the old covenant when it was read publicly in the synagogue on the Sabbath. This understanding is strengthened by the combination of the preposition ἐπὶ with the dative τῇ ἀναγνώσει. According to BDAG, this phrase probably means "at the time of reading" (= a communal reading event).

Staying with this communal reading theme, Paul tells them in 4:2 not to tamper with God's word. As elsewhere, this refers to the Jewish Scriptures, the Christian message, or the gospel, but again the context suggests something that is in writing that can be read communally. Among the interpretative options, Ralph Martin argues, "More likely, what was questioned was Paul's handling of the OT and his claim that 'the veil' of 3:14–16 was removed only in Christ" (cf. Rom 9:6).[134]

There is also an interesting allegation that Paul addresses in this letter: the allegation that his speaking is unimpressive but his letters are weighty and forceful (10:10). One important thing this suggests is that the communal reading of what Paul wrote might have differed significantly from the way he would have expressed it in person. It is also likely that this allegation reveals that the written content was more important than the presentation of it in Christian communities, especially in comparison with certain Jewish communal reading event expectations, such as the ones mentioned in Qumran's Damascus Document (4Q266), even though there is a certain level of rhetoric and exaggeration to consider.[135] Such comparisons, though, remain outside the scope of our study. For our present purposes, part

132. Ibid., 262.
133. Guthrie, *2 Corinthians*, 189.
134. *2 Corinthians*, 2nd ed., WBC 40 (Grand Rapids: Zondervan, 2014), 221.
135. The elitist attitude of the community is marked by expressions throughout the docu-

of Paul's response in 11:6 to their allegation is important to consider. He states that he may be unskilled in speaking but not in knowledge. This suggests that content was paramount and style peripheral. Harris puts it this way, "From this verse we learn that for Paul matter was more significant than manner. An accurate knowledge of the gospel (cf. v. 4) was more important than eloquence in preaching it."[136] Paul even concludes by stating this is one reason why he writes: "So that when I come, I may not have to be severe in using the authority that the Lord has given me" (13:10).

GALATIANS

Paul's letter to the Galatians is addressed to multiple churches in the region of Galatia. Several implicit indicators suggest that he expected it to be read communally among them. A few of these indicators would include such terminology as ἀκοῆς (3:2) and "brothers" (4:31). He connects the gospel firmly to Scripture, even claiming in this letter that Scripture announced the gospel ahead of time (3:8). Martinus de Boer asks at this very juncture, "Paul surely is quoting from Genesis 15:6, but will the Gentile Galatians know this, at least on a first reading? . . . We do not know what Paul intends nor whether the person who shall read the letter aloud to the Galatians will pause or wink knowingly, nor then how the Galatians will hear these words."[137] Regardless of whether the audience would identify his use of Scripture,[138] the significant point here is that this letter would have been read communally from inception and that the main way Scripture was made known to people was via the communal reading of it.

In addition to these implicit indicators, however, there are some stronger indications. For Paul to advance in Judaism, especially in light of the traditions handed down via his ancestors (1:14), his advancement must have included access to the written law, or at least portions of it, as well as the hearing of it being read during communal reading events. It is not difficult to surmise, then, that Paul replicated and assumed these two aspects in his ministry (written tes-

---

ment. For a few examples of such language, see Jonathan G. Campbell, *The Use of Scripture in the Damascus Document 1–8, 19–20*, BZAW 228 (Berlin: De Gruyter, 1995).

136. Harris, *The Second Epistle to the Corinthians*, 750.

137. *Galatians: A Commentary* (Louisville: Westminster John Knox, 2011), 189.

138. See Ciampa, *Scripture in Galatians 1 and 2*; Dan Batovici, "A Few Notes on the Use of the Scripture in Galatians," *Sacra Scripta* 11, no. 2 (2013): 287–301.

timony handed down and the reading of it), as seen in this letter. Five examples should suffice here. First, he explicitly references the Book of the Law (3:10). Second, he quotes Scripture (3:13). Third, he uses first-person plural pronouns and verbs (3:13–4). Fourth, he continues mounting his arguments from Scripture, even down to a single word (3:16). According to Douglas Moo, "While Paul's claim resembles Jewish interpretation of his day at the level of his exegetical technique, he is, in fact, operating with certain hermeneutical axioms that provide warrant for his interpretation."[139] Fifth, one purpose for providing "warrant for his interpretation" is that his audience will be hearing Paul's letter read communally, and they apparently have not exercised a quality control over the same traditions they have heard, since he is attempting to persuade them that they are wrong.

In chapter 4, at least three verses support the contention that this letter was read communally: 20, 21, and 30. In verse 20, Paul wishes he could be present with them so that they would actually hear the tone of his voice. Beyond the simple rhetoric, this also suggests that the reader would not match his intended tone perfectly, or an additional aspect would be conveyed via his own tone of voice. In other words, it is not the content or message that might be different in person but rather the tone of voice with which he would deliver it. In verse 21, Paul poses a question: "Tell me, you who desire to be subject to the law, will you not listen to the law?" The answer is yes and no. Yes, they "hear [= listen to]" the law read every week. But no, they do not "hear [= understand and obey]" what is being read every week. He concludes this section by asking another question in verse 30: "But what does the scripture say?" He cites scriptural warrant for how he wants the Galatians to apply what they are hearing. Paul's letter, then, should not sound like new words simply from Paul, but rather old ones from the Pentateuch that they have already heard communally.

The final two indicators addressed here are in 5:2 and 6:6. In 5:2, Paul again wants them to imagine Paul is speaking to them as they all hear his letter being read communally: "Listen!" This reader and audience assumption complements well Paul's command in 6:6: "Those who are taught the word must share in all good things with their teacher." Regardless of whether the command is passive or active, the point in relation to our study is that there is a shared responsibility

---

139. *Galatians* (Grand Rapids: Baker Academic, 2013), 230.

during Christian communal reading events, and this is further evidence of such assumed communal reading practices (cf. 1 Cor 9:14).

EPHESIANS

More than many other New Testament writings, there is strong evidence to suggest that the letter to the Ephesians was meant to be a circular letter.[140] The strongest external evidence for this interpretation is the textual tradition of the first verse (1:1), which often omits the words "in Ephesus." Internally, many of the impersonal features, general characterizations, and lack of situational details found in the letter strengthen this interpretation. Yet even if the words "in Ephesus" are original, scholars such as Rainer Schwindt still argue from this view that the circular-letter hypothesis is correct—not least of all because the word *church* is absent.[141]

The importance of this letter circulating among the churches throughout the whole Roman province of Asia is obvious in relation to our study, but only if it can also be demonstrated that it was meant to be read communally. Several specific passages will be noted here that buttress such a claim.

Regardless of how many churches actually received this letter, there is no doubt that the author was addressing a community of believers (1:1), and not any one individual. Likewise, as seen elsewhere in our study, the appearance of second-person plural pronouns and verbs, along with common phrases and terms used of the believers collectively hearing words of truth, such as in 1:13, are indicators of communal reading events. Fortunately, however, the author does not just presume this context but explicitly states his assumption that this community is also reading texts such as this letter communally. In 3:4, he states, "When you read this, you can perceive my understanding of the mystery of Christ." His statement here comes right after he presumably refers to another document that the audience would have also received and read communally ("you have already heard of the commission . . . as I wrote above in a few words"; 3:2–3).

---

140. Although authorship debates are outside the scope of our study, for a few key reasons why I accept Pauline authorship, see Harold W. Hoehner, *Ephesians: An Exegetical Commentary* (Grand Rapids: Baker Academic, 2002), 2–61.

141. *Das Weltbild des Epheserbriefes*, WUNT 148 (Tübingen: Mohr Siebeck, 2002), 55–62, esp. 60. Cf. Clinton E. Arnold, *Ephesians: Exegetical Commentary on the New Testament* (Grand Rapids: Zondervan, 2010), 23–29.

PHILIPPIANS

Paul's letter to the Philippians is written to "all the saints in Christ Jesus" at Philippi. By addressing "all" multiple times in his introduction (vv. 1, 3, 7, 8), he is not only promoting unity but also assuming that his letter will be read communally. Further evidence for this same assumption can be seen in the final verse of the opening chapter. In v. 30, Paul reminds the saints of the previous suffering they saw with their eyes (1 Thess 2:2; Acts 16:16–40), but he also refers to his current suffering that they "now hear."

As Paul continues, he includes a poem or hymn in chapter 2 (vv. 6–11).[142] Matters of authorship, interpretation, and literary form, do not affect our present concern. Whoever authored this work, whatever it means, and whether it was a poem or a hymn do not change the fact that there is widespread agreement that it was at least heard communally in Pauline circles. The communal reading of the letter to the Philippians supports this view.

As the congregation continues to hear this letter read communally, Paul gives them a visual image of himself in chapter 3. In verse 18, he says, "And now I tell you even with tears." John Reumann argues, "I now speak (legō) reflects how the letter was to be read aloud in Philippi. . . . The apostle speaks authoritatively through letter and messenger."[143] Assuming his letter is being read communally, Paul speaks to them directly, as if he is present with them.[144] Similarly, while addressing the entire community, Paul can and does on occa-

142. Benjamin Edsall and Jennifer R. Strawbridge recently argued that these verses should not be called a hymn, but rather heightened prose. "The Songs We Used to Sing? Hymn 'Traditions' and Reception in Pauline Letters," *JSNT* 37, no. 3 (2015): 290–311. They reach this conclusion by surveying ancient pagan definitions of ὕμνος and the reception of these classical passages in early Christian writings. Though they rightly note in their conclusion that their argument is largely based on silence (306), it is interesting that they did not incorporate many other pagan authors who use the terminology in the first century, such as Plutarch (*Mor.* 4.36), Philo (*Agr.* 18; *Plant.* 33; *Somn.* 1.7), and Arrian (*Alex.* 1.4.11), or more importantly Jewish Scripture, such as the Psalms, but rather seem to rely solely on figures like Plato, Theon, and Quintilian. The burden of proof, then, does not necessarily shift to those who still see it as a poem or hymn as they suggest (306). Cf. also Michael W. Martin and Bryan A. Nash, "Philippians 2:6–11 as Subversive *Hymnos*: A Study in the Light of Ancient Rhetorical Theory," *JTS* 66, no. 1 (2015): 90–138.

143. *Philippians: A New Translation with Introduction and Commentary* (New Haven: Yale University Press, 2008), 593.

144. For some more observations of this feature in letter writing, see Mathilde Cambron-Goulet, "Orality in Philosophical Epistles," in *Between Orality and Literacy: Communication and the Adaptation in Antiquity*, ed. Ruth Scodel, MnS 367 (Leiden: Brill, 2014), 10:148–74.

sion speak to specific people, such as Euodia and Syntyche, through the letter as if he is there (4:2). Regarding these women, G. Walter Hansen notes, "[Paul's] reference to them by name in a letter to be read to the whole church appropriately and understandably identifies a major cause of the problem of disunity addressed in numerous ways throughout the entire letter. Paul's call for these two women to *be of the same mind* in the Lord repeats his major challenge to the entire community [in 2:2]."[145]

Before ending with his final greetings, Paul commands the church in Philippi to put into practice what they learned, received, heard, and saw in him (4:9). All four of these verbs are important for many reasons, but "received" will be singled out here, since it can be used for receiving written tradition (Mark 7:4; 1 Cor 15:3; 1 Thess 2:13; 2 Thess 3:6).[146] Here are just two extra-biblical examples:

> And I suppose that the thing will seem incredible to those who will read [παραληψομένοις] my narrative in the future. (*Letter of Aristeas* 296)

> It is too much to set forth now the quotations of Heracleon taken from the book entitled *The Preaching of Peter* and read them [παραλαμβανόμενα], inquiring about the book whether it is genuine or spurious or compounded of both elements. (*Keryg.* 6)

Turning back to Philippians, up to this point, Paul assumes his letter is being read communally and that what he is sharing will be received in a way that the people are moved to action. This does not mean "received" only connotes the reception of *written* tradition,[147] but it appears to here.

COLOSSIANS

While the letter to the church at Colossae was probably an "occasional" letter, there is little doubt that it was read communally beyond just this location.[148] In fact, Paul explicitly states, "And when this let-

---

145. *The Letter to the Philippians* (Grand Rapids: Eerdmans, 2009), 282.

146. BDAG, 768. *TDNT* 4.13 = "To receive the fixed form, in the chain of Christian tradition, . . . To inherit the formulated laws of Christian morality, the Christian Halaka."

147. BDAG, 767–8. Cf. *NIDNTTE*, 79–85; *TDNT* 4.11–4.

148. The continuous debate about Pauline authorship is outside the scope of the issues here, but I find most persuasive the discussion and defense of Pauline authorship by Douglas J. Moo, *The Letters to the Colossians and to Philemon* (Grand Rapids: Eerdmans, 2008), 28–41.

ter has been read among you, have it read also in the church of the Laodiceans" (4:16a–b). James Dunn believes that this shows from the beginning Paul's assumption that at least some of his letters would be read communally beyond the one he specifically addresses.[149] Christopher Seitz adds, "What is not in doubt is that Paul conceives of a single letter having the capacity for further address . . . And I hold to the view that this was Paul's own conscious intention and that it informed the way he composed what he had to say."[150]

This verse also points to a quality control via communal reading groups. Paul authorizes and instructs them to read another specific letter communally: "And see that you read also the letter from Laodicea" (4:16c). More than this just being a communal reading event, then, this is an example of a non-Scriptural document being endorsed by an apostle to be read openly in church. Mathilde Cambron-Goulet compares this verse with a passage in Plato's writings and concludes, "Besides indicating that the author perceives his own epistle as 'open', encouraging the addressees to read the letter in common—rather than just pass on the letter to one another—leads to a strong sense of community, since the readers are gathered together instead of staying on their own."[151] This understanding rightly contradicts Valeriy Alikin's argument, "In the beginning, the reading of apostolic letters was not a liturgical practice. Rather these letters were read just as letters received. A letter brought by a messenger could be read by him to the addressee if he were able to do so." Without defining exactly what he means by liturgical practice, Alikin does not seem to address adequately the various ways multiple New Testament authors assumed or requested that their letters be read communally during public worship gatherings. Furthermore, Paul takes for granted that at least some communities would be ready, willing, and able to read and share such literature among and with other communities during their gatherings, even if it was not placed on the same level as Scripture. Just this one verse, then, provides a unique window into seeing how some literature would have been copied, disseminated, and collected within early Christian communities. Moreover, such apostolic endorsement here adds another dimension to the com-

---

149. James D. G. Dunn, *The Epistles to the Colossians and to Philemon* (Grand Rapids: Eerdmans, 1996), 286.

150. *Colossians* (Grand Rapids: Brazos, 2014), 191.

151. Cambron-Goulet, "Orality in Philosophical Epistles," 10:162.

munal quality control, since the endorsement requires a communal reading to be effective.

While 4:16 is the most oft cited, and explicit, verse in this book regarding communal reading events, and mentions "reading communally" more times per verse than any other verse in the New Testament, it is not the only verse that has important factors to consider in light of communal reading events. For example, the focus of 3:16 is on corporate worship. In fact, Moo states, "This verse is one of the very few that provide us with any window at all into the worship of the earliest Christians."[152] One thing that can been seen, in addition to the emphasis on teaching, is that "the word of Christ" ought to be at the center of worship, regardless of whether the phrase is translated "words from Christ" (if subjective genitive) or "words about Christ" (if objective genitive). Moreover, there are good reasons for understanding the word *Psalms* as written texts—either those of the Old Testament or newly produced Christian ones—especially given the noticeable distinction the author places between psalms and "songs from the spirit," which were more likely extemporaneous compositions. Thus, the assumption that the saints are singing written texts communally points again to the principle of reading, even if read with voice inflection and melody (cf. Rev 15:3–4; Luke 1:46b–55e). In other words, singing a written text assumes that either the text is either read enough communally to be memorized by everyone so that they can participate in unison, or participants have copies of the text, or both.

1 AND 2 THESSALONIANS

1 and 2 Thessalonians contain some of the most explicit language and indicators of communal reading events found in the New Testament.[153] In fact, no scholar to my knowledge has argued against these two letters testifying to communal reading events. Timothy Milinovich goes as far as to argue that 1 Thessalonians should be viewed

152. *The Letters to the Colossians and to Philemon* (Grand Rapids: Eerdmans, 2008), 290.

153. No one doubts that Paul wrote 1 Thessalonians, but there is a common misconception that the scholarly consensus concerning 2 Thessalonians is that it is non-Pauline. As Jeffery Weima and Paul Foster have recently demonstrated, this supposed consensus does not exist. In fact, the prevailing view across both English and German works, and that of our study, is still that it is a genuine Pauline letter. See Jeffery A. D. Weima, *1–2 Thessalonians* (Grand Rapids: Baker Academic, 2014), 46–54; Paul Foster, "Who Wrote 2 Thessalonians? A Fresh Look at an Old Problem," *JSNT* 35, no. 2 (2012): 150–75.

as an oratorical performance, given its structure, and coupled with the topics covered in the letter, he writes, "The ecclesial gathering of the community for worship stands as the context of the letter's implied performance. As they listen to the letter being read, they are aware of the empty spaces left by those now absent and departed."[154] This picture is especially noteworthy if, as many interpreters agree, 1 Thessalonians is the first Pauline letter to have been written, sometime in the 40s.[155]

With that in mind, one major aspect will be examined here regarding how widespread communal reading events may have been according to Paul. In addition, the clearest texts related to communal reading events in these two letters will be noted.

The author of these letters seems to have a genuine concern for all believers who are gathering together, even in places beyond Thessalonica. In 2:14, he mentions the "churches" that are "in Judea." Likewise, in 4:10, the author includes "all the brothers and sisters throughout Macedonia." Gordon Fee notes, "The surprising element in the sentence [v. 10], if not the whole paragraph, is his reminder of the broad nature of their current love . . . since the 'whole of Macedonia' at this time reached as far east as Philippi in the Macedonian plain and as far west as the Adriatic Sea, and thus included Berea in the middle . . . [and so] it was an ongoing concern of Paul's that his communities be aware of each other."[156]

This awareness, as seen elsewhere, included written correspondences that the churches were expected to exchange with each other and read communally (e.g., Col 4:16). The awareness of each other also suggests another feature for our study to consider: similar communal reading practices. One way in which the church in Thessalonica and the churches across the "whole of Macedonia" were unified was by the content of what they were reading. Not only does the author go on to tell them to "encourage one another with these words" (4:18), but he strongly asserts, "I solemnly command you by the Lord that this letter be read to all of them" (5:27).

Two main points are in order regarding 5:27. First, this verse is

---

154. "Memory and Hope in the Midst of Chaos: Reconsidering the Structure of 1 Thessalonians," *CBQ* 76, no. 3 (2014): 498–518, here 517.

155. Gerd Lüdemann challenges the scholarly consensus concerning the late-40s date (ca. 49 CE) and posits an early-40s date (ca. 41 CE) in his recent work, *The Earliest Christian Text: 1 Thessalonians*, rev. ed. (Salem, OR: Polebridge, 2013), esp. 75–112.

156. *The First and Second Letters to the Thessalonians* (Grand Rapids: Eerdmans, 2009), 160–61.

one of only five verses in both letters that shift from the first person plural to the first person singular (presumably the apostle Paul). Since Paul expects his letters to be read communally but does not include his typical "in my own hand" here (1 Cor 16:21; Gal 6:11; Col 4:18; 2 Thess 3:17; Philemon 19), "there are good reasons for viewing this second hortatory section and the subsequent grace benediction as an autograph."[157] Second, the charge to read (ἀναγνωσθῆναι) is not meant to be heard as merely coming from one author, but one made before "the Lord."[158] Taking these points together, one of the author's goals is to ensure his letters will be read communally, and in order to ensure this, he affirms its apostolic and divine sanction. Bernhard Oestreich further highlights a few implications the directive in this verse probably had on this community. He essentially argues that everyone was meant to have the same information and type of access to the apostle Paul, thus unifying believers.[159]

Given Paul's appeals in 1 Thessalonians to read his letters communally, 2 Thessalonians seems to assume they did read the first one communally (esp. 2:15), and will do the same with this one. In fact, one purpose of this letter appears to be a clarification and underlining of the first letter's importance—regardless of who wrote it. Bart Ehrman, for example, summarizes his view this way: "To use the language that has recently come to be in vogue, 2 Thessalonians appears to be providing 'reading instructions' for 1 Thessalonians."[160]

On top of these implicit indications, there are at least four specific verses to highlight. First, the authors state that they are aware of forged letters "as though from us" (2:2). It is not difficult to imagine that these forged letters were actually read communally. One reason they would have been read communally is that they were apparently from an apostle or other authoritative figure, like Silas or Timothy. Among other things, it is important to note in relation to our study

---

157. Weima, *1–2 Thessalonians*, 429.

158. As F. F. Bruce points out, it was an "appeal to those addressed to act in this matter as responsible to the Lord himself." *1 & 2 Thessalonians*, WBC 45 (Nashville: Thomas Nelson, 1982), 135.

159. "Leseanweisungen in Briefen als Mittel der Gestaltung von Beziehungen (1 Thess 5.27)," *NTS* 50, no. 2 (2004): 224–45.

160. *Forgery and Counterforgery: The Use of Literary Deceit in Early Christian Polemics* (New York: Oxford University Press, 2013), 169. This study, however, hesitates in using the phrase "reading instructions" here (or elsewhere), since it is often used to promote the view that a letter is inauthentic. For example, see Eckhart Reinmuth, "Die Briefe an die Thessalonicher," in *Die Briefe an die Philipper, Thessalonicher und an Philemon*, NTD 8.2 (Göttingen: Vandenhoeck & Ruprecht, 1998), 105–204, esp. 161–62.

that already in the first century, letters were being forged so that they would be read communally—where it mattered most. In turn, this probably generated and increased the communal reading sensitivities that are even more in evidence in the second century. A key reason to forge a document was that communal reading events were a societal gateway to penetrate. In light of how many forgeries there probably were,[161] the real or assumed communal readings of these texts would not have been a trivial matter. In fact, if this topic is examined in light of several common assumptions operative in New Testament research—such as the consensus that so few people could read,[162] the cost was too expensive for most people to individually own manuscripts,[163] and the impact would have been minimal at best[164]—one ought to wonder why there were so many ancient forgeries. Stanley Porter and Bryan Dean identified this when they wrote, "There was a large enough book market that forgery was a distinct possibility."[165] I would further argue that a high level of forgeries seems indicative of a high level of communal reading events.

Second, the authors use the terminology of tradition. The first instance is in 2:15, where it is plural, and they add "our," which is in the emphatic position. The statement assumes that multiple written accounts have already become tradition by the time this document was written. Fee notes, "The use of the word 'traditions' here, which has a long history in the Judaism in which Paul was raised, is his way of indicating that his teaching at the same time belongs to the much larger community of faith."[166] He uses the same term in 3:6, where he is again clearly addressing the entire congregation via his letter being read communally. His point seems to be that they are to expect no surprises or new teachings. The mere reading of his letter simply parallels common teaching in early Christian communities, demonstrat-

---

161. Ehrman, in *Forgery and Counterforgery*, argues for over fifty forgeries.

162. Joel B. Green, Jeannine K. Brown, and Nicholas Perrin, *Dictionary of Jesus and the Gospels*, 2nd ed. (Downers Grove: IVP Academic, 2013), 644–45.

163. Randolph E. Richards, *Paul and First-Century Letter Writing: Secretaries, Composition and Collection* (Downers Grove: InterVarsity, 2004).

164. In addition to Royalty, mentioned above, Harry Gamble notes, "As a marginal, largely uncultivated, and indeed counter-cultural minority whose texts had no broad appeal for outsiders, Christianity held no interest for the commercial book trade." "The Book Trade in the Roman Empire," in *The Early Text of the New Testament* (New York: Oxford University Press, 2012), 23–36, here 32.

165. "Oral Texts? A Reassessment of the Oral and Rhetorical Nature of Paul's Letters in Light of Recent Studies," *JETS* 55, no. 2 (2012): 323–41, here 329.

166. Fee, *The First and Second Letters to the Thessalonians*, 305.

ing a type of conserving force on a literary tradition via communal reading events. Weima adds, "The proof or evidence that the Thessalonian believers accepted the word of Paul as the word of God and that this word is presently at work in their lives is found in their imitation of the persecuted churches in Judea."[167]

Third, although merely a brief comment, 3:14 speaks about their message through this letter, and how the churches especially need to watch out for anyone who does not obey the letter's instructions. This assumes a community that hears these texts read communally, as well as a further quality control related to communal reading events.

Fourth, Paul concludes this letter by highlighting his other letters. In 3:17, he states, "I, Paul, write this greeting with my own hand. This is the mark in every letter of mine; it is the way I write." Although we cannot determine with certainty how many prior letters they would have received, from Paul or others, it is certain that by the time he is penning this letter, he was in the habit of sending letters to his churches with the intent of both communal reading and further distribution for communal reading. It also is meant to be a distinguishing feature between his authentic writings, and the writings of false teachers (e.g., the forged letters mentioned earlier in this section).

1 TIMOTHY

In this letter, there are multiple references to educational activities, such as preaching (1 Tim 4:13; 5:17) and teaching (1 Tim 3:2; 4:11, 13; 5:17; 6:2). [168] The most explicit passage regarding Christian com-

---

167. Weima, *1–2 Thessalonians*, 165.

168. Debates continue regarding the dating and authorship of the Pastoral Epistles. Space does not permit a fuller discussion of the issues here. For a helpful overview of the competing positions and, in my mind persuasive, defense of Pauline authorship and first-century dating of all three, see William D. Mounce, *Pastoral Epistles*, WBC 46 (Nashville: Thomas Nelson, 2000), civ–cxiii. Cf. George W. Knight, *The Pastoral Epistles* (Grand Rapids: Eerdmans, 1992), 28–32; Peter Walker, "Revisiting the Pastoral Epistles, Part I," *EJT* 21, no. 1 (2012): 4–16; idem, "Revisiting the Pastoral Epistles, Part II," *EJT* 21, no. 2 (2012): 120–32; Preston T. Massey, "Cicero, the Pastoral Epistles, and the Issue of Pseudonymity," *ResQ* 56, no. 2 (2014): 65–84. It is also important to highlight here, especially in light of our study, that Smith adequately demonstrates that the educational environment and priority in all four letters she examined (1 Corinthians, 1–2 Timothy, and Titus) were consistent, with no significant difference noted. Smith, *Pauline Communities as 'Scholastic Communities.'* Benjamin Wolfe also compared the author's doctrine of Scripture with that of Paul, 2 Peter, and Philo, and demonstrated that there is nothing regarding the author's doctrine of Scripture to justify the view that it is outside the Pauline tradition. "The Place and Use of Scripture in the Pastoral Epistles" (PhD diss.,

munal gatherings (1 Tim 4:13) has the activity of "reading" in the emphatic position. It also seems likely that Paul is addressing a wider audience than merely Timothy or Titus. George Knight III discusses three features he believes suggest a wider audience than simply Timothy and Titus. First, the author directly addresses the church as a whole (1 Tim 2:1ff), women (1 Tim 2:9ff), bishops and deacons (1 Tim 3:1ff), and slaves (1 Tim 6:1ff). Second, he indirectly addresses broader groups at times (Tit 2:6; 3:1). Third, all three letters contain benedictions beyond the stated individual addressee at the beginning of the letters (1 Tim 6:21; 2 Tim 4:22; Tit 3:15).[169] Martin Dibelius and Hans Conzelmann highlight this final point when they write, "The plural 'with you' (ὑμῶν) reflects the acknowledgement that a writing with this particular content is directed to a wider circle, despite the address."[170] Certainly, this does not prove the case. Mounce, for example, lists four alternative options: (1) it was a pseudepigraphical mistake, (2) some other papyri demonstrate this same feature of writing to one person but concluding in the plural, (3) it was meant for communal reading, or (4) it only pertained to the benediction.[171] Several of these would equally help explain the manuscript tradition of 1 Tim 6:21 when there are changes from the plural ("with you all") to the singular ("with you") in order to match the singular addressee (D 1739 sy).

Beyond these observations, however, a strong argument can be made that by reading this letter communally, the churches will understand the roles and authority of Timothy and Titus as the apostle's delegates among the various communities around them. Paul even mentions his purpose for writing in 3:14–15: "I am writing these instructions to you so that, if I am delayed, you may know how one ought to behave in the household of God, which is the church of the living God, the pillar and bulwark of the truth." As Towner notes:

It was not at all unusual for Paul to use the letter as a means of commu-

University of Aberdeen, 1990), esp. 157–307. In other words, in terms of dating and authorship, these additional factors that support the position of our study need to be brought into the equation.

169. *The Pastoral Epistles: A Commentary on the Greek Text* (Grand Rapids: Eerdmans, 1992), 6.

170. *The Pastoral Epistles: A Commentary on the Pastoral Epistles*, ed. Helmut Koester, trans. Philip Buttolph and Adela Yarbro (Philadelphia: Fortress Press, 1972), 93.

171. Mounce, *Pastoral Epistles*, 373.

nicating parenetic instruction to a church while absent from it. In fact, the language and style of this note are completely consistent with the similarly intended notes in other Pauline letters [e.g., 2 Cor 13:10; Rom 15:24; Phil 2:23–24]. . . . Here it serves a formal purpose corresponding to the mandate dimension of the letter, mainly to remind the wider readership of Timothy's role and authority as the apostle's delegate in the community.[172]

Mounce argues similarly, "Although Paul has written to Timothy, he intends the letter to be read to the church as a whole. This has been evident throughout the epistle and explains why much of 1 Timothy is directed not so much toward a trusted and informed coworker as to the troublesome Ephesian church."[173]

Yet even if these letters were solely written for individual reading, there certainly seems to be knowledge of communal reading events. To be sure, some of these indicators are clearer than others. For example, it is not precisely clear what the author means by myths and genealogies (1:4), but there are strong reasons to believe that the opposing group was reading, teaching, and spending their time in other writings of that period—whether they be philosophical, Jewish, or other (cf. 2 Tim 4:4; Titus 1:14). For example, 1:7 refers to some people desiring to be "teachers of the law" (νομοδιδάσκαλοι) even though they are not, and this word is used only three times in the New Testament (cf. Luke 5:17; Acts 5:34). In Acts 5, the word is used by Luke to describe the only named rabbi, Gamaliel (5:34; 22:3). In addition, the opposing group seems to want to be teachers of the written law (1:6–7), but they are not interpreting it correctly. Abasciano argues, "Given the likelihood of repeated readings, it is possible that Paul could have expected his letters to be used for teaching, and that teachers would have studied his scriptural allusions and shared their understanding with their Christian community."[174]

It is also likely that many other passages have not been read in light of communal reading events. For example, an overseer "must" (δεῖ) be able to teach (3:2). As seen elsewhere in our study, teaching often involved reading communally. Similarly, women are called to be faithful in all things (3:11). Part of that is educating their children.

---

172. Philip Towner, *The Letters to Timothy and Titus* (Grand Rapids, MI: Eerdmans, 2006), 271–72.

173. Mounce, *Pastoral Epistles*, 373.

174. Abasciano, "Diamonds in the Rough," 170.

Jewish Scripture, such as Proverbs 31:26–7,[175] other Jewish writings, like Testament of Levi 13:2,[176] and writings that later became a part of the New Testament, such as 2 Timothy 1:5, harmonize well with this point. Paul also assumes that Timothy will point "these things" out to the church if he is a good minister (4:6). While "these things" can, and probably do, refer to the surrounding literary context, they can also refer to the whole of the apostle's teaching that he wants to be faithfully communicated to the church. There are a number of other expressions that would complement this interpretation, such as "the word of God" in the previous verse (4:5). This expression could refer to specific texts, like Romans 3:4; entire sections of the Old Testament, like ones in Genesis; the gospel message, like 1 Corinthians 14:36; or Jesus' words, like those in Mark 7. Regardless of which one specifically, the reference is likely to a written text.

Following these implicit passages is arguably the most explicit text in the entire New Testament emphasizing communal reading: 1 Timothy 4:13. However, at least two details need mentioning beyond the simple fact that the author commands Timothy to prioritize communal reading. First, he is not addressing a synagogue community. This Pauline church has separated from the synagogue (Acts 19). Thus, this emphasis on communal reading was not merely for Jewish communities but for all Christian communities, in Paul's mind. Second, he does not explicitly qualify what ought to be read, even though the definite article helps our understanding (τῇ ἀναγνώσει). Since the Greek text does *not* say "Scripture," even though most translations add it, "the author is at least as likely to have had Paul's own writings in mind as what was to become the Old Testament."[177] Luke Johnson writes that Paul is directing Timothy to devote himself "to the public life of the community, beginning with the practice of reading within the *ekklēsia*. . . . It was in the context of such public reading, in fact, that Paul's own letters were undoubtedly first read."[178] And if Timothy would only follow what Paul lays out

175. See Bruce K. Waltke, *The Book of Proverbs: Chapters 15–31* (Grand Rapids: Eerdmans, 2005), 532–33.

176. "Teach your children letters also, so that they might have understanding throughout all their lives as they ceaselessly read the Law of God." H. C. Kee, "Testaments of the Twelve Patriarchs," in *Old Testament Pseudepigrapha*, 1.792–3.

177. Andrew B. McGowan, *Ancient Christian Worship: Early Church Practices in Social, Historical, and Theological Perspective* (Grand Rapids: Baker Academic, 2014), 80.

178. *The First and Second Letters to Timothy: A New Translation with Introduction and Commentary* (New York: Doubleday, 2001), 252.

here, and share it with his community, it would save both Timothy and his hearers (4:16).

Finally, yet worthy of note, Michael Kruger discusses the probabilities of Paul quoting gospel tradition (Luke 10:7) as Scripture in 5:18. He gives three key reasons for affirming it: First, the quote from Luke is placed alongside Deuteronomy 25:4, and both are referred to as "the scripture." Second, the author uses other written texts besides Luke without using this phrase in this form. And third, there are strong historical connections between Luke and Paul.[179] Kruger is not alone in his assessment. In fact, in his study on the place and use of Scripture in the Pastoral Epistles, Wolfe remarks, "All indications are that it [the saying of the Lord in 1 Tim 5:18] came from the gospel of Luke."[180] In light of our study, their persuasive arguments can now add another reason for affirming the probability that the author's source was the gospel of Luke: the widespread nature of communal reading events.

2 TIMOTHY

As in 1 Timothy, there are many indications that 2 Timothy was meant to be read communally in Ephesus. Towner believes Paul's self-identification in the beginning of the body of the letter is one of them (1:3). He states, "As a letter to be read also by the church(es) in which Timothy was working, Paul's claim . . . may well be directed to those who are opponents or to those who are being influenced by opponents to reject the apostle's authority."[181] There are many other points to consider in 1:13–14. The first word (ὑποτύπωσιν) emphasizes an established tradition and doctrine. Next, the "good deposit" from Paul has already been accepted and embraced by Timothy. It is also being lifted up as a model, form, or standard that is meant to serve as a reliable guide or pattern. Together, all this seems to suggest that there was meant to be continuity and purity in this message for

---

179. "Early Christian Attitudes toward the Reproduction of Texts," in *The Early Text of the New Testament*, ed. Charles E. Hill and Michael J. Kruger (New York: Oxford University Press, 2012), 61–80, here 67–69.

180. Wolfe, "Scripture in the Pastoral Epistles," 105. For an example of the broad dissemination of literature in the first century, see my article, "Ancient Rome's Daily News Publication with Some Likely Implications for Early Christian Studies," *TynBull* 67, no. 1 (2016): 145–60.

181. Towner, *The Letters to Timothy and Titus*, 450.

future generations. In essence, the same gospel that God entrusted to Paul, Paul entrusts to others, and so forth.

In chapter 2, there were apparently many witnesses listening to his message (v. 2), a message that they are instructed to teach others. Towner notes, "This qualification places the emphasis on the presence of others who can authenticate the message."[182] Moreover, in 2:8, he asks them again to remember "my gospel." What the author writes here may be part of a formula the audience would have already heard read communally in the past. The author then gives the introductory phrase "the word is reliable" in 2:11–3. He is probably reciting material that has become traditional by the time of this letter—whether Paul has nuanced it for his own purposes or not. As in 1 Timothy, the author commands Timothy to keep reminding (present tense) God's people of these things (2:14). It is assumed that at least part of the current letter is to be included in this teaching. Rightly handling the word of God, then, in 2:15 continues the author's string of speech act terminology ("remind," "words," "hearers," "the word of truth," "babble," "saying"; 2:14–18). For our purposes, these can be viewed as the author's emphasis on communal reading practices. For example, the content and correct conveying of it were to epitomize Timothy's teaching. The author has already established elsewhere that the public reading of Scripture and the sharing of his own letters are exemplars.

Moving on to chapter 3, two verses in particular ought to be observed. First, in 3:15, the author suggests that from "childhood" Timothy was acquainted with the sacred writings. It seems most probable from 1:5 that his Jewish mother and grandmother would have been the main ones who brought him up in traditional Jewish fashion (Deut 6:2, 7, 20). They would have been the ones to read and teach him the Jewish Scriptures in his formative years.[183] Second, "the gospel" the author is promoting finds its basis in Scripture (3:16). In other words, Timothy's training in the same Scriptures ought to form a base that he stands on in contrast to the false teachers. Again, it

---

182. Ibid., 490.

183. For additional sources on educated mothers and women in the first century, see Bruce W. Winter, *Roman Wives, Roman Widows: The Appearance of New Women and the Pauline Communities* (Grand Rapids: Eerdmans, 2003); Craig Keener, "Women's Education and Public Speech in Antiquity," *JETS* 50, no. 4 (2007): 747–59; Linda Belleville, "Ἰουνίαν . . . ἐπίσημοι ἐν τοῖς ἀποστόλοις: A Re-examination of Romans 16:7 in Light of Primary Source Materials," *NTS* 51 (2005): 231–49.

seems the communal reading of these texts throughout Jewish history is in the background and certainly should remain in the foreground.

In chapter 4, this emphasis on writings read communally appears to continue. The author commands Timothy to preach the word (4:2) and that his teaching must be sound (4:3). What standard, though, is considered sound if there is no stability? The ministry activity of teaching the author is conveying here is meant to encourage believers because it is stable like the holy writings of the Old Testament. In fact, according to Mark 14:9, Christ uses a slight variation of the phrase "preach the word" when he states, "The good news is preached."

Towner makes another observation regarding 2 Timothy 4:2–3 that is worth considering: "It encompasses the sort of teaching (from Scripture) that seeks the forward movement of believers toward maturity and is generally positive in tone."[184] This interpretation seems to fit well with the contrast the author sets up in 4:4 regarding myths that are being presented to people. The language here of listening suggests that they will gather around them a group of teachers. It gives the impression of amassing teachers, which would have been easy in such a context that included widespread communal reading events. The metaphorical use of "ears" suggests that they are hearing a message or report, even though they are unable to judge for themselves between truth and error. This description certainly invites a comparison with communal reading events, especially pagan ones, even if it is not explicit. Rather than hearing myths, they should be listening to the truth that is being described in this letter and disseminated throughout the churches.

Paul also requests Timothy to bring him the very materials often used in communal reading events. In 4:13, he requests τὰ βιβλία μάλιστα τὰς μεμβράνας. This phrase has typically been translated, "the books, especially the parchments." But in 1979, T. C. Skeat proposed that μάλιστα ought to be taken epexegetically.[185] Thus, the entire phrase should be rendered something like this: "the books, that is, the notebooks." Since his publication, many scholars have adequately overturned his proposal. For example, Hong Bom Kim and Vern Poythress argue persuasively that the traditional understanding ("especially") is the best.[186] Despite all this, though, John Kloppenborg

---

184. Towner, *The Letters to Timothy and Titus*, 602.

185. "Especially the Parchments: A Note on 2 Timothy 4:13," *JTS* 30 (1979): 173–77.

186. Hong Bom Kim, "The Interpretation of Μάλιστα in 1 Timothy 5:17," *NovT* 66 (2004):

more recently argued that this entire phrase was an attempt to high-light Paul as a writer, possibly just for Paul's personal use while in jail. "It is thus beside the point," he argues, "to inquire whether the βιβλία were books of the Torah or whether the μεμβράνα were blank or filled."[187] However, especially in light of our study, that could be the very point. If the phrase is speaking about specific Scripture and parchments, then it might have nothing to do with Paul being iden-tified as either a reader or writer, as Kloppenborg argues, but rather offers another signal of the emphasis on communal reading events.[188] This would be consistent with other accounts of Christians sending from prison written correspondences to be read communally (Phile-mon). Moreover, there is no clear indication that the purpose of this passage is about the writing capabilities of Paul, or that he merely wanted to write some personal letters apart from his mission. The only persuasive way to argue for this verse addressing the writing capabilities of Paul is to base the entire argument off of one way to understand the term μεμβράνα—that the material was blank—and to assume he had all the other materials in order to write on the parch-ment; none of which are mentioned. Whatever we are to make of this, it is at least clear that the materials mentioned here fit the pur-poses of communal reading events; thus increasing the likelihood that Paul and the communities he addresses are didactic, textually based, and intimately familiar with communal reading events.

Finally yet importantly, the letter ends with the plural "you" (4:22). This probably included Timothy's associates—Priscilla, Aquila, and the household of Onesiphorus.[189] And Johnson notes, "It is fascinating that the text read by three early commentators—Chrysostom, Theodoret of Cyr, and Theodore of Mopsuestia—all had *meth' hēmōn* (with us)."[190] The understanding of this phrase specifically, and the letter generally, seems to have always been the communal reading nature of it—not a pseudepigrapher's mistake, conventional letter

360–68; Vern Poythress, "The Meaning of μάλιστα in 2 Timothy 4:13 and Related Verses," *JTS* 53, no. 2 (2002): 523–32.

187. "Literate Media in Early Christ Groups: The Creation of a Christian Book Culture," *JECS* 22, no. 1 (2014): 21–59, here 33.

188. For example, Dietrich-Alex Koch, who Kloppenborg does not interact with, sees this passage referring specifically to Scripture scrolls, especially since they were not expensive. *Die Schrift als Zeuge des Evangeliums: Untersuchungen zur Verwendung und zum Verständnis der Schrift dei Paulus*, BHT 69 (Tübingen: Mohr Siebeck, 1986), 99–100.

189. Mounce, *Pastoral Epistles*, 601.

190. Johnson, *Letters to Timothy*, 445.

writing feature, or pertaining only to the benediction, as noted above under 1 Timothy.

TITUS

Though Paul identifies Titus on the island of Crete as the sole recipient of his letter, he also seems to have other readers, hearers, and churches under Titus's care in mind as recipients. Philip Towner observes several clues just in the opening greeting that point to a wider audience being addressed (1:1–4). For example, the Old Testament language of "God's elect" in verse 1 "probably infers readers (besides Titus) who are sufficiently familiar with Jewish ideas."[191] Towner argues that this is in keeping with the rest of Paul's letter to Titus, especially since the care of the church is Paul's main concern. In verse 3, there seems to be a strong emphasis on the written gospel of Christ's revelation, which has been entrusted to Paul (like the oracles of God to the Jews in Rom 3:2) and is meant to be preached (similar to Rom 16:25–26). In addition, by calling Titus "my loyal child in the faith" in verse 4, Paul is authenticating the ministry of Titus, "and the primary implication for those who read or hear the letter is that Titus (and not false claimants) may represent the apostle."[192]

Beyond the opening greeting, there seem to be other indications that Paul assumes this letter will be read communally. Three examples will be given here. First, in the body of the letter, Paul discusses the qualifications for elders. One of the qualifications is the ability to teach the congregation and protect them from false teaching (1:9). One way to know that the message is accurate is that it is linked with an apostle whose source is God, such as Paul, who is writing this letter (1:3). Another way to know that the message is accurate is the content. In practice, this accurate teaching is to be presented to the churches in Crete, and the letter Titus holds in his hand from Paul is a perfect exemplar.

Second, Paul commands Titus to do or share certain things in this letter with his people, and it can be assumed that Titus would have read this letter communally to validate his authority in following the apostle Paul's instructions. For example, in 1:13, Paul commands Titus to "rebuke them sharply"—presumably to model the eldership

191. Towner, *The Letters to Timothy and Titus*, 667.
192. Ibid., 674.

instructions Paul just gave, such as in 1:9 mentioned above. In 2:1, Paul commands Titus to teach—implicitly the church. Then in verse 6 of the same chapter, Titus is commanded to teach a specific group within the church: "the younger men." In the last verse of chapter 2 (verse 15), Titus is commanded again to "Declare these things; exhort and reprove with all authority." Though some scholars see the final command ("rebuke") as directly addressing the church (as in 1 Cor 16:11),[193] the immediate context still seems to trump that assessment. For example, the first word of the next verse is Paul's next command specifically for Titus: "remind." Paul goes on to write in verse 8, "The word is reliable. I desire that you insist on these things, so that those who have come to believe in God may be careful to devote themselves to good works; these things are excellent and profitable to everyone." The word here often translated as "insist" (διαβεβαιοῦσθαι) has strong overtones of passing on written communication via teaching—which also appears evident from the context.

Third, Paul's final greetings and benediction offer another indication that his letter would be read communally. The focus here will be on verse 15. In addition to having Titus pass along greetings from one community to another community, he says, "Grace be with all of you." As almost every commentary notes, this ending differs from the ending of the other pastoral letters (1 Tim 6:21 and 2 Tim 4:22) in that it adds the word *all*. William Mounce states, "[The plural here] suggests that despite its personal appearance, the epistle to Titus is more public than private, or that Paul recognizes that it eventually will become public."[194] By offering a prayer and blessing to "all," we come the closest to identifying Paul's inclusion of additional recipients—most probably multiple churches under Titus's care.

PHILEMON

From Roman imprisonment in the early 60s CE (Acts 28:11–31), the apostle Paul writes to Philemon in Colossae (Col 4:7–9). According to ancient letter-writing practices, Philemon was Paul's primary addressee, even though Paul addresses three other recipients: Apphia,

---

193. Norbert Brox, *Die Pastoralbriefe* (Regensburg: Friedrich Pustet, 1963), 302.
194. Mounce, *Pastoral Epistles*, 459.

Archippus, and the church meeting in Philemon's house.[195] While all addressees require specific attention, the entire community will be the focus of this section, because the letter as a whole reflects social—in addition to individual—realities present in this closely knit group.[196] In other words, although the issue addressed in this letter is personal, it is not private—reinforcing N. T. Wright's view that the central theme of Philemon is communal fellowship.[197] By putting the issue between Onesimus and Philemon into the gaze of the church, everyone looks to see how Philemon will respond. Thus, there is an additional honor/shame dimension here, too.

Beyond the communal aspects of the letter, such as the multiple addressees and the central theme of fellowship, the three clearest indications that this letter was read communally are found in the closing of the letter. First, he states that he is writing it with his own hand (19). As noted above, this would be a moot point if only addressed to one person who could see the change in handwriting. Fitzmyer writes, "This is also an indication that the letter is not merely a private communication to Philemon, but was envisaged by Paul as something that would be read to the church that gathered at Philemon's house."[198] Second, Paul writes in verse 22, "through your prayers to be restored to you." According to Paul, the only way he is going to make it to Colossae is if the entire church prays for him. Both pronouns used here are plural (ὑμῶν and ὑμῖν). This matches well with the initial addressees listed at the opening of the letter. In light of this, Moo concludes, "The letter is focused on Philemon and Paul's request of him, but we again see that he assumes that it will be read within the context of the community as a whole."[199]

Third, Paul writes in verse 25, "The grace of the Lord Jesus Christ be with your spirit." Besides being a typical closing for Paul, the pronoun *your* is plural, which Markus Barth and Helmut Blanke

195. Peter Arzt-Grabner, *Philemon* (Göttingen: Vandenhoeck-Ruprecht, 2003), 112–14.

196. Douglas Moo provides a good and balanced survey regarding the importance of identifying both the primary and secondary audience. For example, it is important to observe the use of second-person pronouns and verbal forms and the switches between them throughout this short letter. There is also a false dichotomy at times between "private" and "public" situations. For more information regarding these matters, see Moo, *Colossians and Philemon*, 361–78.

197. Nicholas T. Wright, *Paul and the Faithfulness of God: Parts I and II* (Minneapolis: Fortress Press, 2013), 16–22. He has maintained this position for decades; see, for example, *The Epistles of Paul to the Colossians and to Philemon* (Leicester: InterVarsity, 1986), 183–87.

198. *The Letter to Philemon: A New Translation with Introduction and Commentary* (London: Doubleday, 2000), 118.

199. Moo, *Colossians and Philemon*, 437.

believe "makes clear once more that Paul has understood his letter not as a private one, but as one to the *community* in Colossae."[200] By addressing the whole congregation meeting in Philemon's house, Paul assumes the entire letter will be read among them. Even more, combining "your" with "spirit" seems to suggest that the entire community—and not just Philemon—will need to embrace the Onesimus ordeal, which will require "grace."

In sum, Philemon is also further evidence that "there were structures that allowed texts to circulate independently of traveling performers," since this text would never have been intended to be performed.[201]

HEBREWS

While there is still debate over whether the written account known as Hebrews was sermonic or epistolary, there does not seem to be much debate over whether it was read communally. There are simply too many indicators in the work itself to rule out the probability. Nevertheless, a few of these features will be noted here.

The author's overall literary assumptions on the part of the audience seem to abound, even though they are not identified as such. For instance, the author assumes a high degree of familiarity with many Old Testament narratives and other Jewish texts, such as 1 Maccabees 2 and 2 Maccabees 7.[202] One reason he was able to assume such literary familiarity is that he knows the probabilities are high that these texts were frequently read communally. In fact, after presenting multiple Old Testament passages in the first chapter, he states, "Therefore we must pay greater attention to what we have heard, so that we do not drift away from it" (2:1). This helps explain the way the author references the Old Testament, as when he says, "But someone has testified somewhere" in 2:6. For the author, it matters less who spoke in or wrote down Scripture, since the reading (or reciting) of the authoritative witness is as if God is speaking to the community.

200. *The Letter to Philemon: A New Translation with Notes and Commentary* (Grand Rapids: Eerdmans, 2000), 498.

201. O'Loughlin, "Luke 1:2."

202. See Christian M. M. Brady, "What Shall We Remember, the Deeds or the Faith of Our Ancestors? A Comparison of 1 Maccabees 2 and Hebrews 11," in *Earliest Christianity within the Boundaries of Judaism: Essays in Honor of Bruce Chilton*, ed. Alan Avery-Peck, Craig A. Evans, and Jacob Neusner, Brill Reference Library of Judaism 49 (Leiden: Brill, 2016), 107–19.

Addressing the group in 3:1 as "holy brothers," who have a common confession, and by admonishing them to "consider . . . Jesus," the author emphasizes both the closeness of the community as God's household and the fact that they are hearing this letter read in their presence. These listeners are then exhorted to heed the warning of another text, Psalm 95, as it is read communally. If, however, they are sluggish and dull when hearing communal readings (5:11), and thus not obeying the written oracles of God (5:12), then they are still a "child" (5:13). By the time this letter was written (ca. 60–100 CE),[203] then, the author assumes ample communal reading and is not wanting to start over with elementary things.

There are many other communal reading features throughout this letter, though the ones already noted ought to suffice in showing that this letter was written to be read communally. Nevertheless, even if the features noted are not overly persuasive, the author's conclusion explicitly characterizes itself as a written exhortation to a congregation of "brothers" (13:22), rather than a letter to an individual. The presumed context—especially given the terminology—is similar to the one found in Acts 13:15 (cf. 1 Pet 5:12), where there is a communal reading event within a synagogue in Pisidian Antioch. They also both use the phrase "word of exhortation," as well as similar concepts concerning Jesus and Israel. In addition, the author's final greetings, which include a third party, suggest that the communal reading of these types of letters were more widespread than just this specific community: "Those from Italy send you greetings" (13:24). As many scholars note, greetings of this nature between similar communities highlight their communal nature and concern for each other.[204]

JAMES

By the third-fourth century AD, Eusebius notes that the Epistle of James was among the letters "constantly used communally in many churches." (*Hist. eccl.* 3:31; cf. 3:25). This later picture coincides well

---

203. See Harold W. Attridge, *The Epistle to the Hebrews: A Commentary on The Epistle to the Hebrews*, ed. Helmut Koester (Philadelphia: Fortress Press, 1989), 6–9. I adopt the early end of this date range (pre-70 CE), especially given that the entire Levitical system in this work is spoken of in the present tense. Attridge's two reasons for rejecting this argument and consequential dating seem inadequate to me. Ibid., 8.

204. David L. Allen, *Hebrews: An Exegetical and Theological Exposition of Holy Scripture*, NAC 35 (Nashville: B&H, 2010), 631–32.

with what the author of the Epistle of James states regarding his original audience: "To the twelve tribes of the Dispersion." [205] Though
no one today can be certain as to where exactly these communities existed geographically, there is no doubt the intended audience
was widespread (see the discussion of "the Dispersion" below).[206] The
communal orientation of the book is also not difficult to imagine.
Patrick Hartin even sees "socialization" as the purpose of James's letter,[207] and Peter-Ben Smit argues that many features in James's letter
suggest "a symposiastically organized community."[208] The constant
use of second-person plural pronouns, addressing the readers as "my
brothers," referencing teachers and teaching, are further indications
implying a communal reading environment—not to mention the
strong Jewish background of the author and his writing.[209]

Beyond the letter's stated intent for general circulation, the communal nature, and the plural terminology, there are a number of specific verses that assume, suggest, or address this idea of communal
reading. In chapter 1, Dan McCartney argues, "the word of truth"
in verse 18 is almost certainly referring to Scripture.[210] This fits well
with the immediate context, especially verses 21–23, regarding what
they are hearing: "the word." Allison argues cogently that "the word"
refers to the Jewish Torah.[211] Thus, we have a community hearing
Scripture read aloud. This emphasis on reading Scripture is also especially telling if, as William Oesterley noted in relation to verse 25, the

205. Without outlining all the debates regarding authorship here, suffice it to say that I accept
the letter's own claim that the author is James the brother of the Lord. This view is further supported by early Christian evidence.

206. This point would remain even if the group is taken figuratively and not literally. See
Dale C. Allison, *The Epistle of James: A Critical and Exegetical Commentary* (New York: T&T
Clark, 2013), 115–16.

207. *James*, SP 14 (Collegeville, MN: Liturgical Press, 2003), 13.

208. "A Symposiastic Background to James?," *NTS* 58 (2011): 105–122, here 122. The Epistle
of James is not the only New Testament writing that reveals the eminent position given to
meals regarding influential social gatherings. Scholars have even compared Jesus's feedings to
symposia, as with the possible contrast the author of Mark intends between Herod's birthday
celebration and Jesus's public feast that follows in Mark 6. See, among others, David H. Sick,
"The Symposium of the 5,000," *JTS* 66, no. 1 (2015): 1–27; Susan Marks and Hal Taussig, eds.,
Meals in Early Judaism: Social Formation at the Table (New York: Palgrave Macmillan, 2014). See
also apocryphal works, such as *Acts Thom.* 29, 49–50, 121, 133, 158; *Acts John* 4–85, 89, 109–10.

209. See Scot McKnight, *The Letter of James* (Grand Rapids: Eerdmans, 2011).

210. *James* (Grand Rapids: Baker Academic, 2009), 110.

211. Allison, *James*, 319.

imagery is of a person bent over a Torah roll: "to bend over for the purpose of looking [παρακύψας] into the perfect law."[212]

As we saw in chapter 4 of our study, Scripture was regularly read communally in Jewish synagogues, which subsequently influenced early Christian assemblies. Here, the author is quick to instruct his audience to "receive the word implanted" (1:21). Ἔμφυτος ("implanted") is a unique word in the New Testament, only here in James. Christians ought to regularly listen to, believe, and act upon the word of God.[213] Otherwise, according to the author, they may become "hearers who forget" (1:25), "a malady to which all are prone and requires the remedy of constant, continuous attentiveness to the word of God."[214] The spiritual formation of these communities, then, was directly linked to communal reading events.

At the outset of James 2, the author provides an illustration that supports the idea that his intended audience was widespread—likely written to both Judeans and Christ believers.[215] In fact, he assumes it could take place in any of the synagogues among his audience: "the Dispersion." He does not merely say "synagogue," but rather calls it "your synagogue"—without the definite article (2:2). Since this is an encyclical letter, this reference is important for the case being made here. Whether or not it is an echo of Jewish synagogue practices, the author at least assumes his letter will find its way to multiple communities that are already involved in communal reading events. In support of this assumption on the author's part is another key statement. The author assumes "the Dispersion" have heard the story of Job (5:11). This is not the only Scripture the author assumes the audience has "heard," but it is representative of this communal reading event focus. Just from these two verses, then, the author appears to assume that the current and previous experiences of "the Dispersion" have included the communal reading of Scripture.

---

212. "The General Epistle of James," in *The Expositor's Greek New Testament*, rev. ed., ed. W. Robertson Nicoll (New York: Eerdmans, 1960), 4:385–476, here 4:434.

213. McCartney, *James*, 118.

214. Ibid., 124.

215. See, among others, John S. Kloppenborg, "Diaspora Discourse: The Construction of *Ethos* in James," *NTS* (2007): 242–70.

THE PETRINE EPISTLES

1 PETER

First Peter is another example of a circular letter. This is evident in 1:1, where the author is addressing many communities in many different cultures: "To the exiles of the Dispersion in Pontus, Galatia, Cappadocia, Asia, and Bithynia." And even though the author is addressing various communities, one common denominator is his assumption that they all have heard Scripture read communally, and probably other literary traditions.[216] Benjamin Sargent even argues that there are some similarities between the Qumran community and Petrine communities, such as their special interest in Scripture.[217]

One of the author's opening analogies (1:24–25) comes from the Jewish scriptures, which he states will endure forever and assumes his readers have already heard and believed. Although it is uncertain exactly what he means when he says, "That word is the good news that was announced to you," it is not difficult to argue that it would have included the reading or recitation of the Jewish scriptures or apostolic letters such as his. He also mentions that the word is abiding. Part of the reason it is abiding is his assumption that it is frequently read communally. Additional support for this can be seen in 4:11, where the author says that whoever speaks ought to make sure it is "the very words of God." Again, the author's precise meaning of this is unclear, sense speech activity included evangelism, teaching, prophesying, singing words, testimonies, and reading Scriptures/letters communally. Nevertheless, as we have seen throughout our study, one cannot rule out the widespread practice of communal reading.

The author concludes the letter by mentioning Silvanius (5:12), through whom he sent the letter to "you" (plural).[218] As Davids notes,

---

216. Peter Davids, for example, cogently argues that the reference to Sarah calling Abraham "her lord" in 3:6 almost certainly refers to the extrabiblical literary tradition(s) of the *Testament of Abraham* familiar to the contemporary audience. *A Theology of James, Peter, and Jude* (Grand Rapids: Zondervan, 2014), 143–44. Cf. Troy W. Martin, "The *TestAbr* and the Background of 1 Pet 3:6," *ZAW* 90 (1999):139–46.

217. *Written to Serve: The Use of Scripture in 1 Peter*, ed. Chris Keith, LNTS 547 (London: T&T Clark, 2015).

218. That Silvanus was Peter's letter carrier, not secretary, see E. Randolph Richards, "Silvanus Was Not Peter's Secretary: Theological Bias in Interpreting διὰ Σιλουανοῦ . . . ἔγραψα in 1 Peter 5:12," *JETS* 43, no. 3 (2000): 417–32.

"the letter carrier would not only deliver the letter, but usually read it aloud."[219] In fact, studies continue to show that ancient letter carriers often mediated the very presence of the author(s), often playing a significant role in helping a person or community understand the authorial intent.[220] Douglas Harink argues for this understanding in his commentary. After pointing to passages such as Acts 15:32 and identifying other texts linking Silvanus—likely the same person—with the ministry of Paul, he states, "Silvanus, as a 'faithful brother,' carries Peter's letter to the various churches in Asia Minor bearing the commission of Peter himself and the authority to read it and expound it in those congregations in the power of the Holy Spirit."[221]

In the reading of this letter, whether by Silvanius or someone in each community, the author also sends his greetings (5:13–14). These greetings reveal an additional closeness the author feels with these communities, as if they are blood family or some of his closest of friends—in this case, true believers in Christ listening to this letter read communally. Even more, though, as Lewis Donelson notes, "While the imperative to 'greet one another with a kiss of love' may refer to greetings in all moments and places, it is more likely that this is a liturgical moment. The letter is being read during the gathering of the community, perhaps in worship itself. The call for the kiss of love is a call to end the reading and to greet one another."[222]

2 PETER

The beginning of this Greek letter "serves as a proper opening to a speech."[223] Not only is there identifiable Greek rhetoric, but he is addressing a specific congregation or group of congregations (1:1) that have already received and communally read a previous letter he

219. Davids, *A Theology of James, Peter, and Jude*, 156.

220. See, among others, Akio Ito, "Paul the 'Herald' and the 'Teacher'," in *Sacred Words: Orality, Literacy, and Religion* (Leiden: Brill, 2011), 351–70, esp. 351–52; Peter M. Head, "Letter Carriers in Ancient Jewish Epistolary Material," in *Jewish and Christian Scripture as Artifact and Canon*, ed. Craig A. Evans and H. Daniel Zacharias, LSTS 70 (London: T&T Clark, 2009), 203–19; idem., "'Witnesses between You and Us': The Role of the Letter-Carriers in *1 Clement*," in *Studies on the Text of the New Testament and Early Christianity in Honor of Michael W. Holmes*, ed. Daniel M. Gurtner, Juan Hernández, and Paul Foster, NTTSD 50 (Leiden: Brill, 2015), 477–93.

221. *1 and 2 Peter* (London: SCM, 2009), 129.

222. *I and II Peter and Jude: A Commentary* (Louisville: Westminster John Knox, 2010), 156.

223. Peter H. Davids, *The Letters of 2 Peter and Jude* (Grand Rapids: Eerdmans, 2006), 159.

wrote to them: "This is now, beloved, the second letter I am writing to you" (3:1).[224] Regardless of what the specific purposes of each letter was, both were meant to be communicated via communal reading and teaching.

One of the most explicit signs that the author assumes his letters are being read communally is found in 1:15. In fact, Peter Davids suggests that this verse is "the core purpose of the letter."[225] By leaving them a written record, the congregation will be able to continually read his letter at any time, and by doing so will be constantly reminded of his teaching even after he dies: "And I will make every effort so that after my departure you may be able at any time to recall these things." Likewise, in verses 12–13, he seems to assume the readers already know the things he is sharing, and that this letter "will be a constant reminder as it is repeatedly read in the community."[226] And as Richard Bauckham adds, the constant reminder would not only be for "those who read it immediately but also those who will read it after the testator's death (as 1:12–15 makes very clear)."[227] The author of 2 Peter also makes a contrast between his letter and other written stories that are being read and heard (1:16).[228] The former is truth based on eyewitness testimony, including that of the author, while the latter are false and based on nothing other than authorial creativity.

Moving beyond chapter 1, at least three other verses—all from chapter 3—offer strong support for seeing this letter as the focal point of a communal reading event or a number of communal reading events. First, the author wants the congregation to remember, at the very least, the prophecies of the holy prophets and apostles (3:2). "The result," says Davids, "was that their 'command' was something to be 'recalled' along with the words of the 'holy prophets,' the writings of

---

224. Scholars often note that 2 Peter is characterized by Hellenistic thought, but there is still no consensus as to where the addressees are specifically located. Asia Minor, Greece, and the Eastern end of the Mediterranean remain the most probable locations.

225. Davids, *The Letters of 2 Peter and Jude*, 196.

226. Ibid., 192.

227. *Jude, 2 Peter*, WBC 50 (Nashville: Thomas Nelson, 1983), 133. The context of Bauckham's reference to these verses is in his discussion of the "combination of genres" the author employed, which further suggest the concept of widespread distribution of this letter.

228. While it is possible that he is referring to purely oral stories, it does not seem probable for many reasons. For a few specific first-century examples and contrasts from authors such as Philo, Plutarch, Strabo, and Josephus, see Bauckham, *Jude, 2 Peter*, 213–17. See also Davids, *The Letters of 2 Peter and Jude*, 200–203.

whom they probably read in their gatherings from week to week."[229] Linking the NT apostles and Old Testament prophets arguably provides another strong connection between the communal reading of the Hebrew Scriptures and the writings of the apostles. This idea is further strengthened in verses 15 and 16, which clearly indicate that Paul has written to them (15), and that his writings, which the author cites alongside "the other Scriptures," are presumably being collected and distributed together.[230] According to the author, even those who are ignorant and unstable have access to and read his works (16). This statement serves as both an endorsement of Pauline writings and a warning about the possibility of misreading his letters.

THE JOHANNINE EPISTLES

1 JOHN

The author of 1 John begins his letter with an allusion to the prologue of the Gospel of John:

"Ὃ ἦν ἀπ᾽ ἀρχῆς (1 John 1:1a)
᾽Εν ἀρχῇ ἦν ὁ λόγος (John 1:1a)

Even if some of the meanings and expressions are different, and words few, the echoes appear strong enough for some scholars to suggest a literary connection.[231] If that is the case, then there is an indication that the community has already heard this gospel read communally.[232] Judith Lieu writes, "Given that the majority of an ancient audience would hear rather than read a text, it may be difficult to identify techniques specifically designed to draw the attention of or to persuade *readers* . . . , but there is a sense in which many of

---

229. Davids, *The Letters of 2 Peter and Jude*, 262.

230. The ability to determine which Pauline letter(s) the author is referring to has so far found no consensus. At the same time, Paul does periodically indicate his own view concerning the status of his writings in relation to divine Scripture, such as in 1 Cor 14:37. See E. Randolph Richards, "The Codex and the Early Collection of Paul's Letters," *BBR* 8 (1998): 151–66.

231. Colin G. Kruse, *The Letters of John* (Grand Rapids: Eerdmans, 2000), 51–57.

232. All three Johannine epistles address communities in Asia Minor. This tradition goes back at least as far as Irenaeus. See I. Howard Marshall, *The Epistles of John* (Grand Rapids: Eerdmans, 1978), 47.

1 John's persuasive strategies are literary in that they appeal to textual echoes both within and external to this writing."[233]

What is clearer, however, is the liturgical setting of this apostolic letter. The author clearly provides a written communication that he assumes will be read communally in Asia Minor. In 2:1, for example, he explicitly states this: "My little children, I am writing these things to you so that you may not sin." Later in the same chapter (1:12–17), he even singles out various groups within the church that he assumes will hear this letter being read: children, fathers, and young men. Furthermore, one imperative the author gives his hearers is to test the spirits (4:1). This testing of the spirits seems to be in relation to false prophets. The most probable explanation, then, is that the communities were to test and discuss critically the messages delivered congregationally. This aspect of testing false teachers can also be seen in other early Christian literature. In the Didache, for example, one way the author suggests that they could know a false teacher is by the content of their teaching (11.1–12.1).

2 JOHN

The first two words of this letter ("the elder") already indicate something important. Use of "the elder" signifies more than just an individual writing a letter. The terminology denotes an individual who has authority over a group—in this case, a church and its members—and typically provides oversight and leadership, as seen elsewhere in the New Testament (cf. Acts 11:30; Phil 1:1; 1 Tim 5:17; Titus 1:5; 1 Pet 5:1, et al.). One reason the author does not include his name, according to I. Howard Marshall, is for this very reason: his position is more important than his name, even if we cannot know precisely what he means by the term ecclesialogically.[234]

From there, the elder addresses his readers: "to the elect lady and her children." By personifying his addressees, he prepares them to receive his written message communally in their local church. The written message, however, is not a new one, according to the author, but one they have had since the beginning (v. 5). Using the vocative form of address, "lady," the entire church is again in view. The exhortations that follow are something the author believes they all should

233. *I, II, III John: A Commentary* (Louisville: Westminster John Knox, 2008), 5.
234. Marshall, *Epistles of John*, 59–62.

already know and have heard "from the beginning" (v. 6) and they should remain "in the teaching" (v. 9).

Furthermore, the final few verses all have other important indicators to consider regarding written texts being read communally. In verse 10, he is contrasting the letter he is sending with other itinerant teachers bringing their texts to read. For example, the verb "to bring" (φέρω) can refer to something literally—not figuratively—being brought (Luke 23:26). The author's warning not to "welcome" these heretical teachers into their church specifically chooses the word "greeting" (χαίρειν), which is a typical greeting at the beginning of Greek letters.[235] In verse 11, Marshall highlights the author's target audience again when he states, "It should be noted, however, that the elder's injunctions are addressed to the church rather than merely to the individuals who compose it."[236] Rounding out this emphasis on written communication, the author tells them that although there is still much more he wants to write to them (v. 12), his preference is to be able to visit them in person. The letter ends with a greeting from his church to their church (v. 13).

3 JOHN

As in 2 John, the author starts 3 John with "the elder." This time, however, the letter is not to a community, but rather an individual: "to the beloved Gaius." The combination of these two features suggests that this was not exclusively a private letter, but rather an official church communication by way of a personal letter.[237] In relation to our study, there are two key indicators—though not explicit—that suggest this letter was read communally from inception. These indicators are found in verses 9 and 15.

In verse 9, the author mentions a letter he wrote "to the church." Unfortunately, according to the author, a man named Diotrephes suppressed the letter. Though modern scholars have reconstructed this incident many different ways, one common understanding seems to be that 3 John is another attempt to address the church even though it is not explicitly addressed to one. The elder, then, can only hope Gaius will read it to them communally.

---

235. Kruse, *Letters of John*, 214.
236. Marshall, *Epistles of John*, 74.
237. Among others, see ibid., 82.

Verse 15 also seems to fit well with this interpretation, adding at least two more factors to the prospects of a communal reading event. First, it seems probable that the elder shared the letter with his congregation before sending it, since the members of his church (i.e., friends) send their greetings as well, meaning they at least had to know about the writing, even if it was never read to them. Likewise, there seems to be an assumption on the part of the author and his church that their greetings will be shared with the members of Gaius's church (i.e., friends) who are not following Diotrephes. Both congregations, then, probably heard this letter read to them communally.

JUDE

The community the author of Jude addresses is not specifically identified. Rather, "to those who are called" designates any Christian group in any location (v. 1).[238] We can discern a few things about his audience, though. According to Peter Davids, one detail is that they are "expected to be familiar with the narratives of the Hebrew scriptures . . . [and] both *1 Enoch* and the *Testament of Moses*."[239] Richard Bauckham is more specific when he states that the author's "use of Jewish apocryphal works is at least as extensive as his use of the OT."[240] This supports the contention that the community was bookish, the circulation and reception of these literary works were more widespread than some scholars have suggested, or both.[241] The former seems especially strong if the author of 2 Peter purposefully omits the references to 1 Enoch due to "unfamiliarity rather than distrust,"[242] given the fact that 1 Enoch was popular at Qumran.[243]

After addressing them as "beloved" (v. 3),[244] the author reminds

238. Even if the location of Palestine is not accurate, the eastern Mediterranean is still the most probable location, with Syria, Asia Minor, and Egypt being other conceivable options.

239. *The Letters of 2 Peter and Jude* (Grand Rapids: Eerdmans, 2006), 18.

240. Bauckham, *Jude, 2 Peter*, 7.

241. For a recent assessment of the reception of Jude and 1 Enoch in the early Church, see Nicholas J. Moore, "Is Enoch Also among the Prophets? The Impact of Jude's Citation of *1 Enoch* on the Reception of Both Texts in the Early Church," *JTS* 64, no. 2 (2013): 498–515. Cf. Fiona Grierson, "The Testament of Moses," *JSP* 17, no. 4 (2008): 265–80; Gene L. Green, *Jude & 2 Peter* (Grand Rapids: Baker Academic, 2008), 26–33.

242. Moore, "Is Enoch Also among the Prophets?," 513.

243. Mark A. Jason, *Repentance at Qumran: The Penitential Framework of Religious Experience in the Dead Sea Scrolls* (Minneapolis: Fortress Press, 2015), 25.

244. Curtis Giese correctly points out that this is the only occurrence of the plural form of

them (5) of texts and traditions they had probably heard read communally ("fully informed") on multiple occasions. This seems to be a safe assumption, since it was likely that not everyone in the audience had the ability to read, nor would the majority of people have also owned their own copies of or had access to all the texts and traditions the author references. This is another indication—even if not explicit—of reading practices within early Christian gatherings, meaning there would have been more works read communally in the first century than merely the Law, Prophets, and Writings in the Hebrew Scriptures.

REVELATION

The Book of Revelation contains one of the most explicit statements regarding communal reading events in the entire New Testament: "Blessed is the one who reads aloud the words of the prophecy, and blessed are those who hear and who keep what is written in it" (1:3). This statement alone demonstrates that the author foresees his work being read aloud communally. Furthermore, it comes right after the opening verse, which states that this revelation is for all Christ's "slaves" (= Christians). Following the prologue are seven individual epistolary sermons given through 2:1–3:22 that are addressed to seven historical churches in Asia Minor (i.e., Ephesus, Smyrna, Pergamum, Thyatira, Sardis, Philadelphia, and Laodicea; 1:4), but which are also intended for a wider audience, given their inclusion in this book. Gregory Beale notes, "The number here [seven, in 1:4] must also be figurative for 'fullness' . . . a figure of speech in which the part is put for the whole: the seven historical churches are viewed as representative of all the churches in Asia Minor and probably, by extension, the church universal."[245] He goes on to suggest that the worldwide judgments throughout the book also points to the fact that the universal church is the true addressee, coupled with the fact that the seven congregations are no longer mentioned elsewhere in the book.

As the text continues, there is also a focus on false teaching, which was probably found in more churches than simply the ones explicitly highlighted, as in Pergamum and Thyatira. This idea of writing

this word at the opening of a New Testament letter, suggesting the term maintains a number of functions. *2 Peter and Jude* (St. Louis: Concordia, 2012), 243.

245. *The Book of Revelation* (Grand Rapids: Eerdmans, 1999), 186.

God's revelation in a book for God's covenant people (1:11) is mentioned throughout the Old Testament, especially in texts about coming judgment (Exod 34:27; Isa 8:1; 30:8; Jer 36:2, 32; Hab 2:2), as well as in other Jewish writings. For example, in the seventh and final vision in 4 Ezra 14:1–48, God orders Ezra to restore the holy scriptures, making some public (twenty-four books) while saving others solely for the wise (seventy books). Then Ezra is taken up to heaven (see fuller discussion in chapter 3).

Revelation is also saturated with previously written testimony, even if the author never explicitly acknowledges the references—so much so that it has been especially challenging for its modern readers to interpret many of the ancient images and symbols throughout the book. Nevertheless, for our purposes, the author's intentional use of and identification with previously written accounts, such as the Jewish Scriptures, in a letter written to be read communally in churches makes complete sense. The same can be said for the numerous editorial notes provided for future readers (17:9) and the numerous remarks about books (1:11; 3:5; 13:8; 17:8; 20:12, 15; 21:27; 22:7, 9, 10, 18, 19).

A few more points, however, are worth noting here regarding the seven epistolary sermons just mentioned. First, exactly as many times as there is a command to write to a church (2:1, 8, 12, 18; 3:1, 7, 14), there is an equal number of times the churches are instructed to hear what has been written (2:7, 11, 17, 29; 3:6, 13, 22). Second, the stress on the necessity of hearing *these* written words suggests the churches are hearing other false teaching. This indication is strengthened by the fact that many of the churches addressed are identified with false teachers, who have Old Testament scriptural referents nonetheless,[246] such as those following the teaching of Balaam (2:14), the Nicolaitans (2:15), Jezebel (2:20), and Satan (2:24). Another indication, and even identified quality control, is that some of the churches are commended for testing the teaching of so-called apostles and finding them to be false (2:2). Yet this assumes that they all have a measure by which to test the teaching (cf. 19:10). It seems safe, from the overall context and several phrases—such as the command to "remember what you received and heard" (3:3)—that one of the measures is Jewish Scripture. The fact that the church was able to discern doctrinal inconsistency, even among a group associated with

246. See Aune, *Revelation 1–5*, 149.

the church who called themselves apostles, strongly points to a quality control. Beale states, "Such alertness to doctrinal error may reflect the Pauline admonition to the first-generation Ephesian Christians to be on guard against false teachers. . . . Consequently, the emphasis is on persevering in guarding the internal doctrinal purity of the church's faith."[247] This picture fits well with what we see in some of the earliest Christian documents written outside the New Testament, such as the Didache mentioned earlier (11.1–12.1).

Third, the repeated phrase to hear what the Spirit says via a written text connects with the ability to conquer and receive the promised inheritance that comes along with salvation; that is, the inheritance is based on the hearers obeying the written revelation that was designed to be read communally. This is all the more telling regarding communal reading events in that Revelation is the only book in the New Testament boldly claiming to be equal to Scripture. Tobias Nicklas states, "More than any other New Testament text, this book [Revelation] wants to be understood as God's and Christ's word respectively, which has been revealed to John, the seer of Patmos."[248] Still more, later in this work (Rev 7:14),[249] the author hints that at least the Gospel of Matthew is among its equals, fitting comfortably alongside Jewish Scriptures that are read communally. To put this another way, this recognition of the Gospel of Matthew, toward the end of the first century, suggests a quality control of the contents already being read communally.

Fourth, there are two references to synagogues of Satan in Asia Minor: 2:9 and 3:9. Regardless of the specific or general identification of these synagogues historically,[250] these references at least point to places of communal reading events that are contrary to those of Christ's slaves. And according to later documents, such as Ign. *Phld.* 6.1, conflicts seem to remain a problem between these Christian and Jewish communities at this location. There are also several texts from Qumran that draw similar parallels between different reading communities beyond those of Christians (1QM I, 1; IV, 9; XV, 9; 1QS

---

247. Beale, *Revelation*, 229.

248. "'The Words of the Prophecy of This Book': Playing with Scriptural Authority in the Book of Revelation," in *Authoritative Scriptures in Ancient Judaism* (ed. Mladen Popović; Leiden: Brill, 2010), 309–26, here 309.

249. This verse cites Matt 24:21; the reference to the "great tribulation."

250. Siang-Nuan Leong, "Windows to the Polemics against the So-Called Jews and Jezebel in Revelation: Insights from Historical and Co(n)textual Analysis" (PhD diss., University of Edinburgh, 2009).

V, 1–2, 10–20; 1QH II, 22; VII, 34; cf. CD I, 12; XI, 7–9),[251] but the main point here is the presence of even more locations and opportunities for communal reading events.

Beyond these seven epistolary sermons, there are still other features to consider in the Book of Revelation that suggest widespread communal reading events in the first century. A few of them will be noted here. First, the analogies given often depict materials found at communal reading events, such as scrolls. Even the mere appearance of not being able to read a scroll that contains writing causes the author to weep bitterly (5:4). Then one of the elders comforts him by saying that there is someone who can open the scroll (5:5) and presumably read it. Moreover, after the opening of the penultimate seal, the imagery that is given is that of the sky opening up as if a scroll is being rolled up (6:14). The point being made here is that the author often describes the visions he sees with something his audience was sure to have seen at some point in their life: the rolling up of a scroll at a communal reading event (cf. 10:9–11; the idea of eating a scroll and then prophesying to many peoples).

Second, the author states that he sees an angel flying above him with an eternal gospel to proclaim to everyone on earth (14:6). The fact that he is able to *see* the eternal gospel the angel "has" (or "holds"; ἔχω) suggests that there is a tangible referent point for the angel's proclamation to everyone. Although ἔχω has a large semantic range, as evidenced by its roughly one hundred uses just in Revelation and over six hundred times throughout the New Testament, it can mean "to hold, carry, possess, grip."[252] For example, in 1:16, the Son of Man is holding (ἔχων) seven stars, and in 1:18 he is holding (ἔχω) the keys of death and Hades. In 10:2, a mighty angel holds (ἔχων) a little scroll open in his hand. In other words, as at a communal reading event, there is the picture of someone having something with him or her as the person presents the gospel communally. In both cases, a written text seems most probable.[253]

Third, and as the account continues, there is a picture of people singing the song of Moses and of the Lamb in heaven (15:3–4). This

---

251. For further explanation and comparison, see W. Schrage, "συναγωγή," in *Theologisches Wörterbuch zum Neuen Testament* (eds. Gerhard Kittel, et al.; Stuttgart: Kohlhammer, 1949–79), 7:798–850, esp. 827.

252. *NIDNTTE*, 2.346–49. Cf. *TDNT*, 2.816–32; BDAG, 420–22.

253. There is a noticeable absence of commentators considering or examining this option in their critical commentaries, but not for good or stated reasons.

may provide further imagery taken from communal worship events. The communal singing of written odes or texts, such as the Song of Moses, can be found in both Jewish and Christian communal worship events.[254] Given this emphasis on liturgical practices, the various heavenly songs in Revelation may have even had their origin in early communal worship events where these portions were sung (e.g., 4:8b, 11; 5:9–10, 12, 13b; 7:10b, 12; 11:15, 17–18; 12:10–12; 19:1b–3, 6b–8; 21:3b–4).

Fourth, many speeches in Revelation use terminology associated with writing, reading, and texts, either implicitly or explicitly. There is even a relatively short discourse attributed to God in 21:5–8, and even there, his speech is immersed in written Scripture. At the least, this further suggests that speeches not strictly defined as a reading event had written texts as their basis (cf. Simeon in Luke 2), even if the speech was a literary-theological creation by an author.

In the final chapter (22), John returns to the communal reading focus that he began with in the opening of his work. For example, he purposefully seems to connect his opening exhortation in 1:3 with several statements—both explicitly and implicitly—in his conclusion. He recaps that the words of this book are for Christ's slaves, with whom he is a fellow slave (22:9). He reiterates the blessing that comes to the one who keeps (= hears and obeys) the words of this book (22:7). The angel commands him not to seal the book, since "the time is near," implying that everyone needs to have the opportunity to hear it read communally (22:10). This command might not have been seen as that explicit, were it not for previous commands throughout the book to do the opposite, like the command to seal up what the seven thunders had spoken (10:4).

In addition, Jesus gives his testimony that "these things" are for the churches (22:16).[255] One interesting historical note regarding the transmission of this text is that some manuscripts change the

---

254. See Jennifer Knust and Tommy Wasserman, "The Biblical Odes and the Text of the Christian Bible: A Reconsideration of the Impact of Liturgical Singing on the Transmission of the Gospel of Luke," JBL 133, no. 2 (2014): 341–65.

255. Regarding Jesus's testimony in Revelation, Kenneth Strand creatively argues that the two witnesses found in Rev 11:3–12 "are, namely, 'the word of God' and 'the testimony of Jesus Christ,' or what we today would call the OT prophetic message and the NT apostolic witness." "The Two Witnesses of Rev 11:3–12," *Andrews University Seminary Studies* 19, no. 2 (1981): 127–35, here 134. While that interpretation is certainly appealing, especially in light of our study, it should probably be rejected, since the witnesses are depicted as people, who are conquered and killed (11:7) before ultimately being taken away from the people (11:12).

angel's "testifying" to "teaching" them.[256] This probably connotes the instruction of the churches as understood in the history of interpretation, given that they receive "these things" by hearing the communal reading of the book (see further discussion below). Likewise, the interpretation of the last phrase can be affected by the different ways the preposition ἐπί can be rendered: over, too, against, for, because of, for the sake of, in, among, concerning, etc. While the use and meanings of prepositions are very fluid in Revelation, it seems that this letter is written to all true churches, as symbolized in the seven historical churches in Asia Minor. If that is the case, then it is probably best to understand the preposition as "for," "to," or "among." Additional contextual support for this rendering can be found in the final few verses. In 22:18a, Jesus again confirms his testimony to those who hear this book read communally. This confirms again the importance of communal reading (cf. Gal 3:15; 2 Pet 3:16). But he also adds a strong warning to "anyone [locationless/universal] who adds [. . . or] takes away from" this book, which is being read communally (22:18b–9). This type of warning is not typical in scriptural texts, but rather appears in public documents and inscriptions.[257] This quality control has important implications not just for Christians, but for anyone. As Royalty states, "Reading is not a passive act of reciting words aloud but rather an active process of interpretation and understanding. Reading is above all a political act, and that is why it's a threat."[258]

The final verse, and word, confirms again that this book was intended to be read communally: "The grace of the Lord Jesus be with all the saints" (22:21).[259] Mitchell Reddish pushes this one step further when he argues, "The final words in the book prior to the benediction were possibly the words spoken in response by the congregation, including those in Pergamum: 'Amen. Come, Lord Jesus!'"[260]

---

256. For further details and discussion about the epilogue, see Beale, *The Book of Revelation*, 1122–57.

257. See David E. Aune, *Revelation 17–22* (Nashville: Thomas Nelson, 1998), 1208–16.

258. Robert M. Royalty, "Don't Touch This Book! Revelation 22:18–19 and the Rhetoric of Reading (in) the Apocalypse of John," *BibInt* 12, no. 3 (2004): 282–99, here 295.

259. Most manuscripts have "amen" as the last word, but several of the most important manuscripts do not (A 1006 1841). Given that it is too easily explained as a predictable variant and is found at the end of many other New Testament books, it should not be accepted as original.

260. "Hearing the Apocalypse in Pergamum," *PRSt* 41, no. 1 (2014): 3–12, here 12.

SUMMARY

The main claim of this study is that communal reading events were widespread in the first century. In this chapter, we set out to determine how widespread communal reading events were according to the New Testament writings. As alluded to in chapter 2, if we had merely searched for words such as ἀναγινώσκω or for places like synagogues, many communal reading events and their respective locations would have been missed. A prime example of this is Luke 1:63, which does not mention a synagogue or use the term ἀναγινώσκω, but should be considered a communal reading event in a town in Judah.

As we found in the works discussed in the previous chapter, the locations experiencing some level of exposure to communal reading events were widespread. Granted, some places are specific (Nazareth), while others are not certain (Samaria), and still other places are divided depending on the details provided by the New Testament author(s). For example, Philippi is suggested by Paul's letter to the Philippians in Philippi, but the evidence is not strong enough to conclude that Luke was aware of communal reading events in this location according to Acts 16. Nevertheless, more than two dozen specific locations are identified (albeit to differing degrees at various times): Rome, Corinth, Achaia, Philippi, Thessalonica, Crete, Galatia, Ephesus, Colossae, Laodicea, Capernaum, Nazareth, Jerusalem, Galilee, Damascus, Cyprus, Pisidian Antioch, Iconium, Derbe, Lystra, Berea, Athens, Miletus, Smyrna, Pergamum, Thyatira, Sardis, and Philadelphia. It is noteworthy that several of these locations correspond with places already noted in chapter 3, such as Athens, Asia Minor, Jerusalem, Corinth, Tarsus, and Rome. At the geographical extremes, some level of exposure to communal reading events can be claimed as far west as Rome, as far east as Damascus, as far north as Philippi, and as far south as a desert road between Jerusalem and Gaza.

In addition, more than a dozen broader, more generalized areas were separately identified. These general descriptions, according to the New Testament authors, included the provinces of Asia, Judea, Macedonia, Pontus, Cappadocia, Bithynia, Greece, Galilee, and Nazareth, as well as many other unnamed towns, cities, and villages, such as those between Gaza and Jerusalem—not to mention many vague addressees, like the "diaspora," wherever these dispersed people might be living. Clearly, then, *not* every location mentioned in the New Testament exhibited evidence of communal reading events. In fact, I specifically argued that several locations, including Amphipolis and Apollonia, did *not* have exposure to communal reading events, as described by the New Testament authors.

It was also noted that the direct reading from a manuscript was probably *not* involved in several passages, such as Luke 19:47, 20:1, and 21:37–38. But at other times, beyond the instances of reading directly from a scroll, as in Luke 4:17–20 and Acts 8:28, some form of notes, excerpts, or collections was probably used, such as in Acts 17:2–4, 18:24–28, and 28:23–31. Additionally, I highlighted several occasions where a group of people read something but it should *not* be considered a communal reading event (John 19:19-20), just as, at other times when an individual is said to be reading (ἀναγινώσκω) something, it should *not* be considered a reading event (Acts 23:34; cf. Luke 10:26). Therefore, regardless of whether every New Testament writing or episode discussed points explicitly to a communal *reading* event, there seems to be enough support collectively to support the notion that communal reading events were geographically widespread, according to the New Testament authors, and not only associated with urban settings.

Beyond merely mapping the plausible locations of communal reading events, I provided several new insights regarding how this topic potentially affects the interpretation of many specific New Testament passages. Examples include Mark 14:9; Acts 19:20; Romans 10:18; 1 Corinthians 11:2; 2 Corinthians 3:2; 4:2; Ephesians 5:26; 2 Timothy 4:2–4, 13; Hebrews 2:6; and Revelation 14:6; 22:16. In addition, even where a new (or nuanced) interpretation was not offered, we still clarified and enhanced the historical background of many New Testament writings and episodes, such as the Gospel of Luke and the events in Revelation.

It was further revealed that at least some Christian texts experienced rapid and wide circulation via communal reading events, contributing to Christianity's rapid expansion in the first few centuries CE. Some writings, such as 1 Peter and Jude, even assumed a bookish community with knowledge of non-Christian texts such as 1 Enoch and the Testament of Abraham. The evangelists probably expected their works to be disseminated widely and to be read in communal settings (Mark 14:9).

We also noted that certain New Testament writings as a whole, such as Acts, Galatians, 1 Peter, and James, were oriented to wider circulation and communal reading even though they do not explicitly state it. Christian communities were often defined through and in communal reading events. In fact, already in the first and oldest undisputed Pauline letter, Paul is fully aware of the social context in which his letters will be used: communal reading events (1 Thess 5:27). In Galatians, Paul shares his frustration that they have not exercised a quality control over the traditions that they have heard and that Paul attempts to persuade them are wrong. One purpose for providing warrant for his interpretation, then, is that his audience will be hearing his letter read communally and ought to compare it with these other traditions.

Many, if not all, Christian communities sought to find the best way to read correctly their common literary inheritance (Acts 19:9–10). Here are just a few texts we noted that indicate how communal reading events helped control a particular tradition, interpretation, or both: Luke 4:28–29; 13:14–15; 19:47–48; John 7:40–44; 12:34; 18:21; Acts 13:42; 17:18; 18:26; 20:30–31; 1 Corinthians 14:26; Galatians 3:13–14; 2 Thessalonians 3:14; 2 Peter 3:16; Revelation 22:18–19. This overall reading culture creates the expectation that these events were a viable quality control of the Christian tradition. Moreover, in 1 John, the community was required to test false prophets by critically assessing their messages (4:1–6). Other times, there was an endorsement from an apostle (Col 4:16; 2 Pet 3:15–16), a decree from a council (Acts 16:4), or scrolls examined (Acts 17:11) in order to validate what was read at communal gatherings. Taken collectively, there was a sustained focus on such events in relation to controlling traditions.

Teaching (Luke 4:14), proclamation (Acts 15:21), debating (Acts 17:2), and the circulation of reports (Luke 7:17) were all connected with written texts at certain points. Written texts came in many different forms according to the authors of the New Testament (see table).

Sampling of Terms

Type of Text or Writing	Passage	Greek Text

Book of life	Rev 3:5	τῆς βίβλου τῆς ζωῆς
Book of Moses	Mark 12:26	τῇ βίβλῳ Μωϋσέως
Book of Psalms	Luke 20:42	βίβλῳ ψαλμῶν
Book of the genealogy	Matt 1:1	Βίβλος γενέσεως
Book of the Law	Gal 3:10	τῷ βιβλίῳ τοῦ νόμου
Book of the prophets	Acts 7:42	βίβλῳ τῶν προφητῶν
Book of the words of Isaiah	Luke 3:4	βίβλῳ λόγων Ἠσαΐου
Book of this	John 20:30	τῷ βιβλίῳ τούτῳ
Book of this prophecy	Rev 22:19	τοῦ βιβλίου τῆς προφητείας ταύτης
Currency	Luke 20:24	ἐπιγραφήν
Divorce certificate	Mark 10:4	βιβλίον ἀποστασίου
Forged letters	2 Thess 2:2	ἐπιστολῆς ὡς δι᾽ ἡμῶν
Future inscriptions	Rev 21:12	ἐπιγεγραμμένα
Handwritten decrees	Col 2:14	χειρόγραφον
Handwritten greetings	1 Cor 16:21	ἀσπασμὸς τῇ ἐμῇ χειρὶ
Letters	2 Pet 3:16	ἐπιστολαῖς
Magical works	Acts 19:19	βίβλους
Metaphorical tablets	2 Cor 3:2	πλαξὶν
Narrative	Luke 1:1	διήγησιν
Parchments	2 Tim 4:13	τὰς μεμβράνας
Passage of Scripture	Acts 8:32	ἡ περιοχὴ τῆς γραφῆς
Present inscription	Luke 23:38	ἐπιγραφὴ
Promissory note	Luke 16:6–7	τὰ γράμματα
Prophetic writings	Rom 16:26	γραφῶν προφητικῶν
Registration	Luke 2:2	ἀπογραφὴ
Roll of the book	Heb 10:7	κεφαλίδι βιβλίου
Sacred writings	2 Tim 3:15	ἱερὰ γράμματα
Scriptural scroll	Luke 4:17	τὸ βιβλίον

Writing tablet	Luke 1:63	πινακίδιον
Written code	Rom 2:27	γράμματος
Written oracles	Rom 3:2 (cf. Acts 7:38)	τὰ λόγια

The broad range of venues, participants, and cultures also confirmed the widespread nature of communal reading events. There were public communal reading events (Acts 17 in Athens) and private communal reading events (Acts 5:42 in Jerusalem). They could be small (Acts 8), as well as large (John 6:59). There were formal settings, such as synagogues (Matt 4:23). There were informal venues, such as open-air marketplaces (Acts 17:17). There were also numerous places just about everywhere in between, such as private homes (Luke 1:40), the Bema (Acts 18:12–3), Paul's apartment (Acts 28:23), Solomon's colonnade (Acts 3:11), the temple courts (Mark 12:25), the Hall of Tyrannus (Acts 19:9), temple of the Lord (Luke 1:9), holy places (Luke 1:21–22), the ἐκκλησία (Acts 11:26), and public assemblies (Acts 19:30–31). Social inferiors were often portrayed as participating in them (John 6:31; Acts 8:27); this shows how communal reading events also crossed class boundaries.

In addition, there were examples of outsiders being interested in or even imitating Christian communal reading events, such as in Acts 19:13 or 2 Thess 2:2 (cf. Acts 20:30). Christians sometimes started new venues (Acts 18:7; 19:8). Reading and quoting Scripture beyond the typical worship settings strengthens the idea that these were didactic, textual communities. Travelers from distant lands, such as Ethiopia, had writings with them and assumed communal reading events were the best way to understand the texts (Acts 8). Many analogies were drawn from communal reading events (2 Corinthians 3). There were stated and assumed readings or recitations of texts of various genres, such as Old Testament Scripture (Psalm 110), Jewish writings (1 Enoch), pagan poets (Aratus), apostolic decrees (Acts 15:30), apostolic letters (Romans), and myths (1 Tim 1:4). The evidence of Christian communal reading events further revealed that there was not just the reading of the Old Testament, as one might already expect, but new writings, like Colossians 4:16 or 1 Thessalonians 5:27.

On top of this widespread diversity from every stratum of society, the New Testament authors not only attested to their own communal reading events, but also assumed the audience had participated in others. For example, they often assumed or reminded their respective audiences of what the audiences presumably had already heard read communally (Eph 3:2–3). In fact, it was argued that all the New Testament writings were meant to be read communally from inception. Regardless of geographical locations, every New Testament author experienced and/or assumed exposure to communal reading events. In fact, some Christian authors explicitly commanded them (1 Tim 4:13). Others noted the blessings of them (Rev 1:3). Still others noted the pervasiveness of them among both Jews and Christians (Luke-Acts). Other similarities with Jewish communities include strong literacy and a high view of sacred texts. We showed the distinctiveness of Christian reading culture by noting such things as the inclusion of new writings. Thus, communal reading events were customary even among the far-flung Christian communities, although the exact form may have differed from place to place and from time to time.

Last but not least, there were also several noteworthy similarities with the preceding chapter regarding what the Greco-Roman authors wrote, beyond just the widespread scope of these events. In both literary registers, for instance, there were examples of or remarks made concerning forgeries, comparisons, controls, settings, levels of reading, a gamut of genres, and the same work being read multiple times in multiple locations.

In sum, the New Testament writings not only help establish a historical framework for understanding first-century communal reading events, but they also display the widespread nature of them geographically, in keeping with wider Greco-Roman and Jewish patterns. It was also demonstrated by texts such as John 12:32–34, Acts 18:26, Colossians 4:16, 1 Thessalonians 5:27, 1 John 4:1, Revelation 2:2, and Revelation 22:18–19 that communal reading events acted as a medium for quality control over literary traditions. While certain details may still be questioned, the overall framework seems well founded. It is reasonable to suggest, then, that communal reading events were widespread in the first century CE.

7.

Concluding Remarks

This is the end of this letter, really the end—I won't add another syllable even if I think of something else I have forgotten.
—Pliny, *Letters* 3.9.37 (ca. 61–113 CE)

The lack of attention given to communal reading events in the first century has resulted in an impoverished understanding of the Greco-Roman socio-historical context within which Christianity emerged. Beyond merely assuming a second-century practice emulated an earlier tradition, I have argued that communal reading events were already a prevailing practice over a wide geographic range in the first century CE. In other words, communal reading events were a widespread phenomenon in the Roman Empire during the first century CE. By examining the prevalence of these events, scholars can enhance their understanding of ancient reading practices and the kinds of quality controls related to literary traditions to reconstruct a more accurate picture of the way in which the Christian tradition was controlled and shaped during the same time period.

In chapter 1, it was necessary to draw attention to the flawed assumptions and the noticeable lacuna that negatively affect current scholarship regarding communal reading events. It was shown that many scholars operate under the assumption that communal reading events were not widespread in the Roman Empire, at least until the second century CE, and very few scholars even note the possibility that such events may have acted as a medium for quality control over literary traditions. It was also determined that the best way to scrutinize this assumption and address the lacuna is to locate and map communal reading events. Much more could be made of the actual concepts and controls, but locations were the focus.

In chapters 2–4, we focused on several prosaic forces that shaped the Greco-Roman socio-historical context: economic, political, and social. We concluded that such conditions within which communal reading events occurred were favorable to the spread of these events. While analyzing the first-century milieu, I offered several preliminary texts that confirm communal reading events were an available means of controlling traditions, leaving us the necessary task of determining the extent to which these events took place geographically. Chapter 4 also discussed the Jewish background to Christian communal reading events. It was determined that early Christian communities inherited, at least in part, the literary culture and practices of Judaism, even if they modified or transformed them in diverse ways.

In chapter 5, the cumulative weight of twenty first-century authors demonstrated that communal reading events were widespread across the Roman Empire. Various quality controls were also identified, such as the textual differences Strabo highlights and critiques among poets reciting their literary works communally, and Seneca the Elder's invited guests critically examining and discussing what was being read communally. But the more than two dozen locations were the focal point, given the main thesis of this study.

In chapter 6, we concluded from the New Testament writings that communal reading events were geographically widespread. It was also argued that the authors wrote about such events because they experienced similar reading communities themselves, irrespective of the provenance of each writing. Several other implications were drawn from this, such as the stated necessity for communities to discern doctrinal inconsistency from what was being read communally. But the central thesis once again found merit.

Overall, the findings show that communal reading events were more common and widespread geographically in the first century CE than the current academic consensus assumes. It was demonstrated that the sociological settings were wide-ranging. Letters were read at funerals and legal trials. Sacred texts were read for edification. Passages were read in a school context. Poetic texts were read in public.

The evidence presented in this study also indicates that there were necessarily more kinds of quality controls embedded early on in literary traditions. Whereas we did not attempt to differentiate between the different kinds of quality controls, nor did we track exactly how each literary tradition was affected by such events, the various use of quality controls has implications for such studies, especially those related to the historical setting of nascent Christianity.

This study makes at least two important contributions to New Testament studies and early Christian origins. First, the prevalence of communal reading events raises important new questions regarding the formation of the Jesus tradition, the contours of book culture in early Christianity, and factors shaping the transmission of the text of the New Testament: What do communal reading events suggest about ancient literacy levels? To what extent did communal reading events control a tradition? How early did Christian communities start rejecting written competitors via communal reading events? Did communal reading events provide a unity that transcends other differences and controls?

Second, another quality control that was operative and pervasive in the first century CE has been confirmed. The simplistic notion that only a small segment of society in certain urban areas could have been involved in such communal reading events during the first century has been overturned. Rather, communal reading events permeated a complex, multifaceted cultural field in which early Christians, Philo, and many others participated. It has been determined that even among an evolving tradition, a broad spectrum of society, and a variety of literary forms in a far-flung Christian world, one of the common denominators was communal reading events, and that these events were a widespread controlling factor in the transmission of the Christian tradition. These fresh insights have the potential to inform historical reconstructions of the nature of the earliest churches, as well as the story of canon formation and textual transmission.

Appendix: Some Additional Evidence

All of the following texts illustrate communal reading events to some extent. My aim is merely to offer an additional set of selected texts that were not specifically examined in this study. In other words, beyond the 20 first-century authors in chapter 5 and the 27 first-century literary works in chapter 6, there are at least another 142 texts from 60 additional authors to factor into this discussion. Granted, I have somewhat broadened the time frame to include some examples from the centuries before and after the first century CE (i.e., ca. 100 BCE–200 CE). And I have necessarily limited the amount of text and context reproduced here.[1] Nevertheless, the number of references to communal reading events in and around the first century CE, as well as the radical diversity of sources, further indicates just how broad a footprint of influence communal reading events had during the time of Jesus.

ANCIENT RABBINIC WRITINGS

MISHNAH (CA. 2ND CENT. CE)

1. [The priests] would <u>lead through the reading</u> [both] those who know [how to read] and those who do not know [how to read]. (Bik. 3:7e)

2. On the fifteenth day of that month <u>they read the Megillah</u> [Scroll of Esther] in walled cities. (Seqal. 1:1b)

---

1. The primary sources will remain the same as noted earlier in our study.

3. They handed over to him elders belonging to the court, and they read for him the prescribed rite of the day. (Yoma 1:3a)

4. If he was used to reading [Scriptures], he read. And if not, they read for him. (Yoma 1:6c–d).

5. The high priest came to read [in the Women's Court]. If he wanted to read while wearing linen garments, he reads [wearing them]. If not, he reads wearing his own white vestment. The beadle of the community takes the scroll of the Torah and gives it to the head of the community, and the head of the community gives it to the prefect [of the priests], and the prefect gives it to the high priest. The high priest rises and receives it and reads. (Yoma 7:1a–d)

6. He for whom a slave, woman, or minor read answers after them by saying what they say. But it is a curse to him. If an adult male read for him, he answers after him [only] "Halleluyah." (Sukkah 3:10)

7. He who was going along behind a synagogue, or whose house was near a synagogue, and who heard the sound of the shofar or the sound of the reading of the Scroll of Esther, if he paid attention [thereby intending to carry out his obligation], he has fulfilled his obligation. (Ros Has. 3:7d–h)

8. The Scroll [of Esther] is read on the eleventh, twelfth, thirteenth, fourteenth, [or] fifteenth [of Adar] . . . . [If] the fourteenth coincided with a Monday, both villages and large towns read it on that day. (Meg. 1:1a, 2b)

9. The minister of the assembly takes a scroll of the Torah and gives it to the head of the assembly, and the head of the assembly gives it to the prefect, and the prefect gives it to the high priest. And the high priest stands and receives it and reads in it. (Sotah 7:7b)

10. Agrippa the King stood up and received it and read it standing up, and sages praised him on that account. (Sotah 7:8g)

11. A priest reads first, and afterward a Levite, and afterward an Israelite, in the interests of peace. (Git. 5:8b)

12. And a reader reads. (Mak. 3:14)

13. This exegesis did R. Eleazar b. Azariah expound before sages in

the vineyard of Yabneh. (Ketub. 4:6b)

14. Said R. Aqiba, "What do we find in the synagogue? It is the same whether there are many or few present. [The reader] says, 'Bless the Lord.'" (Ber. 7:3k)

APOCRYPHA AND PSEUDEPIGRAPHA

1 ENOCH (CA. 2ND CENT. BCE–1ST CENT. CE)

15. And they asked that I may write for them records of requests, that forgiveness may be theirs, and that I will read for them the record of request before the Lord of heaven. (13:4)

3 MACCABEES (CA. 1ST CENT. BCE)

16. Then they read the law to him; but he persisted in obtruding himself, exclaiming, that he ought to be allowed: and saying, Be it that they were deprived of this honor, I ought not to be. (1:12)

4 BARUCH (CA. 1ST–2ND CENT. CE)

17. And the eagle said: "To you I say, Jeremiah, come, release this epistle, and let it be read to the people." Then, having released the epistles, he read it to the people. (7:21)

ARISTEAS (CA. 3RD CENT. BCE–1ST CENT. CE)

18. When the decree was brought to be read over to the king for his approval, it contained all the other provisions except the phrase "any captives who were in the land before that time or were brought near afterwards," and in his magnanimity and the largeness of his heart the king inserted this clause and gave orders that the grant of money required for the redemption should be deposited in full with the paymasters of the forces and the royal bankers. (26)

19. Having summoned together the whole people we read it to them that they might know of your devotion to our God. (42)

20. And as is the custom of all the Jews, they [washed] their hands in the sea and prayed to God and then <u>devoted themselves to reading</u> and translating the particular passage upon which they were engaged. (305)

21. When the work was completed, Demetrius collected together the Jewish population in the place where the translation had been made, and <u>read it over to all</u>, in the presence of the translators, who met with a great reception also from the people, because of the great benefits which they had conferred upon them. (308)

22. After <u>the books had been read</u>, the priests and the elders of the translators and the Jewish community and the leaders of the people stood up and said, that since so excellent and sacred and accurate a translation had been made, it was only right that it should remain as it was and no alteration should be made in it. (310)

23. When the matter was reported to the king, he rejoiced greatly, for he felt that the design that he had formed had been safely carried out. <u>The whole book was read over to him</u> and he was greatly astonished at the spirit of the lawgiver. And he said to Demetrius: "How is it that none of the historians or the poets have ever thought it worth their while to allude to such a wonderful achievement?" (312)

PSEUDO–HECATAEUS
(CA. 2ND CENT. BCE–1ST CENT. CE)

24. Later, mentioning the man who was already spoken of, he says, "This man, having attained this respected [position], and becoming our close friend, gathered some of the [people] together with himself and <u>read the entire ["scroll"?] to them</u>. For it contained the record of their settlement and citizenship." (6:8)

RECHABITES (CA. 1ST–4TH CENT. CE)

25. All the monks and all who heard were gathered together, and this covenant <u>was read to all</u>. (22:4)

SIBYLLINE ORACLES (CA. 2ND CENT. BCE–1ST CENT. CE)

26. That they may be <u>easily read by readers</u> and partake their use to them. (0:11)

TESTAMENT OF SOLOMON (CA. 1ST–3RD CENT. CE)

27. Then <u>the one who reads</u> speaks from the third time of the one who was talking loudly over the crowded room. (2)

EARLY CHRISTIAN WRITINGS

2 CLEMENT (CA. 2ND CENT. CE)

28. Therefore, brothers and sisters, following the God of truth <u>I am reading you an exhortation</u> to pay attention to what is written, in order that you may save both yourselves and your reader. (19:1)

DIOGNETUS (CA. 2ND CENT. CE)

29. <u>When you have read these truths</u> and listened attentively to them, you will know what God bestows on those who love him as they should. (12:1)

IRENAEUS (CA. 130–202 CE)

30. And in their writings <u>we read as follows</u>, the interpretation which they give. (*Haer.* 1.25.5)

31. And then shall every word also seem consistent to him, if he for his part <u>diligently read the Scriptures in company</u> with those who are presbyters in the Church, among whom is the apostolic doctrine, as I have pointed out. (*Haer.* 4.32.1)

32. True knowledge is [that which consists in] the doctrine of the apostles, and the ancient constitution of the Church throughout all the world, and the distinctive manifestation of the body of Christ according to the successions of the bishops, by which they

have handed down that Church which exists in every place, and has come even to us, being guarded and preserved without any forging of Scriptures, by a very complete system of doctrine, and neither receiving addition nor [suffering] curtailment [in the truths which she believes]; and [it consists in] <u>reading [the word of God] without falsification</u>, and a lawful and diligent exposition in harmony with the Scriptures, both without danger and without blasphemy; and [above all, it consists in] the pre–eminent gift of love, which is more precious than knowledge, more glorious than prophecy, and which excels all the other gifts [of God]. (*Haer.* 4.33.8)

33. Such are the variations existing among them with regard to one [passage], holding discordant opinions as to the same Scriptures; and <u>when the same identical passage is read out</u>, they all begin to purse up their eyebrows, and to shake their heads, and they say that they might indeed utter a discourse transcendently lofty, but that all cannot comprehend the greatness of that thought which is implied in it; and that, therefore, among the wise the chief thing is silence. (*Haer.* 4.35.4)

JUSTIN MARTYR (CA. 100–165 CE)

34. For not only do <u>we fearlessly read them</u>, but, as you see, bring them for your inspection, knowing that their contents will be pleasing to all. (*Apol.* 1:44)

PAPIAS (CA. 1ST–2ND CENT. CE)

35. And Papias, of whom we are now speaking, acknowledges that he had received the words of the apostles from those who had followed them, but he says that he was himself a hearer of Aristion and John the Elder. In any event he frequently mentions them by name and includes their traditions in his writings as well. Let these statements of ours not be wasted on <u>the reader</u>. (3.7)

SHEPHERD OF HERMAS (CA. 2ND CENT. CE)

36. Therefore you will write two little books, and you will send one to Clement and one to Grapte. Then Clement will send it to the cities abroad, because that is his job. . . . But you yourself will <u>read it to this city</u>, along with the elders who preside over the church. (8.3)

TERTULLIAN (CA. 160–220 CE)

37. We come together to <u>read the divine writings</u>. (*Apol.* 39)

GRECO–ROMAN ASSOCIATIONS

LETTER OF THE TYRIAN SETTLERS AT PUTEOLI TO THE CITY OF TYRE (174 CE)

38. The letter of the Tyrian station <u>was read</u>, having been brought by Laches. (AGRW 317)

REGULATIONS OF THE IOBACCHOI (164/165 CE)

39. He (the vice priest) <u>read the statutes</u> drawn up by the former priests. . . . And the president (*proedros*), Rufus son of Aphrodisios, put the question: "To whomever it seems good that the statutes that <u>have been read out</u> should be ratified and inscribed on a monument (stele), raise your hand. (AGRW 7)

GREEK AND ROMAN AUTHORS

APOLLODORUS OF ATHENS (CA. 1ST–2ND CENT. CE)

40. Now the Thebans were in possession of an oracle which declared that they should be rid of the Sphinx <u>whenever they had read her riddle</u>. (LCL 121: 348–49)

APOLLONIUS OF TYANA (CA. 15–100 CE)

41. After that, in an assembly of the commons, two of the regular politicians, Cylon and Ninon, one from the party of the rich and the other from the people's, denounced the Pythagoreans, dividing the charges between them. When these two had made their speeches, the longer one being Cylon's, the other continued, claiming that he had investigated the secrets of the Pythagoreans, though in fact he had forged and written the charges with which he intended to slander them most, and gave the document to the scribe, <u>telling him to read it out</u>. (LCL 458: 102–103)

APPIAN (CA. 95–165 CE)

42. <u>Upon reading these letters</u>, some thought that they were not to be trusted. Others put faith in them. (LCL 2: 192–193)

43. In Rome <u>Cicero read to the people</u> the report of the consul. (LCL 5: 92–93)

44. Then he stationed near himself a sufficient guard, as if to force Octavius against his will, and <u>ordered the clerk with threats to read the proposed law to the multitude</u>. He began to read, but when Octavius again forbade he stopped. (LCL 4: 24–25)

45. <u>I will read</u>, so that I may voice your sentiments rather than my own (LCL 4: 492–93)

APULEIUS (CA. 125–170 CE)

46. Then from a lofty platform he <u>read aloud from a book</u> verbatim. (LCL 453: 266–67).

ATHENAEUS (CA. LATE 2ND–EARLY 3RD CENT. CE)

47. After <u>the letter was read to the Chians</u>, the sophist Theocritus, who was there, said that he now understood the Homeric line. (LCL 327: 142–45)

48. When Mnesiptolemus, for example, <u>gave a reading of his History</u>. (LCL 274: 64–65)

DIO CASSIUS (CA. 155–235 CE)

49. After this he convened the senate, and though he made no address himself by reason of hoarseness, <u>he gave his manuscript to the quaestor to read</u>. (LCL 83: 348–49)

50. He was seventeen years of age when he began to rule. He first entered the camp, and <u>after reading to the soldiers</u> the speech that Seneca had written for him he promised them all that Claudius had given them. Before the senate, too, <u>he read a similar speech</u>,—this one also written by Seneca,—with the result that it was voted that his address should be inscribed on a silver tablet and <u>should be read every time the new consuls entered upon their office</u>. (LCL 176: 36–37)

DIODORUS SICULUS (CA. 90–30 BCE)

51. Theramenes opposed him and <u>read to him</u> the terms of the peace. (LCL 399: 16–17)

52. The priests . . . <u>read to the king</u>, out of the record of acts preserved in their sacred books, those which can be of assistance. (LCL 279: 252–53)

53. <u>At the reading of this letter</u> the commanders and all the Macedonians found themselves in great perplexity. (LCL 377: 184–85)

DIONYSIUS OF HALICARNASSUS (CA. 60–7 BCE)

54. Then, assembling the people, he informed them of everything which had happened during the battle and <u>read to them</u> the decree of the Roman senate. (LCL 347: 136–37)

FRONTO, MARCUS CORNELIUS (CA. 100–160S CE)

55. Samples of my speech, which I had picked out for you, you <u>read to your father</u> yourself, and took the pains to declaim them. (LCL 112: 164–65)

56. You went about in public gatherings with too serious a face, as when you used to <u>read books either in the theatre or at a ban-</u>

quet. (LCL 112: 206–7)

GELLIUS (CA. 125–180 CE)

57. Herodes, speaking in Greek as was his general custom, said: "Allow me, mightiest of philosophers, since we, whom you call laymen, cannot answer you, to read from a book of Epictetus, greatest of Stoics, what he thought and said about such big talk as that of yours." And he bade them bring the first volume of the Discourses of Epictetus. . . . Then, when the book was brought, there was read the passage which I have appended. (LCL 195: 8–9)

58. The Symposium of Plato was being read before the philosopher Taurus. (LCL 212: 268–69).

GREEK ANTHOLOGY
(CA. 1ST CENT. BCE–2ND CENT. CE)

59. He is really the most excellent of poets who gives supper to those who have listened to his recitation. But if he reads to them and sends them home fasting, let him turn his own madness on his own head. (LCL 85: 258–59)

60. Elissus, full of the years ripe for love, just at that fatal age of sixteen, and having withal every charm, small and great, a voice which is honey when he reads. (LCL 85: 290–93)

HORACE (CA. 65–8 BCE)

61. He puts learned and unlearned alike to flight by the scourge of his recitals. If he catches a man, he holds him fast and reads him to death—a leech that will not let go the skin, till gorged with blood. (LCL 194: 488–89)

JUVENAL (CA. LATE 1ST–EARLY 2ND CENT. CE)

62. My party today will offer other forms of entertainment. We'll have a recitation from the author of the Iliad and from the poems

of sublime Maro which challenge Homer's supremacy. With poetry like this, <u>it hardly matters how it's read</u>. (LCL 91: 414–15)

63. The hopes and incentives of literature depend upon Caesar alone.... To work, young men!... If you're looking to get support for your fortunes from anywhere else, and if that makes you fill up the parchment of your yellow page, you'd better get some firewood right away, Telesinus, and offer your compositions to Venus' husband, or else lock away your booklets in the store and let them be pierced by worms. Break your pen and wipe out those battles you spent all night over, you poor thing, <u>writing sublime poetry in your tiny attic, just to win an ivy crown and a scrawny statue</u>. (LCL 91: 298–300)

LIVY (CA. 59 BCE–17 CE)

64. While these things were going on, Quintus Fabius Pictor returned to Rome from his embassy to Delphi and <u>read from a manuscript</u> the response of the oracle (LCL 355: 32–33)

65. Some authorities say that the decree of the senate also <u>was read before he beheaded them</u>. (LCL 367: 60–61)

66. They immediately <u>demanded the book and then allowed him to read it</u>. (LCL 313: 368–69)

67. The conditions being then recited, he cries, "Hear, Jupiter; hear, pater patratus of the Alban People: hear ye, People of Alba: From these terms, as they have been <u>publicly rehearsed</u> from beginning to end, without fraud, <u>from these tablets, or this wax</u>, and as they have been this day clearly understood, the Roman People will not be the first to depart." (LCL 114: 84–85)

68. The people rush up to the doors of the Curia . . . shouting that the letter should be read from the Rostra before the reading in the senate. . . . <u>The letter was read in the senate first, then in the assembly</u>. (LCL 367: 408–9)

69. The decree of the senate was <u>read to the envoys</u>. (LCL 396: 6–7)

70. The letter which was sent and <u>read to the assembly</u> contained, first, a review of his acts of generosity towards Athens; second, an account of the campaigns he had carried on against Philip,

and, lastly, an exhortation to undertake the war against Philip while they had him. (LCL 295: 46–47)

71. This letter was read to the senate by Marcus Sergius, the praetor. (LCL 295: 336–37)

LUCIAN (CA. 2ND CENT. CE)

72. Long before the festival the rich shall write on a tablet the name of each of their friends. . . . They shall keep this ready at hand. . . . Then in the late afternoon, that list of friends shall be read to them. (LCL 430: 108–109)

73. Hippias the sophist was a native of the place, and he and Prodicus from Ceos and Anaximenes from Chios and Polus from Acragas and scores of others always gave their recitations [λόγους ἔλεγον] in person before the assembled spectators and by this means soon won reputations (LCL 430: 144–45)

74. But as to faults in historical writing, you will probably find by observation that they are of the same sort as I have noticed in many attendances at readings, especially if you open your ears to everyone. But it will not be out of place in the meantime to recall by way of example some of the histories already written in this faulty manner (LCL 430: 10–11)

MARCUS AURELIUS (CA. 121–180 CE)

75. And as he listened to their case, at many points he was secretly grieved, but when the complaint of the Athenian Assembly was being read to him, in which they openly attacked Herodes for trying to win over the Governors of Greece with many honeyed words, and somewhere or other even cried out, "O bitter honey!" and again, "Happy they that perish in the pestilence!" he was so deeply moved by what he heard, that he was brought to tears in the sight of all. (LCL 58: 368–69)

76. And so I have sent a letter to be read to the troops. (LCL 113: 314–15)

PAUSANIAS (CA. 110–180 CE)

77. Entering the chamber a magician piles dry wood upon the altar; he first places a tiara upon his head and then sings to some god or other an invocation in a foreign tongue unintelligible to Greeks, reciting the invocation from a book. (LCL 188: 546–47)

PERSIUS (CA. 34–62 CE)

78. What do you think? That poetry now at last flows with smooth rhythm, so that critical fingernails glide smoothly over the joins [iunctura]. The modern poet knows how to make a line as straight as if he were stretching a plumb line with one eye closed. Whether his project is to speak against morality, luxury, or the banquets of lords, the Muse provides our poet with grand material. Look! We're now teaching people who used to dabble in Greek doggerel to produce heroic sentiments, people not skilful [sic] enough to depict a grove or to praise the plentiful countryside. (LCL 91: 54–55)

PLINY THE YOUNGER (CA. 61–113 CE)

79. She is highly intelligent. . . . In addition, this love has given her an interest in literature: she keeps copies of my works to read again and again and even learn by heart. . . . If I am giving a reading she sits behind a curtain near by and greedily drinks in every word of appreciation. (LCL 55: 296–97)

80. The fact that you are one of my readers is no small encouragement to new work. (LCL 55: 310–11)

81. After his bath he lies down for a short rest before dinner, and listens while something light and soothing is read aloud. (LCL 55: 160–61)

82. An author had begun a reading of a work of exceptional candour, and had left part to be read another day. Up came the friends of someone I won't name, begging and praying him not to read the remainder; such is the shame people feel at hearing about their conduct, though they felt none at the time of doing

what they blush to hear. The author complied with their request, as he could well do without loss of sincerity, but the book, like their deeds, remains and will remain; <u>it will always be read</u>, and all the more for this delay, for information withheld only sharpens men's curiosity to hear it. (LCL 59: 136–37)

83. You urge me to give <u>a reading of my speech to a group of friends</u>. . . . It is certainly my intention, if I agree to this reading, to invite all the legal experts. (LCL 55: 146–47)

84. This was his routine in the midst of his public duties and the bustle of the city. In the country, the only time he took from his work was for his bath, and by bath I mean his actual immersion, for while he was being rubbed down and dried <u>he had a book read to him</u> or dictated notes. When travelling he felt free from other responsibilities to give every minute to work; he kept a secretary at his side with book and notebook, and in winter saw that his hands were protected by long sleeves, so that even bitter weather should not rob him of a working hour. (LCL 55: 176–77)

85. You live in a lovely spot, you can take exercise on the shore and in the sea, and have <u>no lack of conversation or books to read and have read to you</u>. (LCL 55: 304–5)

86. Nothing can satisfy my desire for perfection; I can never forget the importance of putting anything into the hands of the public, and I am positive that any work must be revised more than once and <u>read to a number of people</u> if it is intended to give permanent and universal satisfaction. (LCL 55: 522–23)

87. Personally, I do not seek praise for my speech <u>when it is read aloud</u>, but when the text can be read after publication (LCL 55: 518–19)

88. If I am dining alone with my wife or with a few friends, <u>a book is read aloud</u> during the meal. (LCL 59: 154–55)

89. While I was staying in my house at Laurentum I had Asinius Gallus's <u>works read aloud to me</u>. . . . Afterwards, when I returned to Rome, I read them to my friends, who were appreciative. . . . <u>My verses are read and copied, they are even sung</u>, and set to the cithara or lyre by Greeks who have learned Latin out of liking for my little book. (LCL 55: 490–91)

90. He had helped with the prosecution of Arulenus Rusticus and proclaimed his delight in Rusticus's death by giving a public reading of his speech against him (which he afterwards published) where he used the words "Stoics' ape" branded with Vitellius's mark." (LCL 55: 10–11)

91. Paulus was giving a public reading and began by saying. (LCL 55: 424–25)

PLUTARCH (CA. 46–120 CE)

92. This, then, according to Hermippus, is the story which Stroebus, the slave who read aloud for Callisthenes, told to Aristotle. (LCL 99: 380–81)

93. He also wrote poems and sundry speeches which he read aloud to them, and those who did not admire these he would call to their faces illiterate Barbarians, and often laughingly threatened to hang them all. (LCL 99: 444–45)

94. The speeches of Demosthenes, when read aloud, were far superior in point of arrangement and power. Now, it is needless to remark that his written speeches have much in them that is harsh and bitter; but in his extempore rejoinders he was also humorous. (LCL 99: 28–29)

95. Well, then, the rest of the letters were read aloud to the Syracusans, and contained many supplications and entreaties from the women. . . . When all this had been read aloud, it did not occur to the Syracusans, as it should have done, to be astonished at the firmness and magnanimity of Dion.(LCL 98: 68–69)

96. They also brought back another response from Delphi, and caused it to be circulated in Sparta, which declared that sundry very ancient oracles were kept in secret writings by the priests there, and that it was not possible to get these, nor even lawful to read them, unless someone born of Apollo should come after a long lapse of time, give the keepers an intelligible token of his birth, and obtain the tablets containing the oracles. The way being thus prepared, Silenus was to come and demand the oracles as Apollo's son, and the priests who were in the secret were to insist on precise answers to all their questions about his birth,

and finally, persuaded, forsooth, that he was the son of Apollo, were to show him the writing. Then Silenus, <u>in the presence of many witnesses, was to read aloud the prophecies</u>, especially the one relating to the kingdom, for the sake of which the whole scheme had been invented, and which declared that it was more for the honour and interest of the Spartans to choose their kings from the best citizens. (LCL 80: 306–7)

97. After the letter of the king <u>had been read aloud</u>. (LCL 100: 224–25)

98. This letter Dionysius <u>read to Philistus</u>. (LCL 98: 28–29)

99. Demetrius, who had the loudest voice of any herald of the time, <u>read from manuscript</u> the following decree. (LCL 98: 354–55)

100. What will you do when a friend <u>reads a wretched poem</u> or declaims a silly and preposterous speech? (LCL 405: 60–61)

101. For this is right and useful . . . when the precepts of Chilon and of Bias lead to the same conclusions as <u>our children's readings in poetry</u>. (LCL 197: 188–89)

102. And it is said that Sophocles, when defending himself against the charge of dementia brought by his sons, <u>read aloud the entrance song</u> of the chorus in the Oedipus at Colonus. (LCL 321: 86–87)

103. When we have had <u>readings from Plato in company</u>. (LCL 425: 20–21)

104. For just as the teachers of letters or of music themselves first play the notes or <u>read to their pupils</u> and thus show them the way. (LCL 321: 116–17)

105. <u>He read to the Rhodians</u> his oration against Ctesiphon as an exhibition of his powers. (LCL 321: 392–93)

106. The sacred writings are being <u>read to the perfumers</u> as they mix the ingredients. (LCL 306: 186–87)

107. But Hagnonides <u>read aloud an edict</u> which he had prepared. . . . After the edict had been read aloud . . . . (LCL 100: 226–27)

108. The letters <u>were read aloud</u>, and the accused had no courage to reply. (LCL 46: 514–15)

109. For Antony, in defiance of the senate, had <u>read before the people</u>

a letter of Caesar containing propositions which were attractive to the multitude. (LCL 87: 270–71)

110. And I am very much afraid, my friends, that the Praise of Huntinge which was <u>read aloud to us yesterday</u> may so immoderately inflame our young men who like the sport that they will come to consider all other occupations as of minor, or of no, importance and concentrate on this. (LCL 406: 318–19)

PROPERTIUS (CA. 48–15 BCE)

111. 'Do you talk thus, now that your famous book has made you a legend, and your "Cynthia" [Propertius's first book] <u>is read all over the forum</u>?' (LCL 18: 170–71)

QUINTUS CURTIUS (CA. 1ST CENT. CE)

112. Cleander ordered their leaders to be admitted, and <u>read to the soldiers</u> the letters which the king had written. (LCL 369: 138–39)

113. Then letters of Darius were intercepted, in which the Greek soldiers were tempted either to kill or to betray their king, and Alexander was in doubt whether to <u>read them before an assembly</u>, since he thoroughly trusted the goodwill and loyalty towards him of the Greek troops also. (LCL 368: 256–57)

SELECT PAPYRI (41 CE)

114. Seeing that all the populace, owing to its numbers, was unable to be <u>present at the reading</u> of the most sacred and most beneficent letter to the city, I have deemed it necessary to <u>display the letter publicly</u> in order that reading it one by one you may admire the majesty of our god Caesar and feel gratitude for his goodwill towards the city. (LCL 282: 78–79)

SENECA THE YOUNGER (CA. 4 BCE–65 CE)

115. A lecturer sometimes brings upon the platform a huge work of

research, written in the tiniest hand and very closely folded; after <u>reading off a large portion</u>, he says: "I shall stop, if you wish;" and a shout arises: "<u>Read on, read on!</u>" from the lips of those who are anxious for the speaker to hold his peace then and there. (LCL 77: 58–61)

STATIUS (CA. 45–96 CE)

116. As for his polished verses, what youths, <u>what girls in all Rome do not have them by heart</u>? (LCL 206: 52–53)

SUETONIUS (CA. 69–140 CE)

117. Marcus Annaeus Lucanus of Corduba made his first appearance as a poet with a "Eulogy of Nero" at the emperor's Quinquennial Contests, and then <u>gave a public reading</u> of his poem on the "Civil War" waged between Pompey and Caesar. . . . Nero had suddenly called a meeting of the senate and gone out when he <u>was giving a reading</u>, with no other motive than to throw cold water on the performance. (LCL 38: 482–83)

118. Maecenas <u>taking his turn at the reading</u> whenever the poet was interrupted by the failure of his voice. . . . But it was not until long afterwards, when the material was at last in shape, that <u>Virgil read to him</u> three books in all, the first, fourth, and sixth. The last of these produced a remarkable effect on Octavia, who was <u>present at the reading</u>; for it is said that when he reached the verses about her son, "Thou shalt be Marcellus," she fainted and was with difficulty revived. <u>He gave readings also to various others</u>, but never before a large company, selecting for the most part passages about which he was in doubt, in order to get the benefit of criticism. (LCL 38: 456–57)

119. He wrote numerous works of various kinds in prose, some of which <u>he read to a group</u> of his intimate friends, as others did in a lecture-room; for example, his "Reply to Brutus on Cato." <u>At the reading of these volumes</u> he had all but come to the end, when he grew tired and handed them to Tiberius to finish, for he was well on in years. (LCL 31: 274–75)

120. For there were <u>competitions in prose declamation</u> both in Greek

and in Latin. (LCL 38: 332–33)

121. He even read entire volumes to the senate and called the attention of the people to them by proclamations. . . . He gave every encouragement to the men of talent of his own age, listening with courtesy and patience to their readings, not only of poetry and history, but of speeches and dialogues as well. But he took offence at being made the subject of any composition except in serious earnest and by the most eminent writers, often charging the praetors not to let his name be cheapened in prize declamations. (LCL 31: 278–80)

122. He even gave readings in public. (LCL 38: 326–27)

TACITUS (CA. 56–120 CE)

123. Tiberius . . . ordered the bill . . . to be read aloud, together with the decree registered against him by the senate. He then asked Lucius Piso for his opinion. (LCL 249: 630–31)

124. Now I do not want you to take what I am saying as though I am trying to frighten away from verse composition those who are constitutionally devoid of oratorical talent, if they really can find agreeable entertainment for their spare time in this branch of literature, and gain for themselves a niche in the temple of fame. My belief is that there is something sacred and august about every form and every department of literary expression. (LCL 35: 252–53)

125. These observations, and their like, were read aloud, and the imperial displeasure was evident. (LCL 322: 184–85)

126. It was the day following that on which Curiatius Maternus had given a reading of his "Cato." . . . The thing was the talk of the town. (LCL 35: 232–33)

127. Then some letters of Antonius to Civilis, being read before the assembled troops, roused their suspicions. (LCL 249: 58–59)

128. The speeches they delivered on those occasions are read to this day with admiration. (LCL 35: 322)

129. When they had already roused one another by such exhortations, they were further inflamed by a letter from Vespasian,

which Flaccus, being unable to conceal it, <u>read aloud before a general assembly</u>. (LCL 249: 46–47)

130. This correspondence the Flavian leaders <u>read to their soldiers in assembly</u> and thereby inspired their troops with additional confidence; for Caecina had written in humble terms, as if afraid of offending Vespasian, while their generals had written in scorn and with the evident desire to insult Vitellius. (LCL 111: 344–45)

131. Moreover, he established the worst kind of precedent by turning over all letters to the eagle-bearers of the legions, <u>who read them to the common soldiers</u> before they were disclosed to the commanders. (LCL 249: 48–49)

OTHER ANCIENT WRITINGS

GOSPEL OF THE EBIONITES (CA. 2ND CENT. CE)

132. But they, on their own having erased the order of truth, altered the saying, as is plain to all from <u>the attached readings</u>. (7)

GOSPEL OF THE HEBREWS (CA. 2ND CENT. CE)

133. According to the Gospel written in the Hebrew language, which <u>the Nazaraeans read</u>. . . . Further in the Gospel which we have just mentioned we find the following written. (2)

134. As <u>we have read</u> in the Hebrew Gospel, the Lord says to his disciples. (5)

135. In the Gospel according to the Hebrews, which the <u>Nazaraeans are accustomed to read</u>. (6)

GOSPEL OF THE NAZARENES (CA. 2ND CENT. CE)

136. In the Gospel, of which we have made frequent mention, <u>we read that</u> a lintel of wondrous size was broken and divided. — variant: But in the Gospel, which is written in Hebrew letters, <u>we do not read that</u> "the veil of the Temple" was torn, but "the lintel of the Temple of wondrous size collapsed." (21)

137. In the Gospel books that the Nazarenes use <u>we read</u>: "Rays went
      forth from his eyes, by which they were frightened and fled."
      (25)

INFANCY GOSPEL OF THOMAS (CA. 2ND CENT. CE)

138. And going with boldness into the school he found a book lying
      on the lectern, and taking it <u>he did not read the letters that were
      in it</u>. (1.15.2)

139. And when he came to the house of the doctor, he found a book
      lying in that place and took it and opened (it), and <u>read not those
      things which were written in the book</u>. (3.13.2)

PREACHING OF PETER (CA. 2ND CENT. CE)

140. Peter in the Preaching, speaking of the apostles, says, "But,
      having opened the books of the prophets which we had, we
      found, sometimes expressed by parables, sometimes by riddles,
      and sometimes directly and in so many words the name Jesus
      Christ, both his coming and his death and the cross and all the
      other torments which the Jews inflicted on him, and his resur-
      rection and assumption into the heavens before Jerusalem was
      founded, all these things that had been written, what he must
      suffer and what shall be after him. When, therefore, we gained
      knowledge of these things, we believed in God through that
      which had been written of him." And a little after he adds that
      the prophecies came by divine providence, in these terms, "For
      we know what God commanded them, and <u>without the Scrip-
      ture we say nothing</u>." (4)

141. It is too much to <u>set forth now the quotations of Heracleon taken
      from the book</u> entitled The Preaching of Peter and dwell on
      them, inquiring about the book whether it is genuine or spuri-
      ous or compounded of both elements. (6)

142. But if any would produce to us from that book which is called
      The Doctrine of Peter, the passage where the Savior is repre-
      sented as saying to the disciples, "I am not a bodiless demon," he
      must be answered in the first place that <u>that book is not reckoned
      among the books of the church</u>. (7)

Bibliography

Abasciano, Brian J. "Diamonds in the Rough: A Reply to Christopher Stanley Concerning the Reader Competency of Paul's Original Audiences." *NovT* 49 (2007): 153–83.

Achtemeier, Paul J. "*Omne verbum sonat*: The New Testament and the Oral Environment of Late Western Antiquity." *JBL* 109 (1990): 3–27.

Adams, Edward. *The Earliest Christian Meeting Places: Almost Exclusively Houses?* LNTS 450. London: T&T Clark, 2013.

_____. "Placing the Corinthian Communal Meal." In *Text, Image, and Christians in the Graeco-Roman World: A Festschrift in Honor of David Lee Balch*, edited by Aliou Cissé Niang and Carolyn Osiek, 22–37. PTMS 176. Eugene, OR: Wipf and Stock, 2012.

Albl, Martin C. "The Testimonia Hypothesis and Composite Citations." In *Composite Citations in Antiquity*. Volume 1, *Jewish, Graeco-Roman, and Early Christian Uses*, edited by Sean A. Adams and Seth M. Ehorn, 182–202. London: T&T Clark, 2015.

Alexander, Loveday. *Acts in Its Ancient Literary Context: A Classicist Looks at the Acts of the Apostles.* LNTS 298. London: T&T Clark, 2005.

_____. "Ancient Book Production and the Circulation of the Gospels." In *The Gospels for All Christians: Rethinking the Gospel Audiences*, edited by Richard Bauckham, 71–112. Grand Rapids: Eerdmans, 1998.

_____. "What if Luke Had Never Met Theophilus?" *BibInt* 8 (2000): 161–70.

Alikin, Valeriy A. *The Earliest History of the Christian Gathering: Origin, Development and Content of the Christian Gathering in the First to Third Centuries.* Leiden: Brill, 2010.

Allan, Donald J. "ΑΝΑΓΙΓΝΩΣΚΩ and Some Cognate Words." *CQ* 30, no. 1 (1980): 244–51.

Allen, David L. *Hebrews: An Exegetical and Theological Exposition of Holy Scripture.* NAC 35. Nashville: B&H, 2010.

Allison, Dale C. *The Epistle of James: A Critical and Exegetical Commentary.* New York: T&T Clark, 2013.

Apicella, Catherine, Marie-Laurence Haack, and François Lerouxel, eds. *Les affaires de Monsieur Andreau: Économie et société du monde romain.* Scripta antiqua 61. Bordeaux: Ausonius Éditions, 2014.

Arafat, K. W. "Treasure, Treasuries and Value in Pausanias." *CQ* 59, no. 2 (2009): 578–92.

Arnal, William E. "Itinerants and Householders in the Earliest Jesus Movement." In *Whose Historical Jesus?* William E. Arnal and Michael R. Desjardins, 7–24. SCJ 7. Waterloo, ON: Wilfred Laurier University Press, 1997.

Arnaldo Marcone. "Scrittura quotidiana e relazioni sociali nel mondo romano." In *Les affaires de Monsieur Andreau: économie et société du monde romain,* edited by Catherine Apicella, Marie-Laurence Haack, and François Lerouxel, 301–10. Scripta antiqua 61. Bordeaux: Ausonius Éditions, 2014.

Arnold, Clinton E. *Ephesians: Exegetical Commentary on the New Testament.* Grand Rapids: Zondervan, 2010.

Arzt-Grabner, Peter. *Philemon.* Göttingen: Vandenhoeck-Ruprecht, 2003.

Ascough, Richard S., Philip A. Harland, and John S. Kloppenborg, eds. *Associations in the Greco-Roman World: A Sourcebook.* Waco, TX: Baylor University, 2012.

Attridge, Harold W. *Hebrews: A Commentary on the Epistle to the Hebrews.* Hermeneia. Philadelphia: Fortress Press, 1989.

Aune, David E. "Prolegomena to the Study of Oral Tradition in the Hellenistic World." In *Jesus, Gospel Tradition and Paul in the Context of Jewish and Greco-Roman Antiquity,* 220–55. WUNT 303. Tübingen: Mohr Siebeck, 2013.

_____. *Revelation 17–22.* Nashville: Thomas Nelson, 1998.

Autero, Esa. "Social Status in Luke's Infancy Narrative: Zechariah the Priest." *BTB* 41, no. 1 (2011): 36–45.

Averna, Daniela. "La suasoria nelle preghiere agli dei: Percorso diacronico dalla commedia alla tragedia." *Rhetorica* 27, no. 1 (2009): 19–46.

Aviam, Mordechai. "The Decorated Stone from the Synagogue at Migdal: A Holistic Interpretation and a Glimpse into the Life of Galilean Jews at the Time of Jesus." *NovT* 55 (2013): 205–20.

Backhaus, Knut. "Im Hörsaal des Tyrannus (Apg 19.9): Von der Langlebigkeit des Evangeliums in kurzatmiger Zeit." *ThGl* 91, no. 1 (2001): 4–23.

Bagnall, Roger S. "The Effects of Plague: Model and Evidence." *JRA* 15 (2002): 114–20.

_____. *Everyday Writing in the Graeco-Roman East*. Berkeley: University of California, 2011.

Bailey, Kenneth. "Informal Controlled Oral Tradition and the Synoptic Gospels." *AJT* 5 (1991): 34–54.

Baird, Jennifer A. "Scratching the Walls of Houses at Dura-Europos." in *Proceedings of the XIV Congressus Internationalis Epigraphiae Graecae et Latinae: Öffentlichkeit—Monument—Text*, edited by Werner Eck, 489–91. Berlin: de Gruyter, 2014.

Baird, Jennifer, and Claire Taylor, eds. *Ancient Graffiti in Context*. New York: Routledge, 2010.

Balch, David L., and Annette Weissenrieder, eds. *Contested Spaces: Houses and Temples in Roman Antiquity and the New Testament*. WUNT 285. Tübingen: Mohr Siebeck, 2012.

Bar-Ilan, Meir. "Review of *Jewish Literacy in Roman Palestine*." *HS* 44 (2003): 217–22.

Barrett, C. K. *A Critical and Exegetical Commentary on the Acts of the Apostles*. 2 vols. New York: T&T Clark, 2004.

Barth, Markus, and Helmut Blanke. *The Letter to Philemon: A New Translation with Notes and Commentary*. Grand Rapids: Eerdmans, 2000.

Batluck, Mark. "Religious Experience in New Testament Research." *CBR* 9, no. 3 (2011): 339–63.

Batovici, Dan. "A Few Notes on the Use of the Scripture in Galatians." *Sacra Scripta* 11, no. 2 (2013): 287–301.

Bauckham, Richard. "Eyewitnesses and Critical History: A Response to Jens Schröter and Craig Evans." *JSNT* 31, no. 2 (2008): 221–35.

_____. "For Whom Were Gospels Written?" *HTS* 55, no. 4 (1999): 865–82.

_____. "In Response to My Respondents: Jesus and the Eyewitnesses in Review." *JSHJ* 6 (2008): 225–53.

_____. *Jesus and the Eyewitnesses: The Gospels as Eyewitness Testimony*. Grand Rapids: Eerdmans, 2006.

_____. *Jude, 2 Peter*. WBC 50. Nashville: Thomas Nelson, 1983.

Bauckham, Richard, and Stefano De Luca. "Magdala as We Know It." *EC* 6 (2015): 91–118.

Beale, Gregory. *The Book of Revelation*. Grand Rapids: Eerdmans, 1999.

Beale, G. K., and D. A. Carson, eds. *Commentary on the New Testament Use of the Old Testament*. Grand Rapids: Baker Academic, 2007.

Bede. *Expositio Actuum Apostolorum*, edited by Max L. W. Laistner. Brepols: Turnholt, 1983.

Begg, Christopher. "Josephus' and Pseudo-Philo's Rewritings of the Book of Joshua." In *The Book of Joshua*, edited by Ed Noort, 555–88. BETL 250. Leuven: Peeters, 2012.

Belleville, Linda. "Ἰουνίαν . . . ἐπίσημοι ἐν τοῖς ἀποστόλοις: A Re-examination of Romans 16:7 in Light of Primary Source Materials." *NTS* 51 (2005): 231–49.

Ben Ezra, Daniel Stökl. "Canonization—a Non-linear Process?: Observing the Process of Canonization through the Christian (and Jewish) Papyri from Egypt." *ZAC* 12 (2008): 193–214.

_____. "Old Caves and Young Caves: A Statistical Reevaluation of a Qumran Consensus." *DSD* 14, no. 3 (2007): 313–33.

Ben-Ami, Doron, and Yana Tchekhanovets. "The Lower City of Jerusalem on the Eve of Its Destruction, 70 C.E.: A View from Hanyon Givati." *BASOR* 364 (2011): 81.

Benefiel, Rebecca R. "*Litora mundi hospita*: Mobility and Social Interaction in Roman Campania." PhD diss., Harvard University, 2005.

Berder, Michel. "'Ne soyez pas comme…', 'Ne faites pas comme…': Étude des formules rhétoriques de demarcation attribuées à Jésus dans l'Évangile de Matthieu." *Transversalités* 129 (2014): 61–75.

Bernier, Jonathan. *Aposynagōgos and the Historical Jesus in John: Rethinking the Historicity of the Johannine Expulsion Passages*. BIS 122. Leiden: Brill, 2013.

Bexley, Erica M. "Performing Oratory in Early Imperial Rome: Courtroom, Schoolroom, Stage." PhD diss., Cornell University, 2013.

Bird, Michael F. *The Gospel of the Lord: How the Early Church Wrote the Story of Jesus*. Grand Rapids: Eerdmans, 2014.

_____. "The Purpose and Preservation of the Jesus Tradition: Moderate Evidence for a Conserving Force in Its Transmission." *BBR* 15, no. 2 (2005): 161–85.

Bloomer, W. Martin. "Quintilian on the Child as Learning Subject." *Classical World* 105, no. 1 (2011): 109–37.

_____. *Valerius Maximus and the Rhetoric of the New Nobility*. Chapel Hill: University of North Carolina Press, 1992.

Bloomfield, Ronald. "Reading Sacred Texts Aloud in the Old Testament." ThM thesis, Southern Baptist Theological Seminary, 1991.

Blunt, Alfred W. F. *The Apologies of Justin Martyr.* Cambridge Patristic Texts. Cambridge: Cambridge University Press, 1911.

Bock, Darrell L. *Acts.* Grand Rapids: Baker, 2007.

_____. *Luke.* Vol. 2, *9:51–24:53.* Grand Rapids: Baker, 1996.

Bockmuehl, Markus. "New Testament *Wirkungsgeschichte* and the Early Christian Appeal to Living Memory." In *Memory in the Bible and Antiquity: The Fifth Durham-Tuebingen Research Symposium,* edited by Stephen C. Barton, Loren T. Stuckenbruck, and Benjamin G. Wold, 341–68. WUNT 212. Tübingen: Mohr-Siebeck, 2007.

Boesenberg, Dulcinea. "Philo's Descriptions of Jewish Sabbath Practice." *Studia Philonica Annual* 22 (2010): 143–63.

Bokedal, Tomas. *The Formation and Significance of the Christian Biblical Canon: A Study in Text, Ritual and Interpretation.* London: T&T Clark, 2014.

Botha, Pieter J. J. "'I Am Writing This with My Own Hand . . .': Writing in New Testament Times." *Verbum et Ecclesia* 30, no. 2 (2009): 1–11.

_____. *Orality and Literacy in Early Christianity.* Biblical Performance Criticism 5. Eugene, OR: Cascade, 2012.

Bovon, François. "The Emergence of Christianity." *ASE* 24, no. 1 (2007): 13–29.

_____. *Luke 1: A Commentary on the Gospel of Luke 1:1–9:50.* Edited by Helmut Koester. Translated by Christine M. Thomas. Hermeneia. Minneapolis: Fortress Press, 2002.

Bowman, A. K., and A. Wilson, eds. *Settlement, Urbanisation and Population: Oxford Studies in the Roman Economy.* Vol. 2. Oxford: Oxford University Press, 2011.

Bradley, Keith. "Roman Society: A Review." *CJ* 107, no. 2 (2011): 230–36.

Brady, Christian M. M. "What Shall We Remember, the Deeds or the Faith of Our Ancestors? A Comparison of 1 Maccabees 2 and Hebrews 11." In *Earliest Christianity within the Boundaries of Judaism: Essays in Honor of Bruce Chilton,* edited by Alan Avery-Peck, Craig A. Evans, and Jacob Neusner, 107–19. Brill Reference Library of Judaism 49. Leiden: Brill, 2016.

Braund, Susanna. "Seneca Multiplex: The Phases (and Phrases) of Seneca's Life and Works." In *The Cambridge Companion to Seneca,* edited by Shadi Bartsch and Alessandro Schiesaro, 15–28. Cambridge: Cambridge University Press, 2015.

Bremmer, Jan N. *Initiation into the Mysteries of the Ancient World*. Berlin: De Gruyter, 2014.

Brox, Norbert. *Die Pastoralbriefe*. Regensburg: Friedrich Pustet, 1963.

Bruce, F. F. *1 and 2 Thessalonians*. WBC 45. Nashville: Thomas Nelson, 1982.

Bullard, Collin B. *Jesus and the Thoughts of Many Hearts: Implicit Christology and Jesus' Knowledge in the Gospel of Luke*. LNTS 530. London: T&T Clark, 2015.

Bultmann, Rudolf. *Jesus and the Word*. New York: Scribner's, 1934.

Burtchaell, James T. *From Synagogue to Church: Public Services and Offices in the Earliest Christian Communities*. Cambridge: Cambridge University Press, 1992.

Burton-Christie, Douglas. *The Word in the Desert: Scripture and the Quest for Holiness in Early Christian Monasticism*. Oxford: Oxford University Press, 1993.

Butts, James R. "The *Progymnasmata* of Theon: A New Text with Translation and Commentary." PhD diss., Claremont Graduate School, 1986.

Byatt, Anthony. "Josephus and Population Numbers in First Century Palestine." *PEQ* 105 (1973): 51–60.

Byrskog, Samuel. "A New Perspective on the Jesus Tradition: Reflections on James D. G. Dunn's *Jesus Remembered*." *JSNT* 26, no. 4 (2004): 459–71.

_____. *Story as History—History as Story: The Gospel Tradition in the Context of Ancient Oral History*. WUNT 123. Tübingen: Mohr-Siebeck, 2000.

Cambron-Goulet, Mathilde. "Orality in Philosophical Epistles." In *Between Orality and Literacy: Communication and Adaptation in Antiquity*, edited by Ruth Scodel, 10:148–74. MnS 367. Leiden: Brill, 2014.

Campbell, Jonathan G. *The Use of Scripture in the Damascus Document 1–8, 19–20*. BZAW 228. Berlin: De Gruyter, 1995.

Carcopino, Jérôme. *Daily Life in Ancient Rome: The People and the City at the Height of the Empire*. Edited by Henry T. Rowell. Translated by E. O. Lorimer. Mitchham, Victoria, Australia: Penguin, 1956.

_____. *La Vie quotidienne à Rome à l'apogée de l'Empire*. Paris: Hachette, 1939.

Cargill, Robert R. "The State of the Archaeological Debate at Qumran." *CBR* 10, no. 1 (2011): 101–18.

Caro, José Manuel Sánchez. "La Biblia, libro de la Iglesia, libro de la Humanidad." *Salm* 59 (2012): 15–39.

Carr, David M. *Writing on the Tablet of the Heart: Origins of Scripture and Literature*. New York: Oxford University Press, 2005.

Carras, George. "Dependence or Common Tradition in Philo *Hypothetica* VIII 6.10–7.20 and Josephus *Contra Apionem* 2.190–219." *Studia Philonica Annual* 5 (1993): 24–47.

Carrié, Jean-Marie. "Le livre comme objet d'usage, le livre comme valeur symbolique." *Antiquité Tardive* 18 (2010): 181–90.

Chan, Samuel S. H. "The Preached Gospel as the Word of God: An Old Question Revisited with Special Reference to Speech Act Theory." PhD diss., Trinity Evangelical Divinity School, 2006.

Chancey, Mark A. "Disputed Issues in the Study of Cities, Villages, and the Economy in Jesus' Galilee." In *The World of Jesus and the Early Church: Identity and Interpretation in Early Communities of Faith*, edited by Craig A. Evans, 53–68. Peabody, MA: Hendrickson, 2011.

Chapman, David W., and Eckhard J. Schnabel. *The Trial and Crucifixion of Jesus: Texts and Commentary*. WUNT 344. Tübingen: Mohr Siebeck, 2015.

Chapple, Allan. "Getting Romans to the Right Romans: Phoebe and the Delivery of Paul's Letter." *TynBull* 62, no. 2 (2011): 195–214.

Charlesworth, James H. "4 Maccabees: A New Translation and Introduction." In *The Old Testament Pseudepigrapha*, edited by James H. Charlesworth, 2:531–64. Peabody, MA: Hendrickson, 2009.

———, ed. and trans. *The Odes of Solomon: The Syriac Texts*. Missoula, MT: Scholars, 1977.

———, ed. *The Old Testament Pseudepigrapha*. Vol. 2. Peabody, MA: Hendrickson, 2009.

———, ed. *Papyri and Leather Manuscripts of the Odes of Solomon*. Durham, NC: Duke University Press, 1981.

Charlesworth, James H., and Mordechai Aviam. "Reconstructing First-Century Galilee: Reflections on Ten Major Problems." In *Jesus Research: New Methodologies and Perceptions*, edited by James H. Charlesworth and Brian Rhea, 103–37. The Second Princeton-Prague Symposium on Jesus Research, Princeton 2007. Grand Rapids: Eerdmans, 2014.

Charlesworth, Scott D. "Public and Private: Second- and Third-Century Gospel Manuscripts." In *Jewish and Christian Scripture as Artifact and Canon*, edited by Craig A. Evans and H. Daniel Zacharias, 148–75. London: T&T Clark, 2009.

Childs, Brevard S. *The Church's Guide to Reading Paul: The Canonical Shape of the Pauline Corpus*. Grand Rapids: Eerdmans, 2008.

Chilton, Bruce, Darrell Bock, Daniel M. Gurtner, Jacob Neusner, Lawrence

H. Schiffman, and Daniel Oden, eds. *A Comparative Handbook to the Gospel of Mark: Comparisons with Pseudepigrapha, the Qumran Scrolls, and Rabbinic Literature*. NTGJC 1. Leiden: Brill, 2010.

Choi, Agnes. "Urban-Rural Interaction and the Economy of Lower Galilee." PhD diss., University of St. Michael's College, 2010.

Ciampa, Roy E. *The Presence and Function of Scripture in Galatians 1 and 2*. WUNT 2, book 102. Tübingen: Mohr Siebeck, 1998.

Cohen, Naomi G. *Philo's Scriptures: Citations from the Prophets and Writings, Evidence for a Haftarah Cycle in Second Temple Judaism*. JSJSup 123. Leiden: Brill, 2007.

Collar, Anna. *Religious Networks in the Roman Empire*. Cambridge: Cambridge University Press, 2013.

Collins, Adela. *Mark: A Commentary*. Edited by Harold W. Attridge. Minneapolis: Fortress Press, 2007.

Collins, John J. "The Site of Qumran and the Sectarian Communities in the Dead Sea Scrolls." In *The World of Jesus and the Early Church: Identity and Interpretation in Early Communities of Faith*. Edited by Craig A. Evans, 9–22. Peabody, MA: Hendrickson, 2011.

Corbett, Joey. "New Synagogue Excavations in Israel and Beyond." *BAR* 37, no. 4 (2011): 52–59.

Corbier, Mireille. *Donner à voir, donner à lire: Memoire et communication dans la Rome ancienne*. Paris: CNRS, 2006.

Courtney, Edward. *A Companion to Petronius*. Reprint ed. Oxford: Oxford University Press, 2010.

Craffert, Pieter F. and Pieter J. J. Botha. "Why Jesus Could Walk on the Sea but He Could Not Read and Write: Reflections on Historicity and Interpretation in Historical Jesus Research." *Neot* 39, no. 1 (2005): 5–35.

Cribiore, Raffaella. "Education in the Papyri." In *The Oxford Handbook of Papyrology*, edited by Roger S. Bagnall, 320–37. Oxford: Oxford University Press, 2009.

_____. *Gymnastics of the Mind: Greek Education in Hellenistic and Roman Egypt*. Princeton, NJ: Princeton University Press, 2001.

Crossan, John Dominic, and Jonathan L. Reed. *Excavating Jesus: Beneath the Stones, behind the Texts*. San Francisco: HarperCollins, 2001.

Dalzell, A. "C. Asinius Pollio and the Early History of Public Recitation at Rome." *Hermathena* 86 (1955): 20–28.

Dark, K. R. "Archaeological Evidence for a Previously Unrecognised Roman Town near the Sea of Galilee." *PEQ* 145, no. 3 (2013): 185–202.

Davids, Peter H. *The Letters of 2 Peter and Jude*. Grand Rapids: Eerdmans, 2006.

_____. *A Theology of James, Peter, and Jude*. Grand Rapids: Zondervan, 2014.

Davies, Andrew. "What Does It Mean to Read the Bible as a Pentecostal?" *JPT* 18 (2009): 216–29.

Davies, William, and Dale Allison. *A Critical and Exegetical Commentary on the Gospel According to Saint Matthew*. Vol. 3, *Commentary on Matthew XIX–XXVIII*. Edinburgh: T&T Clark, 1997.

Davis, P. J. "Roman Games." In *The Oxford Encyclopedia of Ancient Greece and Rome*, edited by Michael Gagarin, 3:264–71. Oxford: Oxford University, 2010.

de Boer, Martinus. *Galatians: A Commentary*. Louisville: Westminster John Knox, 2011.

de Jonge, Henk Jan. "The Use of the Old Testament in Scripture Readings in Early Christian Assemblies." In *The Scriptures of Israel in Jewish and Christian Tradition: Essays in Honour of Maarten J. J. Menken*, edited by Steve Moyise, Bart J. Koet, and Joseph Verheyden, 376–92. SNT 148. Leiden: Brill, 2013.

de Luca, Stefano, and Anna Lena. "The Mosaic of the Thermal Bath Complex of Magdala Reconsidered: Archaeological Context, Epigraphy and Iconography." In *Knowledge and Wisdom: Archaeological and Historical Essays in Honour of Leah Di Segni*, edited by G. C. Bottini, L. D. Crupcala, and J. Patrich, 1–33. SBF Collectio Maior 54. Milan: Terra Santa, 2014.

den Hollander, William. *Josephus, the Emperors, and the City of Rome: From Hostage to Historian*. AJEC 86. Leiden: Brill, 2014.

deSilva, David A. *4 Maccabees*. Sheffield: Sheffield Academic, 1998.

DeSmidt, David B. "The Declamatory Origin of Petronius' *Satyrica*." PhD diss., Columbia University, 2006.

Deutsch, R. "Roman Coins Boast 'Judaea Capta.'" *BAR* 36, no. 1 (2010): 51–53.

Dibelius, Martin, and Hans Conzelmann. *The Pastoral Epistles: A Commentary on the Pastoral Epistles*. Edited by Helmut Koester. Translated by Philip Buttolph and Adela Yarbro. Philadelphia: Fortress Press, 1972.

Dickerson, Patrick L. "Apollos in Acts and First Corinthians." PhD diss., University of Virginia, 1998.

Dobbin, Robert F. *Epictetus, Discourses Book I: Translated with an Introduction and Commentary*. Oxford: Oxford University Press, 1998.

Doering, Lutz. *Ancient Jewish Letters and the Beginnings of Christian Epistolography*. WUNT 298. Tübingen: Mohr Siebeck, 2012.

Donelson, Lewis. *I and II Peter and Jude: A Commentary*. Louisville: Westminster John Knox, 2010.

Dorsey, David. *The Roads and Highways of Ancient Israel*. Baltimore: John Hopkins University Press, 1991.

Downs, David J. "Economics, Taxes, and Tithes." in *The World of the New Testament: Cultural, Social, and Historical Contexts*. Edited by Joel B. Green and Lee Martin McDonald, 156–68. Grand Rapids: Baker Academic, 2013.

du Toit, Jacqueline S. *Textual Memory: Ancient Archives, Libraries and the Hebrew Bible*. Social World of Biblical Antiquity 2.6. Sheffield: Sheffield Phoenix, 2011.

Duncan, Carrie E. "The Rhetoric of Participation: Gender and Representation in Ancient Synagogues." PhD diss., University of North Carolina at Chapel Hill, 2012.

Dunn, James D. G. "Altering the Default Setting: Re-envisaging the Early Transmission of the Jesus Tradition." *NTS* 49 (2003): 139–75.

_____. "Did Jesus Attend the Synagogue?" In *Jesus and Archaeology*, edited by James H. Charlesworth, 206–22. Grand Rapids: Eerdmans, 2006.

_____. *The Epistles to the Colossians and to Philemon*. Grand Rapids: Eerdmans, 1996.

_____. *Jesus Remembered: Christianity in the Making*. Vol. 1. Grand Rapids: Eerdmans, 2003.

_____. "On History, Memory and Eyewitnesses: In Response to Bengt Holmberg and Samuel Byrskog." *JSNT* 26, no. 4 (2004): 473–87.

Dupont, Dom Jacques. "Notes sur les Actes des Apôtres." *RB* 66 (1955): 45–59.

Dupont, Florence. "The Corrupted Boy and the Crowned Poet: or, The Material Reality and the Symbolic Status of the Literary Book at Rome." in *Ancient Literacies: The Culture of Reading in Greece and Rome*, edited by William A. Johnson and Holt N. Parker, translated by Holt N. Parker, 143–63. Oxford: Oxford University Press, 2009.

_____. "*Recitatio* and the Space of Public Discourse." In *The Roman Cultural Revolution*, edited by T. Habinek and A. Schiesaro, 44–59. Cambridge: Cambridge University Press, 1997.

Eddy, Paul. "Orality and Oral Transmission." In *Dictionary of Jesus and the*

Gospels, 2nd ed., edited by Joel B. Green, Jeannine K. Brown, and Nicholas Perrin, 641–50. Downers Grove: IVP Academic, 2013.

Edsall, Benjamin, and Jennifer R. Strawbridge. "The Songs We Used to Sing? Hymn 'Traditions' and Reception in Pauline Letters." *JSNT* 37, no. 3 (2015): 290–311.

Edwards, James. *The Gospel according to Luke*. Grand Rapids: Eerdmans, 2015.

Ehrman, Bart. *Forgery and Counterforgery: The Use of Literary Deceit in Early Christian Polemics*. New York: Oxford University Press, 2013.

Elizur, Zeev. "The Book and the Holy: Chapters in the History of the Concept of Holy Book from the Second Temple Period to Late Antiquity." PhD diss., Ben Gurion University, 2012 (Hebrew).

Elliott, David J. "4 Maccabees." In *The Apocrypha*, edited by Martin Goodman, 239–42. Oxford: Oxford University Press, 2012.

Elliott, J. K. *New Testament Textual Criticism: The Application of Thoroughgoing Principles*. NovTSup 137. Leiden: Brill, 2010.

Enos, Richard, and Terry Peterman. "Writing Instruction for the 'Young Ladies' of Teos: A Note on Women and Literacy in Antiquity." *Rhetoric Review* 33, no. 1 (2014): 1–20.

Erdkamp, P. "Beyond the Limits of the 'Consumer City': A Model of the Urban and Rural Economy in the Roman World." *Historia* 50 (2001): 332–56.

Evans, Craig. "How Long Were Late Antique Books in Use? Possible Implications for New Testament Textual Criticism." *BBR* 25.1 (2015): 23–37.

Eve, Eric. *Behind the Gospels: Understanding the Oral Tradition*. Minneapolis: Fortress Press, 2014.

Falk, Daniel K. *Daily, Sabbath, and Festival Prayers in the Dead Sea Scrolls*. Edited by F. García Martínez and A. S. van der Woude. STDJ 27. Leiden: Brill, 1998.

Fantham, Elaine. *Roman Literary Culture: From Plautus to Macrobius*. 2nd ed. Baltimore, MD: Johns Hopkins University Press, 2013.

Fee, Gordon. *The First and Second Letters to the Thessalonians*. Grand Rapids: Eerdmans, 2009.

_____. *The First Epistle to the Corinthians*. Grand Rapids: Eerdmans, 1987.

Ferguson, Everett. *Backgrounds of Early Christianity*. 3rd ed. Grand Rapids: Eerdmans, 2003.

Fiensy, David A., and James Riley Strange. "The Galilean Village in the Late Second Temple and Mishnaic Periods." In *Galilee in the Late Second Temple and Mishnaic Periods*. Vol. 1, *Life, Culture, and Society*, edited by David A. Fiensy and James Riley Strange, 177–207. Minneapolis: Fortress Press, 2014.

Finley, Susan. "Celsus Library of Ephesus: The Man and the City behind the Famous Façade." *Libri* 64, no. 3 (2014): 277–92.

Finnegan, Ruth. *Literacy and Orality*. Oxford: Basil Blackwell, 1988.

Fisk, Bruce N. "Retelling Israel's Story: Scripture, Exegesis and Transformation in Pseudo-Philo's *Liber Antiquitatum Biblicarum* 12–24." PhD diss., Duke University, 1997.

_____. "Synagogue Influence and Scriptural Knowledge among the Christians of Rome." In *As It Is Written: Studying Paul's Use of Scripture*, edited by Stanley E. Porter and Christopher D. Stanley, 157–85. Atlanta: SBL, 2008.

Fitzgerald, William. *Martial: The World of the Epigram*. Chicago: University of Chicago Press, 2007.

Fitzmyer, Joseph A. *The Gospel according to Luke I–IX*. New York: Doubleday, 1981.

_____. *The Letter to Philemon: A New Translation with Introduction and Commentary*. London: Doubleday, 2000.

Focant, Camille. *The Gospel according to Mark: A Commentary*. Translated by Leslie Robert Keylock. Eugene, OR: Wipf and Stock, 2012.

_____. *Marc, un évangile étonnant: Recueil d'essais*. BETL 194. Leuven: Peeters, 2006.

Foley, John M. "Verbal Marketplaces and the Oral-Literate Continuum." In *Along the Oral-Written Continuum: Types of Texts, Relations and Their Implications*, edited by Slavica Ranković, Leidulf Melve, and Else Mundal 17–37. Turnhout, Belgium: Brepols, 2010.

Fontenrose, Joseph. *The Delphic Oracle: Its Responses and Operations, with a Catalogue of Respsonses*. Berkeley: University of California Press, 1978.

Foster, Paul. *The Gospel of Peter: Introduction, Critical Edition and Commentary*. TENTS 4, edited by Stanley E. Porter and Wendy J. Porter. Leiden: Brill, 2010.

_____. "Who Wrote 2 Thessalonians? A Fresh Look at an Old Problem." *JSNT* 35, no. 2 (2012): 150–75.

Fotopoulos, John. "Paul's Curse of Corinthians: Restraining Rivals with Fear and *Voces Mysticae* (1 Cor 16:22)." *NovT* 56 (2014): 275–309.

Frampton, Stephanie A. "Towards a Media History of Writing in Ancient Italy." PhD diss., Harvard University, 2011.

France, Richard T. *The Gospel of Mark*. Grand Rapids: Eerdmans, 2002.

_____. *Luke*. Edited by Mark L. Strauss and John H. Walton. Grand Rapids: Baker, 2013.

Fredriksen, Paula. "How Later Contexts Affect Pauline Content, or: Retrospect Is the Mother of Anachronism." In *Jews and Christians in the First and Second Centuries*, 17–51. Leiden: Brill, 2015.

Friedländer, Ludwig. *Roman Life and Manners under the Early Empire*, authorized translation of *Sittengeschichte Roms,* 7th edition, volume 3. Translated by J. H. Freese. New York: E. P. Dutton, 1910.

Friesen, Steve. "Poverty in Pauline Studies: Beyond the So-Called New Consensus." *JSNT* 26 (2004): 323–61.

Fuhrmann, Christopher. "Dio Chrysostom as a Local Politician: A Critical Reappraisal." In *Aspects of Ancient Institutions and Geography*, edited by Lee L. Brice and Daniëlle Slootjes, 161–76. IE 19. Leiden: Brill, 2015.

Funaioli, Giovanni B. "Recitationes." Pages 435–46 in *Paulys Realencyclopädie der classischen Altertumswissenschaft*. Stuttgart: Druckenmüller, 1949.

Gamble, Harry Y. "The Book Trade in the Roman Empire." In *The Early Text of the New Testament*, edited by Charles E. Hill and Michael J. Kruger, 23–36. New York: Oxford University Press, 2012.

_____. *Books and Readers in the Early Church: A History of Early Christian Texts*. New Haven: Yale University Press, 1995.

_____. "Literacy, Liturgy, and the Shaping of the New Testament Canon." in *The Earliest Gospels: The Origins and Transmission of the Earliest Christian Gospels; The Contribution of the Chester Beatty Gospel Codex P45*, edited by Charles Horton, 27–39. London: T&T Clark, 2004.

Gavrilov, A. K. "Techniques of Reading in Classical Antiquity." *CQ* 47, no. 1 (1997): 56–73.

Gerhardsson, Birger. *Memory and Manuscript: Oral Tradition and Written Transmission in Rabbinic Judaism and Early Christianity*. ASNU 22. Copenhagen, Denmark: Munksgaard, 1961.

_____. "The Secret of the Transmission of the Unwritten Jesus Tradition." *NTS* 51 (2005): 1–18.

Gibson, Craig. "How (Not) to Learn Rhetoric: Lucian's *Rhetorum Praeceptor* as Rebuttal of a School Exercise." *GRBS* 52 (2012): 89–110.

Giese, Curtis. *2 Peter and Jude*. St. Louis: Concordia, 2012.

Giesen, Heinz. "Poverty and Wealth in Jesus and the Jesus Tradition." In *Handbook for the Study of the Historical Jesus: How to Study the Historical*

Jesus, edited by Tom Holmén and Stanley E. Porter, 4:3269–303. Leiden: Brill, 2011.

Gillam, Robyn. *Performance and Drama in Ancient Egypt*. London: Duckworth, 2005.

Gilliard, Frank D. "More Silent Reading in Antiquity: *Non Omne Verbum Sonabat*." *JBL* 112, no. 4 (1993): 689–96.

González, José Miguel. "*Rhapsōidos, Prophētēs*, and *Hypokritēs*: A Diachronic Study of the Performance of Homeric Poetry in Ancient Greece." PhD diss., Harvard University, 2005.

Goodacre, Mark. "Did Thomas Know the Synoptic Gospels? A Response to Denzey Lewis, Kloppenborg and Patterson." *JSNT* 36, no. 3 (2014): 282–93.

––––––. *Thomas and the Gospels: The Making of an Apocryphal Text*. Grand Rapids: Eerdmans, 2012.

Goodman, Martin. "Religious Variety and the Temple in the Late Second Temple Period and Its Aftermath." *JJS* 60, no. 2 (2009): 202–13.

Goswell, Gregory. "Titles without Texts: What the Lost Books of the Bible Tell Us about the Books We Have." *Colloq* 41, no. 1 (2009): 73–93.

Grant, Michael. *History of Rome*. New York: Scribner's, 1978.

Graudin, Arthur F. "Mark's Portrait of Jesus as Teacher." PhD diss., Claremont, 1972.

Graves, Michael. "The Public Reading of Scripture in Early Judaism." *JETS* 50, no. 3 (2007): 467–87.

Green, Gene L. *Jude and 2 Peter*. Grand Rapids: Baker Academic, 2008.

Green, Joel B., Jeannine K. Brown, and Nicholas Perrin. *Dictionary of Jesus and the Gospels*. 2nd ed. Downers Grove: IVP Academic, 2013.

Grierson, Fiona. "The Testament of Moses." *JSP* 17, no. 4 (2008): 265–80.

Gruber, Mayer. "Review Essay: The Tannaitic Synagogue Revisted." *RRJ* 5, no. 1 (2002): 113–25.

Gurd, Sean. *Work in Progress: Literary Revision as Social Performance in Ancient Rome*. Oxford: Oxford University Press, 2012.

Guthrie, George H. *2 Corinthians*. Grand Rapids: Baker Academic, 2015.

Haber, Susan. "Common Judaism, Common Synagogue? Purity, Holiness, and Sacred Space at the Turn of the Common Era." In *Common Judaism: Explorations in Second-Temple Judaism*, edited by Wayne O. McCready and Adele Reinhartz, 69–71. Minneapolis: Fortress Press, 2008.

Hadas, Moses. *The Third and Fourth Books of Maccabees*. Edited and translated by Moses Hadas. New York: Harper & Brothers, 1953.

Hadas-Lebel, Mireille. *Philo of Alexandria: A Thinker in the Jewish Diaspora*. Translated by Robyn Fréchet. SPA 7. Leiden: Brill, 2012.

Haenchen, Ernst. *The Acts of the Apostles: A Commentary*. Philadelphia: Westminster, 1971.

Haines-Eitzen, Kim. *The Gendered Palimpsest: Women, Writing, and Representation in Early Christianity*. Oxford: Oxford University Press, 2012.

Hansen, G. Walter. *The Letter to the Philippians*. Grand Rapids: Eerdmans, 2009.

Harink, Douglas. *1 and 2 Peter*. London: SCM, 2009.

Harland, Philip A. "Pausing at the Intersection of Religion and Travel." In *Travel and Religion in Antiquity*, edited by Philip A. Harland, 1–26. SCJ 21. Waterloo: Wilfrid Laurier University Press, 2011.

Harmon, Matthew S. "Letter Carriers and Paul's Use of Scripture." *JSPL* 4, no. 2 (2014): 129–48.

Harris, Murray J. *The Second Epistle to the Corinthians*. Grand Rapids: Eerdmans, 2005.

Hartin, Patrick. *James*. SP 14. Collegeville, MN: Liturgical Press, 2003.

Hartman, Lars. "On Reading Others' Letters." *HTR* 79 (1986): 137–46.

Harvey, R. A. *A Commentary on Persius*. Leiden: Brill, 1981.

Hawes, Greta. "Story Time at the Library: Palaephatus and the Emergence of Highly Literate Mythology." In *Between Orality and Literacy: Communication and Adaptation in Antiquity*, edited by Ruth Scodel, 10:125–47. MnS 367. Leiden: Brill, 2014.

Head, Peter M. "Letter Carriers in Ancient Jewish Epistolary Material." In *Jewish and Christian Scripture as Artifact and Canon*, edited by Craig A. Evans and H. Daniel Zacharias, 203–19. LSTS 70. London: T&T Clark, 2009.

———. "'Witnesses between You and Us': The Role of the Letter-Carriers in *1 Clement*." In *Studies on the Text of the New Testament and Early Christianity in Honor of Michael W. Holmes*, edited by Daniel M. Gurtner, Juan Hernández, and Paul Foster, 477–93. NTTSD 50. Leiden: Brill, 2015.

Helzle, Martin. *Ovids Epistulae ex Ponto: Buch I–II Kommentar*. Heidelberg: Universitätsverlag C. Winter, 2002.

Hendrickson, G. L. "Ancient Reading." *CJ* 25, no. 3 (1929): 182–96.

Hengel, Martin. *Studies in the Gospel of Mark*. London: SCM Press, 1985.

Henze, Matthias. "4 Ezra and 2 Baruch: Literary Composition and Oral Performance in First-Century Apocalyptic Literature." *JBL* 131, no. 1 (2012): 181–200.

Hezser, Catherine. "The Torah versus Homer: Jewish and Greco-Roman Education in Late Roman Palestine." In *Ancient Education and Early Christianity*, edited by Matthew Ryan Hauge and Andrew W. Pitts, 5–24. London: T&T Clark, 2016.

Hickey, Todd M. "Writing Histories from the Papyri." In *The Oxford Handbook of Papyrology*, edited by Roger S. Bagnall, 495–520. Oxford: Oxford University Press, 2009.

Hill, Charles E., and Michael J. Kruger. *The Early Text of the New Testament.* New York: Oxford University Press, 2012.

Hill, David. "On the Use and Meaning of Hosea 6:6 in Matthew's Gospel." *NTS* 24, no. 1 (1977): 107–19.

Hoehner, Harold W. *Ephesians: An Exegetical Commentary.* Grand Rapids: Baker Academic, 2002.

Hogan, Karina M. *Theologies in Conflict in 4 Ezra: Wisdom Debate and Apocalyptic Solution.* JSJSup 130. Leiden: Brill, 2008.

Hollingsworth, Anthony L. "Recitation and the Stage: The Performance of Senecan Tragedy." PhD diss., Brown University, 1998.

Holmberg, Bengt. "Questions of Method in James Dunn's *Jesus Remembered*." *JSNT* 26, no. 4 (2004): 445–57.

Holmes, Michael W., ed. and trans. *The Apostolic Fathers: Greek Texts and English Translations.* 3rd ed. Grand Rapids: Baker, 2007.

———. "Working with an Open Textual Tradition: Challenges in Theory and Practice." in *The Textual History of the Greek New Testament: Changing Views in Contemporary Research*, edited by Klaus Wachtel and Michael W. Holmes, 65–78. Text-Critical Studies 8. Atlanta: SBL, 2011.

Horrell, David. "Domestic Space and Christian Meetings at Corinth: Imagining New Contexts and the Buildings East of the Theatre." *NTS* 50 (2004): 349–69.

Horsfall, Nicholas. "Rome without Spectacles." *Greece and Rome* 42, no. 1 (1995): 49–56.

Horsley, G. H. R. *Homer in Pisidia: Degrees of Literateness in a Backwoods Province of the Roman Empire.* New South Wales, Australia: University of New England, 1999.

Horsley, Richard A. *Archaeology, History and Society in Galilee: The Social Context of Jesus and the Rabbis.* Harrisburg, PA: Trinity Press International, 1996.

Houston, George W. *Inside Roman Libraries: Book Collections and Their Man-*

agement in Antiquity. Chapel Hill: University of North Carolina Press, 2014.

Howell, Peter. *A Commentary on Book One of the Epigrams of Martial*. London: Athlone, 1980.

Huffmon, Herbert B. "The Oracular Process: Delphi and the Near East." *VT* 57 (2007): 449–90.

Hultgren, S. J. *From the Damascus Covenant to the Covenant of the Community: Literary, Historical, and Theological Studies in the Dead Sea Scrolls*. STDJ 66. Leiden: Brill, 2007.

Hurtado, Larry W. *The Earliest Christian Artifacts: Manuscripts and Christian Origins*. Grand Rapids: Eerdmans, 2006.

_____. "The New Testament in the Second Century: Text, Collections and Canon." In *Transmission and Reception: New Testament Text-Critical and Exegetical Studies*, edited by J. W. Childers and D. C. Parker, 3–27. Piscataway, NJ: Gorgias, 2006.

_____. "Oral Fixation and New Testament Studies? 'Orality', 'Performance' and Reading Texts in Early Christianity." *NTS* 60 (2014): 321–40.

Hurtado, Larry W., and Chris Keith. "Writing and Book Production in the Hellenistic and Roman Periods." In *The New Cambridge History of the Bible: The Bible, from the Beginnings to 600*, edited by James C. Paget and J. Schaper, 63–80. Cambridge: Cambridge University Press, 2013.

Huskey, Samuel J. "Ovid's *Tristia* I and III: An Intertextual Katabasis." PhD diss., University of Iowa, 2002.

Huttner, Ulrich. *Early Christianity in the Lycus Valley*. Translated by David Green. AJEC 85. Leiden: Brill, 2013.

Hvalvik, Reidar. "All Those Who in Every Place Call on the Name of Our Lord Jesus Christ: The Unity of the Pauline Churches." In *The Formation of the Early Church*, edited by Jostein Ådna 123–44. WUNT 183. Tübingen: Mohr Siebeck, 2005.

Iddeng, Jon W. "*Publica aut Peri!*: The Releasing and Distribution of Roman Books." *Symbolae Osloenses* 81 (2006): 58–84.

Inwood, Brad, trans. *Seneca: Selected Philosophical Letters*. Oxford: Oxford University Press, 2007.

Ito, Akio. "Paul the 'Herald' and the 'Teacher.'" In *Sacred Words: Orality, Literacy, and Religion*, 351–70. Leiden: Brill, 2011.

Jacobson, Howard. *A Commentary on Pseudo-Philo's* Liber Antiquitatum Biblicarum *with Latin Text and English Translation*. Vol. 2. Leiden: Brill, 1996.

Janzen, Anna. "Der Friede im lukanischen Doppelwerk vor dem Hintergrund der Pax Romana." PhD diss., Toronto School of Theology, 2001.

Jason, Mark A. *Repentance at Qumran: The Penitential Framework of Religious Experience in the Dead Sea Scrolls*. Minneapolis: Fortress Press, 2015.

Jensen, Morten Hørning. "Antipas: The Herod Jesus Knew." *BAR* 38, no. 5 (2012): 42–46.

_____. *Herod Antipas in Galilee: The Literary and Archaeological Sources on the Reign of Herod Antipas and Its Socio-economic Impact on Galilee*. WUNT 2.215: Tübingen: Mohr Siebeck, 2006.

_____. "Rural Galilee and Rapid Changes: An Investigation of the Socio-Economic Dynamics and Developments in Roman Galilee." *Biblica* 93, no. 1 (2012): 43–67.

Jervell, Jacob. *Die Apostelgeschichte: Übersetzt und erklärt*. Göttingen: Vandenhoeck & Ruprecht, 1998.

Johansson, Egil. "Literacy Campaigns in Sweden." *Interchange* 19 (1988): 135–62.

Johnson, Lee A. "Social Stratification." *BTB* 43, no. 3 (2013): 155–68.

Johnson, Luke. *The First and Second Letters to Timothy: A New Translation with Introduction and Commentary*. New York: Doubleday, 2001.

Johnson, William A. *Bookrolls and Scribes in Oxyrhynchus*. Reprinted paperback. Toronto: University of Toronto Press, 2013.

_____. *Readers and Reading Culture in the High Roman Empire: A Study on Elite Communities*. New York: Oxford University Press, 2010.

_____. "Toward a Sociology of Reading in Classical Antiquity." *AJP* 121, no. 4 (2000): 593–627.

Jones, Christopher. "Books and Libraries in a Newly-Discovered Treatise of Galen." *JRA* 22 (2009): 390–97.

_____. "Towards a Chronology of Plutarch's Works." *JRS* 56, nos. 1–2 (1966): 61–74.

Judge, Edwin A. *The First Christians in the Roman World: Augustan and New Testament Essays*, edited by James R. Harrison. WUNT 229. Tübingen: Mohr Siebeck, 2008.

Kaiser, Otto. *Philo von Alexandrien: Denkender Glaube—eine Einführung*. Göttingen: Vandenhoeck & Ruprecht, 2015.

Kaster, Robert A. *Guardians of Language: The Grammarian and Society in Late Antiquity*. The Transformation of the Classical Heritage 11. Los Angeles: University of California Press, 1988.

Kee, Howard. "Testaments of the Twelve Patriarchs." In *The Old Testament*

Pseudepigrapha, vol. 1, *Apocalyptic Literature and Testaments*, edited by James H. Charlesworth, 792–93. Peabody, MA: Hendrickson, 2009.

_____. "The Changing Meaning of Synagogue: A Response to Richard Oster." *NTS* 40 (1994): 281–83.

_____. "The Transformation of the Synagogue after 70 C.E.: Its Import for Early Christianity." *NTS* 36 (1990): 1–24.

Keegan, Peter. *Graffiti in Antiquity*. New York: Routledge, 2014.

Keener, Craig. *Acts: An Exegetical Commentary*. Vol. 2, *3:1–14:28*. Grand Rapids: Baker Academic, 2013.

_____. *Acts: An Exegetical Commentary*. Vol. 3, *15:1–23:35*. Grand Rapids: Baker Academic, 2014.

_____. "Women's Education and Public Speech in Antiquity." *JETS* 50.4 (2007): 747–59.

Keith, Chris. *Jesus against the Scribal Elite: The Origins of the Conflict*. Grand Rapids: Baker Academic, 2014.

_____. *Jesus' Literacy: Scribal Culture and the Teacher from Galilee*. Reprint ed., LNTS 413 / LHJS 8. New York: T&T Clark, 2013.

Kelhoffer, James A. "'How Soon a Book' Revisited: ΕΥΑΓΓΕΛΙΟΝ as a Reference to 'Gospel' Materials in the First Half of the Second Century." *ZNW* 95 (2004): 1–34.

_____. "If Second Clement Really Were a 'Sermon,' How Would We Know, and Why Would We Care? Prolegomena to Analyses of the Writing's Genre and Community." In *Early Christian Communities between Ideal and Reality*, edited by Mark Grundeken and Joseph Verheyden, 83–108. WUNT 342. Tübingen: Mohr Siebeck, 2015.

Kennedy, George A. *Progymnasmata: Greek Textbooks of Prose Composition and Rhetoric*, edited by George A. Kennedy. Atlanta: SBL, 2003.

Kennerly, Michele Jean. "Editorial Bodies in Ancient Roman Rhetorical Culture." PhD diss., University of Pittsburgh, 2010.

Kenney, Edward J. "Books and Readers in the Roman World", in *The Cambridge History of Classical Literature*. Vol. 2, *Latin Literature, Part 1: The Early Republic*, edited by W. V. Clausen and E. J. Kenney, 3–31. Cambridge: Cambridge University Press, 1983.

Kenyon, Frederic G. *Book and Readers in Ancient Greece and Rome*. Chicago: Ares, 1980.

Kim, Hong Bom. "The Interpretation of Μάλιστα in 1 Timothy 5:17." *NovT* 66 (2004): 360–68.

Klauck, Hans-Josef. *Ancient Letters and the New Testament: A Guide to Context and Exegesis.* Waco, TX: Baylor University Press, 2006.

Klein, Hans. *Das Lukasevangelium: übersetzt und erklärt.* Göttingen: Vandenhoeck & Ruprecht, 2006.

Klinghardt, Matthias. "Prayer Formularies for Public Recitation: Their Use and Function in Ancient Religion." *Numen* 46 (1999): 1–52.

Klink, Edward W., III, ed. *The Audience of the Gospels: The Origin and Function of the Gospels in Early Christianity.* LNTS 353. London: T&T Clark, 2010.

Kloppenborg, John S. "Diaspora Discourse: The Construction of Ethos in James." *NTS* (2007): 242–70.

———. "Did Thomas Know the Synoptic Gospels?: A Response to Denzey Lewis, Kloppenborg, and Patterson." *JSNT* 36, no. 3 (2014): 282–93.

———. "Literate Media in Early Christ Groups: The Creation of a Christian Book Culture." *JECS* 22, no. 1 (2014): 21–59.

———. "A New Synoptic Problem: Mark Goodacre and Simon Gathercole on Thomas." *JSNT* 36, no. 3 (2014): 199–239.

Knapp, Robert. *Invisible Romans: Prostitutes, Outlaws, Slaves, Gladiators, Ordinary Men and Women . . . the Romans That History Forgot.* London: Profile, 2011.

Knauer, Elfriede R. "Roman Wall Paintings from Boscotrecase: Three Studies in the Relationship between Writing and Painting." *Metropolitan Museum Journal* 28 (1993): 13–46.

Knight III, George. *The Pastoral Epistles: A Commentary on the Greek Text.* Grand Rapids: Eerdmans, 1992.

Knust, Jennifer, and Tommy Wasserman. "The Biblical Odes and the Text of the Christian Bible: A Reconsideration of the Impact of Liturgical Singing on the Transmission of the Gospel of Luke." *JBL* 133, no. 2 (2014): 341–65.

Koch, Dietrich-Alex. *Die Schrift als Zeuge des Evangeliums: Untersuchungen zur Verwendung und zum Verständnis der Schrift dei Paulus.* BHT 69. Tübingen: Mohr Siebeck, 1986.

König, Jason, Katerina Oikonomopoulou, and Greg Woolf, eds. *Ancient Libraries.* Cambridge: Cambridge University Press, 2013.

Kruger, Michael J. "Early Christian Attitudes toward the Reproduction of Texts." In *The Early Text of the New Testament,* edited by Charles E. Hill and Michael J. Kruger, 61–81. New York: Oxford University Press, 2012.

_____. "Manuscripts, Scribes, and Book Production within Early Christianity." In *Christian Origins and Classical Culture: Social and Literacy Contexts for the New Testament*, edited by Stanley E. Porter and Andrew W. Pitts, 15–40. Leiden: Brill, 2012.

Kruse, Colin G. *The Letters of John*. Grand Rapids: Eerdmans, 2000.

Lampe, Peter. *From Paul to Valentinus: Christians at Rome in the First Two Centuries*. Edited by Marshall D. Johnson. Translated by Michael Steinhauser. Minneapolis: Fortress Press, 2003.

_____. "Quintilian's Psychological Insights in His Institutio Oratoria." In *Paul and Rhetoric*, edited by J. Paul Sampley and Peter Lampe, 180–99. London: T&T Clark, 2010.

Larash, Patricia. "Martial's Lector, the Practice of Reading, and the Emergence of the General Reader in Flavian Rome." PhD diss., University of California at Berkeley, 2004.

Laronde, André, and Jean Leclant, eds. *La Méditerranée d'une rive á l'autre: Culture classique et cultures périphériques*. Paris: Académie des Inscriptions et Belles-Lettres, 2007.

Last, Richard. "Communities That Write: Christ-Groups, Associations, and Gospel Communities." *NTS* 58 (2012): 173–98.

_____. "The Social Relationships of Gospel Writers: New Insights from Inscriptions Commending Greek Historiographers." *JSNT* 37, no. 3 (2015): 223–52.

Lathrop, Gordon. *The Four Gospels on Sunday: The New Testament and the Reform of Christian Worship*. Minneapolis: Fortress Press, 2011.

Lattke, Michael. *Oden Salomos: Text, Übersetzung, Kommentar*. Part 2, *Oden 15–28*. NTOA 41.2. Göttingen: Vandenhoeck & Ruprecht, 2001.

_____. *Odes of Solomon: A Commentary*. Edited by Harold W. Attridge. Translated by Marianne Ehrhardt. Minneapolis: Fortress Press, 2009.

Leaf, Walter, ed. *Strabo on the Troad, Book XIII, Cap. 1*. Cambridge: Cambridge University Press, 1923.

Lee, Guy, and William Barr. *The Satires of Persius*. Liverpool: Francis Cairns, 1987.

Leibner, Uzi. *Settlement and History in Hellenistic, Roman, and Byzantine Galilee: An Archaeological Survey of the Eastern Galilee*. TSAJ 127. Tübingen: Mohr Siebeck, 2009.

Lenski, Noel. "Assimilation and Revolt in the Territory of Isauria, from the 1st Century BC to the 6th Century AD." *JESHO* 42, no. 4 (1999): 413–65.

Leong, Siang-Nuan. "Windows to the Polemics against the So-Called Jews and Jezebel in Revelation: Insights from Historical and Co(n)textual Analysis." PhD diss., University of Edinburgh, 2009.

Leppin, Hartmut. "Between Marginality and Celebrity: Entertainers and Entertainments in Roman Society." In *Social Relations in the Roman World*, edited by Michael Peachin, 660–78. Oxford: Oxford University Press, 2011.

Levine, Lee. *The Ancient Synagogue: The First Thousand Years*. New Haven: Yale University Press, 2005.

_____. "The Synagogues of Galilee." In *Galilee in the Late Second Temple and Mishnaic Periods*, vol. 1, *Life, Culture, and Society*, edited by David A. Fiensy and James Riley Strange, 129–50. Minneapolis: Fortress Press, 2014.

Levison, John R. "The Spirit, Simeon, and the Songs of the Servant." In *The Spirit and Christ in the New Testament and Christian Theology*, edited by I. Howard Marshall, Volker Rabens, and Cornelis Bennema, 18–34. Grand Rapids: Eerdmans, 2012.

Lieu, Judith. *I, II, III John: A Commentary*. Louisville: Westminster John Knox, 2008.

Lincicum, David. "Paul and the *Testimonia*: *Quo Vademus?*" *JETS* 51, no. 2 (2008): 297–308.

_____. "Philo's Library." *Studia Philonica Annual* 26 (2014): 99–114.

Lindmark, Daniel, ed. Alphabeta Varia: *Orality, Reading and Writing in the History of Literacy; Festschrift in Honour of Egil Johansson on the Occasion of His 65th Birthday, March 24, 1998*. Album Religionum Umense 1. Umeå, Sweden: Umeå University, 1998.

Löhr, Winrich. "The Theft of the Greeks: Christian Self Definition in the Age of the Schools." *Revue d'histoire ecclésiastique* 95 (2000): 403-26.

Long, Anthony. *Epictetus: A Stoic and Socratic Guide to Life*. Oxford: Oxford University Press, 2002.

Longenecker, Bruce. "Exposing the Economic Middle: A Revised Economy Scale for the Study of Early Urban Christianity." *JSNT* 31, no. 3 (2013): 243–78.

Lozynsky, Yuriy. "Ancient Greek Cult Hymns: Poets, Performers and Rituals." PhD diss., University of Toronto, 2014.

Lüdemann, Gerd. *The Earliest Christian Text: 1 Thessalonians*. Rev. ed. Salem, OR: Polebridge, 2013.

Luz, Ulrich. *Matthew 21–28: A Commentary*. Edited by Helmut Koester. Translated by James E. Crouch. Minneapolis: Fortress Press, 2005.

MacMullen, Ramsey. *Roman Social Relations: 50 B.C. to A.D. 284*. New Haven: Yale University Press, 1974.

Maier, Johann. "Jüdisch-christliches Milieu als Magnet für Intellektuelle in der Antike." *ThPQ* 158, no. 1 (2010): 39–49.

Mallen, Peter. *The Reading and Transformation of Isaiah in Luke-Acts*. Edited by Mark Goodacre. LNTS 367. London: T&T Clark, 2008.

Manuwald, Gesine. "The Speeches to the People in Cicero's Oratorical Corpora." *Rhetorica* 30, no. 2 (2012): 153–75.

Marks, Susan, and Hal Taussig, eds. *Meals in Early Judaism: Social Formation at the Table*. New York: Palgrave Macmillan, 2014.

Markus, Donka D. "Performing the Book: The Recital of Epic in First-Century C.E. Rome." *Classical Antiquity* 19, no. 1 (2000): 138–79.

_____. "The Politics of Entertainment: Tradition and Romanization in Statius' *Thebaid*." PhD diss., University of Michigan, 1997.

Marquis, Timothy. "At Home or Away: Travel and Death in 2 Corinthians 1–9." PhD diss., Yale University, 2008.

Marshall, Anthony J. "Library Resources and Creative Writing at Rome." *Phoenix* 30, no. 3 (1976): 252–64.

Marshall, I. Howard. *The Epistles of John*. Grand Rapids: Eerdmans, 1978.

Martin, Konrad. "Labilität und Festigkeit des überlieferten Textes des Neuen Testaments und des Pastor Hermae: Demonstriert an wichtigen Textzeugen." *Sacra Scripta* 7, no. 1 (2009): 65–97.

Martin, Matthew J. "Interpreting the Theodotos Inscription: Some Reflections on a First Century Jerusalem Synagogue Inscription and E. P. Sanders' 'Common Judaism.'" *ANES* 39 (2002): 160–81.

Martin, Michael W., and Bryan A. Nash. "Philippians 2:6-11 as Subversive *Hymnos*: A Study in the Light of Ancient Rhetorical Theory." *JTS* 66, no. 1 (2015): 90–138.

Martin, Ralph. *2 Corinthians*. 2nd ed. WBC 40. Grand Rapids: Zondervan, 2014.

Mason, Steve. *Flavius Josephus: Translation and Commentary*. Vol. 9, *Life of Josephus*. Leiden: Brill, 2001.

Massey, Preston T. "Cicero, the Pastoral Epistles, and the Issue of Pseudonymity." *ResQ* 56, no. 2 (2014): 65–84.

Mattila, Sharon. "Revisiting Jesus' Capernaum: A Village of Only Subsistence-Level Fishers and Farmers?" In *The Galilean Economy in the Time of Jesus*, edited by David A. Fiensy and Ralph K. Hawkins, 75–138. Atlanta: SBL, 2013.

McCartney, Dan. *James*. Grand Rapids: Baker Academic, 2009.

McDonald, Lee Martin. *The Biblical Canon: Its Origin, Transmission, and Authority*. Peabody, MA: Hendrickson, 2008.

McGowan, Andrew B. *Ancient Christian Worship: Early Church Practices in Social, Historical, and Theological Perspective*. Grand Rapids: Baker Academic, 2014.

———. "'Is There a Liturgical Text in This Gospel?': The Institution Narratives and Their Early Interpretive Communities." *JBL* 118, no. 1 (1999): 73–87.

McGowan, Matthew M. *Ovid in Exile: Power and Poetic Redress in the* Tristia *and* Epistulae ex Ponto. MnS 309. Leiden: Brill, 2009.

McGrath, James F. "On Hearing (Rather than Reading) Intertextual Echoes: Christology and Monotheistic Scriptures in an Oral Culture." *BTB* 43, no. 2 (2013): 74–80.

McIver, Robert K. "Eyewitnesses as Guarantors of the Accuracy of the Gospel Traditions in the Light of Psychological Research." *JBL* 131, no. 3 (2012): 529–46.

McKenzie, John L. "The Word of God in the Old Testament." *TS* 21 (1960): 183–206.

McKnight, Scot. *The Letter of James*. Grand Rapids: Eerdmans, 2011.

McNutt, Walter B. "Philo of Alexandria: An Exegete of Scripture." PhD diss., University of Missouri, 2001.

Meeks, Wayne. *The First Urban Christians. The Social World of the Apostle Paul*. 2nd ed. New Haven: Yale University Press, 2003.

Meier, John P. "Jesus and the Sabbath." In *A Marginal Jew: Rethinking the Historical Jesus*, vol. 4, *Law and Love*, 235–341. New Haven: Yale University Press, 2009.

Metzger, Bruce M. "The Formulas Introducing Quotations of Scripture in the NT and the Mishnah." *JBL* 70, no. 4 (1951): 297–307.

———. "The Fourth Book of Ezra: A New Translation and Introduction." In *The Old Testament Pseudepigrapha*, vol. 1, *Apocalyptic Literature and Testaments*, edited by James H. Charlesworth, 517–59. Peabody, MA: Hendrickson, 2009.

———. "Literary Forgeries and Canonical Pseudepigrapha." *JBL* 91, no. 1 (1972): 3–24.

Meyers, Eric M. "Early and Late Synagogues at Nabratein in Upper Galilee:

Regional and Other Considerations." In *A Wandering Galilean: Essays in Honour of Seán Freyne*, edited by Zuleika Rodgers, Margaret Daly-Denton, and Anne Fitzpatrick McKinley, 257–78. SJSJ 132. Leiden: Brill, 2009.

Michaels, J. Ramsey. *The Gospel of John*. Grand Rapids: Eerdmans, 2010.

Milavec, Aaron. *The* Didache*: Faith, Hope, and Life of the Earliest Christian Communities, 50–70 CE*. New York: Newman, 2003.

Milinovich, Timothy. "Memory and Hope in the Midst of Chaos: Reconsidering the Structure of 1 Thessalonians." *CBQ* 76, no. 3 (2014): 498–518.

Millard, Alan. *Reading and Writing in the Time of Jesus*. New York: New York University Press, 2000.

_____. "Zechariah Wrote (Luke 1:63)." In *The New Testament in Its First Century Setting: Essays on Context and Background in Honour of B. W. Winter on His 65th Birthday*, edited by P. J. Williams et al., 46–55. Grand Rapids: Eerdmans, 2004.

Miller, Robert D., II. *Oral Tradition in Ancient Israel: Biblical Performance Criticism*. Vol. 4. Eugene, OR: Cascade, 2011.

Moloney, Francis. "'For as Yet They Did Not Know the Scripture' (John 20:9): A Study in Narrative Time." *IrTheolQuart* 79, no. 2 (2014): 97–111.

Moo, Douglas J. *The Epistle to the Romans*. Grand Rapids: Eerdmans, 1996.

_____. *Galatians*. Grand Rapids: Baker Academic, 2013.

_____. *The Letters to the Colossians and to Philemon*. Grand Rapids: Eerdmans, 2008.

Moo, Jonathan A. *Creation, Nature and Hope in 4 Ezra*. FRLANT 237. Göttingen: Vandenhoeck & Ruprecht, 2011.

Moodie, Erin Kristine. "Metatheater, Pretense Disruption, and Social Class in Greek and Roman Comedy." PhD diss., University of Pennsylvania, 2007.

Moore, Nicholas J. "Is Enoch among the Prophets? The Impact of Jude's Citation of *1 Enoch* on the Reception of Both Texts in the Early Church." *JTS* 64, no. 2 (2013): 498–515.

Moreland, Milton. "The Inhabitants of Galilee in the Hellenistic and Early Roman Periods: Probes into the Archaeological and Literary Evidence." In *Religion, Ethnicity, and Identity in Ancient Galilee: A Region in Transition*, edited by Jürgen Zangenberg, Harold W. Attridge, and Dale B. Martin, 133–59. WUNT 210. Tübingen: Mohr Siebeck, 2007.

Morley, Neville. *Theories, Models and Concepts in Ancient History.* London: Routledge, 2004.

Morris, Mike, ed. *Concise Dictionary of Social and Cultural Anthropology.* Oxford: Wiley-Blackwell, 2012.

Mosser, Carl. "Torah Instruction, Discussion, and Prophecy in First-Century Synagogues." In *Christian Origins and Hellenistic Judaism: Social and Literary Contexts for the New Testament,* edited by Stanley E. Porter and Wendy J. Porter, 2:523–51. Leiden: Brill, 2013.

Mounce, William D. *Pastoral Epistles.* WBC 46. Nashville: Thomas Nelson, 2000.

Mueller, Hans-Friedrich. *Roman Religion in Valerius Maximus.* London: Routledge, 2002.

_____. "Valerius Maximus and the Social World of the New Testament." *CBQ* 51 (1989): 683–93.

Müller, Peter. *Verstehst du auch, was du liest? Lesen und Verstehen im Neuen Testament.* Darmstadt: Wissenschaftliche Buchgesellschaft, 1994.

Murphy, Fredrick. *Pseudo-Philo: Rewriting the Bible.* New York: Oxford University Press, 1993.

Murphy, Holly L. "Reconstructing Home in Exile: Ovid's *Tristia.*" MA thesis, University of Kansas, 2012.

Najman, Hindy. "How Should We Contextualize Pseudepigrapha? Imitation and Emulation in 4 Ezra." In *Flores Florentino: Dead Sea Scrolls and Other Early Jewish Studies in Honour of Florentino García Martínez,* edited by Anthony Hilhorst, Émile Puech, and Eibert Tigchelaar, 529–36. JSJSup 122. Leiden: Brill, 2007.

Nässelqvist, Dan. "Public Reading and Aural Intensity: An Analysis of the Soundscape in John 1–4." PhD diss., Lund University, 2014.

Nauta, Ruurd. *Poetry for Patrons: Literary Communications in the Age of Domitian.* Leiden: Brill, 2002.

Neusner, Jacob. *The Mishnah: A New Translation.* Repr. ed. New Haven: Yale University Press, 1991.

Newby, Zahra, and Ruth Leader-Newby. *Art and Inscriptions in the Ancient World.* Cambridge: Cambridge University Press, 2007.

Nicholls, Matthew C. "Galen and Libraries in the Peri Alupias." *JRS* 101 (2011): 123–42.

Nicklas, Tobias. "'The Words of the Prophecy of This Book': Playing with Scriptural Authority in the Book of Revelation." In *Authoritative Scrip-*

tures in Ancient Judaism, edited by Mladen Popović, 309–26. Leiden: Brill, 2010.

Niederwimmer, Kurt. *The* Didache*: A Commentary*. Translated by Linda M. Maloney. Minneapolis: Fortress Press, 1998.

Niehoff, Maren R. "Why Compare Homer's Readers to Biblical Readers?" In *Homer and the Bible in the Eyes of Ancient Interpreters*, edited by Maren R. Niehoff, 3–14. JSRC 16. Leiden: Brill, 2012.

Nikiprowetzky, Valentin. *Le commentaire de l'écriture chez Philon d'Alexandrie: Son caractère et sa portée, observations philologiques*. Leiden: Brill, 1977.

Nikitinski, Oleg. *A. Persius Flaccus Saturae: Accedunt varia de Persio iudicia saec. XIV–XX*. Munich: K. G. Saur, 2002.

Noack, Christian. *Gottesbewußtsein: Exegetische Studien zur Soteriologie und Mystik bei Philo von Alexandria*. WUNT 2.116. Tübingen: Mohr Siebeck, 2000.

Nolland, John. "Classical and Rabbinic Parallels to 'Physician, Heal Yourself' (Lk. IV 23)." *NovT* 21, no. 3 (1979): 193–209.

Oakes, Peter. "Constructing Poverty Scales for Graeco-Roman Society: A Response to Steve Friesen's 'Poverty in Pauline Studies.'" *JSNT* 26, no. 3 (2004): 367–71.

Oakman, Douglas E. "Models and Archaeology in the Social Interpretation of Jesus." In *Social Scientific Models for Interpreting the Bible*, edited by John J. Pilch, 102–31. Leiden: Brill, 2001.

Oesterley, William. "The General Epistle of James." In *The Expositor's Greek New Testament*, edited by W. Robertson Nicoll, 4:385–476. Rev. ed. New York: Eerdmans, 1960.

Oestreich, Bernhard. "Leseanweisungen in Briefen als Mittel der Gestaltung von Beziehungen (1 Thess 5.27)." *NTS* 50, no. 2 (2004): 224–45.

Oldfather, W. A. *Epictetus: The Discourses as Reported by Arrian, the Manual, and Fragments*. Vol. 1. London: Heinemann, 1925.

O'Loughlin, Thomas. "Ὑπηρέται . . . τοῦ λόγου: Does Luke 1:2 Throw Light on to the Book Practices of the Late First-Century Churches?" In *Early Readers, Scholars and Editors of the New Testament*, edited by H. A. G. Houghton, 17–32. Piscataway, NJ: Gorgias, 2014.

O'Neill, Peter. "A Culture of Sociability: Popular Speech in Ancient Rome." PhD diss., University of California, 2001.

Oporto, Santiago Guijarro. "'Como está escrito': Las citas de la escritura en los comienzos de los evangelios." *Salmanticensis* 61, no. 1 (2014): 91–115.

Orsini, Pasquale, and Willy Clarysse. "Early New Testament Manuscripts and Their Dates: A Critique of Theological Palaeography." *ETL* (2012): 443–74.

Oster, Richard. "Supposed Anachronism in Luke–Acts' Use of ΣΥΝΑΓΩΓΗ: A Rejoinder to H. C. Kee." *NTS* 39 (1993): 178–208.

Overman, J. Andrew. "The Destruction of the Temple and the Conformation of Judaism and Christianity." In *Jews and Christians in the First and Second Centuries: How to Write Their History*, edited by Peter J. Tomson and Joshua J. Schwartz, 251–77. Compendia Rerum Iudaicarum ad Novum Testamentum 13. Leiden: Brill, 2014.

Pao, David. *Acts and the Isaianic New Exodus*. Grand Rapids: Baker Academic, 2000.

Pappalardo, Carmelo. "Synagogue." In *Encyclopedia of Ancient Christianity*, vol. 3. Downers Grove: InterVarsity, 2014.

Parker, David C. *Textual Scholarship and the Making of the New Testament*. New York: Oxford University Press, 2012.

Parker, Holt. "Books and Reading Latin Poetry." In *Ancient Literacies: The Culture of Reading in Greece and Rome*, edited by William A. Johnson and Holt N. Parker, 186–229. Oxford: Oxford University Press, 2009.

Peck, Harry, ed. *Harper's Dictionary of Classical Literature and Antiquities*. New York: Cooper Square, 1965.

Perkins, Larry. "'Let the Reader Understand': A Contextual Interpretation of Mark 13:14." *BBR* 16 (2006): 95–104.

Perrot, Charles. "The Reading of the Bible in the Ancient Synagogue." In *Mikra: Text, Translation, Reading and Interpretation of the Hebrew Bible in Ancient Judaism and Early Christianity*, edited by Martin Jan Mulder, 137–59. Assen, Netherlands: Van Gorcum, 1988.

Peterson, David G. *The Acts of the Apostles*. Grand Rapids: Eerdmans, 2009.

Phillips, Richard Lynn. "Invisibility Spells in the Greek Magical Papyri: Prolegomena, Texts, and Commentaries." PhD diss., University of Illinois at Urbana-Champaign, 2002.

Pokorný, Petr. *From the Gospel to the Gospels: History, Theology and Impact of the Biblical Term 'Euangelion.'* Beihefte zur Zeitschrift für die neutestamentliche Wissenschaft 195. Boston: De Gruyter, 2013.

Porter, Stanley E. "Paul's Bible, His Education and His Access to the Scriptures of Israel." *JGRChJ* 5 (2008): 9–41.

Porter, Stanley E., and Bryan R. Dyer. "Oral Texts? A Reassessment of the Oral and Rhetorical Nature of Paul's Letters in Light of Recent Studies." *JETS* 55, no. 2 (2012): 323–41.

Pothecary, Sarah. "Strabo, the Tiberian Author: Past, Present and Silence in Strabo's *Geography*." *Mnemosyne* 55, no. 4 (2002): 387–438.

Poythress, Vern. "The Meaning of μάλιστα in 2 Timothy 4:13 and Related Verses." *JTS* 53, no. 2 (2002): 523–32.

Price, Simon. "Religious Mobility in the Roman Empire." *JRS* 102 (2012): 1–19.

Rand, Michael. "Fundamentals of the Study of Piyyut." In *Literature or Liturgy? Early Christian Hymns and Prayers in Their Literary and Liturgical Context in Antiquity*, edited by Clemens Leonhard and Hermut Löhr, 107–25. WUNT 2.363. Tübingen: Mohr Siebeck, 2014.

Reddish, Mitchell. "Hearing the Apocalypse in Pergamum." *PRSt* 41, no. 1 (2014): 3–12.

Redford, Donald. "Literacy." In *The Oxford Encyclopedia of Ancient Egypt*, edited by Donald B. Redford, 2:297. Oxford: Oxford University Press, 2001.

Redman, Judith. "How Accurate Are Eyewitnesses? Bauckham and the Eyewitnesses in the Light of Psychological Research." *JBL* 129 (2010): 177–97.

Reed, Jonathan L. *Archaeology and the Galilean Jesus: A Re-examination of the Evidence*. Harrisburg, PA: Trinity Press International, 2000.

Regev, Eyal. "Flourishing before the Crisis: Mapping Judaean Society in the First Century CE." In *Jews and Christians in the First and Second Centuries*, 52–79. Leiden: Brill, 2015.

Reinmuth, Eckhart. "Die Briefe an die Thessalonicher." In *Die Briefe an die Philipper, Thessalonicher und an Philemon*, 105–204. NTD 8.2. Göttingen: Vandenhoeck & Ruprecht, 1998.

Reumann, John. *Philippians: A New Translation with Introduction and Commentary*. New Haven: Yale University Press, 2008.

Rhoads, David. "Performance Events in Early Christianity: New Testament Writings in an Oral Context." In *The Interface of Orality and Writing*, edited by Annette Weissenrieder and Robert B. Coote, 166–93. WUNT 260. Tübingen: Mohr Siebeck, 2010.

Richards, Randolph E. "The Codex and the Early Collection of Paul's Letters." *BBR* 8 (1998): 151–66.

_____. *Paul and First-Century Letter Writing: Secretaries, Composition and Collection*. Downers Grove: InterVarsity, 2004.

_____. "Silvanus Was Not Peter's Secretary: Theological Bias in Interpreting διὰ Σιλουανοῦ . . . ἔγραψα in 1 Peter 5:12." *JETS* 43, no. 3 (2000): 417–32.

Richardson, Peter. Review of *Alexander to Constantine: Archaeology of the Land of the Bible*, by Eric M. Meyers and Mark A. Chancey. *BASOR* 370 (2013): 242–44.

_____. "Towards a Typology of Levantine/Palestinian Houses." *JSNT* 27, no. 1 (2004): 47–68.

Riesner, Rainer. *Jesus als Lehrer: Eine Untersuchung zum Ursprung der Evangelien-Überlieferung.* WUNT 2.7. Tübingen: Mohr Siebeck, 1988.

Rodriguez, Rafael. *Oral Tradition and the New Testament: A Guide for the Perplexed.* London: T&T Clark, 2014.

_____. "Reading and Hearing in Ancient Contexts." *JSNT* 32, no. 2 (2009): 151–78.

Rohmann, Dirk. *Christianity, Book-Burning and Censorship in Late Antiquity.* Arbeiten zur Kirchengeschichte 135. Berlin: De Gruyter, 2016.

Rohmann, Dirk, and Thomas Völker. "*Praenomen Petronii*: The Date and Author of the *Satyricon* Reconsidered." *CQ* 61, no. 2 (2011): 660–76.

Roller, Duane W. *The Geography of Strabo: An English Translation, with Introduction and Notes.* Cambridge: Cambridge University Press, 2014.

Roman, Luke. "The Representation of Literary Materiality in Martial's *Epigrams*." *JRS* 91 (2001): 113–45.

Root, Bradley. *First Century Galilee: A Fresh Examination of the Sources.* WUNT 2.378. Tübingen: Mohr Siebeck, 2014.

Rossi, Ornella. "Letters from Far Away: Ancient Epistolary Travel Writing and the Case of Cicero's Correspondence." PhD diss., Yale University, 2010.

Rouwhorst, Gerard A. M. "The Reading of Scripture in Early Christian Liturgy." In *What Athens Has to Do with Jerusalem: Essays on Classical, Jewish, and Early Christian Art and Archaeology in Honor of Gideon Foerster*, edited by Leonard V. Rutgers, 305–31. Leuven: Peeters, 2002.

Royalty, Robert M. "Don't Touch This Book! Revelation 22:18–19 and the Rhetoric of Reading (in) the Apocalypse of John." *BibInt* 12, no. 3 (2004): 282–99.

Royse, James R. "Did Philo Publish His Works?" *Studia Philonica Annual* 25 (2013): 75–100.

Ruiz-Montero, Consuelo R. "Chariton von Aphrodisias: Ein Überblick." *ANRW* 2.34.2 (1994): 1006–54.

Runesson, Anders, Donald D. Binder, and Birger Olsson. *The Ancient Synagogue from Its Origins to 200 C.E.: A Source Book*. Leiden: Brill, 2010.

Russell, D. A. *Dio Chrysostom: Orations VII, XII, and XXXVI*. Cambridge: Cambridge University Press, 1992.

Safrai, Ze'ev. "Socio-Economic and Cultural Developments in the Galilee from the Late First to the Early Third Century CE." In *Jews and Christians in the First and Second Centuries*, 278–310. Leiden: Brill, 2015.

Sandmel, Samuel. "Philo Judaeus: An Introduction to the Man, His Writings, and His Significance." *ANRW* 2.21.1 (1984): 3–46.

Sarefield, Daniel C. "'Burning Knowledge': Studies of Bookburning in Ancient Rome." PhD diss., Ohio State University, 2004.

Sargent, Benjamin. *Written to Serve: The Use of Scripture in 1 Peter*. LNTS 547, edited by Chris Keith. London: T&T Clark, 2015.

Scheidel, Walter, and Steven J. Friesen. "The Size of the Economy and the Distribution of Income in the Roman Empire." *JRS* 99 (2009): 61–91.

Schellenberg, Ryan. *Rethinking Paul's Rhetorical Education: Comparative Rhetoric and 2 Corinthians 10–13*. ECL 10. Atlanta: SBL, 2013.

Schenkeveld, Dirk M. "Prose Usages of Ἀκούειν 'To Read.'" *CQ* 42, no. 1 (1992): 129–41.

Schiffman, Lawrence H. "The Early History of Public Reading of the Torah." In *Jews, Christians, and Polytheists in the Ancient Synagogue: Cultural Interaction during the Greco-Roman Period*. edited by Steven Fine, 44–56. London: T&T Clark, 1999.

Schnabel, Eckhard J. *Early Christian Mission: Paul and the Early Church*. Vol. 2. Downers Grove: InterVarsity, 2004.

———. "The Muratorian Fragment: The State of Research." *JETS* 57, no. 2 (2014): 231–64.

Schnelle, Udo. "Das frühe Christentum und die Bildung." *NTS* 61. no. 2 (2015): 113–43.

Schrage, W. "συναγωγή." In *Theologisches Wörterbuch zum Neuen Testament*, edited by Gerhard Kittel et al., 7:798–850. Stuttgart: Kohlhammer, 1949–79.

Schreck, C. J. "The Nazareth Pericope: Luke 4:16–30 in Recent Study." In *L'Évangile de Luc – The Gospel of Luke*, edited by F. Neirynck, 399–471. BETL 32. Leuven: Leuven University Press, 1989.

Schwartz, Matthew Barahal. "Torah Reading in the Ancient Synagogues." PhD diss., Wayne State University, 1975.

Schwartz, Seth. "How Many Judaisms Were There? A Critique of Neusner and Smith on Definition and Mason and Boyarin on Categorization." *JAJ* 2, no. 2 (2011): 208–38.

Schwindt, Rainer. *Das Weltbild des Epheserbriefes: Eine religionsgeschichtlich-exegetische Studie*. WUNT 148. Tübingen: Mohr Siebeck, 2002.

Scott, James C. "Protest and Profanation: Agrarian Revolt and the Little Tradition, Part I." *Theory and Society* 4, no. 1 (1977): 1–38.

_____. "Protest and Profanation: Agrarian Revolt and the Little Tradition, Part II." *Theory and Society* 4, no. 2 (1977): 211–46.

Seitz, Christopher. *Colossians*. Grand Rapids: Brazos, 2014.

_____. "Jewish Scripture for Gentile Churches: Human Destiny and the Future of the Pauline Correspondence, Part 1: Romans." *ProEccl* 23, no. 3 (2014): 294–308.

Seo, J. Mira. "Plagiarism and Poetic Identity in Martial." *AJP* 130, no. 4 (2009): 567–93.

Septimus, Gerald. "On the Boundaries of Prayer: Talmudic Ritual Texts with Addressees Other than God." PhD diss., Yale University, 2008.

Sham, Michael Norman. "Characterization in Petronius' *Satyricon*." PhD diss., University of New York at Buffalo, 1994.

Shauf, Scott. "The 'Word of God' and Retribution Theology in Luke–Acts." In *Scripture and Traditions: Essays on Early Judaism and Christianity in Honor of Carl R. Holladay*, edited by Patrick Gray and Gail R. O'Day, 173–91. NovTSup 129. Leiden: Brill, 2008.

Shaw, Deborah B. "The Power of Assumptions and the Power of Poetry: A Reading of Ovid's *Tristia* 4." PhD diss., University of California at Berkeley, 1994.

Shiell, William D. *Delivering from Memory: The Effect of Performance on the Early Christian Audience*. Eugene, OR: Wipf & Stock, 2011.

_____. *Reading Acts: The Lector and the Early Christian Audience*. Biblical Interpretation Series 70. Leiden: Brill Academic, 2004.

Sick, David H. "The Symposium of the 5,000." *JTS* 66, no. 1 (2015): 1–27.

Siniscalco, Paolo. "Travel—Means of Communication." In *Encyclopedia of Ancient Christianity*, 3:831–32. Downers Grove: InterVarsity, 2014.

Skeat, T. C. "Especially the Parchments: A Note on 2 Timothy 4:13." *JTS* 30 (1979): 173–77.

_____. "The Use of Dictation in Ancient Book-Production." *Proceedings of the British Academy* 42 (1956): 179–208.

Skidmore, Clive. *Practical Ethics for Roman Gentlemen: The Work of Valerius Maximus*. Liverpool: Liverpool University Press, 1996.

Smit, Peter-Ben. "A Symposiastic Background to James?" *NTS* 58 (2011): 105–122.

Smith, Adrian. *The Representation of Speech Events in Chariton's* Callirhoe *and the Acts of the Apostles.* LBS 10. Leiden: Brill, 2014.

Smith, Claire S. *Pauline Communities as 'Scholastic Communities': A Study of the Vocabulary of 'Teaching' in 1 Corinthians, 1 and 2 Timothy and Titus.* WUNT 335. Tübingen: Mohr Siebeck, 2012.

Snyder, H. Gregory. "The Classroom in the Text: Exegetical Practices in Justin and Galen." In *Christian Origins and Greco-Roman Culture: Social and Literary Contexts for the New Testament*, edited by Stanley E. Porter and Andrew W. Pitts, 663–85. Leiden: Brill, 2013.

_____. *Teachers and Texts in the Ancient World: Philosophers, Jews and Christians.* New York: Routledge, 2000.

Spence, Stephen. "The Separation of the Church and the Synagogue in First-Century Rome." PhD diss., Fuller Theological Seminary, 2001.

Spigel, Chad S. *Ancient Synagogue Seating Capacities: Methodology, Analysis and Limits.* TSAJ 149. Tübingen: Mohr Siebeck, 2012.

_____. "Reconsidering the Question of Separate Seating in Ancient Synagogues." *JJS* 63, no. 1 (2012): 62–83.

Stanley, Christopher. "'Pearls before Swine': Did Paul's Audiences Understand His Biblical Quotations?" *NovT* 41, no. 2 (1999): 124–44.

Starr, Raymond J. "The Circulation of Literary Texts in the Roman World." *CQ* 37 (1987): 213–23.

_____. "Reading Aloud: *Lectores* and Roman Reading." *CJ* 86, no. 4 (1991): 337–43.

Steele, R. B. "Quintus Curtius Rufus." *AJP* 36, no. 4 (1915): 402–23.

Stegemann, Wolfgang. "Background III: The Social and Political Climate in Which Jesus of Nazareth Preached." In *Handbook for the Study of the Historical Jesus: How to Study the Historical Jesus*, edited by Tom Holmén and Stanley E. Porter, 3:2291–314. Leiden: Brill, 2011.

Stein, Robert H. *Mark.* Grand Rapids: Baker Academic, 2008.

Sterling, Gregory E. "The *Hypothetica*: Introduction." *Studia Philonica Annual* 20 (2008): 139–42.

_____. "Philo's Ancient Readers: Introduction." *Studia Philonica Annual* 25 (2013): 69–73.

Stern, Karen B. "Graffiti as Gift: Mortuary and Devotional Graffiti in the Late Ancient Levant." In *The Gift in Antiquity*, edited by Michael L. Satlow, 137–57. Oxford: Wiley-Blackwell, 2013.

Stevens, Benjamin. "*Per gestum res est significanda mihi*: Ovid and Language in Exile." *CP* 104, no. 2 (2009): 162–83.

Stewart, Alexander E. "Narrative World, Rhetorical Logic, and the Voice of the Author in 4 Ezra." *JBL* 132, no. 2 (2013): 373–91.

Stewart, Robert B., and Gary R. Habermas. *Memories of Jesus: A Critical Appraisal of James D. G. Dunn's Jesus Remembered*. Nashville: B&H Academic, 2010.

Stirewalt, M. Luther, Jr. "Greek Terms for Letter and Letter-Writing from Homer through the Second Century C.E." In *Studies in Ancient Greek Epistolography*, edited by Marvin A. Sweeney, 67–87. Atlanta: Scholars, 1993.

Stone, Michael E., and Matthias Henze. *4 Ezra and 2 Baruch: Translations, Introductions, and Notes*. Minneapolis: Fortress Press, 2013.

Stowers, Stanley K. "The Concept of 'Community' and the History of Early Christianity." *MTSR* 23 (2011): 238–56.

_____. *Letter Writing in Greco-Roman Antiquity*. Edited by Wayne A. Meeks. Philadelphia: Westminster, 1986.

Strand, Kenneth. "The Two Witnesses of Rev 11:3–12." *Andrews University Seminary Studies* 19, no. 2 (1981): 127–35.

Stroumsa, Guy. "The New Self and Reading Practices in Late Antique Christianity." *CHRC* 95 (2015): 1–18.

Struck, Peter T. "Reading Symbols: Traces of the Gods in the Ancient Greek-Speaking World." PhD diss., University of Chicago, 1997.

Sullivan, J. P. *Martial: The Unexpected Classic*. Cambridge: Cambridge University, 1992.

Sussman, Lewis A. *The Elder Seneca*. Leiden: Brill, 1978.

Tabbernee, Williams. "Material Evidence for Early Christian Groups during the First Two Centuries C.E." *ASE* 30, no. 2 (2013): 287–301.

Tellbe, Mikael. *Christ-Believers in Ephesus*. WUNT 242. Tübingen: Mohr Siebeck, 2009.

Theissen, Gerd. *The Social Setting of Pauline Christianity: Essays on Corinth*. Translated by John H. Schultz. Philadelphia: Fortress Press, 1982.

Thompson, Michael B. "The Holy Internet: Communication between Churches in the First Christian Generation." In *The Gospels for All Christians: Rethinking the Gospel Audiences*, edited by Richard Bauckham, 49–70. Edinburgh: T&T Clark, 1998.

Tomson, Peter J., and Joshua J. Schwartz. "The Destruction of the Temple and the Conformation of Judaism and Christianity." In *Jews and Chris-*

tians in the First and Second Centuries: How to Write Their History, edited by Peter J. Tomson and Joshua J. Schwartz, 251–77. Compendia Rerum Iudaicarum ad Novum Testamentum 13. Leiden: Brill, 2014.

Toner, Jerry. *Popular Culture in Ancient Rome*. Cambridge: Polity, 2009.

Tov, Emanuel. "A Qumran Origin for the Masada Non-biblical Texts?" *DSD* 7, no. 1 (2000): 58–63.

_____. *Scribal Practices and Approaches Reflected in the Texts Found in the Judean Desert*. STDJ 54. Leiden, Brill, 2004.

_____. *Textual Criticism of the Hebrew Bible, Qumran, Septuagint: Collected Essays*. Vol. 3. VTSup 167. Leiden: Brill, 2015.

Towner, Philip. *The Letters to Timothy and Titus*. Grand Rapids: Eerdmans, 2006.

Trebilco, Paul. *Self-Designations and Group Identity in the New Testament*. Cambridge: Cambridge University Press, 2012.

Tuckett, Christopher. "Jesus and the Sabbath." In *Jesus in Continuum*, edited by Tom Holmén, 411–42. WUNT 289. Tübingen: Mohr Siebeck, 2012.

Twelftree, Graham. "Jesus and Synagogue." In *Handbook for the Study of the Historical Jesus: How to Study the Historical Jesus*, edited by Tom Holmén and Stanley E. Porter, 3:2105–34. Leiden: Brill, 2011.

Vakayil, Prema. "'Go and Teach the Word of God': Paul's Missionary Command to Thecla." *Indian Theological Studies* 49 (2012): 23–29.

van Dam, Harm-Jan. *P. Papinius Statius, Silvae, Book II: A Commentary*. Leiden: Brill, 1984.

van der Kooij, Arie. "The Public Reading of Scriptures at Feasts." In *Feasts and Festivals*, edited by Christopher Tuckett, 27–44. CBET 53. Leuven: Peeters, 2009.

van der Minde, Hans-Jürgen. *Schrift und Tradition bei Paulu*. Paderborn: Schöningh, 1976.

van Henten, Jan Willem. *The Maccabean Martyrs as Saviours of the Jewish People: A Study of 2 and 4 Maccabees*. JSJSup 57. Leiden: Brill, 1997.

Vatri, Alessandro. "Ancient Greek Writing for Memory: Textual Features as Mnemonic Facilitators." *Mnemosyne* 68 (2015): 750–73.

Vine, Cedric. *The Audience of Matthew: An Appraisal of the Local Audience Thesis*. LNTS. London: T&T Clark, 2014.

Voderholzer, Rudolf. "Liest Du noch oder glaubst Du schon? Überlegungen zur Benennung des Christentums als 'Buchreligion.'" *TTZ* 2 (2012): 101–11.

Walker, Henry John. *Valerius Maximus: Memorable Deeds and Sayings; One Thousand Tales from Ancient Rome*. Cambridge: Hackett, 2004.

Walker, Peter. "Revisiting the Pastoral Epistles, Part I." *EJT* 21, no. 1 (2012): 4–16.

_____. "Revisiting the Pastoral Epistles, Part II." *EJT* 21, no. 2 (2012): 120–32.

Wallace, Daniel B. *Granville Sharp's Canon and Its Kin: Semantics and Significance*. SBG 14. New York: Peter Lang, 2008.

Waltke, Bruce K. *The Book of Proverbs: Chapters 15–31*. Grand Rapids: Eerdmans, 2005.

Walton, John H., and D. Brent Sandy. *The Lost World of Scripture: Ancient Literary Culture and Biblical Authority*. Downers Grove: InterVarsity, 2013.

Ward, Richard F., and David J. Trobisch. *Bringing the Word to Life: Engaging the New Testament through Performing It*. Grand Rapids: Eerdmans, 2013.

Wasserman, Tommy. "The Early Text of Matthew." in *The Early Text of the New Testament*, edited by Charles E. Hill and Michael J. Kruger, 83–107. New York: Oxford University Press, 2012.

Watson, Francis. *Gospel Writing: A Canonical Perspective*. Grand Rapids: Eerdmans, 2013.

_____. *Paul and the Hermeneutics of Faith*. London: T&T Clark, 2004.

Webb, Kerry. "'The House of Books': Libraries and Archives in Ancient Egypt." *Libri* 63, no. 1 (2013): 21–32.

Weeden, Theodore. "Kenneth Bailey's Theory of Oral Tradition: A Theory Contested by Its Evidence." *JSNT* 7 (2009): 3–43.

Weima, Jeffery A. D. *1–2 Thessalonians*. Grand Rapids: Baker Academic, 2014.

_____. "Sincerely, Paul: The Significance of the Pauline Letter Closings." In *Paul and the Ancient Letter Form*, edited by Stanley E. Porter and Sean A. Adams, 307–45. PAST 6. Leiden: Brill Academic, 2010.

Weiss, Herold. "The Sabbath in the Fourth Gospel." *JBL* 110, no. 2 (1991): 311–21.

_____. "The Sabbath in the Synoptic Gospels." *JSNT* 38 (1990): 13–27.

Weiss, Zeev. "Theatres, Hippodromes, Amphitheaters, and Performances." In *The Oxford Handbook of Jewish Daily Life in Roman Palestine*, edited by Catherine Hezser, 623–40. Oxford: Oxford University Press, 2010.

White, Peter. "Bookshops in the Literary Culture of Rome." In *Ancient Literacies: The Culture of Reading in Greece and Rome*, edited by William

A. Johnson and Holt N. Parker, translated by Holt N. Parker, 268–87. Oxford: Oxford University Press, 2009.

Wilburn, Andrew T. *The Greek Magical Papyri in Translation, Including the Demotic Spells*. Edited by Hans Dieter Betz. Chicago: University of Chicago Press, 1986.

_____. Materia Magica*: The Archaeology of Magic in Roman Egypt, Cyprus, and Spain; New Texts from Ancient Cultures*. Ann Arbor: University of Michigan Press, 2013.

Williams, Craig A., ed. *Martial,* Epigrams*, Book Two*. Oxford: Oxford University Press, 2004.

Wilson, Brittany E. "'Neither Male nor Female': The Ethiopian Eunuch in Acts 8.26–40." *NTS* 60 (2014): 403–22.

Winter, Bruce W. *Roman Wives, Roman Widows: The Appearance of New Women and the Pauline Communities*. Grand Rapids: Eerdmans, 2003.

Winterbottom, Michael, ed. *The Minor Declamations Ascribed to Quintilian*. Berlin: De Gruyter, 1984.

_____. "Recitatio." In *The Oxford Classical Dictionary*, 4th ed, edited by Simon Hornblower, Antony Spawforth, and Esther Eidinow, 1258. Oxford: Oxford University Press, 2012.

Wise, Christy N. "Banished to the Black Sea: Ovid's Poetic Transformations in *Tristia* 1:1." PhD diss., Georgetown University, 2014.

Wiseman, Timothy P. "Practice and Theory in Roman Historiography." In *Roman Studies: Literary and Historical*, vol. 1 of *Collected Classical Papers*, 244–62. Liverpool: Francis Cairns, 1987.

Witherington, Ben, III. "'Almost Thou Persuadest Me . . .': The Importance of Greco-Roman Rhetoric for the Understanding of the Text and Context of the NT." *JETS* 58, no. 1 (2015): 63–88.

Wolfe, Benjamin. "The Place and Use of Scripture in the Pastoral Epistles." PhD diss., University of Aberdeen, 1990.

Wright, Brian J. "Ancient Literacy in New Testament Research: Incorporating A Few More Lines of Enquiry." *TrinJ* 36, no. 2 (2015): 161–89.

_____. "'Ancient Rome's Daily News Publication with Some Likely Implications for Early Christian Studies." *TynBull* 67, no. 1 (2016): 145–60.

_____. "The First-Century Inscription of Quintus Sulpicius Maximus: An Initial Catalogue of Lexical Parallels with the New Testament." *BBR* 27, no. 1 (2017): 53–63.

Wright, N. T. *The Epistles of Paul to the Colossians and to Philemon*. Leicester: InterVarsity, 1986.

_____. *Paul and the Faithfulness of God: Parts I and II*. Minneapolis: Fortress Press, 2013.

Wycislo, William E. "The *De Ira*: Seneca's Satire of Roman Law." PhD diss., University of Chicago, 1996.

Young, Stephen E. *Jesus Tradition in the Apostolic Fathers*. WUNT 311. Tübingen: Mohr Siebeck, 2011.

Yueh-Han Yieh, John. "One Teacher: Jesus' Teaching Role in Matthew's Gospel." PhD diss., Yale University, 2003.

Zangenberg, Jürgen K. "Archaeological News from the Galilee: Tiberias, Magdala and Rural Galilee." *EC* 1 (2010): 471–84.

_____. "Climate, Droughts, Wars, and Famines in Galilee as a Background for Understanding the Historical Jesus." *JBL* 131, no. 2 (2012): 307–24.

_____. "Das Galiläa des Josephus und das Galiläa der Archäologie: Tendenzen und Probleme der neueren Forschung." In *Josephus und das Neue Testament: Wechselseitige Wahrnehmungen, II. Internationales Symposium zum Corpus Judaeo-Hellenisticum, 25–28, Mai 2006, Greifswald*, 265–94. WUNT 209. Tübingen: Mohr Siebeck, 2007.

_____. "Jesus der Galiläer und die Archäologie: Beobachtungen zur Bedeutung der Archäologie für die historische Jesusforschung." *MTZ* 64, no. 2 (2013): 123–56.

Zelnick-Abramovitz, Rachel. "Look and Listen: History Performed and Inscribed." In *Between Orality and Literacy: Communication and Adaptation in Antiquity*, edited by Ruth Scodel, 10:175–96. MnS 367. Leiden: Brill, 2014.

Subject Index

Author Index

Scripture Index